SPEAKING FOR
MYSELF

SPEAKING FOR MYSELF

My Life from Liverpool to Downing Street

CHERIE BLAIR

Little, Brown and Company
New York   Boston   London

Little, Brown and Company
Hachette Book Group
237 Park Avenue, New York, NY 10017
Visit our Web site at www.HachetteBookGroup.com

First North American Edition: October 2008
Originally published in Great Britain by Little, Brown and Company in 2008

Little, Brown and Company is a division of Hachette Book Group, Inc. The Little, Brown name and logo are trademarks of Hachette Book Group, Inc.

Permission to quote from *In My Liverpool Home* by Peter McGovern © 1961 Spin Publications is gratefully acknowledged.

Library of Congress Cataloging-in-Publication Data
Blair, Cherie.
    Speaking for myself : my life from Liverpool to Downing Street / Cherie Blair. — 1st North American ed.
        p. cm.
    Includes index.
    ISBN 978-0-316-03145-5
    1. Blair, Cherie. 2. Prime ministers' spouses — Great Britain — Biography.
3. Lawyers — Great Britain — Biography. 4. Blair, Tony, 1953-   1. Title.
    DA566.9.B565A3 2008
    941.085'9092 — dc22
    [B]
                                                                    2008032825

10 9 8 7 6 5 4 3 2 1

RRD-IN

Printed in the United States of America

To my mother, Gale, and my grandmother Vera

CONTENTS

My memory is not infallible, and this is not a history book. It is simply one woman's attempt to recollect her life — a memoir of someone who, for a period of time, had a walk-on part in history.

Cherie Blair
April 2008

June 2007

O kay, guys, that's it. Let's do the business."

The time had finally come: our good-byes had all been said, tears wiped away. At a nod from Tony, the custodian opened the famous front door with a little mock bow, and the six of us trooped out into the June sunshine to face the cameras: Euan, Nicky, Kathryn, Leo, Tony, and me, all of us dressed in what my grandma would have called our Sunday best, exiting that historic building to "do the business" for the last time. I smiled, older and wiser than on the occasion of that first press call in Downing Street on that bright May morning ten years earlier, when we hadn't even seen inside our new home and anything seemed possible.

Although I hadn't wanted Tony to step down, I accepted that now was the right time to go. With a renewed sense of purpose, I kissed each of the children and saw them back into Number 10, where Jackie, our nanny, was waiting. She would take them to Chequers, the Prime Minister's country house an hour outside London, for our last family weekend there. Tony and I had first to go up to the constituency in Sedgefield. He had decided to make a clean break and needed to resign his seat as soon as possible so that a by-election could be held before the summer recess.

All that remained was for the Right Honourable Tony Blair, member of Parliament for Sedgefield, Prime Minister of the United Kingdom of Great Britain and Northern Ireland, officially to deliver his resignation to the Queen. As protocol decrees, while he was ushered into the waiting car by the door nearest the pavement — the principal seat, as it's called — I walked round to the other side behind the driver, closer to the waiting photographers shouting my name. With the renewed frenzy of snapping came the sarcasm: "Miss it, will you? . . . We'll miss you!"

The sunlight glinted on their long lenses, and I thought, not for the first time, how threatening they were, how like weapons. I'd just said good-bye to all these people we loved and who loved us, and I thought, *Actually, I am going to miss all of them, but not you lot, no.* So that's what came out. I couldn't help myself. "Bye. I won't miss you!" I said and laughed.

"You can't resist it, can you?" Tony said through clenched teeth as the door closed behind me. "For God's sake, you're supposed to be dignified; you're supposed to be gracious."

As the car swung out into Whitehall, I heard a helicopter overhead, and suddenly I was filled with a sense of déjà vu. I remembered coming out of our house in Richmond Crescent, our home in north London, in 1997, self-conscious in that red suit bought especially for the occasion. I heard a voice shouting, "Hey, Mum!" and looked up to see Kathryn and Lucy, her cousin, waving down to us from the top floor. I also saw the silhouette of a helicopter against the blue sky and wondered what it was doing there, not realizing that it was filming us. All our neighbors were out on the street to see us off, and all the way down to the Euston Road and on to Buckingham Palace, the pavements were lined with people waving and cheering. And overlaying it all was the sound of the helicopter, pounding the air above our heads, the dark shadow that followed us all the way along the route.

Sitting in the back of the Daimler ten years later, Tony stone-faced beside me, I sighed. He could hardly be surprised by my outburst. It wasn't the first time he'd witnessed such a response, and it was unlikely to be the last. He even calls me his "bolshie Scouser" — slang for a belligerent Liverpudlian. Liverpudlians may be a tough, touchy, and belligerent lot, but they have other qualities, too. They are risk takers, fiercely loyal and proud, and they look after their own. They have to: Scousers have always been outsiders, hence the humor. There's an old Liverpool saying: "If you can't change it, take pride in it."

As for the press and its relentless campaign to paint me as a grasping, scheming embarrassment, I knew, for all my faults, it was simply using me as a way at getting at my husband. I had been born into a hard world and raised by strong women, and I had learned to cope. The paradox was that in my work as a barrister — the English term for a trial lawyer — or a judge I spoke on behalf of other people and was used to being heard. Yet in this other life as the Prime Minister's wife, my voice had virtually been silenced. As we drove down the Mall, I realized with a sudden surge of spirit that those constraints were no longer there. I had traveled a long way and learned so much. The time had come, I decided, to speak for myself.

SPEAKING FOR
MYSELF

CHAPTER 1

The Beginning

The story starts in the early 1950s, when two young actors meet on tour in the provinces. As happens in such stories, they fall in love and are soon in the family way. When a daughter is born, they are overjoyed and overwhelmed at the same time. Sadly, the strain of living in shabby digs, short of money and work, and with a small baby in tow, proves too much. Thus, when their baby is six weeks old, they leave her in the care of the father's parents in Liverpool and go off to the big city to seek their fortune.

The year was 1954, the baby was me, and I never grew tired of hearing how my parents met, of their respective childhoods, and, of course, of how I got my unusual name.

My father, Tony Booth, fell into acting largely by accident. While doing his national service, he conducted a prolonged flirtation with a colonel's wife. As she was heavily into amateur dramatics, he decided that this was the way in. And so the stage was set for the rest of his life. Although he regularly complained that the theater was dominated by gay men, this state of affairs presented him with plenty of opportunities in terms of the ladies.

My mum took her profession a good deal more seriously. One year younger than my father, Joyce Smith had been born and brought up in Ilkeston, a mining village west of Nottingham.

Her mother, born Hannah Meer, remains something of an enigma. Beyond her unusual maiden name and the fact that she was a local beauty with lustrous blue-black hair, I know nothing about her. My mum's father, however, was an extraordinary man, totally self-educated. Jack Smith first went down the pit at the age of fourteen as an ordinary miner, but he was soon promoted to shotfirer — first into the mine at the beginning of a shift, armed solely with a miner's lamp. His job was to test for gas. By the end of his career, Jack had made mine manager.

From time to time we would go over to Ilkeston to visit my grandfather, who was still living in the house where my mother had grown up. I remember being terrified of the huge blue scar on his face. If you had an accident down in the pit, he later explained, the wound could never be adequately cleaned of coal dust, which turned the scar tissue blue. Another thing that intrigued me was the huge amount of water he used to wash himself. He no longer worked underground by then, so he had no need to douse himself in this excessive manner, but old habits die hard. The bathroom where Hannah would have scrubbed his back was still downstairs, and the toilet paper was still squares of newspaper on a hook.

Grandad Jack had always wanted to be a doctor, but for the eldest of eleven children, this was impossible. The nearest he got to it was joining the St. John's Ambulance Brigade and becoming involved with pit rescue. Later he gave lessons in first aid, using my reluctant mother as a guinea pig. He was a man of prodigious energy, active in the Labour Party and Salvation Army. He also wrote poetry and toward the end of his life obtained a degree from the Open University, Britain's state-run distance-learning university for mature students. He worked until he was eighty, becoming a night watchman after he retired from the mines.

As if that wasn't enough, he was also a soccer referee and ran sports clubs for young people. My mother would be obliged to join in, though she always hated these activities. What she enjoyed more was the youth club that he ran during World War II. He was a considerable musician — there wasn't a brass instrument he couldn't play — and having trained the boys and girls in the club, he would visit old people's homes and hospitals and put on little shows. My mum played the piano, flute, and violin.

Mum had an unusual education for the time, attending one of the first Rudolf Steiner schools, Michael House. Everything about it was avant-garde. She began school in 1936, at the age of three and a half. Music and movement, known as Eurythmy, was central to Steiner's ethos. Michael House even boasted its own theater, and from the beginning, my mum was involved in school plays.

But then tragedy struck. Shortly after the war ended, the grandmother I never met died at the age of forty-two. Although Hannah was a local girl, the Meer family wasn't close, and no help was forthcoming from her sisters after her death. So on top of going to school, fourteen-year-old Joyce now had the house, her ten-year-old brother, and her father to look after. Before leaving home early in the morning, my grandfather would ensure that the fire was lit, but that was the extent of his involvement in household chores. It fell to my mother to do everything else: shopping, cooking, washing, ironing, and cleaning, not to mention scrubbing her father's back when he got home from the pit. Being a clever girl, she planned to stay in school until she was eighteen and do her "Matric," the exams that were then the passport to university and beyond. But after a year of attempting to marry schooling and housekeeping, she was asked to leave Michael House.

Meanwhile she had met a woman called Beryl John, whose career on the stage had been cut short by illness but who ran an amateur dramatic society and gave private lessons. How my grandfather could pay for these lessons, I have no idea, but he did. All went well until, out of the blue, he announced he was marrying a woman named Mabel, whom my mother had never met and knew nothing about beyond her name. Not unreasonably, perhaps, my mum took complete umbrage at this interloper, and the day her father married, she packed her suitcase and left. She never lived under their roof again.

Encouraged by my auntie Beryl (as I later called her), Mum applied to and was accepted by the Royal Academy of Dramatic Art, better known as RADA, as prestigious then as it is now. Her father paid the tuition not because he thought it was a sensible thing to do, she believes, but out of guilt.

At the end of her first year at RADA, she jumped at a summer job with the Earl Armstrong Repertory Company. Run by a husband-and-wife team, the company was based in Yorkshire. After one week of rehearsals, the company set out for Wales, and the newly named Gale Howard (Beryl John had planned to use Gay Howard for her own thwarted career) was soon playing romantic leads opposite

Tony Booth, a young actor from Liverpool with no training but charisma to burn. It proved a real baptism of fire. At one time, my mum recalls, the troupe had thirty shows under their belts and still had to do everything themselves: sew costumes, sell tickets, make and paint the scenery, and change the sets. Performing was just the icing on the cake. If a larger cast was called for, there would be any number of keen amateurs, wherever they went, at no cost.

September arrived all too quickly, and a new term at RADA was beckoning. Drama schools are all very well, but as any professional actor will tell you, there is nothing like the real thing, and Gale Howard never went back. More Welsh towns followed, and in one of them — possibly in Rhayader — I was conceived. Next to the only local theater was a café the company used to frequent, run by the mother and grandmother of an eight-year-old girl so taken with the theater that every night she would climb out of her bedroom window on the ground floor and persuade somebody at the stage door to let her in. After the show Tony and Gale — at twenty-one and twenty, barely more than kids themselves — would escort the little imp home, with no one any the wiser. That Christmas found them back in Rhayader, where the run comprised three pantomimes and one Christmas play. The name of the play is now lost, but the cast included two dogs called Schmozzle and Kerfuffle. In the pantomimes my mother played Cinderella, the princess in *The Princess and the Swineherd*, and one of the babes in *The Babes in the Wood*. The other babe was played by the ecstatic café owner's daughter, achieving her dream of appearing onstage, albeit with no lines.

By the end of the season my parents knew that my mother was pregnant, and when the Armstrongs refused to increase their wages, they had no option but to head back to London. The café owner's daughter was devastated that she was about to lose her newfound friends. Mum promised that she would never forget her, and if their baby turned out to be a girl, she said, they would name it after her. And they did: Cherie.

Tony Booth and Gale Howard were married in Marylebone Registry Office in London, a decent six months before I was born. In the end it was all a bit of a rush: a job had come up at Castleford Rep, and they were due to start rehearsals the next day. Their witnesses were the brother of the landlady my mother had had when she was a student at RADA and the registrar's assistant, a Mr. Christmas.

Afterward the landlady's brother took the newlyweds to the top floor of Lyons Corner House, then a landmark restaurant, cheerful but cheap, on the corner of Piccadilly Circus. There, to the strains of a string quartet, they celebrated with tea and cakes in preparation for the four-hour train journey to Yorkshire.

They were still in the north the following autumn, my father now with the Frank H. Fortescue Famous Players. According to my birth certificate, Cherie Booth was born on September 23, 1954, in Fairfield Hospital, in the town of Bury, Lancashire — an event my father announced from the stage that evening to a rather bemused audience. His request for two weeks off to help with the new arrival was turned down, so in true Tony Booth fashion, he gave his employer the finger. With no work forthcoming and rent still needing to be paid, the young couple tucked their daughter into a basket padded with nappies and smelling of greasepaint, and boarded the train for Liverpool.

Crosby lies at the northern end of Liverpool, the Catholic end, where thousands, if not millions, of Irish families disembarked from ships that brought them from their homeland, convinced they wouldn't be staying longer than a few weeks — months at the worst — until they'd be sailing across the Atlantic toward a new life in America. For some the dream came true, but for many it didn't. Instead of Manhattan's skyline, they had to make do with the Liver Building and the cranes and derricks of the Liverpool docks.

Crosby itself had aspirations. My paternal grandparents, Vera and George Booth, lived in a terraced house in Waterloo, the poorer part of Crosby. Upstairs were two and a half bedrooms (the half was a boxroom above the front door with barely enough room for a single bed); downstairs were a front room (the parlor), a back room (the sitting room), and the kitchen and scullery. It was fully plumbed, if basic. It was by no means a house to be ashamed of; indeed they owned it — an uncommon occurrence in those parts. Working-class people such as my grandparents rarely owned houses in those days. At the end of our road was a park with swings and a roundabout. This marked the demarcation line between Waterloo (terraced) and Great Crosby (semidetached). Our street, Ferndale Road, was the last of a grid of other "dales" — Thorndale, Oakdale, and so on — that all abutted St. John's Road. This bustling shopping street, with its butcher, pawnbroker, grocers, barbers, and secondhand shops, seemed to me then to be the center of the universe.

Like all the other houses in our street, Number 15 had a bay window, a small garden at the front, and a slightly larger garden at the rear, made smaller by the presence of an air-raid shelter left over from the war. Unlike the other yellow-brick houses in Ferndale Road, ours was painted cream and green, from the time when, so legend has it, my great-grandfather decided to show where his political allegiances lay — the green a nod to his Irish nationalism — in as ostentatious a manner as possible.

With the largest Catholic population in England, Liverpool has always been a highly politicized city. It prided itself on having no industry — that was left to lesser places like Manchester — no idle boast when the industrial north was shrouded in smoke and washing hung out only when the wind was blowing in the right direction. First and last, Liverpool was a port, and Merseyside (for the river Mersey, which ran through the city) was thus built on transient labor. Unemployment was the baseline. You helped your neighbor out today because God help you tomorrow. In the years before the Labour Party's general election victory in 1945 and the coming of the National Health Service and the British welfare state, Liverpool's communities survived through networks of voluntary effort, and that habit never died. Lending a hand to those in trouble was not an option in our house; it was simply what you did, even if in doing so you went a few shillings short yourself.

Fifteen Ferndale Road was a very Catholic household. My grandmother, born Vera Thompson, was an Irish matriarch of the old school, though Liverpool-born and with a rich Scouse accent. She had two brothers, Edgar and William, and by the time I arrived, Uncle Bill was the proud owner of three small grocer's shops, an empire started by selling tea off a bike with a box strapped on the back. Vera's mother — my great-grandma Matilda, known as Tilly, the youngest of seventeen — came over with her family from County Mayo (or Cork, depending on whom you believe) on their way to America. But like so many others, the McNamaras got no farther than the Liverpool docks. At some point she met my great-grandfather, and that was that.

Her husband Robert Thompson's roots have been the subject of much family debate. The version my grandma told was that he was from Yorkshire, a young man from a family called Tankard. After deserting in the First World War, the hightailed it to Ireland, where he changed his name to Thompson to escape detection. Another version is that he was simply another Irish immigrant who failed to get a passage to the promised land.

What is not in dispute is that he was a fiery character with a talent for drinking, going to horse races, and losing money. He was also a radical. He had been a local leader of the nationwide general strike that crippled the country for nine days in 1926. From then on, he earned his money as a barber, sitting on an orange box outside the dock gates, shaving sailors and cutting their hair when they returned from months at sea with money in their pockets and an urge to spend it. (Not everyone was willing to part with his cash, and my great-grandma would tell stories of how he'd end up accepting the strangest things in lieu, including a parrot that lived with them for years and a monkey she wouldn't let inside the front door.) Eventually he opened his own barber's shop on the corner of Denmark Street in the area known as Little Scandinavia, whose narrow, cobbled streets — back-to-back houses with outside toilets — were to become my route to primary school.

Sadly, I never met him. Robert Thompson died in 1946, and my dad, who adored his grandfather, said the streets of Waterloo were lined with mourners from Ferndale Road as far as St. Edmund's Church when his coffin passed by.

On her husband's death, Matilda moved in with her daughter. The little bedroom above the front door became her private domain. She remained there until she died, when I was seven. She was the only person in the household who had a room to herself, and yet in the years she lived with us, I don't remember ever seeing her lift a finger to help, although occasionally you might catch sight of her flicking a feather duster to show she was willing. Her major preoccupation was watching the comings and goings in the street below from behind her lace curtains. She was tiny, like a bird, and gray-haired, but with a hint of the fiery redhead she had once been. Her legendary temper, however, was still firmly in place. Nevertheless, she was remarkably tolerant when, dressed in my nurse's uniform, I would "inject" her arm with a plastic syringe, and she was always a good source of a sixpence.

From the perspective of an imaginative young girl, my grandfather's ancestors had led far less exciting lives. They were resolutely English, with no unresolved mysteries — or so I thought then. My great-grandmother's family ran a small fishing fleet out of Formby, about thirty miles north of Liverpool up the Lancashire coast, while my great-grandfather's family were hill farmers from Westmorland, the English Lake District, just south of the border with Scotland. Nothing in our family is that straightforward, however, and after my grandad's death I discovered that in the First World War, his father — my great-grandfather Booth — had been a pacifist and had gone to prison for it. He later served as a stretcher-bearer in the trenches in Flanders, where he was severely gassed. My great-grandmother's father turned out to be a famous smuggler who ran a protection racket on the side.

In contrast to the Irish branch of the family, George Booth, my grandfather, was never a great talker, though it didn't help that he was absent more often than he was at home. By the time I was living in Ferndale Road, this translated into ten days on shore for every six weeks away at sea. He was then the chief steward's writer on the MV *Auriel*, which sailed from Liverpool to Nigeria, and his tales of the sights and sounds of Lagos brought Africa vividly to life. He only truly came into his own when playing the piano, which he did at every opportunity. My father claims that he'd had to turn down a scholarship to the Royal Academy of Music in London when he was a boy and that later he had been offered a job with a famous bandleader. It may be true, but Grandad never mentioned it to me. He was much more than just a pub pianist, however. The piano stool was full of sheet music that he'd bought in New York on his sailings with Cunard, and it's thanks to him that I can still sing most of the show songs of the 1950s and 1960s (though whether this is a good thing is another matter).

My grandfather was a gentle and sensitive man, with the most beautiful, but tiny, copperplate handwriting. He hadn't been my grandmother's first choice for a husband. Grandma would tell me how she'd married him on the rebound after the love of her life — a Protestant — refused to convert. It was only then that piano-playing George made his move. He was a friend of her brother's, and it turned out he'd been nursing this secret passion for years. Although the proposed marriage was frowned on by both families, time was running out for the twenty-nine-year-old Vera, who probably realized that the love of a good man was worth any amount of family tut-tutting. Love her he clearly did, though whenever he tried to kiss her in front of us, she'd push him away with a fond "Don't be so daft." Only years later did it emerge that *he* wasn't a Catholic either. On paper, yes: he had converted — my grandmother would never have married him otherwise — but religion was nothing to him. He hardly ever went to church, but as he was away so much, it didn't seem that strange, and the family had plenty of priests to smooth its way into heaven. (I can still remember the mystique that surrounded my cousin Paul — Father Paul as he later became — when he visited from the seminary and how Grandma would insist that we girls keep our distance, to avoid corrupting him with our presence!)

My own relationship with the Catholic Church, though very important to me, has never been entirely conventional. It began with my baptism. Even though my parents had registered my birth in Bury, to a Catholic like my grandma, an unbaptized child was tantamount to a mortal sin. Luckily she knew that her cousin Father Bernard Harvey would quickly rectify the situation, and within hours of my arrival in Ferndale Road, she had been to see him.

"So what would the little one's name be then, Vera?"

"Cherie."

"What was that?"

"Cherie."

"Is that it?"

"That's it."

"Now, Vera, I don't have to tell you, of all people, that the Holy Church . . ."

He didn't. This was 1954, ten years before the Second Vatican Council. Services were still in Latin. Nuns were still fully veiled in habits that reached down to the ground. And Vera Booth knew only too well that a Catholic child could be baptized only with the name of a Catholic saint. Although there are more than seven thousand of them, no amount of scanning unusual saints' names (and there are many) would have revealed a Saint Cherie.

A compromise was eventually reached, and I was baptized Theresa Cara: Theresa being a bona fide saint, and Cara being Latin for Cherie, which was probably Father Bernard's attempt at keeping the peace. At the same time, my grandma opened a savings account for me in the name of T. C. Booth, which I used right up until 1997.

11

My mother, needless to say, had no voice in these decisions. Although she came from a religious background herself — her father was in the Salvation Army, and she'd gone to Sunday school as a child — she claims that she was quite happy for me to be baptized a Catholic, having no strong feelings one way or the other. There may have been another reason for her acquiescence, however. Locking horns with one of the most formidable women on the planet was not something anyone would do voluntarily — particularly if they were now living under the same roof. Nobody messed with Vera Booth.

People who lived through the depression have never entirely forgotten it. Make do and mend wasn't some green-friendly exercise for my grandmother; it was the result of years of draconian economy. For the decade preceding the war, my grandad had virtually no work. Trade between England and America was at a standstill — no ships, empty docks, work only for those who knew somebody who knew somebody else. In those circumstances the women became the breadwinners. My grandma did anything she could, cleaning the houses of the well-to-do who lived in nearby Blundellsands — only a short distance away geographically but light-years from Crosby in terms of money and horizons. Her world was divided between the rich and the poor — and the Booths were definitely the poor. Before she married, she had worked in a draper's in Blundellsands, and she would tell the story of how one day a young woman came in with a new baby. My grandma could never resist a baby, and after chucking him under the chin, she asked what he was called.

"Anthony" came the answer, pronounced with a soft "th," rather than a "t."

"Oh," she said. "I love that name. If I have a little boy, I think I'll call him Anthony."

She said she would never forget the expression on the woman's face — a "people like you don't have Anthonys like my Anthony" expression.

My grandma remained class-conscious all her life and continued to believe that there was one law for the rich and one law for the poor. When my dad was about ten, he came down with scarlet fever and, as happened in those days, was sent to an isolation hospital, where his mother could only look at him through a window. When he was eventually allowed home, he asked her why she had never been to visit his bedside. "Because it wasn't allowed," she said. Then he told her how the boy in the next bed had had regular visits from his parents: a boy who came from Blundellsands. I don't know how long my dad was in there, weeks certainly, if not months, and it undoubtedly affected him. I also think it affected my grandmother's attitude toward him, as she felt so guilty that she had simply accepted what she'd been told and hadn't insisted on seeing him.

When I was growing up, my source of stories about my father's early life was my grandmother, because by the time I was old enough to savor and enjoy them, he had disappeared from our lives. He was born in 1931 and named, of course, after that superior baby in Blundellsands. Then came my auntie Audrey in 1935, and finally my uncle Bob, who was born during the first Luftwaffe bombing raid on Liverpool in May 1940.

With the outbreak of the war, everything changed. For a start, suddenly the docks were alive again. The merchant navy was desperate for men to work the Atlantic convoys, and so that's what Grandad did. Dangerous though it was — more merchant seamen died than members of the Royal Navy — it was work, and it was patriotic. In fact, it was no safer to stay in Liverpool, where the docks were a prime target of the Luftwaffe. The attacks reached their peak in May 1941 with a weeklong blitz, when 4,000 people were killed, 10,000 homes were destroyed, and 70,000 people were made homeless.

War or no war, my dad was growing up. In 1943 he got a scholarship to St. Mary's College, a Catholic grammar school run by the Christian Brothers, about half a mile along the Liverpool Road into Crosby proper. He was clearly destined for great things. St. Mary's boys were famous for going into the church and higher education.

An academic future was not to be his, however. Shortly after my grandad returned from the war in 1946, he was hit by a crane and plunged eighty feet into the hold of a ship, breaking his pelvis. He was lucky not to have been killed. His pay was stopped immediately, and he was off work for nearly two years. Through the union he was eventually awarded compensation, but as soon as he was fit enough to go back, Cunard's response was to lay him off.

In the days following the accident, my grandma did everything she could to find a job herself, but nothing would pay enough. The Booth family now had five mouths to feed, including a seven-year-old (Bob) and a twelve-year-old (Audrey), and no money to do it with. Eventually my grandma had to accept the inevitable, and my father left St. Mary's. At fifteen he began working on the Cunard transatlantic route.

I remained with my grandparents for about two years following my arrival as a babe in arms, my parents coming and going as work allowed. At one point they did a summer season in Blackpool, close enough for them to come down to see me on weekends (which meant Sunday to Monday). Sometimes my mother stayed with me in Crosby, but usually not, and I certainly never traveled with them. I was left with my grandma, my mum now says, because she wanted me to have continuity, "a steady place," though I suspect she already knew that to keep my dad, she'd have to stick to him like glue. And of course she wanted to be with him: he was witty and handsome, and she was in her early twenties and in love.

By late 1956 my father found the beginnings of fame, if not of fortune, with the play No Time for Sergeants, based on a best-selling novel. The play ran for eighteen months in the West End, and by the time my sister Lyndsey was born, he and Gale (as my mother is always called) were living in a settled way in a large Victorian house in Stoke Newington, north London. When Lyndsey was about three months old, my grandparents took me down to meet her.

On arrival, my grandma went straight to the nearest Catholic church and arranged to have the baby baptized the following day. The only Catholic my mother knew, another actress, was roped in to be Lyndsey's godmother. This duty done, my grandparents left, at which point I discovered the hideous truth: I wasn't going with them. According to my mother, my grandma's last words to me as she and Grandad left the house were "You're going to live with your mother now. You'll probably never see me again."

I was inconsolable: kicking and screaming and generally expressing my anger and distress in the only way I could. The woman I called "Mama" had gone for good. What it must have been like for my poor mother, I can scarcely imagine, overcome as she was, no doubt, with guilt and remorse, and possibly even jealousy. As for my grandmother, traumatic as it was, she had clearly fueled my dependence on her and so exacerbated my sense of abandonment. Later, when we were all happily (from my perspective) back in Crosby, she would repeatedly tell me how she could never listen to "I Could Have Danced All Night," the Julie Andrews classic from *My Fair Lady*, without crying, because it had been playing on the radio when her "baby" had been taken from her.

I stayed in Stoke Newington long enough for photographs to be taken, including one of the toddler Cherie looking bemused, her baby sister propped up in her carriage beside her. The photo is of poor quality, but the general impression is not a happy one, and I think that was probably an accurate reflection of the circumstances. It couldn't have helped that my parents were living in what was essentially a student house with rented rooms and no real structured family life. My dad would come home from the theater late at night, and inevitably I'd be woken up. I have a vague memory of the sporadic presence of another flamboyant actor couple, blessed with an equally cavalier attitude toward children and their needs. Apart from my mother — whom at this juncture I barely knew — the most stable presence in the house was my auntie Diane. Not a real aunt but my mum's friend, Diane lived in the basement with another girl, both of whom were studying design at the North London Polytechnic, as it was then known. To make ends meet, my mum spent hours packing sherbet fountains — an English candy made of sherbet powder and licorice sticks — during the day. In later years I could never bring myself to eat them; the smell alone was enough to bring back twinges of anxiety.

Christmas passed. (The only Christmas I ever missed having with my grandma until she died.) Then spring. I imagine they'd been hoping I'd settle down, but I didn't. For the previous two years I had been the apple of my grandma's eye, and now I was just one of two little girls competing for affection. There is no doubt that, for all my grandmother's iron will, I had been horribly spoiled. Shortly before Christmas my dad's show closed, and having no means of paying the rent in Stoke Newington, our little family returned to Ferndale Road. Even now I can remember the joy of finding myself once again sharing my grandma's bed.

It is only once I returned to Ferndale Road that my own memories really begin, starting with the smells: my grandad's Senior Service cigarettes; the condensed milk he used to sweeten his tea;

coal burning in the grate. In addition to the various humans in the house, we once had a cat and always had dogs — Alsatians, all called Sheba; Quin, a poodle — plus sundry white mice and tortoises. (In those days nobody connected the pets with my frequent asthma attacks.) There are fragments of other memories: A circular ashtray where the cigarette stubs disappeared when you pushed down the plunger. Linoleum that curled up at the edges. The gas meter behind the front door which we fed with shillings. (As a treat, I'd drop them in, and Grandad would turn the knob.) Except when Grandad was at home, I slept in my grandma's bed, while Lyndsey slept in our mum's. In fact, they slept in the same saggy double bed right up until Lyndsey left home.

For a long time I had an ambivalent relationship with my grandad. Of course I loved him, but whenever he came back from sea, I'd be ousted from my place, obliged to sleep on a camp bed in my mother's room. My resentment was always short-lived. Who could resist someone who played all your favorite songs? The first Sunday he was back on shore, our front room would be filled with aunts, uncles, and cousins for a sing-along. Grandad would always start with "Thank Heaven for Little Girls," dedicated to Lyndsey and me. Then one tune would flow into another, and we'd all join in, with people asking for their favorites, Broadway musicals mainly: *My Fair Lady*, *South Pacific*, *West Side Story*, and, best of all, *The Sound of Music*. There was a time when I knew every single word.

Grandad was not without vices. The first was horses: he was always trying different "systems," but he never seemed to win. The second was smoking: cigarettes were cheap at sea, and he would get through forty untipped Senior Service a day. He coughed his guts out the last few years before he died. As a result, I have never touched a cigarette in my life. His third vice was drinking: not alcohol, but very strong tea sweetened with lashings of condensed milk, which also came in handy for sticking tiles on the wall in the bathroom whenever they fell off, a regular occurrence.

For the next eighteen months, my father worked in various theaters around the north, based with us but in reality visiting only on weekends. The only time he actually lived with us was when he did a season at Liverpool Playhouse, but when that came to an end, he headed back to London. Realistically it was the only place he could forge a career. Once he'd found somewhere to live, he told my mum, we'd join him. It never happened. It was during this time that he first played opposite Pat Phoenix, then an unknown actress called Patricia Dean, who would later become an important person in his life — and in mine.

CHAPTER 2

Growing Up

School was naturally St. Edmund's Catholic Primary, where my father, Auntie Audrey, and Uncle Bob had all gone before me. The school was attached to St. Edmund's Church, where Father Bernard Harvey, my grandma's cousin — the one who had baptized me — was the parish priest.

I suppose that for the first day or two, I must have been taken to school, but from then on I would go on my own and later took Lyndsey with me. Hand in hand we would walk or skip down St. John's Road, past Ronnie the cobbler, who had been at school with my dad and who always said hello. Farther along there was the pawnbroker's on the corner, with a window made entirely of black glass that came down to the pavement. If you pressed your nose to the glass and raised an arm and a leg, you looked as if you were flying. Then we'd continue up over the railway. If a train was coming, we would stand on the footbridge and shriek as the steam billowed round us, lifting our skirts and warming our bare legs in winter. On the far side lay Little Scandinavia, a shortcut to school. The streets here were still cobbled, making the game of never stepping on the cracks far more challenging than on the hopscotch sidewalks of Ferndale Road. In the middle of this labyrinth, the rag-and-bone man kept his horse. In Crosby we had had miles and miles of dunes — you could even see the sea from my classroom window — but this was the nearest we got to the country. So whenever the old man wasn't around, we would clamber up and peer over the wall at his poor horse. If the old man found us, he'd yell abuse and we'd scramble down, scraping our knees on the brick, then rubbing them better with lick. Another game was breaking empty milk bottles. All you had to do was pick one up, drop it, and then run down one of the entries before an aproned housewife could reach the door. One morning my friend Margot and I were spotted, and I'll never forget the shame of having to stand in front of the whole school while our hands were rapped with a ruler.

On the way home we might stop at my uncle's shop, a grocer's cum sweetshop, and buy a piece of candy. We had to pay: Uncle Bill was far too canny a businessman to give anything away, even to us. He used to have these little cereal packets for display purposes, though, and when he changed the window, he'd let us have them to play shop.

As soon as I was old enough, I'd be sent out on errands — "messages," as they were called. Grandma made us memorize her requests, and they had to be delivered word perfect or else. "Four nice, lean lamb chops, please, for Mrs. Booth." God help either me or the butcher if they weren't. The question for the baker was "Is it fresh?" If what he gave me turned out not to be, then woe betide. I'd be packed off back with the stale loaf, where my new line would be "Mrs. Booth is not satisfied."

Life could not have been easy for my mother. From the beginning, her mother-in-law made it clear that, grandchildren or no grandchildren, we would have to pay our way. If anyone had expected my dad to support his family, they were mistaken. His career was going well, with work on both the stage and the small screen (television) steadily coming his way, but that made no difference. Thus Mum would get Lyndsey and me up and breakfasted and ready for school before setting off by bicycle toward Seaforth, two miles away. There she would work behind the counter of a small fish-and-chip shop from ten o'clock till two. Grandma would give us our lunch, but Mum would be back in Ferndale Road in time to give us our tea. She would work again from four to six, then come home to get us ready for bed before heading back on the bike for her final stint from eight till midnight. All for a princely four pounds ten shillings a week, enough to cover the rent of a small room.

It's hard to imagine what working at the Seaforth chippie must have felt like for my mum. Only a few years earlier, Gale Howard had been a rising star at RADA, glamorous, accomplished (Jackie Collins had been one of her contemporaries), and with the world at her feet. Now here she was, serving penny packets of cod and chips and sausages to drunken sailors. I can just imagine the leers she got late at night. How long she suffered it, nobody remembers now. Months, certainly. Luckily salvation was at hand in the shape of Auntie Diane, her friend in Stoke Newington. Since qualifying as a designer, she had started work at Selfridges department store as a trainee buyer. Diane managed to get Mum an interview at Lewis's, Selfridges' parent company, whose flagship store was in Liverpool. Mum got the job.

Whereas an ordinary shop assistant's wage was £7 a week, my mum went straight in at £11, nearly three times what the fish-and-chip shop was paying her. Every week from then on, she gave half of whatever she earned to her mother-in-law. In addition, she continued to do the washing and ironing — although the new job meant that we soon got a top-loading washing machine. Naturally she also bought our clothes. Another plus of working for Lewis's was that she was entitled to a discount, which increased the longer she worked there. The bicycle was dispensed with, and from then on Mum took the bus, did a full day's work, and then took the bus back in time to put us to bed. As for her own life, she put it on hold. For a while she kept nursing the hope that her husband would come back, but he didn't. The money stopped; the visits stopped; there were no more telephone calls, or none that I remember, until the fateful one.

It was April 1963. The Easter holidays. I was eight, and Lyndsey was six. As a special treat, Mum had taken us to see *Summer Holiday*, a movie about a bus conductor who takes a London bus all the way to Greece for a holiday. We didn't often go to the movies, and I'd been looking forward to it ever since I'd heard it was coming to Crosby. I already had a poster of Cliff Richard, the film's star, pinned to my bedroom door. When we got back, Lyndsey and I were packed off upstairs to bed and banned from going downstairs again. Instead we played one of our favorite games, which we called "policewoman's training."

My grandma was always obsessed that burglars were about to

come in and steal our nonexistent worldly goods. Policewoman's training involved creeping downstairs, touching the front door, and rushing back up again, before Mum and Grandma, who would be watching television, could catch us. The rules were no noise and no giggling. Sometimes I'd lift Lyndsey onto the banister and give her a little shove so that she slid down to the bottom. On one occasion my hands slipped, so instead of putting her on the rail, I pushed her right over, and she plummeted down into the hallway. There was a sudden scream from downstairs, then Lyndsey was bawling out at the top of her voice, "Cherie tried to kill me!"

Lyndsey was only winded, and neither of us was punished, but I still remember hiding behind my grandma's bedroom door, shaking with fear.

On this particular Thursday night, we were playing policewoman's training when the phone rang. Scuttling hurriedly back upstairs, I crouched outside the bathroom as my mum came into the hall and picked up the phone. She didn't say anything, apart from hello at the beginning. Then suddenly she began to cry. I had seen her cry before, but nothing like this, and it was somehow worse because she didn't say anything to explain it. Then my grandma came out and started hissing, "How could he? . . It's absolutely unforgiveable! . . . As for the *Crosby Herald* . . ." Then she put her arm round my mum, which was something she didn't usually do.

Eventually they went back into the front room, and I just sat there on the landing, feeling my eyes prick as if I was going to cry. Then I found Lyndsey and told her that something terrible had happened, but I didn't know what.

The next morning at breakfast, everyone was quiet. Mum had obviously been crying all night, but nothing was said.

"Why don't you two run along to the park?" Grandma suggested.

So we did. The park was just at the end of our road. It was a lovely, sunny April day, and you could always find somebody to play with. I remember Lyndsey took her jump rope, and there was some discussion about whether we needed sweaters.

As soon as the other children saw us coming, they began staring and whispering. Finally I got up the courage to say something.

"What is it?" I asked one of my friends. "What are you looking at me like that for? What's happened?"

"You should know," she said, then shrugged and looked down at the ground. Then a group of boys started giggling and chanting my dad's name.

"Tony Booth, Tony Booth, Tony Booth!"

Even though he hadn't lived in Crosby for years, everyone knew who my father was. He was on the telly!

And then it all came out: the *Crosby Herald* was published on Friday, but the first edition appeared the night before, and that week, on the announcements page, top of the list, was the following:

BOOTH, Anthony, late of 15 Ferndale Road, Waterloo, and Julie née Allan proudly announce the arrival at the London Clinic of their daughter Jenia, a half sister for Cherie and Lindsay.

We had no idea. Mum had no idea. Grandma had no idea. Crosby had no idea.

It had generally been accepted in the family that my father had abandoned us, and by then Mum knew he was seeing someone else: she was even considering giving him a divorce. But when the new woman, Julie Allan, decided to force her hand with this announcement, it backfired spectacularly. Divorce was the one thing Mum could withhold.

It is difficult to overestimate the humiliation — to my mother, to his mother, and, of course, to his children. This was 1963, in the heart of Catholic Liverpool. People didn't get divorced, or if they did, they didn't talk about it. Girls who had the misfortune to get pregnant were sent away to convents to have their babies, who were then offered for adoption. As for "single parent," it was a term that hadn't yet been invented. To broadcast your sins to the world by placing an announcement in the local paper which everybody would read was a crime against society, against the church, and against everything any decent-minded person stood for.

And he hadn't even spelled Lyndsey's name right.

CHAPTER 3

Girlhood

Shortly after the painful business with my father, Uncle Bob, who had moved in with us, occupying my great-grandmother's former room after her passing in 1961, left home. He, too, had decided that he was going to be an actor and had taken up a place at the Central School of Speech and Drama in London. All at once the house felt very empty. The sole advantage was that I was given his room, which I would gladly have done without to have him back. He had been more like a brother than an uncle, and in a fatherless household, he had contributed a healthy dose of masculinity. I also missed his car, a sparkling Triumph Roadster, which had facilitated numerous adventures.

Children can be horribly cruel to anyone they sense is vulnerable or different, and I remember standing in a corner of the playground, with taunts of the "you're not a proper family" and "your dad doesn't love you" variety ringing in my ears. Newton's third law of physics tells us that for every action there is an equal and opposite reaction, and mine was to fight. I pulled hair. I punched. I bit. Friends stopped knocking at the door to ask if I could come out to play. Whether this was their own decision or their parents deciding that the Booths weren't the kind of people they wanted their kids to mix with, I don't know, but the effect was the same. I remember going down to the swings in the park, swinging as high as I could, my legs pumping away, wishing that a rope would break, and like

Katy in the classic children's book *What Katy Did*, I'd come crashing down, break my neck, and spend a lifetime as a cripple. Then they'd be sorry.

During those dreadful months, reading became my refuge. Although my grandmother had no education worth the name, she had always been a great reader and would pass on books she thought I might like, books that were far more sophisticated than a ten-year-old usually had access to. One of her favorite authors was Daphne du Maurier, and in *Frenchman's Creek* and *Jamaica Inn*, I could escape from the misery of the playground to nineteenth-century Cornwall and beyond. It was thanks to her that I discovered *Wuthering Heights* and fell in love with Heathcliff, Emily Brontë's dark-skinned orphan from Liverpool. Luckily Mrs. Savage, my teacher, was a woman of both sensitivity and sense. I had read my way through all the children's books in the local library, so not only did she arrange with the library to bend the rules and let me borrow adult books, but as the summer term drew to a close, she spoke to my mother and suggested that the following September I skip a year in school. I was bored, she said, and it was no wonder I was getting into trouble. It was simply that I wasn't being stretched.

I remember my mum sitting on my bed that night, holding my hand and telling me what had been decided — and yet warning me at the same time.

"Now remember, Cherie, you're going to be with children a whole year older than you, and it's going to be difficult."

Even so, it seemed as if I had won some sort of small victory, and my recent experience of trial by taunt only served to strengthen my resolve. I was, as my grandma used to say, "contrary." If my mum was saying it would be difficult, I'd show her she was wrong.

I succeeded. At the end of the year, my final year at St. Edmund's, I finished at the top of the class, and I remain convinced that it was the prompt action of this caring and farsighted teacher that stopped me from going completely off the rails.

The only thing that really suffered by my missing a year was my handwriting. To catch up, I had to do extra arithmetic while the others in the class were having handwriting lessons. As a result, it is still absolutely terrible (my grandad would be appalled). By the time I was in secondary school, it was too late for remedial treatment.

That last year at primary school was a magical time for me. Mr. Smerdon was one of those charismatic teachers you never forget. He had been a fighter pilot in the war and would devote hours recounting his experiences. However unconventional his instruction, it certainly did me no harm. A larger-than-life figure, he had theatrical aspirations and would occasionally disappear to London for auditions. He was also in charge of the school choir, of which I became a very enthusiastic member. He became a significant male presence in my life, the sort of man my father might have been if he had not left home.

Now that we didn't have Uncle Bob to take us out, Grandma decided we needed a car of our own. So in 1964, in an uncharacteristic act of generosity and folly combined, she bought a Mini. I can still remember the number plate: ALV 236B. She had no intention of driving it herself; this masterpiece of modern engineering and design was for Grandad.

Grandfather loved that Mini and was ridiculously proud of it. There was one small problem, however: he couldn't pass his driving test. I don't know how many times he took it, but he always failed. It didn't stop him from driving, although he never went very far. He and Grandma would take us down to the seafront, where Lyndsey and I could play on the beach while they watched the great ocean liners, including the *Queen Elizabeth* and *Queen Mary*, make their stately way from the docks to the open sea, bound for New York. Grandad had retired by this time, due to his bad heart, but the sea and ships were still in his blood.

Otherwise life in Ferndale Road continued much as usual: Mum went out to work, and Grandma stayed at home. Mum did the washing and the ironing, while Grandma did the cooking. She was what was known in those days as a plain cook, but a good one. The menu never varied. Sunday: roast shoulder of lamb. Monday: leftovers. Tuesday: mutton stew with potatoes. Wednesday was baking day, and we'd have steak and kidney pudding and apple pie. Nobody could make pastry like my grandma. Thursday was the "four nice, lean lamb chops" I'd learned to ask for. Friday was inevitably fish and chips, and Saturday was mincemeat pie. And so it continued, week in, week out. We rarely had chicken, which, in those days, before factory farming, was expensive. Shoulder of lamb was cheap (if bony), and the great Sunday treat was gnawing the sweet meat off the bone. I will never forget Grandma's mortification when, right in the middle of Mass, my cousin Catherine shouted, "Grandma, are we having bones for dinner?")

Sunday Mass was an important ritual. It wasn't simply our weekly appointment with God; it was the weekly get-together of the various branches of the family. The only person who didn't participate was my mother, although she'd always come to the big celebrations, such as my first Holy Communion and Easter. Whatever the current crisis, standards had to be upheld, so we would always dress up in our best coats and hats. When I was very young, the Mass was entirely in Latin, even the gospel readings. Then, as the Second Vatican Council began to take effect, the gospel at least was in English, though sung High Mass remained in Latin. (This at least had the advantage that I can now understand the service wherever I am in the world.)

During the years immediately following the discovery of my father's other family, he kept in touch with his mother sporadically but rarely came home. There came a point where my mum became a more important part of the household than he was. My grandad was especially fond of her, and he consistently refused to have anything to do with my dad.

From time to time Uncle Bob would see my father in London, and I remember on one visit to Liverpool, he showed me a photograph of my dad smiling broadly with Jenia, still a toddler, and a new addition: Bronwen, who had been born only a year later. I must have been upset — I can't imagine that I wouldn't have been — but whether I kept my feelings hidden at the time I can't remember. As to why Bob showed the photo to me, who can tell? Perhaps he thought it was a way of easing me in gently.

Over the next ten years or so, I saw my father only rarely. The first time, I was in the ninth grade at St. Edmund's. Crosby Baths was a state-of-the-art indoor swimming pool recently built on wasteland behind Crosby beach. St. Edmund's being just down the road, our class had been learning to swim. I have always been very uncoordinated physically and was as hopeless at swimming as I was at riding a bicycle (something I still can't do). Nevertheless, at the end of term there was going to be a gala, and for some reason my dad came along, ostensibly to see me compete.

When he arrived, there was pandemonium, as he had just appeared in the pilot for a new show called *Till Death Us Do Part*. The show had become an instant hit, and Tony Booth would soon become one of the most recognizable faces on television. Playing a left-wing, working-class Scouser (a character based on my father himself) made him a near god in left-wing, working-class Liverpool. But while everyone swarmed about him, I felt nonexistent.

My father is not one of nature's diplomats, and over the years, whenever he was interviewed in the newspapers, it was always his current daughters he talked about. At the time of the Crosby Baths gala, it was Jenia and Bronwen. Later their place would be taken by his next batch, Sarah (later known as Lauren) and Emma. I pretended I didn't care. But I did.

The only time I saw him at home was after my grandad died in September 1968. The death certificate said heart disease, but he'd been going downhill for some time because of his smoking. The heart got him before the lung cancer did.

Grandad's funeral was the first one that really affected me. I'd been only seven when my great-grandma had died, and Mum had decided I was too young to attend. I wasn't unused to the rituals of Irish death, however. As my grandma's favorite, I'd gone to any number of wakes when the various members of the Thompson clan had returned to their Maker. But Grandad was Grandad, and I was devastated. His body was laid out in our front room, and despite my mother's protests, I insisted on seeing him.

So there we all were in church — red-eyed and somber, waiting for the service to begin, while I tried not to stare at that horrible, shiny coffin where I knew his poor old body was lying, wondering what was going to happen to him when it was put into the ground, wondering how long he would have to stay in purgatory, whether God would have mercy on his soul and let him go straight up to heaven — when there was a sudden clattering and banging of the door and the thud of heavy footsteps crashing down the nave. And there was my dad, barging through the ranks of other family mourners to get to the front. It had been four years since I had last seen him at the Crosby Baths, and I clearly remember my fourteen-year-old self sitting there thinking, *What is he doing here?* It wasn't just outrage that he couldn't even turn up at the right time. My concern was largely for my mum and what she was feeling. I had reached the age where I was beginning to understand the wider implications of what he had done, specifically what it had meant to her. Ironically, although he had abandoned us, my sister and I were very much part of his family, in which he was inevitably a central, if absent, figure, whereas we were not really part of my mother's family at all. That he was late to his own father's funeral was in some ways predictable: Tony Booth was a man who knew how to say hello but never thought much about saying good-bye.

I went on to Seafield Grammar after St. Edmund's. Seafield was run by nuns, a French order called the Sacred Heart of Mary.

From the seventy pupils in my year at St. Edmund's, only four girls got into Seafield Grammar. One couldn't go because her parents couldn't afford the uniform. When Lyndsey followed me to Seafield three years later, she inherited my old blazer, and I got a new one. On her first day at school, she was singled out by the headmistress. "Why are you wearing that shabby blazer?" the headmistress demanded. Poor Lyndsey said later that she had stammered and blushed and wished the ground would open up and swallow her. The truth was, of course, that my mother couldn't afford to buy two new ones, even though she got a discount, Seafield's school outfitters being Lewis's.

By the late sixties, after years of being little more than an embarrassing joke, Liverpool had become the center of the universe. Although I had been too young to go to the Cavern and see the Beatles, we were all very proud to be Scousers. After all, it wasn't only the Beatles; there were also the Searchers, the Swinging Blue Jeans, the Merseybeats, Cilla Black, Gerry and the Pacemakers, and dozens more, now forgotten. By the time I was old enough to go out, however, folk was my music of choice. Together with a friend from Seafield, I had learned to play the guitar, and we would do versions of traditional songs that the Spinners, a homegrown band that revived "Scarborough Fair" long before Simon and Garfunkel recorded it, were bringing to a wider audience. The Spinners became famous for songs about Liverpool, including "Maggie Mae," about a Liverpool sailor and a prostitute — nothing like the later Rod Stewart version. Another favorite was "In My Liverpool Home":

I was born in Liverpool, down by the docks
Me Religion was Catholic, occupation Hard-Knocks
At stealing from lorries I was adept,
And under old overcoats each night I slept

Once I was a Seafield girl, I no longer saw my friends from primary school who had gone to St. Bede's. It wasn't that I was hostile to them; they were hostile to me. I was now "posh."

There were other changes, too, and it took me time to settle down. Relative to St. Edmund's, the regime was strict. Although the majority of the teachers were not nuns, the sisters ran the school and lived in the convent attached to it. Skirts had to be a regulation two inches above the knee (though of course as we got older, we got bolder and were always hiking them up). The moment we got into school, we had to change our outdoor shoes for indoor shoes, and there was no running in the corridors. The nuns used to keep the oak floors polished like mirrors, and heaven help us if we transgressed.

The worst aspect of life at Seafield was the school lunch. At St. Edmund's I had been close enough to go home at midday. Seafield, however, was a good twenty minutes' walk away; by the time I got home, it would be time to go back. Furthermore, I'd only ever had my grandma's cooking, and she encouraged me to think that nobody else could meet her high standards. Faced with this dilemma, I could see only one solution: I didn't eat.

I had always been what in those days was called "painfully thin," and the first sign that something was amiss was an asthma attack. It was then that the doctors decided I was malnourished. I could not go a whole day without food, they said, no matter how good a breakfast I had. By chance, my auntie Audrey lived only about fifty yards from Seafield, on the opposite side of the road. As her third baby had just been born, she was at home during the day and agreed to give me lunch. This arrangement continued until I was fourteen, when Auntie's husband, my uncle Bill, was promoted to bank manager, at which point they sold their house and moved.

Over those three formative years, Auntie Audrey and I became very close. I even started my periods at her house. Back then this was still considered something shameful and not to be discussed, but thanks to her, I was spared all of that. Though never an academic, she had always been politically aware. I was used to my grandad and the other men in the family talking politics, but women largely kept out of these conversations. In retrospect I think it likely that I owe my early interest in politics to her. Whatever the trigger, by the time I was fourteen, when asked what I wanted to be when I grew up, I would answer, "Prime Minister!" Whether it was simply the smart-aleck reply of a teenager who wanted to impress, I don't remember. What is in absolutely no doubt, however, is that in 1970, at the age of sixteen, I was committed enough to join the Labour Party.

CHAPTER 4

Convent Girl

As far as academic progress was concerned, although I was always among the top students, I was never first in the class until I reached the sixth form. I was useless at languages, so until I could drop them, they pulled me down. Looking back, I realize that dropping them was a mistake, as, unusually for the time, I had every opportunity to get practical experience.

Right from when we were small, Lyndsey and I had always gone away on holiday, usually day trips and drives to resorts in Wales. In hindsight I know that it was the one chance our mum had of having us to herself.

Once my mother was transferred to Lewis's travel department, however, our horizons broadened. As a matter of routine, counter staff were encouraged to take advantage of the subsidized travel offered by companies whose holidays they were selling, this being particularly important for new destinations. Mum could go free, and Lyndsey and I could tag along for a nominal cost.

My first taste of "abroad" was a bus tour to Spain when I was around twelve. It was right at the beginning of the package-holiday era, when the Costa Brava was still relatively undeveloped. I was horrified by the toilets we had to use when we stopped, which were hole-in-the-floor affairs. To someone brought up with Grandma's near-holy attitude toward toilet cleanliness, it was a salutary lesson. When we eventually reached Calella, then no more than a fishing village, I remember being astonished at seeing oranges and lemons growing on trees and having fresh juice to drink instead of sweetened concentrate.

The following year we went to Italy, to a village on the Italian Riviera. This time we flew, and the whole thing seemed incredibly glamorous and exciting. I loved flying and still do. Our next trip was even more exotic — to Romania. As this was shortly after Grandad died, Mum felt obliged to take Grandma with us. I had never seen her so unnerved. First time out of England, first time on a plane, first time hearing foreign voices. Romania was still a communist country, and we had been advised to take tights as presents for the chambermaids. We flew into Bucharest, but we were mainly based in a down-at-heel resort on the Black Sea. As part of my mother's research, we visited a health spa, where the treatment consisted of being covered entirely in mud. It was all very un-English, and although it might not have helped my language ability, it certainly gave me a fascination for the wider world.

By this time my social life revolved around the Young Christian Students (YCS) — the best chance a good Catholic girl had of meeting a good Catholic boy, which for Seafield girls meant boys from St. Mary's. Although the two schools faced each other across Liverpool Road, opportunities for getting to know one another were extremely limited. Hanging round the bus shelter rarely did the trick, and debating only really got going in the sixth form.

I joined the YCS at the same time as several friends, who pretended to be scandalized when, at about age fifteen, I began going out with a boy in the year below me named Patrick Taaffe. (In fact, because I had skipped a grade, there was not much difference in our ages.)

Patrick's father was a general practitioner (GP) on the Scotland Road, which in those days was one of the roughest parts of inner Liverpool. The Taaffes were the first middle-class family I had ever come across. They lived in a detached house in Blundellsands, complete with drive, conservatory, and garage. They also had a holiday cottage in North Wales, and during the two years Patrick and I went out, they would take me there on weekends. It was another world.

Patrick's mother, Meriel, was a nurse, and she became very fond of me. (She and her husband even came to my wedding.) "You remind me so much of me when I was your age, Cherie," she would say rather wistfully. She was a really bright woman who, though she would never admit it, had not fully realized her potential, and I think she wanted me to realize mine. Later, when the time came to think about university, it was Meriel who came up with the idea that would change my life.

"You're good at debating," she said. "You're good at drama. Have you ever thought about becoming a lawyer?"

After the end-of-year exams, Dr. Taaffe gave me a job in his office helping out the receptionist over the summer. Occasionally he would give me a lift home after work. He'd usually have one or two visits to make, and rather than wait in the car, I'd go in with him. It was the first time I had come across this level of poverty, and I was shocked: no inside toilets; dirty, damp, and depressing; old back-to-backs and tenements; mold everywhere; too many children, their mothers hollow-eyed and worn down by everything.

"You cannot imagine what they're like," I would tell my grandma after Patrick's father had dropped me off.

"Oh, but I can, young lady. We didn't always live in this kind of luxury, you know." Where she grew up, she said, the doors opened straight onto the street. There weren't even sidewalks. The only people who lived there were fishermen and dockers. She called the women "fishwives" and said it was all they could do in those conditions to feed their kids and keep them clean.

The central pillar of the YCS was community work. In the late sixties, inner-city Liverpool was being torn down, and people were being moved out to new suburbs. Even then it was obvious that the policy was a disaster. These new towns had been built with no social facilities: no doctors' offices, no cinemas, no pubs, no bus links, nothing. They were just dormitories. The residents were completely isolated.

The nearest of these to us was Kirkby, a few miles to the northeast of Crosby, and during the summer the YCS ran a summer school and a whole range of activities for the kids during the holidays. We were based in one of the local primary schools. Each project involved a twenty-four-four-hour commitment, and we slept on the floor in sleeping bags. On one level, of course, it was fun. I'm sorry to say that we probably wouldn't have done it with such gusto if it hadn't been. But I ended up feeling that whatever else you might say about where I lived, it was at least a real community. These new towns were not, and the people there knew it.

The alternative to working in the community was a week of spiritual reflection, and the following summer I went to one such retreat in a town called Rugeley. It was 1971, and peace and love were breaking out all around. The YCS retreat was no exception: there was a lot of scurrying about in the dark while more saintly souls sang songs round the campfire. In the daylight hours the debate was as much political as spiritual. As revolutionaries went, we were pretty tame. Nonetheless, we saw ourselves as part of a kind of "workers of the world unite" movement. It was all vaguely left-wing Christian socialism.

Until then the only boys I'd met through the YCS had gone to St. Mary's. But the boy I was scurrying around with in Rugeley lived in Leeds, a distance that required a certain amount of ingenuity to keep the romance going. His name was Steven Ellis, and he was the national secretary of the YCS, so my friends were dead impressed. We could write to each other, but that took time. Best was the telephone, but in those days it was still very expensive, particularly long distance, and when it came to making calls, Grandma was very strict. She had a specially designed money box on the hall table next to the phone which said, "Phone from here when e'er you will, but don't forget to pay the bill."

As long as you weren't the one doing the phoning, you could talk as long as you liked. So Steve and I developed a wonderful scheme — though with hindsight, scam would be a more appropriate description. Steve would ring from a call box — his family didn't have a phone — I'd answer it, then close the door to the hall. This was considered perfectly reasonable behavior if your young man was phoning you. Then very quietly I'd put down the receiver and dial him straight back — and nobody was the wiser!

After a few months of this mild deception (as I saw it), the inevitable happened. A phone bill arrived. A very substantial phone bill. My grandmother went berserk: the bill for that one quarter exceeded the total of the entire previous year, and she just couldn't account for it. It had to be a mistake, she said. So naturally she called the telephone company to give them an earful.

"There's been a mistake," she said.

"I'm afraid not, Mrs. Booth. There's no mistake."

I genuinely hadn't realized just how much my little chats were costing, and I knew that if I didn't own up, the blame would fall on my mother. I had no choice. To say I got a tongue-lashing is putting it mildly. I couldn't pay because I didn't have any money. In the end it was my poor mum who had to foot the bill, but at least she wasn't blamed. There were no more phone calls after that.

If my relationship with Steve was to continue (and it did, though not for too much longer), hitchhiking was the only answer. In fact, it proved so successful that from then on, I hitched all over the country.

Although the nuns knew that I was doing well in school, they didn't see fit to communicate the good news to either me or my mother. At the final awards ceremony, she was shocked to discover that I had won all the prizes except the one for religion. As I kept going up to the dais to collect the various awards, Mum was falling under the seat with embarrassment, she said. My reports had been nothing exceptional, and as for parents' evenings, when in the normal course of events you might expect a bit more depth, the nuns would tell her nothing beyond the fact that they couldn't read my handwriting, and it was a shame she hadn't done something about it earlier. Why did they treat her like this? Because she didn't have a husband. For all their lip service about independence and individuality, when it came right down to it, they were the same as everybody else, and my poor mother, who had given up her career and worked hard all her life to do the best she could for us, was treated with disdain.

Meriel Taaffe couldn't have known how well her idea of a law career would be received back in Ferndale Road. My grandmother had always been an admirer of strong, independent women who made a mark on the world, and Rose Heilbron, the most famous defense lawyer of her generation, fulfilled those criteria. She was a true pioneer: The first woman to win a scholarship to Gray's Inn, one of the four professional associations to which every English barrister must belong. The first woman to become a King's Counsel, the most senior sort of lawyer. The first woman to be defense counsel in a murder trial. The first woman judge to sit at the Old Bailey. As Rose was married to a Liverpool doctor, she continued to practice on the northern circuit, with chambers (as barristers' offices are called, from the days when they lived in them) in Liverpool. From time to time my grandmother would go down to watch her in action at the Crown Court — when trials were still conducted in the baroque splendor of St. George's Hall — and come back glowing.

If that wasn't enough, Rose was also beautiful, and by the 1950s, with dozens of murder trials to her name, she was a celebrity in her own right, to the extent that a television series was based on her. Called *Justice*, it starred Margaret Lockwood. At my grandmother's instigation, I watched the actress dishing out justice on TV in her wig and gown, and when Meriel Taaffe made her suggestion, that image shot into my mind: I could be another Margaret Lockwood!

The big question now was which university? No one in either the Booth or Thompson family had ever done such a thing, so I had no one to advise me. The London School of Economics (LSE) was the last one on my list of five, put there in part to annoy the nuns, who thought I had rebellious tendencies anyway. In the early 1970s, the LSE was seen as a hotbed of revolution. Many of my Liverpool contemporaries considered London to be one step short of hell, but it wasn't that off-putting to me. My dad lived there. Uncle Bob lived there. My mum went to London regularly for her work. So when the LSE made me an offer, I didn't wait to hear about the other places I'd applied to. I accepted straightaway.

As for the nuns, they continued to disapprove. They didn't understand why I couldn't have stayed in Liverpool. Or if I really wanted to spread my wings, Manchester was very good. "Lots of Seafield girls go there," they said. Exactly.

"You know, Cherie, you could be a good leader, but you're very headstrong. If you go to London, you had better be careful."

They didn't have high expectations of me, and who could blame them? During my time in the sixth form, I set a world record for late marks. I wasn't that keen on assembly and often wouldn't bother to turn up until it was finished. The nuns turned a blind eye because they recognized my academic potential.

I'd always had holiday jobs. The first had been with Dr. Taaffe in the summer of 1969, but as soon as I could, I went to work at Lewis's, for all the obvious reasons. The summer of 1971 they put me in the baby clothes department — about which I knew absolutely nothing. Like my grandma, though, I have always loved children, so it couldn't have been better. The following summer, as soon as I'd finished my A levels (advanced school-leaving exams), I started in the school-outfitting department, about which I knew considerably more. On the same floor, just along from me, was gents' outfitting, where I couldn't help but catch the eye of another student who looked equally bored. His eyes were blue, and he was slim and dark, with hair considerably longer than St. Mary's boys were allowed. He even had a cute-looking beard! With his John Lennon glasses and well-cut clothes, he was the last word in trendiness. We started taking breaks at the same time, chatting over coffee in the canteen. His name was David Attwood, and he was two years older than me and at Liverpool University reading law. His father was a GP who worked in Scotland Road, in the very same practice as Dr. Taaffe. Like the Taaffes, the Attwoods lived in Blundellsands. With all these coincidences, we had plenty to talk about.

Toward the end of the summer, Mum took us off on our annual holiday, this time to Ibiza, when it was just an ordinary holiday island, with none of the hard-drinking, hard-dancing reputation it later gained. Imagine my surprise when whom should I see on the beach but my fellow flirt from gents' outfitting! He was there with a group of friends from university. It was the perfect holiday romance: sun, sea, sand, and sangria. As for my mother, she was putty in his hands.

I was due to leave for the LSE at the end of September, but David and I made full use of the few weeks left to us back in Crosby. The weather was still lovely and the evenings still long. The one fly in this romantic ointment was the Blundellsands–Waterloo divide. With the Taaffes it had never been a problem, but although David's mother had always been fine with me, he thought it prudent to play it safe. He told her only that I lived near Merchant Taylors', the smart Protestant school that is a Crosby landmark, which wasn't entirely a lie. Eventually she would find out exactly where I lived, and just as David had suspected, all hell broke loose.

CHAPTER 5

Student Life

On September 24, 1972, the day after my eighteenth birthday, my mum and I took the train from Liverpool to London. The night before, I'd had a combined birthday and farewell party at home with a few of my YCS friends and made a little speech saying how I owed everything to my mum — sentiments that were overtaken by my embarrassment as she burst into tears when the time came to leave me at the residence hall.

The term didn't start till the following week, but first-year students, called freshers, arrived early to get the hang of things. As the first in my family to go to university, I hadn't considered a few basics — such as where I was going to live. Although the school had found me a place for the short term, I needed a more permanent solution. I was sent to an address in Pembridge Villas, Notting Hill, which turned out to be a lodging house for the Digby Stuart Teacher Training College — run by the nuns of the Sacred Heart: dormitory accommodation and in by ten. I could just imagine what they must have thought: good Catholic girl, barely eighteen — a convent is the very thing. Well, they thought wrong. I was not going into a convent. I did not want to be a good Catholic girl. I intended to put all that behind me and have a bit of fun. I went straight back to Passfield Hall, the residence hall in the heart of Bloomsbury, in central London, where I'd been staying till then. Somehow, after a plea that would not shame a defense counsel in a murder trial, I was squeezed into a room with two other girls: Caroline Grace and Louise Oddy, both of whom were also studying law.

The LSE differs from all other English universities in that it has always been political. Though now part of the University of London, it was originally set up at the end of the nineteenth century by Beatrice and Sidney Webb, founders of the Fabian Society, who believed in advancing socialist causes by reformist rather than revolutionary means. Its full name is the London School of Economics and Political Science, and the Fabians envisioned it as a research institution that would focus on the problems of poverty, inequality, and related issues. Certainly in the seventies, this ethos remained at the heart of the place — one of the reasons I'd decided to go there. Instead of teaching law in order to churn out solicitors (lawyers who advise clients and represent them in lower courts, as opposed to barristers, who try cases before higher courts), the LSE saw the subject more in terms of its impact on every area of political and economic life. This was the kind of work I saw myself doing — helping in the more politically relevant areas where ordinary people were traditionally shortchanged by lawyers.

In fact, during those first few years in London, I was in too much of a hurry to get on in the world to waste my time on fashionable student politics. There was a Labour club, but I wasn't active.

That first term David Attwood came down from Liverpool a couple of times to see me, but sharing a room with two other girls didn't leave much space for romance. Things weren't much easier when I got back to Crosby. He would borrow his mother's car, and we'd park on Marine Road, where street lighting was at a minimum. The sand dunes were still there, of course, but December on the banks of the Mersey is cold, and no amount of youthful passion could cope with the near-zero temperatures.

I'd been so looking forward to coming home that I hadn't realized how quickly I'd got used to my new life. My family was inordinately proud of me but knew nothing about universities, hadn't a clue about what I did or what any of it meant. As for the law, with its arcane vocabulary, that was a foreign country. It was as if a chasm had opened up between us, a split in the earth that would only grow wider.

I began to see how unworldly they were. At Passfield Hall I'd have a shower every day. At Ferndale Road I'd have a bath once a week, because hot water was heated by our coal fire in the sitting room. Lyndsey and I would go first, and then my mum and grandma would use the same water, with a kettle or two added to keep it hot. Meanwhile we'd wash our hair and sit in front of the fire and let it dry. If we needed a heater upstairs — for example, if someone was ill — there was a paraffin stove. I can still remember that smell.

That Christmas David took me out to my first restaurant — a steak house a few miles up the coast. I can remember even now what I had: shrimp cocktail, followed by steak, some sort of ice cream, and an Irish coffee. I imagine there was wine or sherry. I arrived back home in a state of near bliss, swiftly dented by my grandma's comment: "a waste of money when it could have been spent on good home cooking."

On New Year's Eve, David took me to a party given by student friends of his in Liverpool, and we stayed out all night. When we eventually got back, my mum was fine about it. I remember her saying that she hoped I'd been careful.

Later that afternoon there was a knock at the door. It was David's younger brother, Michael. I was upstairs.

"Cherie, there's someone to see you," my mother called. I peered down to see Michael standing on the step looking cold and miserable. I immediately sensed that something was wrong. Michael had never been to our house before.

"What's wrong? Is David okay?" I asked.

"He's okay, but . . ."

"You'd better come in," I said. "You'll catch your death standing out there."

It turned out that David's mum had gone bananas about his seeing me, just as he'd predicted. Although he'd denied that anything had "happened" the previous night, she was not convinced. If he continued to see me, she said, she would cut off his allowance, which would mean an end to his university career. She had already been telling him that she thought I was after his money, and in her eyes "making" him stay out all night showed that my motives were dishonorable.

"He says to tell you that he'll have to lie low for a few days, give her a few days to calm down, but you shouldn't try to call him," Michael said.

"Don't worry," I told him. "It'll be all right. I know it will." I stood on the doorstep and watched him walk back down Ferndale Road toward the park.

Later that night, as we were watching TV, the phone rang. "That'll be for you, Cherie," Grandma said with a nod of her head. I sighed. The idea that I wasn't good enough for Mrs. Attwood would drive her mad. I didn't rush to get it. It wouldn't be the one person I wanted it to be.

I was wrong. I felt a rush of blood to my head when I recognized David's voice. "I thought you weren't going to call," I said.

"I had to," he said, then paused. "Something awful's happened." Gradually I began to make sense of what he was saying. About an hour after Michael had been to see me, he'd collapsed playing golf. They'd taken him to the hospital and found that he had an enlarged spleen. Leukemia. Our little difficulties suddenly seemed unimportant.

From then on, there was no more talk about splitting us up. I didn't see Mrs. Attwood before I went back to London. When I was next in Crosby, she barely noticed I was around. There were more important things in life than worrying about whether David was involved with the right kind of girl.

Nine months later Michael was dead. The funeral was really shocking. I had been to family funerals before, and Grandad's had been painful for all sorts of reasons. But even Grandad, important as he was to me, had been old. This was entirely different. The church was full of boys from St. Mary's — sixteen, the same age as Michael, the same age as Lyndsey. For Dr. Attwood it was terrible. You could sense what he was feeling just by looking at him. There he was, a doctor, and he couldn't even save his own son.

It was around this time that I renewed contact with my dad, perhaps sensing that life is too short to hold grudges against the people you love. My grandma had always wanted me to keep in touch with him, and in her own way so had my mother, though her feelings were obviously more complicated.

Following my grandad's funeral, things had begun to thaw a bit between my parents. By then my dad's relationship with Julie Allan, Jenia and Bronwen's mother, had ended. His drinking had finally become too much for her, and she had gone to America, taking her daughters with her. Her father was a successful Canadian screenwriter, who she knew would provide both practical and emotional

41

support for his grandchildren. From my mum's perspective, this made things easier. For my dad, however, it was devastating. He didn't see his girls for years.

When I was about eleven, my dad started writing to Lyndsey and me. He also sent us books. The first one I remember was a leather-bound *Pride and Prejudice*, which I fell in love with. Most, however, were rather more radical or eccentric in nature. I particularly remember *The Female Eunuch* by Germaine Greer and later *The Doomsday Book: Can the World Survive?* by Gordon Rattray Taylor. (I got off lightly. He sent Lyndsey *Portnoy's Complaint*.) The *Doomsday Book* was an early broadside on the environmental disaster that was about to be unleashed on the world. Not surprisingly, with books like these I found plenty to write back to him about, and so a relationship gradually developed. Not so with Lyndsey; she never replied. Because she was so close to our mother, I think she always felt his betrayal more acutely than I did.

My father was now famous. He was the living embodiment of the opinionated loudmouth he played on the hit TV series *Till Death Us Do Part*. One of the most popular comedy shows in British television history, it ran from 1966 through 1975. As a prominent Labour supporter, Tony Booth had even been invited to Downing Street by Harold Wilson, which made me immensely proud. He completely inhabited the character of the Scouse Git: when he wasn't spurring on left-wing politicians, he was haranguing Tories.

In 1970 he was back in the headlines as one of the original cast of *Oh! Calcutta!* an "erotic revue" in which the actors, male and female, performed naked. The mix of serious, if explicit, writing and full-on nudity was described by critics as groundbreaking. Cringe making would have been my verdict — not that I ever saw it.

My father's potential for embarrassment proved endless. In 1974, in my second year at the LSE, he costarred in *Confessions of a Window Cleaner*, a sort of X-rated version of a more mainstream, low-budget British comedy. Needless to say, I didn't see that either. My grandma wasn't going to pass up the opportunity to see her errant son on-screen, however, and when it came on at the Waterloo Odeon, she informed the box office that she was the star's mother, demanded a free ticket, and got it. She told me afterward that she couldn't see what all the fuss was about. It was a huge commercial success and led to several more *Confessions of . . .* films, each one a source of acute misery for me. Jibes by fellow students were the least of it; most children find their parents' sexuality faintly disturbing. But having it be so public was even more difficult. The paradox is that at the same time I was appalled, I was immensely proud of my father — proud of what he'd achieved in his chosen profession, proud of his forthright views on politics, proud that I was his daughter.

Successful though was in the public perception, he was a complete disaster in his private life. After Julie Allan left him, he started drinking even more heavily and smoking cannabis — another reason my mum was nervous about my seeing him. By then he had fathered two more daughters, Sarah and Emma, by a woman named Susie Riley, whom my dad had met when reeling from Julie's departure. Susie was a model, and my father now describes their relationship as "mutually ruinous." By the time I met Sarah and Emma, they were perhaps five and two. I would regularly go to my father's flat in West Heath Road, Hampstead, to babysit. Things were not good there. There were times when the girls had to get themselves up and dressed. There was no structure in their lives. Even if I hadn't planned to, I'd often stay the night, as I just couldn't leave these so-called parents in charge of my half sisters.

Although I didn't analyze it at the time, I suspect this was one reason I never got involved with drugs myself, although there were plenty of them around. I don't even remember being tempted. If your father is behaving like that, it's guaranteed to put you off. Who wants to look that stupid?

As far as Sarah and Emma were concerned, I did what I could when I could, but an instinct for self-preservation kept me at a reasonable distance. The only stability in their lives was provided by Susie's parents, who would take the girls on weekends and give them some love and affection.

At the end of my third year at the LSE, it was clear that I was going to get a top-class degree, so my tutors were encouraging me to do my bachelor of civil law (BCL), the master of arts (MA) of law. The next stage in my student career should have been straightforward. Following my bachelor's degree at the LSE — a First, the highest grade awarded — I was invited to study for my master's at Wadham College Oxford. But when I was offered a scholarship to study for the Bar exams at Lincoln's Inn, I decided that was a better option. Although an academic career had its attractions, the life of a practicing barrister had more instant appeal.

As an undergraduate, I had been lucky enough to spend three years in residence halls, but "home" was now a hideous bed-sit in Weech Road, West Hampstead. The one time my grandma came down to see me — bringing some pots and pans she thought I might need — she cried her eyes out because she thought it was so awful. For her, cleanliness was everything, and I can see her now, peering round the bathroom door, nearly apoplectic. London water is notoriously full of iron, and the combination of lime scale and rust made everything in the plumbing line look disgusting. Elsewhere, the bedsit was the usual thing for those days: dirty linoleum; peeling paint; windows you couldn't see out of; electric and gas meters into which you'd put a coin and which would always run out at the worst possible moment. I shared a couple of gas rings on the landing with another girl, and I didn't have a fridge; I kept anything that needed to be refrigerated on my windowsill.

At the LSE there had been a fair sprinkling of women, but the Bar was still overwhelmingly masculine. That year was the first time the number of women at Lincoln's Inn exceeded 10 percent. During the formal dinners there, a group of us tended to sit together, and I was the only girl.

The main way of learning to be a barrister is by watching and helping an experienced junior barrister, known as a pupil master. In those days this was very much a hit-and-miss affair. Some pupil masters took their teaching duties seriously; others saw their pupils as unpaid servants. Of all the specialties, commercial law is the most lucrative, but I had already decided it was not for me. In the end I opted for employment law. I thought it would be intellectually challenging, and from a career perspective it had one overriding advantage: it was all very new, so there was a real shortage of people doing it.

When I consulted the professor who had taught me employment law about pupil-master possibilities, he told me that very few practitioners were holding themselves out as employment lawyers, and he could recommend only three names.

One of them was Alexander Irvine, more usually known as "Derry," and he was anything but a traditional barrister. He was larger than life: overweight, bullish, and blunt. Derry spun me the line that he was a down-to-earth, working-class boy who'd gone to Glasgow University and somehow ended up at Cambridge. In many ways I understood where he was coming from.

Because you shadow your pupil master for a year, the relationship is crucially important. Pupil masters form the core of your professional life. If things go well, you hope to be taken on — given tenancy, as it's called — in the same set of chambers, so developing a good personal relationship is crucial.

The interview with Derry didn't start well.

The first thing he said was "Why are you wearing that dress?"

"What's wrong with it?" I asked. It was dark blue with a paisley pattern, and I had been rather pleased with it. I was very thin in those days, and as it was ruched round the waist, it made the most of my not-very-curvy figure.

"Don't you know lady barristers are supposed to wear black and white?"

I remember thinking, *What a nerve! It's all right for you with all your money, but this is the only smart dress I've got, and I have to wear it for other things besides being interviewed by pompous barristers.*

What I actually said was "Well, this is the only decent dress I've got, and I bought it especially for interviews. So sorry it isn't black."

It clearly did me no harm, as he offered me a pupilage there and then, or as he put it, "Okay, you can start in July."

"And just one more minor thing," he added as I was leaving. "I've half-promised this place to somebody else, some fellow from Oxford." Then he paused and gave me a broad smile. "But don't you worry about that. I'll get rid of him, and I'll take you instead."

I had won an entrance scholarship to Lincoln's Inn, but there were also major scholarships intended to help fund the year of pupilage. Once again the blue paisley dress was dusted down, and on the appointed day I found myself in the anteroom sitting next to another scholarship hopeful. His suit was far less appropriate than my blue dress, I decided, being made of some kind of tweed, an old-fashioned thing complete with cuffs. He had obviously been privately educated in what the British rather confusingly call a public school, which is anything but. Equally obviously, he had just had his hair cut. As there were only the two of us sitting there, I decided to break the silence.

"I think we must have names close to each other," I said by way of introduction. "My name's Cherie Booth."

"Then I'll be going in before you," he said. "Tony Blair."

He smiled — a wide, broad smile. His voice wasn't as public school as I thought it would be from his appearance. Indeed, there was a slight accent I couldn't place. Only later did I realize that it was a hint of Scottish left over from his time at Fettes College, a boarding school just outside Edinburgh.

We talked for a few minutes, then I asked him whether he had got pupilage yet.

"Yes, thank goodness. Two Crown Office Row. Derry Irvine. What about you?"

For once in my life I was speechless. I was about to say something when he was called in.

CHAPTER 6

Brief Encounter

In order to boost my limited income I had taken a part-time post teaching law at the Polytechnic of Central London. In the spring and summer of 1976, I spent most of my nonteaching hours in the Lincoln's Inn library. While everyone else took a break at lunchtime, I stayed: reading, making notes, and eating my sandwich. Even with the money I got from teaching, I had to eke things out. Every week I would buy a loaf of bread and a little round box with six triangles of processed cheese wrapped in silver foil. I would keep them out on the windowsill and make up one sandwich every day, the cheese getting softer and softer as the summer built up to a heat wave. It was all I could afford.

Although I didn't know it at the time, my lunchtime eating habits were being watched.

"You know, Tony Blair quite fancies you," an odd but clever chap called Charles Harpum told me one evening as we were dining in the Great Hall — one of the obligatory twelve dinners, an old tradition dating back to the sixteenth century — the only times I would have what my grandma would call a proper meal.

"How could he? I don't even know him."

"Well, he thinks he knows you."

A few days later I heard the same thing from Bruce Roe, one of my regular Great Hall dining companions.

I wasn't interested. I already had a boyfriend. In fact, I had two:

David in Liverpool and John in London. John was another Lincoln's Inn habitué. John knew about David, but David had no idea about John. It might seem odd that a girl with my Catholic upbringing was being so flighty. But fornication is a bit like contraception: most Catholics do it as much as anyone else; you can always go to confession. (To be frank, however, I have never confessed to fornication. Perhaps one day in my old age I will: "Father, forgive me. I am trying to be sorry for it, but I still find it quite difficult!") Nor did it seem that terrible then. We were living in different times, post-Pill and pre-AIDS.

The summer after Bar Finals, John and I managed to go away on holiday. We had a week in Corfu, which in those days was totally unspoiled. When it was over, I went back to Liverpool and had another holiday, this time with David and my mum. Mum had become very fond of David, and there was an assumption by both families, his mother included, that he and I would marry.

During the autumn of 1975, I gave this possibility some long, hard thought. David had always planned to be a solicitor and was expecting me to go back to Liverpool once I'd done my Bar Finals. If I did, that would be the end of a London-based career, and my instincts told me that if I really wanted to do employment law, I wasn't going to be able to do that in Liverpool.

I finished my exams at the end of June, and the following Monday I started work with Derry. Most people didn't begin their pupilage till the results were out and they'd officially been called to the Bar, but there seemed little point in my going back to Liverpool. Why look for a job up there when I could be getting on with it down here?

Derry's chambers were in 2 Crown Office Row, a Georgian terrace in the area of London known as the Temple, between Fleet Street and the Thames. The building had been bombed during the Second World War and had been rebuilt in an approximation of the original style, but with the addition of an elevator. There were no computers, no typewriters even, except in the clerks' rooms. In the squares outside, bat-winged barristers flitted round and gathered in corners, carrying piles of paper tied with pink tape like parcels. Only the occasional ringing of a telephone would remind me that I was living in the twentieth century. Barristers were referred to as Mr. or Miss by the clerks, while we called them by their Christian names, even if they had been in the job all their lives and earned more money than a successful senior counsel. The chief clerk was named David. His formidable wife, Cassie, did the books — one of the few women you saw regularly around the building. There were about sixteen tenants in the chambers, of whom two were women, but their practice wasn't deemed as good as the men's because commercial solicitors (who made the big money) would never take them seriously.

About three weeks into July, the Bar Finals results came out, and by nine o'clock in the morning, I was already at the Council of Legal Education in Gray's Inn. People were several deep trying to find their names on the board, where they were listed alphabetically. I found "Blair, A.," but no "Booth, C."

I was standing there feeling bewildered — could I really have failed completely? — when up came Charles Harpum, the chap who had told me that Tony Blair fancied me. Charles was a highflier who'd got the top First from Cambridge. He was not exactly a friend, but I used to dine with him quite regularly, and we would talk for hours on the law.

"Well, Cherie, I must congratulate you," he said, with an odd expression on his face.

"It would be nice if I could just find my name," I replied.

"You don't know?"

"Know what?"

"You've come top."

He grabbed my shoulder and propelled me toward the end board, where the top names had been put. And there it was, "Booth, C.," the first name on the list. The blood, which had previously descended into the pit of my stomach, came surging up to my face. I could feel myself going bright red. Everyone had assumed it would be Harpum who'd finish on top: public school, Cambridge, and so on. And now, here I was, the grammar-school girl from Liverpool and the LSE.

I ran all the way to Crown Office Row to tell Derry. Next thing he was crowing to everyone about how clever he was to have discovered this pupil who was so brilliant. Somehow or other it was his achievement. It wouldn't be the last time that somebody else's success would miraculously turn out to be Derry's.

Kudos are one thing, but for me there was a distinct practical advantage in coming top: I was the first recipient of the Ede & Ravenscroft Prize. Ede & Ravenscroft is where you get your wig and gown, and as these were essential items, I'd already had my head measured for my wig and been fitted for the gown, though I still had no idea how I was going to pay for them. Now I wouldn't have to, because they would be free. In addition, I got a black and gold wig box, with my name printed in gold letters, which I certainly wouldn't have bothered buying. Also included in the prize was a blue bag with a drawstring, with my initials embroidered in white, which was traditionally used for carrying robes (although in truth I have only ever used it for laundry).

Our ceremony took place a few weeks later, and David came down with my mum and grandma. Because he was being called to the Bar at the same time, John was there as well. Knowing what the situation was, he kept well out of the way. I had invited my dad, but there was some crisis, not entirely unexpected, and he couldn't come. In a way I was pleased; I didn't want any unhappiness for my mum. It was all thanks to her that I had got this far.

A week or so before the swearing in, I'd been asked to provide details as to how I'd be introduced. The form asked for my father's name and occupation, but I crossed it out and wrote my mother's name and occupation instead. I wasn't going to have her stand there and hear me being called to the Bar as the daughter of Tony Booth, when she was the one who had made all the sacrifices. My father had done bugger all to get me to this point. The powers that be raised a few eyebrows, but I was insistent. So at the moment I was admitted, the voice intoned, "Cherie Booth, daughter of Gale Booth, travel agent."

Derry's pupils soon learned the meaning of the term "devil": it meant doing your pupil master's work for him. He would check it and sign it, and from then on it was his.

Chris Carr, Derry's pupil immediately before me and one of my tutors at the LSE, deviled all Derry's commercial stuff. I did the rest. He started me out on some minor things, but once he realized that I knew my employment law, he had me write his opinions for him, then he would sign them off. With Derry, you wrote in longhand, double-spaced, leaving big margins. He would correct the text before sending it off to be typed.

For all his faults, Derry was an extremely good teacher. When it came to an affidavit, for example, he taught me to tell the story. He was obsessive about style and about details such as not splitting infinitives. He kept telling me he thought I was probably dyslexic.

The reason I hadn't been diagnosed, he decided, was that my hand-writing was so bad that nobody had noticed how atrocious my spelling was.

Although Derry's writing style would serve me well, he was distinctly aggressive as an advocate — hardly the ideal template for a twenty-two-year-old lady barrister. But how, as a woman, do you develop a style in a man's world when what works for a man is regarded as inappropriate for a woman? It was difficult to find female role models. Most chambers still had a "women need not apply" attitude, and during the time I was a pupil of Derry, I never once saw a female advocate. Even after I began practicing on my own, I rarely came up against other women, except in the occasional family case. Those I did meet tended to be beginners like me.

One of my friends at the LSE had been Veena Russell. She had originally trained as a ballet dancer at the Royal Ballet School, but having grown too tall, she had moved to the LSE to do law. She was extraordinarily beautiful. Her parents were South African Asians, and they still lived in Durban. They were quite well-off and had managed to buy a flat north of London, in St. John's Wood, where Veena lived. As she had managed to get pupilage in Cardiff, the flat at Abercorn Place would be empty from September on. Her parents came over from time to time, so it couldn't be rented out. She needed somebody to house-sit. Would I be interested?

Overnight my life changed. Good-bye, bed-sit; hello, luxury — certainly by my standards: my own bathroom, a fridge. All I had to do, she said, was pay the bills. There was a double and a single bedroom, the former to be kept for Veena or her parents when they visited. I moved in that September.

At one point Veena's dad came over on business on his own. One evening he suggested that he take me out to dinner. I remember sitting on the bus with this kind, intelligent, cultured man and then realizing that everyone was giving me dirty looks. Here I was, a white girl, with a handsome, older Indian guy. I could feel the hatred blazing from the passengers' eyes like sparks from a ray gun in a children's comic. It was the first time I felt just an inkling of what it must be like to be discriminated against on the basis of skin color.

To some degree, as a Catholic and a Scouser, I was used to feeling like an outsider. But my sense of apartness didn't cause people on a bus to stare at me. In working-class London, race prejudice was still rife. It hadn't been that long since there'd been signs in boarding-houses saying "No Blacks, No Irish, No Dogs." Just a month or so before I was called to the Bar, there had been riots at the Notting Hill Carnival, an annual event put on by locals of West Indian descent.

As befitted his heavy workload, Derry's room on the first floor was larger than most and dominated by a huge partners desk, at which he sat with the window behind him. My much smaller desk was facing his, and the wall between us, opposite the door, was lined with books. Behind the door was a table stacked high with briefs. Above my head was a large oil painting that Derry would stare at when he was thinking.

Sometime in October a familiar face peered round Derry's door. "Hi," the newcomer said, not noticing me sitting at the desk opposite the window. "Just to say I'm here." He was clutching an old briefcase, and his hair was looking considerably longer than before.

"Ah, yes. Tony!" Derry said. Then he waved a hand vaguely in my direction. "Cherie Booth, Tony Blair. You see, Tony, I've got two of you, and I'm afraid young Cherie here beat you to it. I'm putting you upstairs." And that's where he stayed.

Tony had got his pupilage by way of a personal introduction. His father had been a barrister in Newcastle before a stroke ended his career, and his older brother, Bill, was already in practice in a more commercial set of chambers in the Middle Temple, another of the four Inns of Court.

Inevitably, as Derry's two pupils, Tony and I spent a good deal of time together. Apart from anything else, I needed to keep an eye on my rival. It was unlikely that Derry would see both his pupils accepted as tenants. I needed to persuade him that I was the better bet. Tony and I attended numerous cases together, during which there was always a lot of hanging around, and he would regale me with stories about his recent time in France with Bruce Roe. After Bar Finals they'd gone to Paris and worked in a bar. Then, with the money they'd earned, they'd gone round the Dordogne and the Languedoc. He'd also tell me about his love life. He didn't have a permanent girlfriend at the time, but he bragged about the upscale girls who were always asking him out. In all seriousness, I would give him advice. He knew about my London boyfriend, as did

Derry, because occasionally "the worm" (as they called John) would turn up at chambers. Derry was particularly disapproving, but then he was by nature proprietorial. I didn't dare tell them about David.

That Christmas John and his flatmate decided to do a Christmas dinner. John volunteered me as cook. Even then I enjoyed cooking, and the chance to do something properly, as opposed to frying up bacon offcuts on a gas ring on a landing, was something to look forward to. The oven wasn't big enough to roast a turkey, so we had chicken. I was told I could invite someone, so I thought I'd ask Tony.

It was a proper Christmas party with games. One involved putting a balloon under your chin and passing it along. As Tony didn't know any of the other guests, he'd been put next to me, and so we were doing this passing the balloon, and I suddenly thought, *Hang on a minute* . . . I don't know what it was — perhaps the smell of his skin, something so fleeting, a little flicker — but definitely there. Until that moment it had never crossed my mind that he was anything but a rival.

The truth, I began to realize, was that he was a very good-looking young man, tall and slim, yet broad in the shoulders — a really strong body. As for his hair, the short back and sides he'd had when we'd first bumped into each other had grown out into an unruly mess, curling down over his collar in a way that made me want to twist it round my fingers. His eyes, which I'd barely registered before, were a clear, penetrating blue — penetrating because they seemed to see right through me, to the extent that I could feel a blush rise up from some uncharted part of me and flood my face.

Toward the end of term, as it's called, Derry decided to take us out for our Christmas dinner. It wasn't an office party as such — there weren't enough of us for that — it was just Derry being Derry. He loved being expansive. The table was booked for twelve-thirty at Luigi's in Soho — a favorite haunt of Derry's — one of those restaurants where they have photographs of famous people on the walls. The lunch went on and on, with Derry pontificating on the state of the world. I remember four o'clock coming and going. Derry ordered another bottle — and another. Anyway, by ten-thirty we were still there. A lot of drink had been drunk. The remains of the food had been taken away and there I was between these two men, one of whom — Derry — was decidedly inebriated, and the other of whom — Tony — was decidedly amorous. I knew if I said it was time I went, Derry would leap up, and I'd have to take a taxi with him. Tired though I was, I decided to sit it out until Derry went home on his own. Eventually he did. Then Tony and I took the bus in roughly the same direction: he was living in Primrose Hill, on the north side of Regent's Park, with three of his friends from Oxford. The bus was a double-decker, and we went upstairs. It was empty, and by the time we got off, we knew each other better than when we'd got on. And even better the next morning.

The next day Tony came downstairs from the attic annex for the usual morning conference. As chief pupil, I always sat next to Derry, while Tony sat at my desk opposite. He claims (I don't believe this at all) that I spent the entire time winking at him.

Oh, dear.

So that left me with three men in my life. Tony knew about John but not about David. John knew about David but not about Tony. And poor David fondly imagined I was living a quiet life of hard work in dreary London, enlivened by occasional visits to Liverpool.

Inevitably, as the months ticked by, my thoughts turned to the chances of my getting tenancy. One of the things Derry kept repeating was that the Bar was a tough place for a woman. Also, he thought that of the two of us, I was the political animal. It was completely the reverse. Tony was never as committed to the law as I was; I was just much more open about my political affiliations. When I was living in my Weech Road bed-sit, I had joined the local Labour Party and was its nominee governor at the neighborhood primary school. This was common knowledge in chambers. In fact, Tony was already a member of the Wandsworth Labour Party, but he kept it quiet. In not shouting about his political affiliations, he was wiser than me, giving chambers the impression that his energy was entirely focused on a career at the Bar — crucial if it came to a head-to-head for the tenancy. There were also pragmatic reasons for Derry going for Tony over me. Because Tony was focusing on commercial law, he could be more useful and lucrative, and Derry was keen to build up the commercial side of the practice. I was just the leftie who did that other stuff.

There were other names in the hat as well. Not every pupil master can get his or her pupil accepted as a fully fledged tenant in chambers every year — there simply isn't room. And though my position as chief pupil was not in dispute, being constantly in Derry's company had its disadvantages. Up on the top floor, Tony was sharing a room with two junior members. This put him in a much better position to network while I was downstairs with my nose to Derry's grindstone.

It was increasingly clear that in terms of getting a tenancy, my major obstacle was gender: I was the wrong sex. That year only 16 percent of those of us called to the Bar were women. The year before it had been 9 percent, and the year before that, even fewer. Yes, the percentage was growing, but attitudes among senior barristers — the people who decide who gets tenancy — were not changing. A set book in my first year reading law was *Learning the Law* by Professor Glanville Williams, QC (Queen's Counsel). In the 1973 edition, he warned of the difficulties of women succeeding at the Bar. "Practice at the Bar is a demanding task for a man," he wrote. "It's even more difficult for a woman. It's not easy for a young man to get up and face the court; many women find it harder still. A woman's voice does not carry as well as a man's."

I will never forget how, shortly after I was called to the Bar, an entire robing room full of men fell silent in shock and horror when it dawned on them that I was going to go in there and change into my wig and gown along with the chaps.

In many ways Derry was no different from the rest. But he had taken me on, and he had already got considerable mileage out of having miraculously discovered the top law graduate in the country. I had also seen how he pushed his former pupils and found them tenancies. He was someone who honored his obligations. I would have to trust that.

CHAPTER 7

Tenancy

Once both Lyndsey and I had left home (she, following in my footsteps, had headed off to study law, though she did so in Cardiff instead of London), there was no further reason for our mum to stay in Ferndale Road. It's one thing living with your mother-in-law when you have no real option, but Grandma was now well into her seventies, and my mum was more or less looking after her. As it turned out, she wasn't the one to make the decision. One day, when my mum got back from work, Grandma made her sit down. There was something she wanted to say: "Now, Gale, have you thought what you're going to do when I die?"

"Whatever do you mean?"

"Well, when I die, this house is going to be sold and divided among my three children, so what's going to happen to you?"

In fact, my mother owned nothing beyond what was in her wardrobe. Even though by this time the bed she shared with Lyndsey was sagging and everything was falling apart, Grandma hadn't let her have anything. The only thing Grandma had let her buy was a television from Lewis's, and of course she left that there when she moved out.

Housing was controlled by the local authority. Because she still had one daughter in full-time education, my mum was given a two-bedroom flat in Seaforth, down by the docks in a pretty rough area, not far from the fish-and-chip shop where she'd worked all those years before. The flat was on the sixth floor and was actually very nice, with lovely views out across the sea. I stayed there that Christmas, but it never felt like home.

One afternoon shortly before New Year's, the phone rang. My mum answered it, then passed it to me with an odd expression.

"It's for you," she said.

Much to my surprise, it was Tony. He had vaguely suggested that as we would both be in the north, I might go to his father's house near Durham sometime over the holiday. Now he was calling to see what was happening.

"Who was that?" Mum asked accusingly. "No one from round here, in any event. Not with that voice."

"Tony Blair. You remember. Derry's other pupil. You met him at the ceremony." Although I'd warned John to stay well clear, I'd had no qualms about introducing Tony to her.

"I don't remember."

"Well, you did."

"So what did he want, then?"

"He wants me to go over there."

"Where?"

"A village near Durham. Where his dad lives. His sister is there, and he thought I might like to meet her. She's reading law at Oxford."

She was definitely suspicious.

"I told him I'd go."

"I heard. Well, you know what you're doing, I suppose."

"I'll go on my way back to London."

"Just don't you forget, Cherie, an accent like that is as much of an accent as a Liverpool accent."

All went well till I arrived at Durham, when my bag — inconveniently containing a bottle of disinfectant and some cheap bleach I'd picked up back home in an attempt to save money — fell out of the luggage rack. As if that wasn't bad enough, Tony wasn't there to meet me, as he'd promised he would be. I was so irritated that I thought I'd take a taxi and go straight to his father's house. So I got in this cab, reeking of cheap disinfectant, and gave the driver Tony's dad's address. Just as we pulled away, I saw Tony getting out of a car behind me. I was so cross that I said nothing to the taxi driver. But Tony must have seen me get in, because as we drove along, my driver kept saying, "There's a fella behind us keeps flashing his lights." I told him to carry on. I thought, *I've put myself out for him, so he can bloody well lump it.*

We arrived at the same time. It wasn't a great start, admittedly, but at least I had the moral advantage. And he paid for the taxi.

I don't know now what I'd been expecting, but the house wasn't remotely grand. I knew a bit of the backstory already, and it was really tragic. When Tony was only ten, his father had a stroke. He'd been a lecturer in law at Durham University and a part-time barrister in Newcastle. He'd been planning on going into full-time practice as a barrister when it happened, with a view to becoming a Tory member of Parliament (MP). Tony's mother, Hazel, had died of throat cancer the previous year, just two weeks before Tony left university. His parents had always talked about moving to Shincliffe village and had finally found this house, which they really liked. But Tony's mum had died before they could move in, so it was all very sad.

Only a few hours before, I had been in Ferndale Road, and now I was here. I surprised myself at how easy it was to move from one world to the other.

All five of us at the house were "legal": Leo, Tony's father; his brother, Bill, who had a commercial practice in the Middle Temple; Tony and I; and Sarah, who was then at Oxford reading law, though not entirely happy with it, as I soon found out. Looking at the lineup of Blairs in the kitchen, I was surprised at how tall Tony was in comparison with the others. He was a good six feet, while his father and brother were almost six inches shorter, as was Sarah.

She and I hit it off immediately. Leo turned out to be fairly right-wing, so sometimes he would come out with something completely outrageous. I would inevitably rise to the bait, then Sarah would join in, the pair of us taking the feminist stance. But it wasn't just women versus men. I never forgot that Tony was the competition, and I was trying to counteract the notion that anyone who wasn't from public school and Oxbridge didn't cut the mustard.

I can't imagine what his family made of this rather odd girl who, having stunk the kitchen out with the smell of cheap disinfectant, proceeded to harangue their father about why women are as good as men, while their sister cheered from the sidelines. I could certainly hold my own. My mum, having trained at RADA, had always spoken well herself, which had served to temper the Scouse that was all around us — though no one could doubt that I was a northern lass. In addition, the nuns had seen to it that we had elocution lessons. Those things were important if you were going to get on in life.

The moment Tony and I were back in chambers, Derry started a big case. Unusually for him, it was a criminal case concerning a huge scandal in Singapore. Derry was representing the Singapore government, which was trying to extradite a number of British businessmen to stand trial for fraud. The two key individuals involved were Jim Slater, the main protagonist, represented by a famous criminal barrister, and Dick Tarling, managing director of Slater Walker's Singapore subsidiary, represented by Michael Burton, fellow tenant of 2 Crown Office Row. The case was being heard at Horseferry Road Magistrates Court in central London, and Tony and I went along. Our job was to see that Derry had what he needed, passing him the necessary papers, taking notes, and doing whatever else was required. The court was close to the Tate Gallery, so every lunchtime Tony and I would go to the museum, and it was then that he really began to open up.

He talked to me about his mother, whom he missed tremendously. Also about religion, which was obviously very important to him. Although the Blairs were not a churchgoing family, the two boys had been sent to the Chorister School, attached to Durham Cathedral. He told me that he had been confirmed during his time at Oxford. His father wasn't a believer, however, perhaps explaining why Tony hadn't been confirmed earlier.

At Oxford he had met an Australian priest called Peter Thomson, studying theology as a mature student. Their discussions were all about liberation theology: Christ as a radical and how it all fits in and resonates with socialism. That was exactly what had inspired those campfire debates when I was with the YCS.

Even at that very early stage in our relationship, Tony and I spent hours talking about this kind of thing, about God and what we were here for. I don't think it would be too much to say that it was this that drew us together. This and the fact that he had just lost his mother. He was incredibly honest and open about his feelings, which was unusual in a man at that time. He had very firm views on marriage, for example. He genuinely thought that two people could be together for life. Having seen what had happened to my mum, I thought this was a wonderful thing to aim for, though I wasn't sure any man was up to it. I certainly wanted it to be true, not least because I had seen for myself how damaging a wandering male can be to his family. Yet when Tony talked about love and fidelity, there was no sense that these were anything more than general conversations. He always kept me guessing in that department, which I found intriguing and not a little challenging. What I really admired was his honesty, his desire to get to the heart of things, and his belief that we were here for a purpose. I loved talking to him, and on the odd occasion when we couldn't have lunch together at the Tate, I felt as if something was missing.

By now he was introducing me to his friends as his new girlfriend, and I'd say, "I'm not sure I'm your new girlfriend." But I liked his friends.

The house where he was living in Primrose Hill was owned by the mother of a guy he'd known at Oxford called Marc Palley. The family was originally from Rhodesia, where Marc's MP father had been described by Ian Smith, Rhodesia's white supremacist leader prior to independence, as a "one-man opposition." His mother, Claire Palley, was a law professor at Oxford, as vociferous as her ex-husband in terms of African emancipation and an extremely formidable woman, though not a very motherly one. Marc lived in one of the flats with his girlfriend, Bina (short for Sabina), while Bina's brother Dave, who had also been at St. John's, was in the flat below with Tony and another St. John's friend, Martin Stanley. They were all quite posh, but surprisingly, I liked them. At the LSE I had avoided anybody like that. The first time I met Marc, he said, "Oh, Tony's been talking about you. You're not like his usual girlfriends. He usually wears his girlfriends like a flower on his lapel." At the time I thought this was a dig, but later I realized it was meant as a compliment, meaning that I wasn't just a pretty face.

Once Tony's Oxford friends had given me the thumbs-up, it was his school friends' turn. He was really wooing me now. One weekend he wanted to take me to Reading, where Ian Craig, a friend from Fettes, was studying agriculture. In order to go, I told John that a friend from the LSE had been dumped by her boyfriend, so I had to spend the weekend propping her up.

It was around this time that I first met Geoff Gallop and his wife, Beverley. Geoff, who would later become Premier of Western

Australia, was a couple of years older than Tony. They had met at St. John's when Geoff was a Rhodes scholar studying philosophy, politics, and economics. He had been in the International Marxist group at the time, and it was Geoff who had introduced Tony to left-wing politics. It was also Geoff who had introduced him to Peter Thomson, who had rekindled Tony's interest in theology. So Geoff was a very important figure in Tony's life. When I met him, he had just arrived back in Oxford to do a Ph.D. I was totally captivated by him.

Although John had been to Cambridge, I just didn't seem to have the same kind of conversations with his friends. By now he was even more in evidence than ever, always wanting to come to the flat and generally being overkeen and clingy. He must have sensed I was losing interest. He certainly felt that there was something between me and Tony, but he didn't know what. I was beginning to feel very uncomfortable about the whole thing.

And then there was David.

The previous summer David's sister had married her Welsh solicitor boyfriend, and it was just as you'd imagine a wedding at Blundellsands to be: morning suits, frocks, hats, the tent, the flowers, the champagne. Already I must have known it wasn't going to work with David, because I did everything I could to stay out of the photographs. Nothing to do with Tony — I barely knew him then — nor even to do with John. It was simply that although David and I were compatible in so many ways, we disagreed politically. He was definitely a Conservative, and I definitely was not. Although we had never really talked about politics, it was a fundamental difference between us, and it mattered. What made it so difficult was that I was very fond of him and we had a connection, a quite deep connection that went back a long way.

Over that Christmas I tried to tell David how I felt, coming out with things like "There's no future in this." Basically I was a coward, and I didn't have the heart to do what I had to do. It didn't help that he and my mother had become so close. She'd met somebody in Canada on one of her trips abroad and had begun to think about the future — even talked about emigration — and David was helping her get a divorce based on more than five years' separation.

Then one evening, sometime that spring, out of the blue David turned up on my doorstep at Abercorn Place. When he knocked on the door, John answered with a shoe in his hand — mine. (He was one of those men who enjoy cleaning shoes.) At that point David realized that was it. He was very upset and left immediately.

My mum could barely bring herself to talk to me. David had gone back and poured out his heart to her. Not surprisingly, she was really angry, and was probably right to be. There is no doubt that I behaved very badly. I don't regret many things in my life, but I do regret how I treated David. I had known for some time that we weren't going to walk off into the sunset together, yet I couldn't find the courage to tell him. I know that he found it hard to forgive me, and I don't blame him. Fortunately young people are resilient, and two years later David met and fell in love with a friend of my sister's. They married and had two daughters. I am happy to say that a few years ago, David and his wife came to see us in Downing Street. So at some level, anyway, I hope that I've been forgiven.

After this incident, of course, John thought he was in the ascendant. Once again cowardice got the better of me. The more time I spent with Tony, the less I wanted to be with John. The situation was complicated by the fact that Tony and I were still professional rivals and would be until the question of tenancy was settled.

Sometime that spring Derry asked me and Tony to dinner at his house. He didn't often ask his pupils to dinner, but I think someone else had dropped out.

Among the other guests was a painter called Euan Uglow. He was about the same age as my father. A small, wiry man with a neat mustache and a very eclectic dress sense — whatever the weather, he always wore sandals, for example — Euan was charming, intense, and quietly spoken, with the manners of somebody from a previous age. He told me that he was always on the lookout for models and asked if I would like to sit for him. He knew enough about the Bar to know that pupils were usually in need of extra cash. The standard fee, he said, was £3 an hour. *Why not?* I thought. It wouldn't take very long, I surmised, and I was always one for new experiences. I said okay, and he said he would give me a call.

So one afternoon, when nothing very much was happening at chambers, I went along to his studio in Battersea. I had no idea when I went there that he was one of the most important figurative painters of the second half of the century. The pictures in his studio were mostly of women.

"I'm currently doing two paintings of a standing nude," he explained. "One is of a blond girl, and you're going to be the dark girl. Here's the one I've already started."

The blond girl was looking left, and she was wearing practically nothing.

I was going to be facing the other way, he said, then handed me what he called "a blue dress" that he wanted me to wear. The blue dress turned out to be just a piece of material he had stitched together, almost like a hip-length waistcoat. It was completely open down the middle. The pose he wanted was very straightforward. I had to have one leg out in front and the other behind, as if I had been caught in the middle of a stride. It had never occurred to me that I would be expected to pose naked, or as good as. What could I say?

"Fine."

During the first few sessions, as I stood desperately trying to hold the pose, I thought, *What on earth am I doing this for?* But at the same time it went through my head that one day I might want my children to know that I wasn't such a dull-o, bluestocking Goody Two-shoes after all.

To keep me still and engaged, he put pictures of paintings he admired in front of me on another easel, then talked about them. The minuscule amount I know about art was taught to me by Euan Uglow.

A barrister's work, particularly in the first few years, is very hit-and-miss, so when I didn't have anything on, I'd ring up Euan and say, "Can you fit me in?" Then I'd go round to his studio. Or I might be at the magistrates court just down the road in the morning and when I was finished, pop over to the studio. He'd give me lunch and talk about what he was doing and why, about the system of plumb lines he used, how the light changed and its effect on my skin and my stomach, and how he saw the different colors. Over the many months I posed for him, we became very fond of each other. Neither of us had much money, so we agreed to make each other Christmas presents. I gave him two tea cozies, which I religiously knitted in two very different patterns. He made me a miniature lectern with a marble base. It was too heavy to take to court, but I still have it.

I really loved him. He was such a gentle, intelligent man, with a

63

lovely smile. After about eighteen months, or even two years, I realized that I just didn't have the time to continue. Also, Tony had begun to query why I was spending quite so much time with this man.

Not surprisingly, I found it really hard to tell Euan that I had to stop, but in the end I said that I didn't feel it was fair to him. I was thinking, *He makes his living like this, and he's wasting time on me, when actually he could be doing a painting of somebody else.* He told me not to worry and that he'd get another dark model to take my place. He had never got round to doing my face, though you could still see it was me. I think he did try to get a replacement, but it didn't work out, so he decided to leave my painting unfinished. It still exists somewhere, but where I don't know. I would love to have it, of course, but his paintings are very valuable, even more so now that he's no longer alive. He died in 2000, and I was very proud to go to his memorial service.

In all the time I was going to Battersea to model for Euan, Tony never knew that I was posing nude. There came a point when I think Derry hinted at it. Possibly Derry had seen it as a work in progress. I don't know. Either way, Tony, when he eventually learned the truth, was very uncomfortable with it. He still is.

Meanwhile the business of what was to happen when my pupillage came to an end was like a nagging headache that, no matter how many aspirin you take, won't go away. A set of chambers is a bit like a family. Different members have different roles and contribute in different ways. On the one hand, the tenants doing commercial work were earning huge amounts of money, a percentage of which they would pay as "rent." Given that their financial contribution was higher than anyone else's, they wanted more of a say about who came in. On the other hand, those doing crime and family law were saying, "We're providing a good service. You commercial boys are forever insisting we take on your pupils, and yet we also need people to do our work, and the people who come via you don't want to do our work."

So that spring of 1977 there was an internal power struggle going on in 2 Crown Office Row. The last four or five pupils who'd been taken on had all been Derry's, and Michael Burton, who had a highly paid commercial practice, was saying that it was his turn now. Like Derry, he was an up-and-coming junior who would shortly become a Queen's Counsel — the most senior level of barrister, known colloquially as a "silk." Some of it, I suspect, was simply him flexing his muscles.

One evening in late spring Derry took me out for a drink and said that in his view, he couldn't get both Tony and me taken on and that obviously, since one of us was a girl, it would be easier to get the boy taken on. Not that he could guarantee Tony would get it either, because Michael Burton was pushing hard for his pupil, but at least Tony would stand a better chance. He proposed to find me somewhere else to land.

Of course I was hurt. It was the first time I had ever been discriminated against because of my gender, and it was hard to accept that I was being pushed out simply because I wore a skirt. But at the time I thought, *That's life.* I wasn't on a crusade.

Derry put me in touch with Freddie Reynold, whose chambers were in 5 Essex Court. As luck would have it, Freddie and I got on instantly. He came from a family of immigrant German Jews and was about the same age as Derry, whom he had got to know through doing work for the same trade union solicitors. Freddie himself did a lot of trade union work, which was another reason Derry probably thought the arrangement might work — he had me down as a committed leftie. Of course Freddie himself could not offer me tenancy — that right belonged to the head of chambers. But as the senior figure was based in the north of England, Freddie basically said yes.

When Chris Carr heard what had happened, he couldn't believe it. "Listen, Cherie. You are much better qualified than Tony. You are mad even to think about moving. You must stay on and fight for your place, because you deserve a place."

Maybe. But then there was the whole romantic complication, which neither Chris nor anybody else in chambers knew about. Although I wasn't about to admit it even to myself, the truth was that I was in love with my witty, charming rival, and the last thing I wanted was to jeopardize that, even subconsciously. As for the battle of 2 Crown Office Row, in the end Michael Burton didn't get his pupil taken on. Instead Derry, the more senior, got his: Tony.

I probably should have stayed and fought. But I could easily have not got tenancy. Then what would I have done? Hung around like the other squatters for another six months, and then another, living on whatever crumbs Derry and the others decided to throw my way? Put Tony into the equation, and it was a real mess. A tenancy in those days meant you were there for life. In the end, of course, I didn't stay in 5 Essex Court for life, but thanks to Freddie, I was in.

CHAPTER 8

Romance

Moving from 2 Crown Office Row into 5 Essex Court was like going back in time. The lower floors had generous-size rooms, but the upper floors were pure servants' quarters, all creaking floors and ill-fitting windows. In other words, nothing much had changed since it was first built. The wards in Jarndyce would certainly have recognized it, and Mr. Tulkinghorn would have felt quite at home. We even had gas lamps outside, which were lit every night by the Inn's porters. I had a room in the annex, which I shared with Malcolm Knott, a former solicitor who had come to the Bar after having his own firm in north London. He was meticulously tidy and I was not, but he put up with me, even selling me his own small Victorian writing desk and buying himself another, larger version.

So there I was, twenty-two years old, a tenant in my own right, able to take my own cases and give opinions under my own name. I may not have been the lowest of the low (a pupil), but I was at the bottom of the chambers' ladder. In those days the head of chambers was not elected — he was simply the most senior silk. Judges have to leave once they are appointed to the Bench, which is how room is made lower down the ladder for new tenants.

Like any young barrister, my work came primarily through the clerk, who operated much like an agent, taking 10 percent of each fee, which he would negotiate. Solicitors would go to a particular set of chambers because they offered the particular expertise they sought for a particular case. At the English Bar, the "cab-rank" system applies: if the requested barrister can't do the job, it's passed on to somebody who can (usually lower in the hierarchy) within the same set of chambers. This system also dictates that you can't turn down a case because you don't like the looks of it — that is, whether it offends your politics or your sensibilities. You can turn down a case only if you are otherwise engaged, no exceptions.

In this way a young barrister builds up a practice by taking on cases that somebody else can't do, broadening his or her experience in the process. I was very lucky. The most junior tenant until I came along was a talented advocate called Charles Howard, who was already building up a good practice among the burgeoning group of left-inclined legal-aid solicitors. Charles and I became firm friends, and when he was not available, he would recommend me. In that way my practice, too, began to develop.

Five Essex Court was unusual in that the majority of its silks were based in Manchester and Liverpool and hardly ever came down to London. As the other juniors were mainly doing general common law, Freddie felt he needed help with his trade union clients, which is to say employment law, so I suited him perfectly. By the time I joined, there were about twelve juniors of different calls and five or six northern silks. I was the only woman.

In the main I did very lowly stuff. My first case was a bail application at Bow Street Magistrates Court. I was ill prepared; there were no papers. I was simply instructed to appear and ask for bail. ("Counsel will do their best" was the basic instruction in those days.) So I turned up, got there at ten o'clock, and was standing outside the court. Everyone was milling about, as they do. There are dozens of cases listed every day. There are defendants, witnesses, barristers, solicitors, and everyone in between. They all look much the same — solicitors in suits, barristers in gowns, defendants and witnesses in their Sunday best. And there I was, calling out my client's name: Mr. Bloggs? Then it suddenly occurred to me: Mr. Bloggs was not going to be standing outside the court because he was getting a bail application, which meant he was locked up in the cells below the court.

I can't remember whether Mr. Bloggs ever got bail, but I well recall that the morning was nearly a complete disaster.

On another occasion early in my career, I handled a guilty plea. Despite my impassioned argument that the accused be given a second chance, he was sentenced to imprisonment. On his being sent down into the cells, I went down with him, because that's what you do. The sentence was lenient, so I tried to tell him it wasn't too bad. After saying good-bye, I went into what I thought was the elevator. I pressed the button to go up, and when it stopped, I got out, looked round, and realized that I wasn't where I had expected to be. I was in a room with two doors on either side and nothing else. The elevator door closed behind me, and I heard it rumble back down again. At the same moment everything went black.

I had no idea where I was and could see nothing. First I groped round the sides of the lift, looking for a button. Nothing. I groped round the room, looking for a light switch, anything. Then I started banging on the walls, on the lift door, and shouting. I remember thinking, *I'm going to die! They are going to find my body, and my mum will be so upset.* I imagined them hiding this skeleton in the corner, identifiable only by her briefcase, a promising career tragically ended.

Suddenly I heard the elevator rumbling up again. The doors opened, and I practically fell into the arms of two court officials.

"Now then," said one, "you're all right, miss. Got yourself trapped between court one and court two, that's all. You were making such a racket up here, they had to suspend the sitting in court two!" I'd taken the prisoners' elevator and ended up in a holding room.

As 5 Essex Court was in the Middle Temple, we would generally eat in Middle Temple Hall and use the Middle Temple library. In Crown Office Row they tended to go to Inner Temple and use the library there. Yet Tony kept coming to the Middle Temple library, and I started avoiding the Inner Temple library, where John would often be found. Also, because I was still deviling for Derry, I would regularly find myself going back to Crown Office Row.

As far as Essex Court was concerned, John was my boyfriend. John, meanwhile, was aware that Tony was around. He knew that we sometimes went out, but he didn't know how far the going out went, and he was very keen that it stop.

One Saturday afternoon John was round at Veena's flat. It must have been sometime in October. I don't remember what I was doing.

I just remember the knock on the door and a voice saying, "It's me." Tony.

I remember watching as John walked over and looked through the spy hole. Next I heard the click of the lock as he turned the key — not to open it; to lock it. I remember staring at him aghast. John leaned on the door with his head in his hands. It was terrible.

The knocking continued. John shouted at him to get lost, but Tony wasn't budging. If he hadn't known it before, he knew now that John was there. He knew that I would never have turned a lock against him.

"Cherie? What's going on? Just let me in. I promise you that whatever else happens, I will never keep you against your will."

This was my home. It may not have been my flat, but it was my home.

So I got up and walked to the door, turned the key, and opened it. Tony, eyes blazing, came in.

"Right," said John immediately. "You've made your choice. I'm off." And he picked up his bag and left.

There was no showdown. No saying you must choose one or the other of us. John had never been one for the melodramatic. He was always calm. In fact, they both were.

But he was right. I had made my choice.

John should have been the more comfortable choice for me, because he hadn't gone to a posh public school, just the regular local one, and he was clever and kind and all those sorts of things. But I was probably the dominant one in the relationship. This was not the case with Tony. There was no way that Tony was going to be dominated by me, nor was I necessarily going to be dominated by him. It was much more of an equal thing, so much more challenging.

My friend Felicity always says, "You can see why Tony wanted Cherie, but we're not quite sure why Cherie agreed to take Tony!" Perhaps she thought that he needed a working-class girl to give him working-class credibility. But she couldn't understand why I needed a charming public-school boy when my principles were so clearly to the left.

Politics and religion certainly played a part. John wasn't interested in politics, although he would have described himself as left of center. David, while far from left of center, was a Catholic and would have been the safest choice: going back to my hometown and doing okay, but never really being able to spread my wings. Tony might not have been Catholic, but religion was more important to him than to anyone I had ever met outside the priesthood. In terms of politics, we might not always have agreed on the details, but we were never that far apart.

Over the years I have thought about what made me choose Tony. It was partly chemistry — I fancied him rotten and still do — but partly because I thought even then that he had something. Behind the charm there was a steely quality to him. Frankly, he fascinated me, as I had never met anybody quite like him before, somebody who could give me a run for my money. Life with the others would have been easier but not so challenging.

Foolish girl — to think how simple my life could have been . . . .

There turned out to be a curious symmetry between Tony's family history and mine. His paternal grandparents were actors — music-hall performers — who met on tour in the north of England. In 1923, in Yorkshire, a son was born: Tony's dad. A week or so later they arrived in Scotland and decided — no doubt for all the right reasons, just like my parents — that the life of a traveling player was no life for a baby, particularly one born out of wedlock. So the child was fostered out to a Glaswegian electrician and his wife, James and Mary Blair. The little boy's parentage was acknowledged in his new name: Leo Charles Lynton Blair: Charles for his father (born Charles Parsons) and Lynton for his father's stage name, Jimmy Lynton — which strikes me as a bit hard on his mother, who got precious little thanks for her contribution. (For the record, her name was Mary Wilson, née Bridson, stage name Celia Ridgeway.) Although Leo's birth parents eventually married and desperately wanted their only son back, Mary Blair refused to relinquish her much-loved adopted child. If you're looking for a parallel there, think no further than my grandmother, similarly distraught when she had to hand over me.

Another thing Tony and I have in common is ambition. We are both driven. It has been suggested that Tony needed to accomplish what his father couldn't because of his stroke. I certainly felt the need to make it up to my mum and grandma for their disappoint-ments. My mum's father, Grandad Jack, had extraordinary ability, but he was born in the wrong place at the wrong time. As for my dad, for all his success, charm, wit, and innate intelligence, he didn't

71

do his mother proud. Not that she wasn't proud of him. On the contrary, she was immensely proud of him. And with reason: he was a very talented actor. Sadly, though, he never reached his full potential. Perhaps his charm was his undoing. Tony is charming like my dad, but he has the steel my dad lacks.

Did I see in Tony the man my dad might have been? No. I see that in myself.

My mum never got to Canada; the romance fizzled out. In November 1977 she moved down to Oxford. The travel bureau of the Oxford branch of the department store chain Selfridges was in some kind of trouble, and the head office asked her to sort it out and then take over the management. When I was at the LSE, she had been brought in to troubleshoot at Selfridges in London, and they had offered her Oxford then, but she'd turned it down. Lyndsey was still at school; Mum had left a daughter once and wasn't about to do it again. Only now, with both of us having left home and Lyndsey set to come to London for her final two years of practical legal studies, known as Articles, did she feel she could think of herself. It would be a promotion, and with the increase in salary, she would be able to buy a small house. As she said to me at the time, "Well, I either stay in Liverpool for the rest of my life, or I take this one chance to move nearer you and make a better life for myself." Lyndsey had made it clear that she wasn't planning on staying in the north either, so it made sense for Mum to move south.

In the spring of 1978, her finals over, Lyndsey came down to London. I was able to help get her an articled clerkship. It didn't pay much, but thanks to Veena's flat, she could stay in Abercorn Place for nothing.

Once my mum was in Oxford, getting to see her was much easier. Realizing it would take time for her to get to know people and build up her own circle of friends, Tony and I used to go up most weekends. She had bought a little terraced house with two bedrooms, so it was perfect. It seems strange now, but the first friends my mum made in Oxford were Geoff and Beverley Gallop, and we would always meet up with them. They were living in a small flat in north Oxford, and we became like a little family. Geoff was doing his Ph.D. Beverley had been a teacher in Australia and later became a very successful potter. As Gale was only twenty years older than me, the age difference was never an issue. In spite of the David complication, my mum and Tony got on right from the start. In a way, from his point of view, she became a substitute mother. To her, Tony was still a boy.

I was finally beginning to realize how hard it must have been for Mum, living all those years under her mother-in-law's roof. She never really was able to make a life for herself. There was a relative of Grandma's, a chauffeur whose employers lived in the northwest, and sometimes he would take us out in his car for long weekends. I remember a trip to Scotland when I was about nine and my sister was seven. Something was obviously going on between him and my mum. He was a nice man, but Lyndsey and I were not terrifically encouraging, to put it mildly. Mum never complained, however, and it was only much later that I realized what a brake we had been on her love life.

Whenever Veena's parents came to London, Lyndsey would move out and stay with Tony's friend and fellow tenant in 2 Crown Office Row Charlie Falconer in the house he'd recently bought in Wandsworth, across the river in south London. When he'd gone to view it, one of the things Charlie had liked was the little garden. "This will be lovely for breakfast in the morning," he'd said to the woman showing him round. He remembers that she looked at him strangely, but he didn't think anything of it. In fact, his house was just under the railway arches, directly beneath the main flight path to Heathrow, and bang next to the underpass/roundabout/ dual carriageway. You could never go out there.

Tony moved in with Charlie, and as a result, I got to know the house — and their domestic habits — quite well. When it came to basic housework, they were a disgrace. Slobs, the pair of them. Whenever I arrived for a visit, I'd find my feet sticking to the kitchen floor because it was so dirty. So the first thing I'd do was get down on my hands and knees and scrub. Then I'd spend the rest of my time — as did Lyndsey when she was there — straightening up, changing the sheets, and cleaning the bathroom.

That summer Geoff, Bev, Tony, and I went on holiday to Brittany. Unlike me, Tony hated to fly, and since Bev was newly pregnant, we went on the ferry. This venture required a car, and Tony had this

73

idea that he would like a Morris Minor. He managed to find one through an ad in a local newspaper. After only two weeks, it collapsed — completely packed up. Tony was absolutely furious; it was clear he'd been sold a dud. So Tony went back to the chap he'd bought it from and threatened him with legal action if he didn't give Tony his money back. He was about to get into fisticuffs when he had the presence of mind to say, "I'm a barrister," and the chap paid up. Luckily one of my colleagues in Essex Court was selling his old Beetle, so Tony bought that instead.

As my mum had never learned to drive, we'd always gone on package holidays to resorts. This freewheeling was a totally new experience, and I loved it. (Only when it came to reading the map did the jovial atmosphere deteriorate.) Tony was quite used to this pile-everything-into-the-car kind of holiday. His mother had come from Ballyshannon, in County Donegal in the Irish Republic, so when he was a boy, they went every summer to his mother's family's place. When the Troubles began, they switched to France.

All in all, we had a great time. That holiday consolidated a friendship with the Gallops that would continue on down the years, with Tony and I becoming Tom's (Bev's bump) surrogate godparents. (Geoff and Bev were not religious so their children weren't actually christened.)

During that trip we just followed the French coast. Bev's pregnancy wasn't proving easy, and my overriding memory is of inspecting the toilets at the various places where we stayed to ensure they were fit enough for her to be sick in. I also had my first experience of oysters. We marveled at the standing stones at Carnac — rows and rows of them, more than three thousand in all — and the swimming, from little coves to great, sweeping Atlantic beaches of yellow sand (not so different from Crosby, bar the temperature). At Nantes we turned the Beetle inland and headed down the Loire Valley.

Tony and I were now definitely an item. When he introduced me as his girlfriend, I no longer made a face. In spite of my fears that Derry would take umbrage, in the end he was fine about it.

The following September we drove to Italy. Tom Gallop had been born, so this time it was just Tony and me. Love and marriage were definitely in the air. Marc and Bina Palley had tied the knot, with Tony as best man. Everyone said his speech was the best that summer.

Like many other young barristers, we both worked in August. With everyone else away, it was a good time to pick up new cases and clients. Then we were off to Calais, making our way down through France and Switzerland to Italy, to Chianti country, where we had rented the bottom half of a villa. The pale blue Beetle had survived the year, but only just. I can remember us trying to get up St. Bernard's Pass, where it felt as if we were pedaling, and just about making it to the top. In those days the Michelin Guide had a category called "Good Food at Reasonable Prices," marked on the map with a red *R*, and we planned our route following the red *R*s religiously.

Until he met me, Tony's girlfriends had all picked at their food. To go out with a woman who enjoyed her food was a real eye-opener for him.

"It's probably a class thing," he said.

What did he expect? I mean, here was I, a working-class girl, and we'd paid money for this food, so I was jolly well going to eat it. The idea of picking at a few leaves in a ladylike fashion verged on the criminal to me.

Derry, too, liked to see a girl enjoy herself, and when he was feeling expansive, he would take us out to incredibly fancy places, like La Gavroche. He also introduced us to El Vino's, the celebrated drinking haunt of barristers and journalists on Fleet Street. It was incredibly expensive, so the only time I ever drank there was when Derry bought us drinks.

Enjoying eating is only a step away from enjoying cooking, and renting a villa meant that I could buy food at the local market and cook it at home. Although I enjoyed cooking in London, in the seventies it was difficult to get even garlic, let alone the eggplants and peppers piled up in Siena. The pages of the notebook I kept that summer have as many descriptions of meals as they have of churches and architecture.

The two weeks ended all too soon. The last morning I was up early, scrubbing the floors and cleaning so as to leave the villa as I would hope to find it. Naturally Tony was nowhere to be seen. My last task, inevitably, was the toilet.

So there I was, on my knees, cleaning the toilet, when Tony came up behind me and said, "You know, Cherie, I think maybe we should get married." Without hesitation, I said yes.

CHAPTER 9

Marriage

Since early that summer I had no longer been living in Veena's flat. Her parents needed it back. Having lived in luxury for two years rent-free, I could hardly complain.

The Bar is the ultimate nonlinear networking web, with each set of chambers acting as its own mini-hub. Whatever the requirement, chambers is always the best place to start looking, and so it proved in this case. A former pupil, I was told, had just bought a house and was looking for someone to help pay the mortgage.

I already knew Maggie Rae in a professional capacity. Following her pupilage, she had gone off and become a barrister in one of the first chambers set up outside the Inns of Court. Once there she decided that the Bar wasn't for her and retrained as a solicitor. Now qualified, she was a partner in the left-leaning firm of Hodge, Jones and Allan, who regularly sent family law work to our chambers.

The house Maggie had bought was in Wilton Way, Hackney — one street north of London Fields, the only patch of green in the area. I had never been that far east before, and West Hampstead and St. John's Wood were like posh Mayfair in comparison. The area hadn't always been so run-down, as could be seen from the houses themselves, many of which were Georgian. The streets were both wide and wide apart, making for generous gardens. Hackney's proximity to the City (London's financial center), however, had resulted in its being heavily bombed in the Second World War, and where the bomb sites had been filled in at all, it had been with poor-quality housing and tower blocks.

Maggie's house was a complete wreck — in fact, the whole front wall was missing. It had previously been divided into bed-sits, and the only heating was a gas cooker on the top floor (my bedroom) in what had been a little kitchenette. So there we'd be, up in my bed-room, the front wall covered with a tarpaulin and the door of the oven wide-open, with us huddled round it for warmth.

She was heavily into do-it-yourself, and I spent every free moment there with the sandpaper — from floors to doors to skirt-ing boards. Tony got involved as little as possible; he has many fine qualities, but DIY is not among them. Maggie had even constructed her own bed, admittedly from a kit, and persuaded me to do the same. This time I did enlist Tony's help. He would, after all, benefit personally. The result was totally hopeless. Not only was the bed wonky, but it tended to collapse at just the wrong moment. Building that bed had one single advantage: we learned very early on that DIY wasn't for us, and when it came time to look for a house of our own, wrecks were out.

During the long drive back from Siena, my head was full of plans for the future. Tony's proposal might have been a little unusual — definitely the wrong one on her knees — but I hadn't needed to think about my answer. We were best friends and lovers, surely the ultimate combination for a happy and successful marriage. There was a constantly changing dynamic between us, and I knew that life with Tony would never be boring. What more could a girl ask for?

Possibly a ring. But then I have always hated my fingers, and Tony felt we should put everything we had into a house. There was just one thing he wanted to be sure of, he said, as we drove the Beetle off the ferry at Dover.

"What's that, my darling?" I asked, giving his knee a squeeze. Could he want me to tell him how much I loved him yet again?

"Promise me you won't say anything to anyone."

I remember sitting there and thinking, *What?* Instead I said, "I see."

"Nothing to worry about. I just think we need to be sensible about how we handle it, that's all."

As in, just in case I change my mind? My little balloon of happiness instantly deflated.

He did agree that we could tell my mother, and the first weekend we were back, we drove up to Oxford to see her. Even then, my husband-to-be pulled his punches, talking at some length around us buying a house. My mum, being very liberal-minded, thought he was saying, "Cherie and I are going to move in together." Only later, when Tony suggested buying a bottle of champagne, did the penny drop. "You mean you're getting married?" she said. Up till then the m-word hadn't crossed his lips.

What mainly worried Tony was Derry. If he disapproved, it could have really negative consequences, he said. As far as I was concerned, it was not a question of "if." Of course Derry would disapprove. He may have tolerated Tony and me as sweethearts, but marriage was another thing altogether. He'd always had a droit du seigneur attitude toward me, though naturally he didn't put it like that.

"You're much too young to get married," Derry said, to no one's surprise, when Tony eventually told him. "Don't do it."

Paradoxically it was Derry who made it possible, at least from a financial perspective. He brought Tony into a case to do with the Bank of Oman. For the next few months, Tony was always popping back and forth to the Persian Gulf. It was a nice earner, and it brought him his first really big fee, so we were able to start looking for a house.

My personal worry was closer to home. How would my mother react to my father giving me away? Unlike being called to the Bar, there were no precedents for the bride's mother walking her up the aisle.

One morning early in November, I was at home, vaguely listening to the radio, getting ready to leave for chambers, when I heard my father's name.

"Tony Booth, the *Till Death Us Do Part* actor, is in hospital after being severely burnt in a fire at his home. The other occupants of the building were unharmed."

My first thought was to call Susie, though I hadn't seen her or my father in months. She was very angry. He'd been taken to Mount Vernon Hospital, she said. Beyond that all I got was "drunk . . . locked him out . . . tried to burn the place down . . . may he rot in hell."

I then called Mount Vernon. I should try to come in as soon as possible was all they would say.

I went on my own. I had nothing on that morning, and Lyndsey had to go to work. In any event, her feelings toward the man who had betrayed her were still not good.

There are no subways in Hackney, so I took a bus to Liverpool Street, and from there it was direct but slow. Eventually I had to transfer to another bus. The journey took more than two hours.

My father tells a complicated story of what actually happened the previous night. It involves the Special Air Service (SAS), counterespionage, the Irish Republican Army (IRA), and a botched assassination attempt. Two SAS operatives, he claims (whom he met in a pub, naturally), helped him break into his own house by climbing on two paraffin drums to access a trapdoor to the loft. They then decided it would be easier to set fire to the front door, so they put a torch to the paraffin, which subsequently exploded, and flames engulfed him. I've never bought that version of events, and, strange to relate, the two key witnesses have never materialized. Some facts are indisputable, however. He was certainly locked out of the flat; he was certainly burnt; and he was certainly very, very drunk.

I knew the layout of the house from babysitting. His flat was on the top floor of a prewar mansion-house block. Opposite his front door was a storeroom where, among other things, he kept spare paraffin for the heater. He must have climbed up on the drum to access the trapdoor to the loft. Once there he could move about above the rafters and climb down through his own trapdoor. He had done it before. My dad was a heavy smoker and, on this occasion, insensible. Add paraffin into the mix, and what happened is not surprising. In all likelihood he had a cigarette in his hand. As he was hauling himself up into the trapdoor, it fell onto the paraffin drum — probably covered with spilled paraffin — and set it alight. It then exploded, and he fell feetfirst into a furnace of flames.

Apart from his feet and lower legs, the worst burns were on his hands. Even in extremis my dad knew what his most precious asset was, and his first instinct was to protect it. I know that's what he did, because over the months I subsequently visited him, it became an obsession.

When I first saw him, he was in a terrible state. His hands were encased in what looked like plastic bags, and he was rambling. One of the nurses changed me a £1 note for some coins, and I called my grandma from the pay phone in reception. He wasn't as bad as I'd expected, I told her. It was a lie. I couldn't bear to tell her the truth. Just hearing her voice was enough to bring tears to my eyes, in a way that seeing my father hadn't. Then, I had been in shock. Next I called Auntie Audrey. I told her the truth. He was in a desperate state, I said. Everything was desperate. The hospital building was a prefab, and there was a constant noise of people crying out in pain.

When there was nothing more to do, I kissed my dad's head and left. (Later, interestingly, when he was undergoing skin grafts, such ordinary human contact wouldn't be possible.) Meanwhile I had called and left a message for Tony. David, the chief clerk, said he was back from Oman but was with Derry reporting on the case. I said that my dad had had an accident, that I was going into chambers, and that I'd explain when I saw him. Could he please call me.

Back at Essex Court, I sat there waiting for Tony to ring. When he did, it wasn't from chambers. I could hear the noise of a bar in the background.

"I'm having a drink with Derry in El Vino's. Why don't you join us?"

"Tony, my dad's in a really bad way. I need to talk to you."

"So come over."

"But you don't understand. He's ill, really ill."

"Just come over!"

I went over. This was in the days when Fleet Street was still Fleet Street, and El Vino's was packed with its usual crowd of journalists and a sprinkling of lawyers. It was a very masculine world, and women were not very welcome. I remember standing in the doorway looking across this mass of suits, and then I saw Tony sitting at a table with Richard Field, who had been Derry's pupil after me. All three men had their heads back in laughter. I went over, and Richard pulled out a chair.

"Tony, I really need to speak to you," I said. Neither Derry nor he took a blind bit of notice. I tugged at his sleeve and repeated what I'd said. Nothing. Then I burst into tears.

"You know what, my dad is dying, and you won't talk to me," I said, then got up and walked out.

Tony had no reason to like my father, but once he realized that his life was in danger — and, more important, saw how much my father mattered to me — he felt terrible about how he'd behaved. He knew the moment I got up and left, and then, of course, he came running after me. It was just bad timing: there he was, back from his first big job, full of stories of Oman and the rest of it — and my being in a state wasn't what he expected or wanted.

Whatever residual anger I might have felt toward my dad evaporated over the next few weeks. Whatever bad things he'd done in his life, I decided, I would not wish this on my worst enemy. He had nobody now except me, so every Monday I made my way out to the hospital. I felt I owed it to my grandma and to Auntie Audrey to be there. They had to know there was someone from the family looking after him.

My dad was now resident in the burn unit and making very slow progress. His lungs had been damaged by smoke inhalation, and he was having skin graft after skin graft. That was when he was in the most pain: the thicker the graft taken, the less the eventual deformity, but the greater the pain. He was not alone. Everyone in the unit was in pain. You could hear them screaming, and people were dying all the time. When shifts changed, I'd overhear the nurses saying, "So-and-so won't survive the night." One woman, a nurse, had 90 percent burns. She'd been lighting the gas in the oven when it exploded. By the following Monday she was dead. The body can't survive that amount of damage.

My dad nearly died twice from liver failure. He was, of course, an alcoholic. Above all, they had to prevent infection. Before going in to see him, I had to dress completely in plastic. While the grafting was continuing, in order to avoid the skin stretching, he couldn't exercise. His legs and arms were covered with what looked like stockings. We just sat and talked. His one great terror, to which he returned again and again, was whether he would ever have an erection again. I mean, did I want to have this conversation with my dad?

My experiences over those months deeply affected me. My kids know that when I die, I want to be buried. Whatever happens, I do not want to be cremated. Not only that, but my relationship with my dad changed. And he changed.

Dad's accident also affected his relationship with Lyndsey. Her reaction was "Trust my dad always to go for the main chance." Maybe. But he was very ill, and it's only thanks to the wonderful nursing care he received at Mount Vernon that he's alive today.

My father's accident had one unforeseen advantage: no way could he come to the wedding. So it was arranged that my uncle Bill, Audrey's husband, whom I'd known since I first arrived at Ferndale Road when he was just her boyfriend, would give me away.

As Tony and I were both members of Lincoln's Inn, we could easily have had the wedding at Lincoln's Inn chapel. But it was expensive to hire, and as my mum was now living in Oxford, it made sense to have the wedding there. We were incredibly lucky that St. John's College gave us permission to marry in its chapel, where Tony had been confirmed (in itself highly unusual). This was achieved through the intervention of a friend who had done his postgraduate thesis on the history of the chapel and persuaded the chaplain to conduct the service.

The chaplain was named Anthony Phillips. We discussed the issue of my being a Catholic. The Church of England didn't have a problem; the question was whether I did. In fact, since leaving home five years earlier, I had been to Mass only when I was in Liverpool. At the LSE no one even knew that I was a Catholic. I probably should have asked my father's second cousin Father John Thompson to be there alongside the Reverend Phillips, but I didn't want to push my luck. Anthony Phillips was doing us a big favor. I didn't want to say, "Oh, and by the way, I'd rather you didn't officiate at the wedding."

There was no stag night or anything like that. The two families had arranged to have a meal together the night before the wedding and were meeting up at my mum's house. By six o'clock the bridegroom had still not turned up. He eventually arrived around eight, and we had a jolly evening. But next morning, calamity: he'd forgotten to bring any underpants, so he had to scrounge a pair from the hotel. They were hideous, ill-fitting things, with the most peculiar line round his crotch area, clearly visible in the wedding pictures.

Grandma was there, of course, and her face lit up when she saw Tony. "I'm so glad she's marrying you," she said. "I like you." That was a relief.

I had bought my dress on sale at Liberty, the famous store in London's West End. It was very pale ivory silk chiffon with pale lilac binding. It had a medieval feel, the sleeves being split along the top and caught by little pearls. The bodice was satin, hand-painted and sewn with seed pearls. To go with it I had a skullcap with the same pale lilac binding as the dress and more pearls. As for the bridesmaids' dresses, Maggie had volunteered her services as seamstress, as she had a sewing machine. We bought matching silk from Liberty, which she made to her own design. Unfortunately, like a lot of Maggie's DIY activities, it took longer than she anticipated, and we had barely finished hemming the dresses when the car arrived to pick us up for the wedding.

The bridesmaids — Lyndsey; Tony's sister, Sarah; and Auntie Audrey's daughter, Catherine — went first with my mum. As the car was my mother's contribution, I'd decided we needed only one — it could come back and collect me and Uncle Bill. That was a good idea in principle, but Oxford on a Saturday afternoon is a nightmare, and my mum had miscalculated how long the trip would take. We waited and waited. The wedding was supposed to start at two o'clock, but at two the car had only just arrived back to get us.

"Tony will be so cross," I twittered as we crawled through traffic.

"He'll probably just go." I was convinced there would be no one waiting at the altar and a lot of strained faces. Tony hates it when I'm late, and I often am. For once, though, it wasn't my fault. We eventually arrived at the chapel at two-thirty, by which time the poor trainee organist had been through his entire repertoire and had gone back to the beginning.

The bridegroom hadn't left. I learned later that he'd had his last cigarette at five to two. I had never smoked, but I'd watched my grandfather dying as a result of smoking, and I wasn't interested in seeing Tony go the same way. It had been my one condition for us getting married.

At around three o'clock on March 29, 1980, Tony Blair and Cherie Booth were pronounced man and wife. Needless to say, I did not promise to obey. Otherwise it all passed in a blur. All I can remember is that Anthony Phillips preached a really good sermon, about how in marriage you have to keep moving, never stick, never be static; you have to move forward together. When he came to the bit about "those whom God hath joined together let no man put asunder," he bound our wrists together with his stole, which I wasn't expecting and had never seen done before.

"Gosh," Maggie said later, "he really meant that, didn't he!"

The chapel was quite small. Apart from our families, most of the guests were from our chambers. The master of St. John's had offered us the use of his house for the reception, so we could walk there from the chapel, which we did, as the mad March wind blew everyone's hat off.

Tony's brother, Bill, was best man. His ushers were Charlie Falconer, Chris Catto (a friend from Fettes), Geoff Gallop, and Bruce Roe. (Marc and Bina Palley were in Dubai.) In the absence of my father, I had asked Derry to make the speech on my behalf. This was a mistake: it was all about Tony. How marvelous he was and how lucky I was to have him. Naturally he cast himself in the role of Cupid. Afterward Freddie Reynold said he wished I'd asked him. I could have seconded that. Luckily my uncle Bill insisted on saying a few words about me, and very generous they were, too.

As for my dad, his is the one telegram I can now remember: "Congratulations from the proud father of the beautiful bride. Absent wounded."

Late that night Tony sat down on the edge of the bed in our hotel bedroom in the Cotswolds. "Well," he said, still dressed in his striped trousers and braces, "that was the worst day of my life." Nothing to do with me, he explained. He was just overwhelmed with sadness that his mother hadn't been there.

CHAPTER 10

Politics

After months of fruitless searching, we eventually found a house we liked in Mapledene Road, Hackney, due west of London Fields and a stone's throw from Maggie's. Although it was more than we could afford, at least no DIY was involved, as developers were doing the renovation. It was still a building site when we bought it, so Tony moved into Maggie's with me. (He had kept his room at Charlie Falconer's right up till the wedding.)

We moved into our first real home shortly before Christmas 1980, when I persuaded my husband to carry me across the threshold. After the unconventional proposal, it was the least he could do. Number 59 was at the end of a row of four early Georgian houses. Then there was a gap before another row began, this time Victorian. The end one of these was empty when we moved in. The municipal authority, what we call the council, was supposed to be fixing it up, but in the meantime it was attracting vagrants and thieves. During our first six months we were burgled three times. It didn't help that both Tony and I were out all day. The miscreants would climb over the garden wall, then break the back door, which had glass panels. Once a family moved in next door, the stealing stopped.

The first time it happened I lost all my jewelry — nothing that valuable, but it all meant something. David had always given me jewelry for my birthday, and everything went, including a lovely silver and black enamel bracelet he had given me for my twenty-first birthday. I also lost a gold sovereign on a chain that Grandad Jack had given me.

Neither the jewelry nor the culprits were ever found, but it was obvious where the thieves had come from. Across the road from us was one of the poorest housing projects — what we call estates — in Britain. Canvassing there during the local elections was a salutary experience and a real eye-opener for Tony, who had never come across social deprivation on this scale. People were so frightened, they would barricade themselves in their flats behind fortified doors. I had never seen Tony so angry. Night after night he would come back determined to do something about the crime and antisocial behavior that plagued such places.

Yet just across the Queensbridge Road were some of the nicest houses in north London and — thanks to their insalubrious neighbors — still affordable. Like-minded people were moving in. Future Labour cabinet minister Charles Clarke and his wife were near neighbors, and Barry Cox, a producer with London Weekend Television, became a close friend.

Whenever I relocated, I moved my Labour Party membership. When I first moved into Maggie's in Wilton Way, I joined the Hackney Labour Party, in which she was already involved. By the time Tony and I bought Mapledene Road, I was on the local party's General Management Committee. I was also a school governor. I'd been one before, and even though Tony and I had yet to have a child, I wanted to be involved. Governors have a very important role to play in the running of a school, as they are the ones who appoint the teachers and the head teacher. In my view, a school stands or falls on the quality of its teachers, so I wanted to make sure we got it right. I was chair of governors at Queensbridge Road Infant School and on the board of Haggerston Girls School.

Now that I was legally qualified, I could also offer more specialized help. I advised and helped set up the Hackney branch of the Child Poverty Action Group and provided legal advice for the National Council of Civil Liberties. Back in Liverpool, I had followed the local tradition of doing things for charity whenever I could — it was how communities survived. As a teenager, of course, I would stand on street corners rattling tins, as the YCS was regularly involved in collecting money for specific causes. I particularly remember a twenty-four-hour vigil we had in Liverpool City Centre for Biafra during the war and subsequent famine. We slept overnight in the Catholic chaplaincy. Needless to say, a lot of canoodling went on, but nothing too terrible. It was simply a combination of social action and socializing.

As I began to build up experience in family law, I was asked to help out at a law center in Tower Hamlets, an impoverished borough in London's East End. The University House Legal Advice Centre was run by the marvelous Ann Wartuk, a formidable and down-to-earth woman who, in some respects, reminded me of my grandma. She terrified everyone and could be quite a prickly character, but she certainly got things done.

Three of us — myself, Ann, and another lawyer — would go there every Wednesday evening. Ann would have seen people during the week, and our job was to give advice to those who needed to take things a step further or who needed more information than Ann could provide. The place itself was a wreck. No money had been spent on it, and in the winter we would sit there with our coats on as the gas heaters hissed in the background.

I was involved in two major areas. First were the horrendous housing problems. People would come in with bits of wall or wallpaper with plaster attached, stuff that was just rotting away with damp or infested with cockroaches. Some of it was old housing stock, Victorian or even earlier, but equally bad — and even more shameful in some respects — was the newer housing. It was quite hard in those days to get legal aid to take on the housing cases, so I would do what I could in the way of writing letters to the council in an effort to get families rehoused.

Second was domestic violence. I could refer most of that to solicitors, and I would even see some of these people again as formal clients. This was when I saw housing conditions firsthand. The fact that these women were living in terrible physical circumstances was not helping their situations.

In the early 1980s, the Labour Party was going through troubled times. The James Callaghan government of 1976–1979 had failed to deal effectively with the unions, and the country had reeled under strike after strike, leaving the door wide open for the Conservatives and Margaret Thatcher, who had swept into power in May 1979. I remember sitting in the polling station at Abercorn Place just feeling the votes slipping away, while at the same time being fascinated by the idea that Britain was about to get its first female Prime Minister.

In November 1980 Callaghan resigned as Labour leader. The leadership was now up for grabs, and with the election of Michael Foot, the left was clearly ascendant. The spectrum of people who were paid-up members of the Labour Party now ranged from hard-left neo-Trotskyists, known officially as "Militant" (after their magazine) or, rather more disparagingly, the Trots; to those on the right, who, despairing of Foot's ability to deal with Militant, peeled off to form the Social Democratic Party (SDP) in what was known as the Limehouse Declaration in early 1981. While not wanting to move to the right, people like Tony and me found ourselves somewhere in the middle of this arc. We believed that the Trots represented a mad, extreme form of Labour that was never going to do anything for anybody, yet we felt strongly that nothing would be achieved by jumping ship and defecting to the SDP. If we wanted to get rid of the Trots, we had to stay and work internally, we both believed, without the support of the unions and the working class, so the only viable option was to stand and fight within the party. With that firmly in mind, we joined an organization called the Labour Co-ordinating Committee, which was a left-of-center, non-Trotskyist group.

Around the same time, Derry had been approached by his fellow Scot and near contemporary John Smith — a rising star in the Labour firmament and a member of the Shadow Cabinet (the group of senior opposition spokesmen who form a parallel Cabinet) — to advise on the legal status of Militant members within the Labour Party. When Derry brought Tony in to act as his junior, he couldn't have known what the repercussions would be. The more Tony saw what was happening from the inside, the more incensed he became. What Militant was attempting was little short of a takeover, he believed. He would come home at night raging. Tinkering around at the edges was useless, he said. The only way to achieve anything was through mainstream politics: in other words, through becoming an MP. Everything else was a waste of time and effort.

Parliamentary politics is very different from local politics, and it required a change of focus. On a practical level, Tony began to do more trade union work, getting Derry to introduce him to his union solicitors. He also published an article against the need for a Bill of

Rights, his thesis being that with a Bill of Rights, you would be entrusting power to nonelected judges, who are basically white and upper-middle-class.

Union membership was mandatory if you wanted to be a candidate, so while Tony signed up with the Transport and General Workers Union (T & G) in the northeast, I ended up in the central London branch of MATSU, the white-collar arm of the General and Municipal Boilermakers Union (GMB). It was a complete farce. The only people who turned up at board meetings were people like us, who'd basically joined the unions to get credibility and to get on the candidate list.

To get himself known, Tony put himself forward to give lectures at trade union conferences. Barristers were still viewed with suspicion by such audiences, and that was where I came in. I was his passport to working-class acceptability: "I might be posh, but this is my working-class wife, whose father is Tony Booth — you know, the well-known left-winger." At the end of these things, there was usually some kind of sing-along, and inevitably that would be my cue.

"Cherie will now sing you some Liverpool songs," Tony would announce, to tentative applause. Then I would put my hands together, open my mouth, and sing "The Leaving of Liverpool" or "In My Liverpool Home," because Liverpudlians were always powerful in the trade union movement. Thus it was that Tony Blair and Cherie Booth got known within the regional Labour Party, and soon we were both actively looking for seats.

On October 1, 1981, the MP Sir Graham Page died. Though not exactly a household name, he had held my hometown, Crosby, for the Conservatives since 1953, and his death turned our old neighborhood into front-page news (which it had never been while he was alive). Shirley Williams, Secretary of State for Education in the Callaghan government, had lost her seat in the landslide Tory victory of 1979. This could be her chance for a comeback, though not for Labour: she was one of the founders of the SDP. Since she was a good Catholic girl, and the only woman in the Cabinet, her defection had struck me like a slap in the face. When it was announced that she was standing for my hometown (unlike in America, where candidates tend to have long roots in their districts, it is common in England for candidates to choose a race they think can win, even if far from home), I thought, *For goodness' sake. I'll throw my hat in the ring!* My father was incredibly excited, though I knew I wouldn't have a hope in hell.

There was no grand plan, but I have always believed that if an opportunity comes along, you should grab it. Having been fascinated by politics for years, I felt I was at least as good as the other people I had seen put their names forward. If they could, why not me? I saw what was happening to Britain under Thatcher — unemployment and related misery rising inexorably. It wasn't enough just to hope that somebody else would do something about it. That somebody could be me!

I didn't even make the candidate short list, while Shirley Williams romped home to become the first SDP MP. However, it certainly got me thinking.

A few months later, at the end of February 1982, another Tory died: Sir Ronald Bell, MP for Beaconsfield, a small town about twenty miles west of London. This time Tony threw his hat into the ring. My father was partly responsible. Knowing that Tony was interested in getting into mainstream politics, my dad arranged for him to have lunch with an MP called Tom Pendry, and Tony came back that evening very excited. Tom had mentioned Beaconsfield; why didn't he put himself forward for that? He wouldn't win, but it would be good practice, and, more important, it was sure to be very high profile. Tom knew somebody quite senior in the local Labour Party, and he could put Tony in touch.

Beaconsfield had been Disraeli's constituency, and basically it had remained Conservative ever since. The Beaconsfield Labour Party wasn't exactly thriving, and it needed all the help it could get. During the monthlong campaign, Tony put his practice on hold and stayed with my mother in Oxford, driving into Beaconsfield every morning. He didn't come back to Mapledene Road until after the election on May 27. I would join him in Oxford on weekends but otherwise stayed in London, going up by train to help him campaign whenever my commitments in court allowed.

The timing of the election couldn't have been worse for a party in opposition. We were right in the middle of the Falklands War: Argentina had invaded the British-owned island of South Georgia in March, and at the end of April came the sinking of the Argentine cruiser *Belgrano*, with the loss of more than three hundred lives.

The whole of England was in a state of war fever, with Margaret Thatcher cast in the role of Boadicea.

Everyone joined in the campaigning. Even our old friend Bruce Roe, a Conservative from birth, drove round the streets of Beaconsfield in a sports car, blasting out "Vote for Blair." Tony's family was there en masse: Sarah, Bill, and, of course, Tony's dad, along with his new wife, Olwen. Leo and Olwen had married just four months after us. (I had kept the third tier of our wedding cake for them.) Olwen made all the difference in Leo's life, and from my perspective she was a dream mother-in-law.

On the distaff side, Lyndsey, Auntie Audrey, and my mum chipped in. But the stars in the Booth camp were my dad and Pat Phoenix. By this time they were courting, if not actually an item. After he'd been released from the hospital in the summer of 1981, my father had returned to Ferndale Road, there being nowhere else for him to go. One evening when he and Grandma were watching *Coronation Street*, Grandma remembered that he had known Pat Phoenix, who played the show's perennial sex symbol, Elsie Tanner, in the old days. She suggested that he look her up, and they reconnected.

The presence of Tony Booth and Pat Phoenix always guaranteed publicity. She in particular was an inspiration: always beautifully turned out, always with a ready smile, always gracious.

My dad didn't share Pat's innate sense of decorum, however. One afternoon we were touring the district's villages, with Pat and my father leading the way in one car and Tony and I in the car behind. As we were enjoying rural England at its most beautiful — hedges overflowing with bluebells and cow parsley — my dad decided to liven things up a bit by playing "Give Peace a Chance" over the loudspeakers. This was immediately after the sinking of the *Belgrano*, so it was not a good idea on many levels.

Tony was having none of it. "For God's sake, man, turn that racket off!" he yelled out the window. It took some time for my father to comply, because he simply didn't hear: Tony Blair versus John Lennon at full volume was no competition. My husband failed to see the humor in it. Fortunately, the message of peace and love, and the subsequent altercation, was heard only by the cows.

Most campaigning is not that glamorous. Knocking on doors, smile at the ready and leaflet in hand, is not everyone's idea of fun. But I have always loved it, not least because I love meeting people, which ultimately is what it is all about. Whether I have ever persuaded anyone to vote for someone they wouldn't otherwise have voted for is another question. But I could never be accused of being a shrinking violet.

I don't think the Beaconsfield Labour Party had any idea what energy and commitment they had got in Tony Blair. It is hard to imagine a group of party activists more fired with enthusiasm, and the atmosphere was tremendous. Of course, by no stretch of the imagination was Beaconsfield winnable, so the most important job was to identify who the Labour supporters were and to make sure they cast their votes, which was important psychologically both to Tony and to the party at large. I was happy to do anything required of me, particularly asking, in the nicest possible way, whether they were intending to support the young and vibrant Labour candidate, who also happened to be my husband. Whenever we could, Tony and I campaigned together, working our way through the electoral roll of the town and its satellite villages, one street at a time. It was a long process, but we were so happy in our joint endeavor. Tony was in his element. Everyone loved him, even die-hard Tory matrons, who once they saw it was the candidate himself coming down the drive, would personally open their front doors to shake his hand (though a couple did set their dogs on him).

Midway through the campaign, Tony took time off to be best man for his brother. Bill was marrying Katy Tse from Hong Kong. The wedding was behind Manchester Square, just north of Oxford Street, but the timing was very tight. I brought Tony's morning suit with me, so he dashed in from Beaconsfield, changed, performed his duties, and then dashed straight back again, not realizing that he was still in his wedding outfit. A prospective Labour candidate could hardly campaign dressed like that, so as soon as he realized what he had done, he had to dash back to the church again.

Tom Pendry had been right: Beaconsfield was as high profile as they come. Among those who turned up to show their support for the Labour candidate was Michael Foot, then party leader, who came up and had lunch with Tony. Tony had discovered that they were both fans of P. G. Wodehouse, and the poor man was almost in tears, so happy to find someone with whom he could talk about Jeeves and Wooster—much preferred to being harangued about policies by the Labour left.

The whole *Newsnight* team was covering the by-election for BBC TV, and following this lunch, the candidate and the Labour leader were buttonholed outside the restaurant. "Whatever happens tomorrow," Foot said, "in Tony Blair we have a man I know is going to go far in the Labour Party." Not for the first time, P. G. Wodehouse had worked magic.

Tony's campaign had been based on local concerns, not broader Labour mandates. For instance, he'd joined forces with a local pop star's wife on an environmental issue. Indeed, toward the end of the campaign, a leaflet went out headed "Why Tories Are Voting for Blair." It turned out to be prophetic, but not in Beaconsfield.

As expected, Tony lost to the Conservative candidate. But he made his mark and showed his skills at campaigning and bringing people together. I remember one journalist commenting, "In Tony Blair you have the candidate that every Tory mother would love their daughter to bring home as son-in-law."

The night the results came in, the Labour Party–appointed press officer added a final sentence to Tony's "acceptance" speech: "And that's why I pledge that I'll come back and fight this seat again in the eighty-three election." When Tony saw this, he shook his head.

"I can't say this, Cherie," he said. "If I do, then I can wave good-bye to ever becoming an MP."

"So take it out."

"Well — you know, they've all been really great —"

"Don't be silly. Take it out!"

He did.

After the election Michael Foot wrote Tony a very nice letter saying what a good candidate he'd been, that he felt Tony had a lot to offer the Labour Party, and not to despair.

In fact, Tony showed no signs of despair. Quite the contrary. By now he had the bug. He might be doing well at the Bar — he was both incredibly hardworking and proving to be a skilled advocate — but he now knew that what he really wanted was to be in Parliament. The problem was finding a winnable seat. Once an MP is elected, he or she tends to stay put, and deselection is rare.

Over the next eleven months we became like vultures. In June Tony tried for Mitcham and Morden and got nowhere. In February 1983 he went for Bermondsey and was again shut out. We both tried unsuccess-fully for Oxford East — not a by-election, but everyone was now gear-ing up for the general election. I at least made it to the final selection.

Following the Labour candidate's defeat in Bermondsey, all the failed by-election candidates were called in by the party's National Executive Committee (NEC) to analyze what had happened. The view of everyone, apart from Tony, was that "we haven't been left-wing enough." It was then that Tony began to articulate what eventually became the political creed that led to New Labour.

What with all the excitement of Beaconsfield, we had failed to organize our vacation. Not for the first time, my mum came to the rescue with a hotel in Portugal that she could book for us through the office. As neither Tony nor I had been there before, it sounded like the perfect solution.

After his defeat, Tony had decided to concentrate on the north-east. First, a seat in the Labour heartland was more likely to be winnable, and second, it was where his roots were. As usual we worked through August, picking up bits and pieces, then one afternoon Tony called me in chambers.

"Good news and bad news," he said. "The good news is that a seat in Middlesbrough has come up. I've had a word with some of my mates in the T & G, and they think I stand a good chance!"

"But that's fantastic! So what's the bad news?"

"One of the key selection meetings is when we're supposed to be in Portugal. So I'm afraid you'll have to ask your mum to cancel . . ."

My mum was furious. I was simply resigned. It was so late in the game that we lost all the money we'd put down.

In many ways this constituency was exactly what Tony had been hoping for, which was how I came to spend the night of my twenty-eighth birthday in the Middlesbrough Travel Lodge while Tony went to a meeting. I can remember ringing my mum from this miserable hotel room on my rather miserable birthday and her saying, "I don't know why you married that Tony Blair. It's just ridiculous."

Around ten o'clock he was back at the hotel looking hangdog and shamefaced. There was no point staying in Middlesbrough any longer, he said. Another candidate — who duly became the MP — had sewn it all up long before. I have to say it came as a great relief. Middlesbrough had singularly failed to inspire me. Tony was determined not to be downhearted, displaying a character trait that would stand him in good stead. As the Fred Astaire and Ginger Rogers song has it, "Pick yourself up, dust yourself off, and start all over again."

*

*

*

During Tony's Beaconsfield campaign, I had got to know the regional secretary of the Labour Party quite well. He had seen for himself that I was at home canvassing and generally holding forth, and one day in the early spring of 1983 he suggested I drop in and see him. He had some news, he said, that I might be interested in.

"There may be a seat going," he said when I arrived. "They're looking for a woman candidate, so I was wondering if you'd be interested." I never found out why they wanted a woman particularly. It was a safe Tory seat, so perhaps they thought they needed to do something different to generate publicity. "Thanet," he continued, naming the district. It rang a vague bell. Thanet, I hazily recalled, was near Southend, and I knew from the courts that Southend wasn't that far from Hackney.

"Well, why not?" I said. "After all, it's only round the corner."

He gave me a slightly puzzled look.

The more the regional secretary told me, the more I liked the sound of it. The sitting MP was a chap called Billy Rees-Davies, QC, a notorious old criminal lawyer who'd got silk, it was thought, solely because he was an MP. He had only one arm and used to claim that he'd lost the other during enemy action, making himself out to be some sort of war hero, though some said that the circumstances were more dubious.

Rees-Davies was a well-known rogue, one of those barristers who are more famous for the anecdotes about them than anything else. He was a character with a capital C, so I thought, *Well, at least you can have a bit of fun with an opponent like that.*

As I got into my car to go home, I had a thought. "I suppose I had better go to some ward meetings and that kind of thing," I said to the regional secretary.

"Oh, no," he said. "Don't bother with any of that. Just go for the final selection. We'll get you a nomination, and you can take it from there."

Great!

It was only the night before the selection meeting, when I looked up my route on the map, that it dawned on me what a terrible mistake I had made.

Thanet was nowhere near Southend, except possibly as the seagull flies. It was the other side of the Thames, at the far end of Kent — more than a hundred miles away. (This was before the M2 was opened.) During the long drive down, crawling through south-east London, I prayed that I wouldn't be selected.

Fat chance. The constituency party consisted of about three men and a dog. I was the only woman, and the moment I went in, I could tell by their smiles that they really did want a woman candidate and they were going to select me. Sure enough, they did.

I drove back feeling very odd. Marc and Bina had just had their first baby, so I met Tony at the hospital.

"Guess what?" I said. "I've become a candidate."

On one level it was quite a coup. Barristers were not flavor of the month in the Labour Party. At least I was a working-class barrister, which is slightly better than a public-school barrister, and for once being a woman had worked in my favor.

Tony smiled, a bit wanly I thought. He obviously had mixed feelings. Yes, I had a seat to fight — we'd had so many setbacks that we didn't actually think it would happen — but it wasn't that lucky because it was perfectly obvious that Billy Rees-Davies would get straight back in.

I'd rather been looking forward to sparring with him — it was the one bright spot on the horizon — but in the end even that was denied me. The former Thanet West and Thanet East constituencies were changed to north and south to reflect the current demographic. The Tories took full advantage of that to chuck out Billy Rees-Davies, who even they knew had been a hopeless incompetent. My new opponent was named Roger Gale. To take on someone of his background — a former pirate radio DJ and regional television presenter — could have been amusing, but it wasn't.

Thanet's local organization made Beaconsfield seem a powerhouse in comparison. It had no resources and very few members. As a constituency, it was a strange mixture. The main center of population was Margate, and a lot of it was seaside land, full of old people who'd retired there, most of whom were too proud to be Labour. It was a sign of respectability to put a blue Tory sticker in the window.

Even my agent and the councillors were in their sixties and seventies. The few young people around were basically Trots who'd done their usual infiltrating — not that Thanet was exactly a prime target for the radical left.

The local Labour Party was not without ambition, however, and when my dad said he could probably get Tony Benn, the standard bearer of the old left of the Labour Party and a former cabinet minister, to come up and speak, the members were delighted. Of course my dad came along, too. The result was a very strange meeting. I was definitely the most conservative of the three.

For my little speech of introduction, I raised a few smiles when I said how proud I was to be on the platform with these two Tonys, who had been such a great influence on me and the Labour Party. "I give you Tony Booth and Tony Benn!"

The third Tony — my Tony — was there as well, though very much behind the scenes. We had offered to drive Tony Benn down in our car, and on the way back he had really opened up. The three of us had talked nonstop, both politics and, more surprisingly, religion — about liberation theology and the influence of Christianity on socialism. We ended up at his house in Notting Hill still talking, where we met his wife, Caroline, a lovely woman. We all got on very well, and I had the feeling that Tony Benn thought my Tony was an okay guy, although politically, of course, they were on different sides of the debate.

The Thanet Labour Party was delighted with the meeting. It got more publicity than it had had in years, probably ever. Whether it won us any votes is less certain. There was a council election at the same time, however, so it was important.

My husband was supportive right from the beginning. On our way back from France the previous Easter, before the election had even been announced, we had stopped in Margate to have lunch with my agent to talk about the forthcoming campaign. My feelings were a mixture of excitement and dread. The Conservatives were on a high, while the Labour Party was tearing itself apart.

After lunch, it was time for business.

"Tony," he said, "Cherie and I need to talk things over, so perhaps you wouldn't mind helping my wife with the washing up?" Tony ambled off to the kitchen.

My agent's wife was nice enough, but very much the supportive spouse. The conversation during lunch had drifted here and there — the pleasures of the seaside and her belief that seagulls are vermin. While they were washing up, Tony later reported, she said, "So tell me, Tony, are you interested in politics, or are you just doing this for Cherie's sake?"

For him, this was the nadir.

CHAPTER 11

Sedgefield

Tony's thirtieth birthday was on May 6, 1983, a Friday, and I'd decided to organize a surprise party. Then Margaret Thatcher called the election, so I had to start campaigning more or less immediately. I wasn't about to let her spoil the celebrations, however.

I arranged for Richard Field, our old friend from Crown Office Row, to keep the birthday boy busy until about eight o'clock. Maggie and I had spent the whole day cooking, and I'd asked everyone to come at seven-thirty.

Time passed. Eight o'clock came and went. Eight-thirty. Just before nine the pair of them staggered in, having passed a pleasant few hours at El Vino's. I was furious. It wasn't Tony's fault, of course. The man I had relied on to bring him home had himself had one drink too many. When everyone had gone, I apologized to my husband for being less than gracious when they finally showed up.

He had stayed drinking, he said, because he was really depressed.

"The thing is," he said, "I don't really want to be a barrister anymore. I just want to be an MP. And look at me: a general election looming and no seat."

"You've done everything you could —"

"It wasn't enough. At least you've got Thanet."

I laughed.

"There's apparently one seat left in Durham," he said. "I haven't got a hope in hell, of course. But I've nothing to lose, so I may as well go up there anyway."

So that's what he did.

Tony drove up the next day and stayed with friends of his dad's in Shincliffe. For some reason the constituency of Sedgefield had been abolished in 1974, and now they had decided to re-create it, hence the lack of candidates.

As a first step in the selection process, Tony needed a nomination from one of the local party wards. He telephoned John Burton, secretary of the Trimdon Village branch, a few miles to the north of Sedgefield itself, where they had yet to nominate a candidate.

"As it happens, we're having a meeting of the local lads on Wednesday," John told him. "We won all the seats on the council, and we'll be having a bit of a drink to celebrate."

Tony rang me every evening at my agent's house in Margate to tell me how he was getting on. The semi-enthusiasm he had set off with, however, was dissipating rapidly. Although he liked the sound of John's voice, he said, he wasn't convinced it would get him anywhere. It meant hanging around for another two days, and he felt bad about not helping me campaign in Thanet East. He also confessed that he might even be missing me.

"You can't give up now," I told him. "What's two days in the greater scheme of things? From the sound of it, it's exactly the kind of seat you're looking for. And if it's right for you, there's a good chance you'll be right for them."

When Tony arrived at John's house, the lads were watching soccer. So the beers were handed round, and at the end of regulation it was still a draw. Then it went to extra time, then into penalties. Basically they were sitting round the television for two and a half hours without a word of politics being spoken.

When they finally got to talking about the election, Tony told them what a relief it was to find himself among normal people. In London, he said, Labour Party meetings were erupting in violence, plate-glass windows were being smashed, and people were being thrown off balconies. (That, at least, is John's memory of the evening.)

"And now here I am sitting with you lot, watching football, which seems a great deal better than all that infighting."

Indeed it was. Even though it was very late, Tony called me as soon as he got back to his dad's friends' house.

"I've got it!" he said. His voice sounded completely different. I could hardly keep my eyes open, but I listened to him talking about these "normal" people and what a lovely bunch they were. He had told them he thought Britain should remain part of the European Community, which flew in the face of Labour Party policy. He'd also made clear that he did not agree with the Labour Party's campaign for unilateral disarmament. Even so, they had agreed to support him.

He spent the next few days meeting everyone who would have a vote at the selection meeting, from little old ladies to union people. It wasn't enough. The left had organized against him, and he'd failed to make it onto the final list. He was devastated, and John was furious.

But John, it turned out, had one more card up his sleeve. The following night the local party's General Management Committee met. As the selection list was about to be closed, he stood up. "I would like Tony Blair's name added to the short list," he said. "I'm not going to say anything about Tony Blair. I just want to tell you what the leader of our party thinks about Tony Blair," and he read out the letter that Michael Foot had sent Tony after Beaconsfield.

A vote was taken, and Tony got through 42 to 41.

As time was so short, the selection meeting itself was the following night, and Tony won easily, by 73 votes to the runner-up's 46.

The area was very run-down. Coal mining was in decline, and there were fewer and fewer pits. There were some small-scale factories, but the main employer was the local council. John Burton said that people knew something had to change.

When Tony called me that night, he was ecstatic but also rather terrified.

"Knowing my luck," he said, "I'll be the person to lose what is technically an unlosable seat." (Tony has always had the tendency to be pessimistic, while I am incurably optimistic.)

Tony moved into John and Lily Burton's house, sleeping in their daughter Caroline's room. (She was away at college.) When I joined him on the weekends, we took the two single mattresses off the beds and pushed them together on the floor. Lily laughed. It did her heart good, she said, to see two people so in love.

With John's stalwart help, Tony ran a brilliant campaign. The local organization was minimal, and once again the family came to the rescue. Tony's brother, Bill, and his new wife, Katy, came over, as did Lyndsey and my auntie Audrey, all knocking on doors and doing the tedious but crucial stuff of grassroots canvassing and getting the vote out. And, of course, my father and Pat Phoenix were a main attraction.

Everything was brought into play, even my voice. John ran a folk group called Skerne, named after the local river. Because of my folksinging background, I knew all the words to their songs and, with the rest of the audience, would join in. Although John and those close to him knew that Tony wasn't just a posh barrister drafted to run for the seat by the London party bigwigs, it was important to show the constituency as quickly as possible that this wasn't the case.

The day before the election, I sent Tony a card: "From the candidate in Thanet to the candidate in Sedgefield, in the sure knowledge that one of us will be an MP tomorrow."

June 9, 1983, was one of those perfect summer days that politicians pray for. Sunshine brings with it a general air of optimism and not having to pester or ferry people down to the polling booths in the cold or rain. Lyndsey was there to support me at the count, and Bill and Katy sent me a bunch of red roses for luck. At Sedgefield, Tony had his dad and stepmother. It will always be a lasting regret that I couldn't be there with him, but Leo and Olwen could not have been prouder.

My results came in fairly early. I didn't do bad. Basically, Labour was decimated in the southeast, but I got 12 percent of the votes, one of the few Labour candidates to do that well that year. Lyndsey and I drove back to London, listening to the other results on the car radio, trying to work out when Sedgefield would come in. When we arrived back home, I rang up Labour Party headquarters and asked them to call me when the Sedgefield results came in.

The next day Tony told me about the count, how the first boxes to come in were from the outlying villages around Darlington, which were Tory wards. They were all piled up on tables, and he knew from Beaconsfield exactly what that meant: the Conservative candidate was in the lead.

"I was in such a panic," he later admitted, "that I went outside and had a cigarette" (the first since our wedding day). But then new boxes began to arrive, and the tide turned. In the end he won by 8,281 votes.

Tony might have been successful, but the results for the Labour Party as a whole were disastrous. Any idea that going further to the left was the way to revive the party was dented. Michael Foot resigned, and Neil Kinnock took over as leader.

One of Tony's election promises was that if he was elected as the MP for Sedgefield, he would buy a house in the constituency. Thankfully, he didn't say we would move up there permanently, which was what he'd planned to do if he hadn't been elected: he had been determined not to be accused of being a London carpetbagger.

Although Tony might have been happy to move his practice, I knew that if I moved mine, I could wave good-bye to specializing in employment law; it would be back to a diet of family, crime, and accident cases. With Tony now safely elected, I could breathe again. We could have a home in the northeast, but I could continue to work in London.

Immediately we began thinking about where to buy. Even though he had only been there three weeks, Tony had a good idea of the geography, it being so close to where he'd been brought up. Sedgefield is essentially a rural constituency made up of mining villages and farms. The small town of Sedgefield itself, he decided, was a bit posh. As he'd had a lot of support from Trimdon, it made sense to base himself round there, and we could tap into the community through John and Lily Burton.

So while I went back to work, Tony stayed up in Durham, getting to know the people and looking for a house. It would need to be comparatively big, he had decided, as it would double as the constituency office. In the meantime he continued to sleep on the Burtons' floor.

In early July he called me with news. "Cherie, I've found the perfect house. It's fabulous! It's got seven Victorian fireplaces and a hand pump in the kitchen!"

"Does it have anything else?" I asked. "Because we're expecting a baby."

Throughout the campaign, I had been feeling a little peculiar, which I'd put down to anxiety. I still wonder whether it happened the night of his thirtieth birthday party, but we'll never know for sure.

Before we got married, I'd been on the Pill. But Tony always worried about the long-term effects, so after the wedding we practiced other forms of contraception. Once I realized that Thanet was a dead duck, I stopped taking precautions. My future, I decided, did not lie in politics, though I never imagined I would get pregnant immediately. When Tony was selected as candidate, I saw that even thinking about starting a family was not sensible, so I went back to using contraception again . . . a bit late.

As for Myrobella, as the house was called, the answer to my question "Anything else?" was no. The house had been cleaned out. The last occupant had been the mine superintendent's widow. A friend of John Burton's had been planning to buy it, but luckily for us, the reality of the renovation proved too daunting for him. Everything needed to be done: rewiring, replumbing, the lot.

The hamlet of Trimdon Colliery is about two miles from Trimdon Village. It's basically two streets of small terraced houses, at right angles to each other, with Myrobella roughly in the middle. The unusual name is not one of those unwieldy conjunctions of the owners' names (as I first supposed), but a variety of pear that grew in profusion in the garden. We bought it for about £30,000 and spent about the same doing the absolutely necessary improvements. We didn't move in till the following summer, by which time Euan had been born.

When I discovered I was pregnant, I was twenty-nine years old. My career was going pretty well. I had started to do much more employment law and less of the more general stuff. So far, so good. I was only the second woman tenant that 5 Essex Court had ever had. The first one, when she found out she was expecting, left and never came back. That wasn't my intention at all. Nor could it be. Although some barrister MPs continue to work, Tony had decided to give it all up and devote himself to politics. As simple as that. He did one last case and then bowed out for good.

Financially, of course, this had implications. By 1983 he had been earning in the region of £80,000 per year. This would now drop to an MP's salary of less than £20,000 — not bad at all for the times, but not enough to cover our expenses, especially with a baby on the way. It was going to be a struggle. I was about to become the main breadwinner, a status that filled me with anxiety. Not that I had ever indulged in fantasies of being a stay-at-home housewife — quite the reverse. The specter of what had befallen my mother loomed large in my life. I wasn't afraid of abandonment — I didn't think for a moment that Tony would abandon me. (But, then, what new wife does?) However, accidents happen. Behind my mum was the example of my grandma. How often had she drummed into me the need for a woman to have financial independence as she recounted trudging the streets of Crosby and Blundellsands in her desperate attempt to find work after Grandad had his accident on the Liverpool docks after World War II. For two years he was totally incapacitated, which led directly to my dad leaving school long before he should have, which changed his whole life. That was why my education meant so much to her: nothing to do with certificates and diplomas, and everything to do with never being dependent on a man for money.

None of these practical considerations, however, took away from the sheer excitement of realizing that a baby was on the way. I have always loved babies, and the unexpectedness only added to the thrill — like being given a surprise present that you have secretly longed for.

In 1983 there was no such thing as maternity leave, not even a moratorium on the rent. Once the baby was born, I would be able to arrange for child care and continue to work. But before birth comes pregnancy — something I couldn't delegate. My practice was far less lucrative than Tony's, and so I had to work as long as I possibly could. This is where my stubborn streak came to the fore. I would show everybody that I could do it. Completely ridiculous, but there we are.

Just because I was pregnant, I saw no reason to slow down. Now that Tony was MP for Sedgefield, he was up there every weekend, and I'd go with him, though usually on a later train. Then as now, on a Friday night it would be standing room only. Young and healthy as I was, this was a strain the bigger I got, not least because I had usually been on my feet in court earlier in the day.

I was due on January 29, 1984. At my first checkup after Christmas, I was told that the baby was too small. "The baby is not receiving sufficient nourishment," the doctor said. "You are doing too much. At eight months this workload is completely unacceptable."

I was taken to the hospital for bed rest and went nearly mad with boredom. After ten days, there being no improvement, they said they wanted to induce me. I wasn't keen, I said.

"Mrs. Blair, your baby is not growing. It's not a question of not being keen."

Tony and I had gone to all the birthing classes, and I had fully expected to have my baby naturally. But they broke my water and put me on an IV, and immediately I was right into a very painful experience. My firstborn made his appearance at about eleven-thirty, on January 19, 1984, after an epidural and a high-forceps delivery. So much for natural childbirth.

As birth experiences go, it was utterly ghastly, including a third-degree tear, because they yanked him out. It was the human equivalent of going from zero to sixty in five seconds. Lyndsey and Tony's sister, Sarah, were now sharing a flat, and when they arrived at the hospital, I was still in trauma. There was blood all over the place, and Sarah said it put her off having babies forever. Luckily for the future of the planet, a new mother quickly forgets the pain as she is overwhelmed by love for this perfect little person. This was certainly my experience, and from the first blink of those little unfocused eyes, the curl of those tiny fingers, I was hooked. We called this precious creature Euan, after Euan Uglow and also a school friend of Tony's who had died far too young.

Tony had been there since the induction. It would be nice to say that his presence had made all the difference. It would be wrong. He was completely useless. Like practically all new fathers, he hadn't been expecting it to be quite so gory. My husband has always been good at empathizing, but when it comes to childbirth, empathy only goes so far. Once Euan was cleaned and wrapped and smelling delicious, however, Tony's pride and delight in his son was such that you'd think he had taken more than a queasy spectator's role. He made up for it later, becoming as adoring and hands-on a dad as anybody could wish for. That afternoon Tony told me I had a visitor. I was about to have my picture taken, he informed me, by a photographer from the *Northern Echo: Sedgefield MP, wife, and newborn son* being the theme. I think the caption was something like "Euan Brings Labour for Labour."

I was given a rubber ring to sit on so that at least I could force a smile. As the guy went about his business, focusing and clicking, all

I could think was *An appearance before the highest court in the land is a cakewalk compared to this. I am never going to do this again.*

My last thought as I went to sleep that night was of my husband: *I hate this man.*

Euan was comparatively small, so the numerous hats and coatees I had knitted, though far too big, came in handy, as he needed to be kept very warm. He was both families' first grandchild, and we were well looked after: my mum came down, then Auntie Audrey, then Olwen. But it couldn't last. I needed to get back to work; I needed a nanny.

Euan was christened in Sedgefield, and that same weekend I found Angela, who stayed with us for four years. I had advertised in the *Northern Echo* because I wanted someone who wouldn't mind spending time in the northeast. Angela was a farmer's daughter from North Yorkshire with a strong Yorkshire accent and a passion for Manchester United soccer. A down-to-earth girl, then in her midtwenties, she had already worked for a couple of other families. She spoke her mind and was completely trustworthy and sensible, and we just clicked.

No matter how confident I was that Angela would care for Euan as well as, if not better than, I could have, it was incredibly hard for me to leave him. Apart from the first few weeks, I'd had sole care of him; to hand him over to somebody else was torture. We had our own little routine; everything was a pleasure and a game. For four months the center of my world had resided in this small, helpless creature. I was still breast-feeding when I went back to work, and my breasts had no scruples in showing exactly how they felt. Sometimes I'd be sitting in court, aware only of the intense pain of the swelling and knowing that by the time I got out, my bra would be soaked. I would express milk with a breast pump in chambers during the day, put it in the fridge, and then take it home for the next day.

It was hard, but I didn't dare slow down. I'd put in so much effort to build up my practice that it would have been mad to let it go, particularly at a time when Tony had effectively given up his. Tony's election had already put an end to any thoughts of standing for Parliament myself. There wasn't a pact between us, as has been speculated; it was simply impractical. Nor can I say I minded. I loved my job, and with Tony a committed MP (I knew even then he was determined to go as far as he could), I would get all the exposure to politics I wanted — and then some.

Our first summer at Myrobella, in 1984, was the year of an intense and sometimes violent miners' strike, which ultimately resulted in significant damage to trade unions throughout the country. Although there were no longer any mines in the constituency itself, the Fishburn coke works were affected, and a number of Tony's constituents were miners. It was a painful time, not only for the individuals and the families concerned but also for the communities as a whole and ultimately for the Labour Party.

Once we were a family, Nicky came along quite naturally. I didn't want Euan to be an only child, and given that the system was now in place, we thought we might as well get on with it, especially as my practice had definitely flattened out.

I remember our second summer in Myrobella — the summer I was pregnant with Nicky — as a kind of idyll. Driving up the road from Sedgefield, through Fishburn past the coke works, I felt almost as if I was going back to my roots. Perhaps it had to do with being pregnant, but the smell of coal fires — a smell that was there even in the summer — reminded me of my childhood. Living in Trimdon was, in some sense, going back into that community. Just as in Ferndale Road, we always had an open door, and there was a group of local kids — they must have been about age ten — who would come in and play with Euan, by now a sturdy toddler. I used to do cooking with them. At that time garlic was exotic, and I remember introducing them to it, showing them how to peel it.

We went up to the constituency every weekend. Tony would usually go on Thursday, and I'd follow on Friday. Looking back, I don't know how we did it.

When Euan came along, we became a two-car family, Tony had a Rover — Parliament had done a deal with Rover, so MPs got them at a discount — and I had a beat-up Mini Metro, which got progressively more beat-up because I was such a terrible driver. I have no spatial awareness whatsoever.

During my first driving test, the examiner told me to stop after only ten minutes. "In the interests of public safety, I'm terminating this test," he said. "Stay here. Do not touch the car. I'm going to go back and get your driving instructor to come and get you."

On my second attempt, I spent the entire time with my foot hovering over the brake, expecting the examiner to stop me at any second: failure number two. The third time, the test seemed to go on far longer than usual. "I thought you needed settling down," the young examiner explained. I'd put it down to mine being the first test of the day and the lovely spring weather.

On the way home, I called Tony from a phone box. "I passed!" I said.

"You can't have. It's a disgrace. He should never have passed you — you're a hopeless driver."

The following day I volunteered to take Geoff and Beverley Gallop, who were staying with us, on a tour of junk shops round the backstreets of Hackney. At one point another car got a bit too close, and there was a crunch. I found a phone box and rang Tony. "You're going to have to come and get me."

If anything, I found the open spaces of the northeast even more daunting than London, particularly the lack of lighting after dark. On at least three occasions over the years, I landed in a ditch, with the kids screaming in the back.

As far as the people in chambers were concerned, my driving was a standing joke. To accept a lift from me was a rite of passage.

My second pregnancy was a breeze compared with the first. I was fit and well and had a support system with Angela, and we had our own home in the constituency.

On Thursday, December 5, 1985, I woke up feeling unusually anxious. Tony was due to go up to Myrobella, but I didn't want him to leave. I had a feeling the baby might be coming, I told him.

"But you've still got two weeks to go."

"Euan was early."

"Because Euan was induced!"

It wasn't that Tony was being difficult. It was a matter of diplomacy, he explained: Prince Andrew was going to be opening something in the constituency the next day, and he was due to have breakfast with him.

"If you can assure me that the baby's coming this weekend, then of course I won't go. And don't forget you've got your mum coming."

Friday being my mum's day off, most weeks she would take the bus down from Oxford to spend the day with her grandson. She didn't usually stay the night because she had to work on Saturday. In fact, that weekend Auntie Audrey was also expected for her annual Christmas shopping expedition.

Tony left Mapledene Road around 4:00 p.m., and the contractions started in earnest around 8:00. At about 9:00 I called Myrobella. No reply. I called the Burtons' house; Lily answered. The ancient Daimler Tony kept in the constituency for when we went up by train had packed up, so John had gone to collect him at the station.

In the meantime my mum had begun to panic.

Finally the phone rang. "There's no question about it now," I said. "I think you're going to have to come back!"

"How can I? The Daimler's dead, and there are no more trains tonight."

"Well, what am I going to do?" I knew I was in no state to drive myself to the hospital.

"Get Lyndsey to drive," he said. "I'll borrow John's car and get there as soon as I can."

Lyndsey had just passed her driving test that week. She had never driven my car, never driven in the dark, and never driven into central London, and she had no idea where the hospital was. Other than that, it was fine.

The moment Lyndsey arrived, I waddled out of the house in my dressing gown and eased myself across the backseat. Mum sat in the front with the A–Z map of London, and we set off. Between groans I gave directions, wincing at the grinding of gears and the regular stalling. "Push your clutch down!" I yelled as the car bucked and whinnied through east London.

Somehow we got there. As Lyndsey lurched to a stop, I flung open the door and propelled myself toward the entrance. Once in a wheelchair, I was rushed straight to the delivery ward, my mum struggling to keep up. The moment we got there, I dashed to the toilet, and they had to pull me off. Sure enough, I was ten centimeters dilated.

"How fascinating to see it from this angle," I heard my mum say as I was pushing Nicky out.

I'm ashamed to confess that I wasn't very nice to her. "I don't want you here!" I shouted. "Where's my husband?"

Less than half an hour after we arrived, our second son came gliding into the world. He was born incredibly quickly. No drugs, no forceps. It was over in what seemed like minutes, and my mum was the first one to hold him.

Tony arrived about 4:00 a.m., exactly twelve hours after he had left, having borrowed John Burton's old banger and driven through the night on near-empty roads — which was a good thing, as the brakes failed just as he came into London. On the way down, he'd been thinking about what to call our son, he said, and had come up with Colin.

"Colin? You can't call a baby Colin!"

Fortunately my mum agreed, and as he was born on St. Nicholas's Day, Nicholas he was.

The following week we took Nicky on his first plane ride, when the entire family flew up to Sedgefield for Christmas, our second at Myrobella. To have a new baby at Christmas was a joy, and we had a full house, with Mum, Lyndsey, and Grandma somehow all squashing in. Although Grandma was becoming increasingly frail and forgetful, she still loved babies and happily spent the entire holiday cooing with delight over her new great-grandson.

This would be the pattern of our Christmases for the next twelve years: the family all assembled at Myrobella, me cooking a huge turkey from our wonderful local butcher and next-door neighbor Eddie Greaves. It was always over too quickly, and that year — like every other — I was back at work by the beginning of January.

CHAPTER 12

Departures

When Nicky was three months old, we left Mapledene Road and moved to Highbury, in north London. With a baby, a toddler, and a nanny, we simply needed more space. Not only did the new house have four bedrooms and a conservatory — and two bathrooms — but it was also better situated in terms of public transport.

I was rapidly discovering that two children are very different from one. When we had only Euan, I continued to work with the Labour Co-ordinating Committee — to the extent that I would even be breast-feeding at the meetings. But once Nicholas came along, it was just too much. For the same reason, I also had to stop the legal advice sessions I'd been conducting in Tower Hamlets.

Now that Tony was an MP, it wasn't appropriate for him to get involved in the local Labour Party. With two small boys, we decided that joining a church would be a more practical way of becoming active in the community, and we started going to nearby St. Joan of Arc. Not only was it within walking distance, but it had both a primary and a nursery school attached. We were learning that as parents, we had to think ahead. I might not have minded being married in a Protestant church, but I was insistent that the children be brought up Catholic.

In July 1986, Pat Phoenix died. My dad was utterly distraught, not least because it came as such a shock. Among women of that generation, cancer was not something you admitted to, and Pat did not admit how ill she was until the end. My father couldn't bear to think that she might be dying. Although she and my father had been together for six years and the subject of their marital status was regular tabloid fodder, they married only a day or so before she passed away. She had tried to persuade him for some time to "regularize" their relationship, but he had always resisted. Marrying him was her last great kindness: now he would be financially secure.

Indeed, Pat's generosity was boundless, from looking after my dad when he was physically and psychologically at rock bottom to supporting Tony in his campaigns. She was an avid collector, and Myrobella had been largely furnished with what she could not fit into her own house in Cheshire, including a number of risqué William Russell Flint paintings that adorn Myrobella's walls to this day. Her funeral was extraordinary, and the streets of Manchester were lined with her fans.

The news hit me like a brick, not least because she had been having treatments in the same specialist cancer unit where I knew Auntie Audrey was getting her own radiation treatments. Three years earlier, while she and Uncle Bill were in America visiting old friends Gerry and Shirley Quilling, Auntie Audrey told Shirley that she had a lump but didn't want to go to the doctor about it. Shirley took charge at once and arranged for her to see her own doctor. As soon as he saw it, he said, "That's got to come off." She had the operation there and then. She called me at work and told me she had breast cancer. She wanted me to tell her mum, my mum, and Lyndsey.

"But, Cherie, whatever you do, don't say anything to my kids," she said. Catherine was then about twenty, Christopher a year younger, and Robert only fifteen. It seems incredible now that there was still such a taboo against talking about breast cancer. It was as if by not talking about it, you could deny its existence. When I eventually became a patron of Breast Cancer Care and other related charities, talking about it became very important to me, not least because I am convinced that had Auntie Audrey seen someone earlier, the outcome might have been different.

Even though I was one of the only people who knew how ill she was, she never talked about the cancer with me. Sometimes it was obvious that she was having the chemo and that things weren't all that great, which was why it was nice that she was there when

Nicholas was born, but it was never clear how she was faring. She'd be ill, and then she'd be well. She took such pleasure in Euan and Nicky, coming to stay with us whenever she could and boasting that she was the one who fed Euan his first solid food. It was as if she knew she wouldn't live long enough to see her own grandchildren, and the boys were the nearest she would have.

In addition to our Christmas gatherings at Myrobella, the family would always spend Easter with us. In the spring of 1987, Auntie came over on Maundy Thursday, three days earlier than usual, in order to spend time with the boys, and it was obvious that she was very ill. She helped put Euan and Nicky to bed and read them a story, but that night she was in a really bad way. By this time the cancer had spread to her lungs, and they filled up with fluid and needed to be drained. She couldn't breathe and was in pain, so the next morning Uncle Bill took her home. As I held Nicky up to wave her off, I knew this would be the last time I would see her. It was only then that I realized that whereas I thought she had come to spend Easter with us, she had really come to say good-bye.

The following Tuesday they rang to say she had died at home. She was fifty-two, no age at all.

A week or so later, I was driving back from a court case outside London when the dam burst. I pulled over, and as cars swished past me in the rain, I just sobbed and sobbed. When I was a newborn baby, it was Audrey who rushed home from her job as a telephonist to play with me. It was Audrey who took me in at lunch when I was at Seafield. It was Audrey who showed me that politics wasn't just for men. It was Audrey and her husband and children who showed me how a normal family life could be. She was a friend to my mum when my dad left us. She was a vibrant, outgoing person, who always had time for everyone. And now she was gone, and the world was a bleaker place without her.

Easter was late that year, so her funeral was at the end of April, coming up to May, and we sang the May Day procession hymn that is sung when Mary is crowned. It wasn't a funeral hymn — quite the opposite — but we chose it because we knew it was one of her favorites.

In 1987 we also said good-bye to Angela, who had become much more than a nanny. She and I had discovered a shared interest in athletics, and we would regularly go to the National Sports Centre at Crystal Palace in south London together. She was a very good cook, and what she really wanted to do was run a sandwich business. That spring a friend of hers heard that British Rail was starting a hospitality suite for first-class passengers and suggested she contact the company. The idea was that she could learn about running a catering business while being paid for it at the same time. So that was what she did. She is still a family friend.

Having had such success with Angela, I once again advertised in the *Northern Echo*. With no baby to look after and Euan now at St. Joan of Arc nursery school every morning, I decided that a trained nursery nurse wasn't really necessary and took an eighteen-year-old straight from school. She had never been to London, though she did drive. In retrospect I realize it was asking too much. At the interview I was pleased when she told me she was religious. It was only after she came down that I realized she was quite fundamentalist, and she was soon involved with a local sect. One day I got home to find Euan in a terrible state. He was then just over four, and it seemed he had come out with a swearword, and she had squirted liquid soap into his mouth.

I was shocked, and it showed, but beyond telling her that this was unacceptable behavior, I decided to do nothing before discussing it with Tony. That weekend we went up to the constituency, where we talked about sacking her, but by the time we got back on Sunday, she had already left. A note told us that her future lay with her new friends at church and she had decided to join them. So it was back to the *Northern Echo* for the second time in three months.

Luckily we then found Gillian, who came from near Richmond, in Yorkshire. She was a fantastic young woman who stayed for three years, when she left to get married.

I had never yearned for a large family. Once I had Euan and Nicholas, I decided that was quite enough. Yet in those weeks after Audrey died, I found myself thinking, *I want another baby*. What I really wanted — though I never voiced it, even to myself — was a daughter. I was able to tell my grandma that I was pregnant shortly before she died the following August.

Grandma never knew that her own daughter, Audrey, had died. For some time she had been increasingly confused, so in many ways she had already left us. After my mum moved out of Ferndale Road, Uncle Bob moved back in to keep an eye on Grandma. Eventually he couldn't cope, so she went to a retirement home. I wasn't very happy about that, but as she could no longer look after herself, there was no alternative. Realistically, I couldn't bring her down to London.

Grandma wasn't at the retirement home long, perhaps a year, before she passed away. Until I was two years old, these two women, Grandma and Audrey, had been everything to me — one a surrogate mother, one a surrogate sister — and losing both of them within six months marked a watershed in my life.

My father was devastated. In a little over twelve months, he had lost his wife, his sister, and his mother. It could have sent him back to the bottle — which he had forsworn after his brush with death — but thank God, it didn't.

Our daughter, Kathryn — blessed with the auburn hair of both her great-great-grandmother Tilly and Tony's mother, Hazel — was born on March 2, 1988, nine months to the day after the 1987 general election.

That night in June, we had been in a celebratory mood. Although the Labour Party in general had fared barely better than it had five years earlier, Tony had increased his margin of victory.

For a newcomer to Parliament, he had done well in the previous five years. In his maiden speech to the House of Commons, he had said: "I am a socialist, not through reading a textbook that has caught my intellectual fancy, nor through unthinking tradition, but because I believe that, at its best, socialism corresponds most closely to an existence that is both rational and moral. It stands for co-operation, not confrontation; for fellowship, not fear. It stands for equality."

However well this might have gone down in the reformist camp, it did nothing for the harmony of daily life at Westminster. When he arrived, Tony was allocated a room with Dave Nellist, the MP for Coventry South-East, one of three Labour MPs who belonged to Militant. This was a marriage made in hell. Not only was Tony a barrister — in itself a class crime — but he was a barrister who, when working with Derry, had tried to get Militant expelled from the party. It wasn't long before Nellist got himself transferred to another office, which he shared with another, younger Militant, while Tony was allocated a room with a Scottish MP named Gordon Brown. They found common ground immediately. Both were bright, both had been elected in the 1983 general election, and both had fought a previous election in an unwinnable Conservative constituency. Gordon was more established in politics, and he certainly considered himself more senior, which I think Tony would have agreed with, not least because Gordon was older, though only by two years.

As Gordon didn't have a family, we didn't tend to socialize with him. Our Labour milieu was in London, while Gordon spent his time in Scotland, and he wasn't used to the presence of small children.

It was inevitable that Labour would lose the 1987 election. However, the failure at the polls convinced Tony that something had to be done. In British politics the team of senior politicians who head up government departments is known as the Cabinet. The opposition's parallel team is known as the Shadow Cabinet, and both Tony and Gordon were determined to get elected by fellow Labour MPs to this select body in order to move the Labour Party from an unelectable force into an electable one, which was something I fully agreed with.

At the 1987 Labour Party Conference that September, they both stood for the Shadow Cabinet. Gordon got in (becoming Shadow Secretary of State for Trade and Industry), while Tony was the highest runner-up. Their campaign manager was Nick Brown, whom Tony had introduced to Gordon. He, too, had entered Parliament in 1983, when the previous incumbent of Newcastle East went over to the SDP. We had got to know him because, having a local constituency, he would regularly drop in at Myrobella. He was basically a fixer, with fingers in all sorts of pies. He had been a legal officer for the GMB and for a short time had been on the Newcastle City Council. He had future Chief Whip written on his forehead even then. He was unbelievably patronizing, always calling me "love," and clearly felt that women should be seen and not heard in the Labour Party. I saw him as a bit of a political thug.

My career was also in a state of flux, but with things moving so fast in the Labour Party, Tony had other things on his mind. Along with many other young barristers, I believed that we needed to find a new system for paying the clerks. While he was still at Crown Office Row, Tony had pushed for just such a change, and he and Chris Carr had put their case to Derry. The old-fashioned system of a clerk getting 10 percent of each fee when there were nine or ten tenants was one thing, they said. But now that there were twenty-five of them, David was getting paid ridiculously well. Tony and Chris thought that they would all be better off in their own chambers. The split eventually happened, with Derry taking off his people and forming 11 King's Bench Walk. Although Tony had been very active in pushing for it, almost as soon as it happened, he left the Bar for good.

At around the same time, tensions had begun to develop in 5 Essex Court. A split opened up between the silks in the north and the junior barristers down in London, which included me. Normally juniors could hope to build up their practice by picking up work that trickled down from the silks, but as the silks were on an entirely different circuit, that wasn't happening. Then Freddie Reynold, who had originally taken me on, took silk, and he and Alastair Hill — another of the original London members who took silk at the same time — decided that they, too, would do better to cut loose.

Word of this plan eventually got out. The silks whose practices were based entirely in the north didn't really care, but those who had mixed practices were not at all happy. It didn't help when libel and criminal lawyer George Carman, who by this time was famous, suddenly decided that he wanted to join the renegades. On the one hand, we weren't that keen to have him, because "selfish" and "George" were two terms that definitely went together. On the other hand, his income would be useful.

I was for the split from the beginning, and once we moved into our new premises, I became very much a player on the management committee. Also, although I wasn't the only woman, I became the mother hen, with everyone coming to me with their problems. Perhaps because I couldn't channel all my mothering instincts into my children at home, these grown-ups got it instead.

Everything was quite tense in the run-up. The northern silks refused to move out of the building, saying it was theirs; we — the ones who actually worked there — said it was ours. Today it is increasingly common for chambers to set up in premises outside the Inns, but that wasn't the case back then, and space was at a premium. Eventually Gray's Inn — in this case the de facto landlord — managed to find us space in New Court Chambers, as they wanted to avoid a major fallout on their doorstep.

For the first time in my joint career of mother and barrister, I had some financial relief when I was expecting Kathryn. Three months after I fell pregnant, Gail Carrodus, the other female tenant in New Court Chambers, also fell pregnant. Unlike me, she was horribly sick and unable to work. Feeling desperately sorry, chambers offered her a three-month rent-free period, so I said, "Hello! Do you think I should have a rent-free period, too?" They agreed. We were one of the first chambers to do that, and eventually it was enshrined by the Bar Council in the 1990s.

With Gillian's approval, I decided that this time I was going to have a home birth, not least because the hospital I'd used for Euan and Nicholas had closed its maternity wing. Every few weeks I would visit my GP to make sure that all was well, and from time to time I'd have a scan. I should have had one at thirty weeks, but work was picking up and I was just too busy. At thirty-four weeks the doctor said that I couldn't postpone the scan any longer. I couldn't see what all the fuss was about. Scans were necessary for first-time mothers perhaps, but not experienced hands like me. I was feeling fine, and I thought the baby's head was engaged. Nevertheless, I submitted.

"I'm sorry, Mrs. Blair," the technician in charge of the ultrasound said, sweeping my swollen belly. "That's not the baby's head that's engaged; it's the baby's bottom. This is a breech."

The doctor's verdict was unequivocal: "You cannot possibly have a home birth. Indeed, I rather think we're looking at a cesarean."

I was so adamant that I didn't want a cesarean that they took an X-ray of my pelvis.

"Well," the doctor said as I stared at the X-ray, "if you want to kill yourself and your baby, then have a home birth. But otherwise you're going to have a cesarean."

I was booked in on March 3, 1988. A few days earlier, a computer had been delivered from chambers. We had just started to modernize, and I had resolved to teach myself how to use it. (Until then we had written everything by hand, and a typist would type it up.) As soon as I began to get the hang of it, I was hooked.

Tony had arranged to take me to the hospital the evening of March 2, and I decided to use the time beforehand typing an opinion on the computer, though I was barely able to reach the keyboard over the bump. I was aware that contractions had started, but I carried on anyway, while Gillian fussed in the background.

"Are you sure you're all right?" she asked repeatedly.

"Quite sure. I'm just going to finish this advice."

"I'm really not happy about this."

"I'm fine. Really."

"You are not fine, and I'm going to ring Tony to come now."

I was still typing away when Tony arrived. When we got to the hospital, there was a line for emergency cesareans, and at that point I started to worry because of my experience with Nicky.

"I'm warning you," I said to Tony, "if it's a boy, I'm going to cry."

Then came the epidural, which the doctor had agreed I could have rather than a general anesthetic. It took ten attempts to get the needle in, as I watched Tony turn whiter and whiter. Then, more quickly than seemed possible, the surgeon cut me open and scooped up the baby: a gorgeous baby girl. I cried anyway.

In fact, I was soon screaming.

"In about two percent of the population, the epidural doesn't reach there," the surgeon later explained as he immediately stopped stitching me up. He had no alternative, he said, but to knock me out, just briefly, to finish the job. I had to stay in the hospital for five days. When I got home, I read the advice I'd been writing on the computer when I'd left. Fortunately I had not had time to print out. It was complete and utter garbage.

My friend Francesca had also had a cesarean a few months before. She had married John Higham, one of the barristers who had done his Bar Finals at the same time as Tony and me. Like us, they had moved to Hackney, and their first baby had been born around the time I discovered I was pregnant with Euan. During those early days when I was an inexperienced mum at home on my own, she was very kind in showing me the ropes. She had a second baby a year before I had Nicholas. When she was feeding him, she noticed a lump in her breast. Her doctor, who was our doctor, too, thought it was an engorged milk gland. It wasn't. By the time they realized it was cancer, it had already taken hold. She was operated on, and all seemed to go well, although the oncologist told her that she should not get pregnant again. But Francesca, who was half Italian, was a Catholic, and she did get pregnant, and the cancer returned. As soon as the baby was viable, she had her cesarean. It was a boy, and though tiny he lived. His mother did not. I went to her funeral just three days before Kathryn was born and wept for another life lost, another family left devastated by breast cancer.

CHAPTER 13

Moving On

In 1989 I received the ultimate accolade for a junior barrister when the Queen's Counsel who had led me in a very difficult wardship case gave me a red bag. All barristers carry their robes in a blue bag, but a red one can be given only by a Queen's Counsel for what he or she deems exceptional work. There is a whole ritual surrounding the presentation, including the £10 tip you are supposed to give the junior clerk who delivers the bag to your chambers.

Maggie Rae was the instructing solicitor in the case concerned, and everything about it had been difficult. The family of the children who had been taken into care were involved in prostitution. The grandmother was the madam of a brothel, and the mother was now putting her own children "on the game." The evidence was harrowing. Now that I was the mother of a daughter myself, I was finding these family law cases increasingly hard to cope with. I remember one case involving a woman whose newborn baby had been taken into care. She was devoted to her child, but the baby had drug withdrawal symptoms when it was born. The mother was a heroin addict, and the medical view was that she was going to die. She was devastated when the baby was placed for adoption.

In another case, a young woman was accused of injuring her baby, but she denied it. We argued her case, and I convinced the magistrate that it hadn't happened. The baby was delivered back to the woman on a Friday. By the next Monday she had called social services and said, "I did do it, and I can't cope. Please take him back." Otherwise, she said, she feared she'd hurt him again. The saddest thing about it was that now she was going to be prosecuted for perjury on top of everything else, and I thought, *Please, don't do that.*

It was very difficult not to get emotionally involved. I represented one client who was accused of sexually interfering with his children, which he denied, but I was deeply dubious about his denials. His defense was quite straightforward: "Yes, I did beat them, I did commit physical violence against them, but I didn't sexually abuse them." After the second day of the trial, things were looking bad. When we arrived at court the following morning, we were told that he had committed suicide overnight. That wasn't the end of it, however. The judge said that we had to continue with the case. The local authority wanted to make the findings a fact and to take the children into care. They didn't want them to be handed back to the mother, who they believed was, at worst, complicit in the abuse or, at best, prepared to turn a blind eye. So that's what happened: the defendant had given his evidence, and the judge duly found against him.

There came a point where I could no longer face the hideous things that some people do to their children. It seemed rarely to be a matter of simple sexual intercourse. A lot of it involved horrible acts that these people forced their children to perform, things that I then had to stand up and talk about in court as if it were the stuff of everyday life. Although the judges are all family law judges, and thus are familiar with most of these practices, barristers are obliged to go through the evidence point by point. I still think it's a really important job — so many women's issues throughout the world revolve around children and what happens when family relationships break down — but on a day-to-day basis, it was hard going, and luckily I had another string to my bow.

Through my work in employment law, I had come to the notice of Michael Beloff, a brilliant man with impossible handwriting — even worse than mine. When I joined 5 Essex Court back in 1977, I thought I was there for life. Then, during the eighties and certainly by the end of the decade, there was a movement for change at the Bar. It was no longer unheard-of for people to move chambers. Specialization became the hot topic, and life in general common-law sets became more precarious. And not only did commercial members of chambers earn much more money than criminal barristers, but to add insult to injury, they would complain that their well-to-do clients had to sit in the waiting room with people who were quite likely to take their wallets.

Employment law was still a fairly unusual specialty. Like any other area of expertise, the more cases you do, the more people are likely to come to you. If you can't do a case yourself, you want to be able to pass it on — to "return" it — to someone else in chambers, and so it was becoming increasingly difficult to be a lone specialist in chambers.

In addition to employment law, I had also done a bit of public law, which was Michael Beloff's field, and this, too, was starting to build up as an independent specialty. Public law is about challenging government decisions, and education was one of the areas in which I had become involved early on. Foremost among the cases I had worked on were those challenging school closures or the provisions that local authorities made for children with special education needs.

The planning barristers who largely made up Michael Beloff's chambers were great advocates who could cross-examine witnesses till they were screaming for mercy, but their interests did not lie in analyzing and debating the exact meaning of a word in a piece of government legislation. Although I believe I am a good trial lawyer, I enjoyed this type of intellectual argument more. Moving to Michael Beloff's chambers would mean moving into that more stimulating arena, where cases I was involved in would set precedents.

Tony has always been totally supportive of my having a career — he is not one of those men who are threatened by successful women — and by "supportive" I mean real, practical support. Without his help with child care, both on weekends and on holiday, I would have found it much more difficult to cope. As he had a parking space at the House of Commons, we would usually travel to work together, and when he dropped me off that morning for my interview, he said I had to go for it.

"You would be completely and utterly mad to turn down Michael Beloff just because you feel loyal to Freddie and the others," he said.

As it turned out, I didn't turn them down because I wasn't offered the tenancy. Michael rang me later to say the chambers had been very divided, but in the end they had decided against taking me on. He added, however, that he thought this would not be a long-term decision, and he would get back to me. Sure enough, in the following year he did, and I was offered and accepted the place at Gray's Inn Square.

Although my husband was not a senior MP, he was definitely starting to appear on the radar. In 1988 he got into the Shadow Cabinet in charge of energy, and after impressing with that, he was given the employment portfolio. This was a significant appointment. At the time I was first approached by Michael Beloff, the big issue was how we would deal with Thatcherite workplace reforms, in particular those dealing with the closed-shop rules requiring workers to belong to the relevant union. These rules' original purpose had been to protect union members from being discriminated against by employers bringing in cheap nonunion labor. But the Thatcher government was eager to dismantle this tradition. In 1989 Tony committed the Labour Party to accepting the reforms, and the following year closed shops were outlawed by the 1990 Employment Act. He might have outraged the left wing of the party, but he made it far harder for the Tories to attack. These, of course, were all issues that I was familiar with because it was my field of law, and though there were some areas of policy that we disagreed on, this wasn't one of them.

Although being in the Shadow Cabinet did not increase Tony's salary, it did give him access to what is called Short money, named in honor of Edward Short, the Speaker of the House. Short money is allocated on the basis of how many seats the opposition has, so in 1987, when we didn't have that many MPs, we had to get money from other sources, mainly the trade unions. The idea was for Tony and Gordon to pool whatever extra money they raised, but somehow Gordon always seemed to have more staff than Tony. We weren't the only ones who noticed that Gordon put himself first. Mo Mowlam, another northeast MP, was strongly of the opinion that Tony was being taken for a ride by Gordon and should assert himself.

When I was at the LSE, I had a twenty-one-inch waist and was so skinny you could see my ribs. With each pregnancy, I put on twenty pounds, then managed to lose two-thirds of it. So by the autumn of 1989, with Kathryn getting on for eighteen months old, I was about twenty-one pounds overweight and a size 10 instead of a size 6. Intermittently I'd go on a diet, but basically I was stuck. One day I came across a handout in one of those free magazines that come through the door. It was directed at busy working women and/or young mothers who were feeling daunted by not being able to get back into shape. I qualified on both counts. It was a completely different approach to losing weight, "freeing the body and feeding the mind." I knew that I wasn't eating properly. When you have young children, you tend to finish off what they're eating and then sit down for another meal with your husband. But with a full-time job and the constant feeling of guilt that I ought to be at home, I was not thinking about eating sensibly.

The course was called Holistix, and it was run by a mother and daughter, Sylvia and Carole Caplin. Carole was a professional dancer, incredibly fit and with more energy than anyone I had ever met, and she made everything seem both easy and possible. I immediately signed up. The course basically involved exercise classes combined with workshops on healthy eating — a regime that was about as far away from my normal daily routine as could be imagined. "Pamper yourself" was one of Carole's favorite phrases, and she introduced me to Bharti Vyas, who ran a beauty clinic in Chiltern Street. That was the first time I'd ever had a facial. I also had my first massage and signed up for a course to learn how to do it myself, which I thought would be useful. In fact, over the next few years I was able to put my new skill into practice on Tony. I didn't take all of Carole's advice, but I did begin to lose weight. At the end of 1991, Carole moved to New York, and once she was no longer around, I found I didn't keep up with the classes as much as I should have.

Around the same time, Peter Mandelson came into our lives. Although he had been appointed the Labour Party's first director of communications in 1985, I didn't really get to know him until after the 1987 election. Peter was a politician to the ends of his fingernails. His grandfather was Herbert Morrison, who had been Home Secretary in Clement Attlee's government after World War II and who, so it was said, believed that he should have been Prime Minister instead of Attlee. Peter was charming, sympathetic, cultured, funny, and clever, and I got on well with him from the start. Not being an MP, he necessarily worked in the shadow of elected politicians, namely — following the 1987 election defeat — Tony and Gordon. He was closer to Gordon, but he wasn't partial and would make use of whoever was around at the time. As Gordon's base was in Scotland — he was then dating a Scottish advocate — he was often not around when needed, so inevitably Tony did more interviews. Wherever we've lived, we've had an open-door policy, and with Peter regularly dropping in, he gradually became introduced to our social circle.

After Tony had failed to get elected to the Shadow Cabinet in 1987, an unreconstructed veteran Labour MP told him that his mistake had been not being seen around enough in the bars at the House. Unless Tony stopped going home between seven and ten in the evening, the times when votes were taken in the House, he would never get anywhere in politics. Fortunately Tony took no notice. Our children were far too important to him, and indeed, this so-called advice proved utterly wrongheaded. One of the things the public liked about Tony was the fact that he was a family man. The House of Commons' timetable was not designed for fathers who wanted to spend a modicum of time at home with their wives and kids. By now, however, we had developed a routine. We continued our habit of driving in together, with Tony dropping me off at chambers, and this gave us time to talk. Evenings were more complicated and revolved around the time of the vote in the House. If there was an early vote, Tony would come straight home afterwards, by which time I would have returned under my own steam, put the kids to bed, and started dinner. If the vote wasn't till later, he might pick me up at chambers around six o'clock and then put the kids to bed while I cooked dinner. Then we would spend some time together before he had to go back to Westminster to vote at ten o'clock.

Our time with the kids was obviously limited during the week, but we would always take over on the weekend, which the nanny had off. Once Euan was in nursery school, we no longer traveled up to Sedgefield every weekend; we'd spend every other weekend at home in London. In our working lives we met barristers and politicians, and that was about it. But St. Joan of Arc had, as we'd hoped, given us a foot in the local community. Through the church we met all different types of people. I was able to get selected as a Labour

Party governor of the school, and I was also a governor of Highbury Hill, the local girls' comprehensive secondary school.

Around the time I moved to my new chambers, a new building became available for Shadow Cabinet offices. Gordon had assumed that he and Tony would go there together. Although they wouldn't share rooms, they would have offices next to each other. But Anji Hunter, an old friend of Tony's and a political studies graduate, who now ran his office, was of the view that Tony should not move, and Mo and I agreed. Peter didn't express it quite as directly, because of his relationship with Gordon. So when Gordon decamped to the new offices, Tony stayed where he was, with Mo Mowlam and the others down the corridor. It added a physical distance between him and Gordon — there was no more just popping in and out — and it also sent a message that Tony was his own man. I don't think Gordon was very happy, but he had no real alternative but to accept the situation. As far as their ability to work together was concerned, however, nothing really changed.

CHAPTER 14

All Change

I n the run-up to the 1992 election, the mood in the party was curiously subdued. Margaret Thatcher had resigned, and her successor, John Major, was generally seen as a damp squib. The Conservatives were in disarray. One of their biggest issues, a new poll tax, had alienated a huge proportion of the electorate. All in all, it should have been the perfect springboard for a Labour victory. It was not, and critics outside the party offered various reasons for Labour's failure at the ballot box: Neil Kinnock was not seen as a credible Prime Minister, and a major campaign rally, nationally televised for all to see, came off as cocky and triumphalist. Within our group, however, nobody was surprised, and in spite of the traditional upbeat performance of politicians on the campaign trail, no one really believed we were preparing for government.

The press, meanwhile, had been hedging its bets and was on the lookout for Labour's rising stars. The MP for Sedgefield was definitely on the list, and Barbara Amiel (later better known as Mrs. Conrad Black) came up to interview Tony for the *Sunday Times*. She had wanted to stay at Myrobella, but I put my foot down. Although I was happy to be known as Tony's wife in the constituency, I didn't see that I was relevant farther afield, perhaps sensing even then that I would somehow fall short.

I also hated the idea that I would be singled out and treated as some sort of celebrity. I wanted nothing to do with what I called showbiz life. I had always been suspicious of surface glamour, no doubt a view that I absorbed from my grandmother. It was exactly that life — a superficial world filled with frivolous people — that had led my father astray and turned him into a drinker and a womanizer. He had been completely seduced by it, with devastating consequences. It wasn't that I didn't relish the role of political wife. It was being treated as a celebrity that I objected to, as if politics were a strand of show business. It's part of the reason that I tended to come out with "gaffes." It didn't happen when I was in my own world, in chambers or in court. But when I felt uncomfortable and on edge, I would end up talking too much as a result of nervousness, and that's when I would say something untoward.

Barbara Amiel came up, and we took her out to dinner. I can't say I enjoyed the evening. She was very flirtatious around all the men, especially Tony. A few days later she phoned, claiming that she needed more from me. Reluctantly I agreed to see her at chambers. I remember little of our conversation, beyond her saying that she envied me having a career and children, as she had not managed to do both. In the published profile, she wrote that I was prickly and recorded the fact that I hadn't wanted to answer her questions. I hadn't.

The 1992 election was the first time I saw how the kids might be affected by their father's being a politician. There was a huge anti-Labour poster by the school, and I remember them getting very upset. (God knows it was mild compared with what was to come.) As for who should take over from Neil once he stepped down, John Smith, an old drinking buddy of Derry's from Glasgow University and now Shadow Chancellor of the Exchequer, was seen as his inevitable successor: he had gravitas. Tony, however, wasn't convinced that John would put through the necessary reforms. John's line was "Steady as we go"; Labour was slowly crawling its way back, and eventually the electorate would see sense. Tony strongly disagreed. The electorate was not going to turn to Labour, he believed, until we had changed ourselves.

After the defeat, Tony was seriously of the view that Gordon should stand for the leadership against John, but Gordon said no.

"Well, if that's the case," I said to Tony, "why don't you stand as deputy?"

He toyed with the idea, the main question being not "Is this sensible in terms of my career?" but "Is this sensible in terms of the kids?" In the end we decided it wasn't. Besides, Gordon himself was against it. Only later did we discover that he'd done a deal with John right from the outset. In return for Gordon's backing him for the leadership — with Margaret Beckett, an MP with strong links to the unions and the more left-leaning elements of the party, as deputy — Gordon would get Shadow Chancellor. And so it came to pass.

Change was definitely in the air. Tony decided he just couldn't cope with the to-ing and fro-ing from Highbury twice a day. Getting across Holloway Road, the main artery from the north, was a nightmare. We needed to move farther in, he said. Through Margaret Hodge, an MP friend, we heard that a doctor and his wife, down the road from her in Islington, wanted to do a swap for a smaller house. There were a number of pluses: not only would traveling be easier, but we'd be within walking distance of my sister, who had married and had just had her second child. The drawback of the new house was that financially it stretched us right to the hilt, with nothing left over for improvements. This situation was exacerbated when interest rates went to over 15 percent following the financial meltdown of the Black Wednesday stock market crash.

Once we were settled in Richmond Crescent, we began to participate in "state-of-the-party" meetings either at our house or at Margaret Hodge's. Peter Mandelson and Mo Mowlam would often be there, and also Sally Morgan, who was employed by the Labour Party in London.

Under the new regime, Tony became Shadow Home Secretary. At least in government, the Home Office is seen as a poisoned chalice. In opposition, however, it depends on what happens, and what happened in 1993 was the horrific murder of James Bulger. The abduction of this small boy by two older boys, caught on CCTV cameras, was played and replayed on television — the first time I can remember such a thing happening. Law and order had previously been seen as an Achilles' heel for Labour, yet Tony's unequivocal and hard-line response was proof that this was no longer the case. He combined compassion with a streak of steel — that steel I had recognized so early in our relationship. For the most tragic of reasons, Tony became a familiar figure on TV.

He had already shown that he was at ease in front of the cameras — he was the only MP who had been prepared to go on television the day after the 1992 election defeat. He also happened to be young and good-looking, with a growing family, all of which resonated with the public.

Tony was an impressive debater, and in February 1994 two of the most contentious issues in British politics went before Parliament: capital punishment and lowering the age of consent for homosexuals. These were both cross-party issues, and Tony showed in very practical terms how he could work effectively with people of opposing political views when he thought it necessary.

Over the two years of John Smith's leadership, Tony did what he was asked to do, gave policy speeches and so on, but felt increasingly frustrated. On May 11, 1994, Tony went to a Labour Party fund-raising dinner in one of the big London hotels. (I didn't go. For a big party fund-raiser like that, tickets cost hundreds of pounds even then.) Late that night he came back saying that he thought John had looked very ill. The next morning we had to be up early, as he was flying to Aberdeen and I was due in south London at an employment tribunal.

Just as we settled the case, somebody came in and said, "Have you heard?"

John Smith was dead of a heart attack.

I remember standing in the corridor not moving, with people bumping into me. I was in total shock. I went straight back into London. It was only when I was on the train, looking out at the gardens filled with blossoms, that I thought of his wife and daughters. He was only fifty-five. It was a terrible warning about the pressures of public life.

I remembered a conversation Tony and I had had barely a month before, when we'd taken a rare weekend away from the kids. He'd been asked to speak at the European Business School in Fontainebleau, outside Paris. It had been years since we'd been to the French capital, and we did all those things you do in Paris, including going to the movies, something we never had time for in London. We went to see *Schindler's List*, a haunting film that left us feeling disjointed and somehow suspended in time. While we were having dinner afterward, Tony started talking about John Smith and

how frustrated he felt under his leadership. He felt that the modernizers were grinding to a halt.

"It can't go on like this," he said. "But I've got this feeling that it
won't anyway."

"What do you mean?"

"I mean that something's going to happen. Got to happen."

"Like what?"

"Some kind of bust-up. I don't know. But something. It can't go
on like this."

Never could he have imagined anything so tragic or so decisive.
Tony called about two minutes after I got into chambers.

"You've got to stand," I told him.

"It's difficult."

"Listen to me. You have to go for this."

He was about to board the plane. I said I'd meet him at arrivals.
We'd pick up the car and talk about it then.

As I turned into High Holborn on my way to the tube, I bumped
into our friend and former Hackney neighbor Barry Cox.

"Can't stop," I said. "I'm off to Heathrow to get Tony. When you
talk to him, Barry, tell him that he's got to stand. I'm frightened he'll
think that maybe he owes it to Gordon not to."

When I got to Heathrow, I called Anji from a pay phone. Mo
Mowlam had rung, and the influential Scottish MP John Reid, both
saying the same thing: "He's got to go for it."

As usual the arrivals hall was crowded, but it wasn't till I saw
Tony come through on his own that I realized that many of those
waiting were cameramen and reporters. They practically trampled
me underfoot to get to him, shouting "Tony! Tony!" For a moment
it was mayhem, then he gave them a few words on the theme of "It's
a great shock," and of course it was. They may not have agreed on
everything, but John had been good to him, and Tony respected and
liked him. Eventually I managed to get him down to the parking
garage and into the car.

I am a barrister, an advocate, and my job is putting a case coher-
ently. This time it seemed that all my skills had abandoned me. I just
said, "You're the best candidate for the job, and you can't let Gordon seize the moment through some misplaced sense of obligation."

"He'll have all the Scottish MPs tied up."

"No, he won't. John Reid's been on the phone already. Listen, Tony. This is your moment. You've got to take it. Who dares, wins." He sat slumped in the passenger seat with his eyes closed and said, "I know." But it was with no sense of triumph or eager anticipation. It was more resignation.

We both knew the arguments against: the children and Gordon. Tony looked pale. That he let me drive was a sign of how unnerved he was. "John Smith was working too hard," he said, "burning the candle at both ends."

I knew that time was of the essence. My fear was that Gordon would just move in and it would be a fait accompli, but I knew Tony was the right person for the job. By the next general election, there would be people voting who had never known a time when the Tories weren't in power. The new leader had to be someone they could relate to. Tony had always been more appealing to the general public than Gordon, and more grounded in the realities of everyday life. What could be more grounding than bringing up a young family? Ironically, Tony was always saying, "Gordon, if you really want to be leader, you need to get married." Yet he also felt it was a mark of how honorable Gordon was that he didn't marry just for appearances. (In my view, however, if he had, he would inevitably have been a more rounded person, with another dimension to his life.)

Nothing would happen until after the funeral, so to that extent discussions would be ongoing. But we all had to know whether Tony was going to stand. When we got to the office, people were beginning to show their faces. Anji was there, and Mo and Peter Kilfoyle: the two of them would eventually head up his campaign. Also, to my great relief, I saw John Reid, one of Neil Kinnock's close advisers and an early advocate of party reform. Although he and Gordon were both Scottish MPs, I knew he would support Tony. The voices were unanimous: Tony had to stand. And I think he knew in his heart that he was the better person to carry the modernizers' message, if only because he embodied it better. It was about changing the perception of the Labour Party, making it a party of government and actually being relevant to people's lives. Having made my position clear and knowing that I would see him later, I headed back to chambers.

The next day the BBC had Tony as the front-runner. Over the next few days I had plenty of time to think things over. I knew this was a pivotal moment for Tony. I knew that he had what it takes. I knew it would make a huge difference to Tony himself. I knew that he would have less time for the children, but I didn't think it would make much difference to us as a family. My practice was going in the right direction, we had just bought a big family house, and I assumed we would tick on.

My own belief is that he decided to go for it straightaway. For him the real question was not whether he should stand, but how to reconcile Gordon in order to preserve the modernizers' ticket. What he most feared was that if both of them stood, the modernizers would lose out through squabbling among themselves. Tony's main aim over those next few days was to persuade Gordon to give way to him. He wouldn't stand unopposed — the left would see to that — which was even more reason not to risk splitting the moderate vote.

Getting Gordon to stand aside was no easy task. First, he was the more senior. Second, he obviously had his supporters, too. One of the key players was Peter Mandelson. I remember sitting in our kitchen that first night and asking Tony, "What about Peter? What does he think?" Tony said with a sigh, "Peter is very conflicted." I wish now that Peter's ambivalence had been better known at the time, because Gordon's conviction that Peter was instantly in our camp destroyed their relationship.

John Smith's funeral was on May 20 in Scotland. Gordon had gone back to his constituency fairly early on, while Tony just flew up for the funeral. The fact that Gordon hadn't been in London during the early stages was irrelevant to his campaign. We knew from day one that Nick Brown would be his campaign manager and had a good idea of the tricks he would have up his sleeve. Nick is an old-style political campaigner, and his people were basically going around saying, "Gordon is more acceptable to the unions. He is more true Labour than Tony. Tony is a young upstart." He didn't need Gordon in London to do that. In fact, it was more effective if Gordon wasn't there.

After the funeral Tony stayed with Nick Ryden, a friend from Fettes, and that night Gordon went round there to talk. Nick had only recently bought the house, and not everything worked as it should. At one point Gordon disappeared upstairs. He was gone for what seemed like a very long time, and Tony was just wondering

133

what on earth could have happened when the phone rang. It was Gordon calling from the bathroom on his cell phone. The handle had come off the door, and he couldn't get out.

As the week went on, Tony clearly had the momentum, and I was coming to the view that if Gordon wanted to stand, Tony should let him.

"You'll win anyway," I said. "So don't come to a deal. Just let him lose." But Tony said no. The modernizers were a team, and this was a team effort. He didn't want anything to break that up.

Back in London there was yet another get-together with Gordon. This time it was at Lyndsey's house in Richmond Avenue, just round the corner. (One of the conditions of these meetings was that no one should see Gordon coming to our house.) This was the meeting where essentially it was agreed that Tony would stand unopposed and Gordon would be Chancellor; that they would work together and Gordon would support him, and the aim would be to reform the Labour Party and take power. Part of Gordon obviously didn't want to accept that, but another part of him could see that Tony now had the momentum. There were plenty of ways he could have rationalized it to himself: that he had been unlucky in having the economic portfolio, which had failed to give him much exposure, whereas Tony, with law and order, had been able to strike a popular chord. It was always a given that they would work in tandem and that when Tony stood down, Gordon would take over. Tony also made it clear to Gordon that he had no intention of staying leader forever and that when he did stand down, he would support Gordon as his natural successor, assuming they worked well together as Prime Minister and Chancellor in the meantime.

As far as I know, the timing of all this was never discussed, but when Tony left for Lyndsey's, I made my position perfectly clear, even if I framed it as a joke. "If you agree with Gordon that you're going to do this for one term only, don't come back home. Because that's just ridiculous."

But Tony was always very supportive of Gordon having his chance. He used to say that in terms of ability, Gordon was way ahead of everyone, and the irony is that if they'd only worked as closely together as originally agreed, his chance would have come sooner.

*   *   *

Barry Cox raised about £70,000 from various people to support the campaign, and Anji was organizing the campaign events.

Tony never takes anything for granted, but it was soon clear that he was the front-runner. I didn't by any means go to all his meetings, because he was traveling round and I had the children to look after and a career to pursue. I did go to some meetings in London and the southeast, and I went to a couple of the question-and-answer sessions, where he was developing the relaxed style of campaigning that would soon become popular not just with Labour Party members but with the whole British electorate: sitting down on the edge of the stage and rolling up his shirtsleeves to his elbows. He did fantastically. I was so proud of him.

So much was going on, and I was so focused on the job at hand — which was getting Tony to stand and then getting everyone to support him — that perhaps it's not surprising that I forgot about my own role. The "Hang on a minute, if all this is going to happen, I'm going to be a bit in the public eye" moment was late in arriving. One evening, shortly after Tony had decided to stand, the phone rang.

"Hi there, Cherie. Great to hear your voice after so long. So how are you doing?"

It was Carole Caplin.

CHAPTER 15

Nearly There

When Carole called, I couldn't have been more delighted. The twin spindles of my life — politics and the Bar — were rather incestuous, but Carole was completely separate. More to the point, I was still anxious to lose the extra fourteen pounds.

She came round to the house the following Saturday.

"Well, this is all very exciting, isn't it?" she said, as she came in. Her call hadn't been entirely serendipitous. She'd just returned from New York and knew all about what was happening. She wondered if I needed some advice on hair and makeup. I didn't understand what she was talking about. I went to the same hairdresser I'd been going to for years, and as for makeup I just went to Boots, our low-priced pharmacy chain. It would be useful, she said, if we could look through my wardrobe; it would help her determine my style. I didn't really have a style. My clothes divided into two types: casual things to hang round the house in, such as leggings, baggy tops, tennis shoes, and the occasional long skirt; and barrister suits, mainly black or blue, always with skirts, as trousers were not allowed. My work shoes had heels, but they were reasonably chunky, as I spent a lot of time on my feet, both in court and traveling. I also had the odd fashionable dress, which I bought from someone called Ivona Ivons, who ran a shop near one of the courts. She would sort me out a couple of suits for work, perhaps a dress at the same time, and that was that.

I wasn't uninterested in clothes, but I didn't read fashion magazines or keep up with the latest styles. I'd just pop along to Ivona, and whatever was in that year I'd have. I was reasonably objective about my body. My strong points were my hair, which I had in abundance, and my skin. I had always had a neat bust and a small waist, but I had big hips and thighs, so on the whole I avoided trousers, as I thought my bottom was too big. Although I tried to look nice, we had three small children and two houses to keep up, so shopping for me was bottom of the list. The exception was work clothes. Operating in such a public arena, I needed to look sharp. Shoes were not a priority. It wasn't as if Tony and I went out to restaurants or clubs. Our social life consisted of seeing friends and just sitting around a kitchen table, talking. As most of our friends also had young kids, it was hardly a competitive environment.

I didn't have either the time or the knowledge even to think about changing my image. Looking at my wardrobe through Carole's eyes, however, I could sense what was coming. "I think you could do with some help," she said. Of course she was right. Everything was connected, she said: my weight, my clothes, my food. It would take time, but she was convinced that I could begin to see some improvements quickly, certainly in the couple of months we had before the results of the leadership election were announced. We started immediately. She spent the rest of the afternoon at the house.

The first thing that needed attention was what I ate, which soon extended to everyone in the family, as she chucked out half the things in the kitchen. She opened the cupboards and went through everything, saying, "This is bad; this is good." (It was short-lived. The kids would have none of it. Within days the cupboards were restored to their former glory.)

Once that was done, we went upstairs to the sitting room to go over an exercise plan. There was no time to lose. Since I had done her workshops five years previously, I already had the basics, but this was specific. While we were doing this, she met Tony and suggested an exercise plan for him as well.

My wardrobe came in for the same treatment as the kitchen cupboards, and most of what I had went straight into garbage bags. She made me put on some things before making a decision. Long jackets were more flattering, she said. I should go for low necks rather than high necks. Heels were good, and I should wear more of them. On the one hand, it was a fairly horrifying spectacle; on the other hand, it was probably for the best. By nature I'm a hoarder, and this was something that needed to be done. "If you can't remember when you last wore it, chuck it" was one of her mantras.

To sharpen my eye, Carole took me shopping. Browns, on upscale South Molton Street in London, was a revelation. It was the first time I had been anywhere so obviously fashionable. But she was right about making an immediate improvement. I wore the dress I bought at Browns to a party midway through the leadership campaign and bumped into Fiona Millar, the daughter of Audrey Millar, at whose house I had attended meetings of the Marylebone Labour Party years earlier. She was feeling particularly frumpy, she said, as she'd only recently had a baby girl with her partner, a political journalist named Alastair Campbell, who would later play a large role in Tony's life. "But as for you, Cherie, you're looking great. Much more — how shall I put it? — groomed!" How we laughed.

The question of the deputy was still in the air. John Prescott and Margaret Beckett were standing both for the leadership and for deputy leader. The aim was to find the best balance. Tony's membership of the T & G was not treated with any great seriousness, and he was not seen as a union man. He'd got them to accept that the closed-shop agreement would not be reinstated, and he wouldn't be remembered fondly for that. On the other side, he had pushed through a minimum-wage policy. Peter Kilfoyle (MP for Liverpool Walton), Anji, and I were keen on John Prescott — very much a union man — who we felt would make for more of a contrast. Gordon was keen on Margaret Beckett. But it would depend entirely on who won the ballot.

July 21, when the results of the leadership election were to be announced, was a lovely summer day, and come what may, I knew it was important that I look my best. I also had discovered how much more confident I felt when I looked the part.

Downstairs at Richmond Crescent, the combined Blair and Booth clans were gathering. While I was getting ready upstairs, the kids gave me a running commentary about the scruffy-looking types hanging round on the pavement opposite, men mostly, loaded down with cameras and camera bags.

About half an hour before we were due to leave, Tony had a word with them and agreed to do some pictures. He suggested the park behind the house where he and the kids often played soccer. So the photographers got us to sit on a bench while they snapped away: Tony and me looking at each other, Tony looking at the camera and me looking at Tony, and so on. It was the first time I had ever done anything like it. The nearest I'd got to experiencing any kind of press interest was at Pat Phoenix's funeral, when I'd led my father into the church.

The oddest thing of all was being called Mrs. Blair, as they shouted out instructions. Most people called me Cherie. My colleagues at the Bar certainly did, as did those involved with the Labour Party, where I was very much a person in my own right. Even at the children's school, where mothers might be expected to be called Mrs. Whoever, I was known by my Christian name, as both teachers and the head knew me primarily as a school governor. On a day-to-day level the only people who didn't call me Cherie were the clerks. To them I was Miss Booth.

Tony's union, the T & G, had provided a car to take us down to the Westminster Institute of Education, where the results would be announced. The candidates all lined up on the stage, and when I saw Tony's face, I knew he was victorious. He had come top, in fact, in all sections, including the union one, which our people had speculated might prove more difficult. John Prescott was duly elected deputy leader, so it couldn't have been better. Then it was time to celebrate. Cars took us the short distance to Church House, a conference center just behind Westminster Abbey. It was a beautiful afternoon, and both the building and the square outside were thronged with supporters. We were taken straight upstairs and out onto the balcony, where Neil and Glenys Kinnock were already waiting.

Tony made his leadership acceptance speech, in which he thanked everybody who'd worked so hard for his campaign. Although Margaret Beckett had just lost to both Tony and John Prescott, she and her husband, Leo, came up with a warm and ready smile to thank Tony for what he'd said and to wish him well. Just as she was leaving, she added, "I nearly forgot. Sylvie will be waiting for you outside."

I thought, *Sylvie? Who is Sylvie?*

Sylvie turned out to be the backup driver for the Leader of the Opposition. While Margaret had been standing in as leader, she had been driven round in the official car. No one had said anything to us about there being a car. From then on, whenever Tony was involved in official business, either Terry, who became a true family friend, or the wonderful Sylvie would drive him round.

The next day Terry was waiting outside in the Rover to take Tony to the House. And this became the routine: If I was up early enough, I'd get a lift, and they'd drop me at Gray's Inn, which was directly on their route. Similarly, when they were about to leave, I'd get a call, and if I was ready to go, I'd be waiting on the pavement when the familiar red Rover drew up.

The office of the Leader of the Opposition was far grander than anything Tony had had before, certainly in size. It's at the heart of the Palace of Westminster itself, not far from where the Prime Minister has his office on the opposite side of the courtyard. The suite of rooms included the Shadow Cabinet room. Tony decided to use the office Neil Kinnock had used when he was leader; John Smith's was piled high with boxes of papers waiting to be dealt with. After all the excitement over Tony's election, it was a sober reminder.

Tony asked me to take a look at the room he proposed using, and I was not impressed. It was in serious need of redecoration. The House of Commons offered to get it done, but Tony declined. "I don't intend to stay here very long," he said. "I don't want to make these rooms too comfortable, because I don't want to get too comfortable in opposition." The aim was to get into government as soon as possible.

With this in mind, Tony was pretty clear that he wanted Alastair Campbell to join the team as press secretary. Alastair was a political journalist, and Tony had got to know him in the House of Commons when Alastair was a correspondent for the *Daily Mirror*, a popular tabloid newspaper. Although a Labour man through and through, he was never interested in policy, and he had never been part of our discussion groups.

When Peter Mandelson first sounded Alastair out for Tony, he said no. Then Tony talked to Alastair himself a few days after he moved into his new office. Alastair was equivocal, Tony told me, though Tony thought he could be persuaded. When Tony is deter-mined, nothing will stop him, and on this he was determined. We were about to set off for what had now become our usual holiday in France, dropping in on friends. As Alastair and Fiona were spending the summer in a house in Provence, Tony proposed to go down there and talk him into it. He would convince Alastair, and I would convince Fiona. That, at any rate, was the idea. The parents of one of Tony's researchers, Tim Allan, had just bought a cottage in Tuscany, and Tim suggested that we go there for a week or so. We could drop in on Alastair on our way there.

Originally we had started going to France because of Tony's fear of flying. By sheer willpower, however, he'd succeeded in overcoming that, and now we went because it had become a tradition. Some of our old Hackney neighbors had bought a house together in a village called Miradoux, north of Toulouse, in western France. It was a complete wreck, and over the years we had joined in cheerfully, helping to pull it into some sort of shape. But with three growing children, we found it a bit cramped. Then in 1992 David Keene had come to the rescue. David, one of my partners at work, had recently bought a place in the Ariège, just south of Toulouse. We could go there whenever we liked, he said.

David's "place" turned out to be a château in a village called St. Martin d'Oydes, in the foothills of the Pyrenees. To the delight of the kids, it boasted a swimming pool, and as there was plenty of room, Mum and the nanny could come, too. In later years Lyndsey and her family would sometimes join us.

Children like going back to familiar places, seeing familiar faces, and the trips gave Tony and me an opportunity to spend time with each other and with our friends. For years we visited these same two houses, so it's hard to remember what happened when and where. There was the time, I remember, when we sang "These Are a Few of My Favorite Things" for what seemed like hours to drown out a storm that threatened to engulf Miradoux, with the fire engine across the road clanging a merry accompaniment. One year David's swimming pool turned bright green. That didn't stop the Blair family from swimming in it. Swimming was a favorite activity. Our nanny Ros would devise complicated galas — "the summer Olympics," as they were known — which involved convoluted races, "biggest splash" competitions, even the "funniest wet hairstyle" competition, which Tony regularly won. For him, being in surroundings in which he felt so completely at home, practicing his French at the local shops and cafés, playing tennis, and eating out in the local restaurants were the perfect antidote to our busy life in England. There was nobody to collar him on the street; no need to dress the part. He could slob around in shorts and a T-shirt to his heart's content. A true holiday.

Flassan, where Alastair and Fiona had their house, turned out to be as far away from the foothills of the Pyrenees as it's possible to be in France. Tony decided that the drive would be too daunting, so we dropped off the hired car and took the train from Toulouse to Avignon. It's not a journey I'd recommend. We arrived at Avignon late at night, the children understandably grumpy, to find an equally grumpy Alastair waiting for us. We piled into his car for a drive of over an hour into the hills.

I didn't know Alastair that well in those days, though you always knew when he was around. He was tall and handsome, though not the kind of handsome that appealed to me. He had a definite presence, and I knew from Tony that he had a powerful personality. What I didn't know was that he had a temper and an ego you could build a house on.

On the way to Avignon, Tony had been through what he wanted me to do. Alastair was the best man for the job, he said, and he wanted him. It would mean his taking a big cut in salary, so both he and Fiona had to be persuaded that it was worth it. My job was to be nice to Fiona, to reassure her that Tony was a family man, that it would all be all right, that Tony had his priorities and the job wouldn't ruin her family life. So that's what I did, whether we were washing up, watching the children, or chopping vegetables together on the kitchen table.

"This is our chance to do something of real importance, Fiona. Tony feels Alastair has a real contribution to make. He says that Alastair is the best man for the job, and I believe him. It won't be that bad, as I'm not going to let Tony lose sight of the family thing."

In the end Alastair agreed. He didn't say so in so many words — at least not in my hearing — but we left for Tim Allan's parents' place in Italy with Tony confident that he'd got what he came for.

Our onward journey was as chaotic as usual. We left Flassan at four in the morning, the children lying like sacks in the back of Alastair's car. Our train to Italy left Marseille around 6:30 a.m. It was all a great rush, and in the end we got on a local train, though at least we had a carriage to ourselves, meaning we could sing songs — my usual way of keeping at bay the kids' favorite question: "Are we nearly there?"

CHAPTER 16

Hurdles

I n 1993 Tony wrote a pamphlet for the Fabian Society, of which we had both long been members. In it he criticized the continued presence, unchanged since it was written in 1917, of Clause IV of the Labour Party constitution, which read:

To secure for the workers by hand or by brain the full fruits of their industry and the most equitable distribution thereof that may be possible upon the basis of the common ownership of the means of production, distribution and exchange, and the best obtainable system of popular administration and control of each industry or service.

His position was "How can we be a Party who are supposed to be of the modern world when we still have as part of our objective 'the common ownership of the means of production and exchange'?" Everyone accepted that wholesale nationalization was no longer part of our policy, but the fact that Clause IV was still there could be used as a stick to beat us with — either by the Tory press, who could pretend that we really did want to nationalize everything in sight, or Militant, who could berate us for not getting on with what was supposed to be a key objective.

Only those closest to Tony knew what he was planning to do. The occasion, of course, would be the annual Labour Party Conference.

Scrapping Clause IV, he believed, would set the tone for all that would follow. On one level it was only a gesture — it was axing something that was already dead — but gestures are sometimes important, and if he could get the party behind him on this, the left would be out in the cold, and the modernizing process could begin in earnest. If the electorate was to trust us to run the country, we had to show that the Labour Party had made a clean break with the past.

Paradoxically, the Labour Party as then constituted was a very conservative organization. It didn't like change, and Clause IV was seen as part of the family furniture, handed down from generation to generation, a much-loved heirloom but now useless and out-of-date.

Although Tony's personal credit was running high, it was not enough to guarantee agreement. There were plenty of reactionary elements about, especially within union ranks, and he would need all the help he could get. He would even have his Shadow Chancellor to square. Gordon didn't like rocking the boat, and his line was "Why bother, given it doesn't really matter?" Tony's answer to that was "public perception."

Meanwhile I had my own agenda in relation to the 1994 Labour Party Conference. I was determined that the leader's wife would go out on that platform looking good enough to take on the world — or at least the massed ranks of the Tory Party — so I continued with my dietary regime and exercise, and I found a new hairdresser. André Suard worked at Michaeljohn, a hip London salon. He had no idea who I was when I first went in — just a new client with a haircut that needed fixing. A radical attempt by my former hairdresser to give me a more modern look had resulted in what can only be described as a mullet. André was in his midtwenties. Although his father was Italian, he had been brought up and trained in France and as a result had a wonderfully quirky accent.

The spiky fringe was not the look for a woman who wanted to be taken seriously, he decided, and short hair on top with a long bob looked doubly ridiculous after being crammed under a sweaty wig during a hot day in court. Although I had a lot of hair, André explained, it was soft. The difficulty would be holding a style. As I wanted to have something I could handle myself, this became a major problem. Even after hours of blow-drying practice, I was incapable of making it look remotely "done." If I attempted any back-combing, it looked as if a mouse had crawled in to make its nest. It was the same with my makeup. Touching up what had been done earlier had never occurred to me. I had never reapplied makeup nor worried about whether my nose or my forehead was shiny.

My new haircut had its first outing on September 23, 1994, my fortieth birthday. The previous March I had booked Frederick's restaurant for the party. For Tony's fortieth, we had just had a party at home. It was not a surprise party, but a surprise there certainly was. Among his things I had found an old tape recording with a label saying "BBC Radio Oxford: Ugly Rumours." Tony's student band! Halfway through the evening I played it. The lyrics were deeply profound — sadly, not matched by the reedy voice singing the plaintive dirge. Everybody thought it a great hoot. Well, everybody except Tony.

My mum had been warning me for some time that things would change, and not necessarily for the better, but even she was shocked when the *Evening Standard* took her photograph that evening. In fact, everybody was photographed, as if my guest list might provide a clue to who was out and who was in under the new leadership. But my party owed nothing to Labour or even to Tony. I made a little speech about how much I owed my mum — not so different from the one I'd made twenty-two years earlier, the night before I left for the LSE.

Anji had already warned me to block off Labour Party Conference week. She showed me the stage set for the platform, because I'd need to be color coordinated, or at least wear something that wouldn't clash. The previous year, at the party conference in Brighton, I'd heard that John Smith's wife had brought along a hairdresser who was being paid for by the party. My thought then was *Why on earth would Elizabeth Smith need a hairdresser?* Now I was thinking, *I hope to goodness André will be available!* He wasn't, so Carole volunteered to come to ensure that I didn't look a complete disaster. She had never been to a Labour Party Conference — she wasn't even a member of the party — and when she asked if I thought I'd need an evening dress, I burst into laughter.

"This is a Labour Party Conference," I said. "But I would need something for the dozens of functions and receptions I'd have to attend with Tony. There would be media everywhere. It was all about photographs. I'd need something to arrive in, something for Tony's big conference speech, and possibly something to go home in.

I was beginning to realize that the whole business was both expensive and a diplomatic minefield. If I went looking like a slob, it showed a lack of respect. If I wore the same thing all the time, that, too, showed a lack of respect. It was a question of "damned if you do, damned if you don't." I remembered how Norma Major, wife of the current Prime Minister, never seemed to get it right, at least as far as the press was concerned. A further constraint was that whatever designer I went for had to be homegrown, and the look needed to be "modern" to reflect the "modernizer" label.

That year conference was in Blackpool, a seaside resort north of Liverpool. I hadn't been there since I was a little girl riding a donkey on the beach. For the first time, Tony had police security. The whole of one floor of the Imperial Hotel was sealed off. Access was by elevator, and there was a policeman standing outside our door and Labour Party stewards patrolling the corridors. I'd had no idea it was run like this. Tony was permanently holed up with Alastair, Peter, Anji, Gordon, or one of the others. I was feeling particularly unsettled, as I had left Ros in sole charge of the kids. She hadn't even done a night on her own before, and this was for nearly a week. She was incredibly reliable and trustworthy and as mad about soccer as the boys were. All the same . . . Over the next few days, whatever else was happening, Tony and I made sure that we both spoke to them every evening, and we'd hear them arguing about who was going to tell Mum or Dad this or that piece of news.

Anji had told me that on no account could I go down to the conference on my own. If I wanted to go, somebody had to accompany me. At one point I thought, *This is utterly ridiculous. I've been coming to conference for years. What are they talking about? I'm hardly a novice.* So I opened the door, sneaked down the back stairs to avoid the elevator, and emerged into the hotel lobby, where I immediately caught sight of Glenys Thornton, an old friend from LSE days.

We were just having a chat when suddenly there were lights and cameras all round and someone with a microphone asking Glenys who she was. I froze. The next moment I felt a hand on my back and then on my arm, and Hilary Coffman was propelling me toward the lift, saying, "Thank you, Cherie," and it was back to my prison.

The pair of us stood in that lift not saying a word, and I felt my blood pounding. I had known Hilary for years. She had been head of press for John Smith and had also worked for Neil Kinnock. Alastair had brought her in to work for Tony. When the lift stopped at my floor, she handed me over to Anji.

"I thought I told you not to go down there, Cherie," Anji said as she walked me down the corridor. "You really don't understand politics."

"Thank you, Anji, but I do understand politics." If looks could kill, she should have been dead. Our relationship was deteriorating rapidly. I couldn't believe it. I was being treated like a naughty schoolgirl. These people apparently considered themselves empowered to tell me what to do.

For years I had devoted myself to helping the Labour Party — treading freezing streets, even giving up weekends and evenings. I had stood as a candidate, for goodness' sake. As for my husband, he hadn't always been surrounded by acolytes tending to his every need. I had been there from the beginning, encouraging him when he needed encouraging, listening when he needed someone to bounce ideas off, to talk things through with. From first to last, we were a team. Hopes, plans, dreams — ours was a true marriage, a joint endeavor. Yet this wasn't a negotiation with my husband; it was ten other people saying "Cherie will do this." Since I was a teenager, I had been used to having my own political opinions, and not being allowed to voice them publicly was like having a limb cut off. I sensed that I was becoming a nonperson — someone to be wheeled out when appropriate, or perhaps, like an Edwardian child, to be seen but not heard.

My humiliation was made worse by the fact that part of me knew that I couldn't just go down and pretend that I was like any other delegate, because I wasn't. Not anymore. I felt highly unsettled, unable to concentrate on anything. I wanted to be involved, just as I always had been, but how could I be? It had been made perfectly clear that I wasn't wanted.

Then Alastair started fretting about Carole. "We can't have that glamorous-looking creature here," he announced.

"Why on earth not?"

"Because I don't want people to know that you're having help with your hair and makeup."

"Elizabeth Smith did last year."

"That was different."

"Don't be ridiculous, Alastair. How could it be different?"

"I'm telling you, Cherie, it's different, and I don't want the press to know."

"Because she's good-looking, you mean? Is that a crime?"

He stalked off. But Alastair had spoken, and the rest had heard. From then on, Carole was banned from going anywhere. She was stuck either with me or in her room and told not to go out under any circumstances.

That conference was the first intimation I had of what was to come. Only the bathroom was sacrosanct, and then only if you remembered to lock the door. My one way of guaranteeing a bit of peace and quiet was to visit Carole's room.

Conference proceeded in the usual way: going to meetings, listening to debates on the platform, and in the evening attending the various functions, such as Scots Night. I had done a bit of Scottish dancing in school — things like the Gay Gordons and the Eightsome Reel — but to hear it announced that "the leader and his wife will now start the dancing" proved strangely paralyzing, especially with the BBC filming the whole thing for its *Newsnight* program.

Thankfully, dancing was limited to this one occasion. On other occasions we'd simply go in and shake a few hands, Tony would make a little speech, everyone would listen, and then we'd move on to the next one. These talks were basically off-the-cuff remarks that reflected what he was thinking, things that might end up in his keynote speech. Wherever we went, we were followed by film crews, on show the whole time. Meanwhile I tried to follow Pat Phoenix's example: be nice and smile.

It was the first time I had found myself in this position of appendage, and it did not come easily. I am by nature a doer, not a stander-and-watcher. I had already decided that I would do something for the wives of our MPs, a good number of whom were not politically active. I felt that wives generally got a raw deal in Parliament, and the Labour Party in particular didn't look after them. (Indeed, the Tories were much better in their support of wives and children.) The least I could do, I thought, was to invite them to tea. It was agreed that I would host a tea party just for the wives of the northwest regional MPs, because few of the others would be there. This proved to be the start of what became known as Spouse in the House, a support group of which I became one of two honorary patrons.

Tony's speech wasn't until Tuesday. Purgatory, I decided, would be a cinch compared with this. Tony had been working on his speech for days, and it still wasn't finished. The slogan "New Labour, New Britain" had only been agreed on the previous week, just in time to get the banners up for the conference. The trickle of people around my husband gradually became a whirlpool, and the debate about his speech became more frenetic and tense with every passing hour. The speech went through between twenty-five to forty drafts, with everyone chipping in, including me, though Tony and Alastair did the final tinkering.

On Sunday we went to church. Every year there was a nondenominational service organized by the Christian Socialist Movement. I remember how that first year I didn't have anything to wear and had to borrow a cream outfit of Carole's, which shows how effective the diet was and how disorganized I was. I had always enjoyed going to those conference services. There was usually a good crowd and a good preacher, who would give a thoughtful sermon, and there is nothing I like more than a rousing hymn. Tony and I both believe that we have an obligation to God in determining what we should do, and the sermon frequently dealt with serious issues, such as Third World debt or, later, asylum seekers, issues that the church has a right to be concerned about but that maybe don't entirely chime with Labour Party or, later, government policy. We always listened seriously to what the preacher said.

The Labour Party Conference is the biggest of the party conferences, not least because of the union involvement. That year I discovered for the first time how it's funded. Basically, interested parties rent stalls that act as shop windows for what they do. Some smaller stalls are given rent-free to charities. One thing Labour Party Conferences are not short on is opinion formers, so this is a great opportunity for the organizations or businesses concerned to get themselves seen and talked about. One of the incentives given them to return year after year is the "best stall" competition, judged by — yes! — the leader's wife. There are various categories — public sector, private sector, voluntary sectors, and so on.

It took me at least two half days to get round to all the stalls. I wasn't overly enamored with the prospect. How would I judge? What were the criteria? That first year someone came along to show me the ropes, and surprisingly I really enjoyed it. Apart from anything else, it was something to do. It was completely out of the limelight, and a little bit nonsensical, but the stallholders genuinely seemed to value my visit. What they really wanted, of course, was a piece of their glamorous new leader, but if they couldn't have that, they'd settle for a piece of his wife. There were usually about two hundred stalls, and I made sure I went round to all of them, having a little chat and my picture taken with everybody.

Over the years there were inevitably some hiccups in my visits to the stalls, even though I was always closely shepherded — usually by Fiona, sometimes by Roz Preston, who later took over running Tony's office from Anji. One year a stand had Viagra on display, and my comment "Oh, we don't need that!" was duly trumpeted across the next day's newspapers. Every stall would press me to take its mug or pencil or its mouse pad, so naturally I did, getting increasingly weighed down, not daring to refuse the kind offers, in case doing so would show favoritism. At the end of the week we'd divvy up this "booty" among the staff who had been working so hard for Tony, they'd had no time to find anything to take home to their kids. My sense of fairness would later come back to haunt me when the *Daily Mail* claimed that "Cherie used to go round the conference and Hoover up every freebie she could find."

By Monday night, when the speech was into its nth draft, Tony was getting tenser and tenser. Gordon had given his speech that morning, and apparently he had said something that Tony had been planning to say. While I was drifting off to sleep, the voices in the sitting room next door continued to rise and fall. Eventually I could stand it no longer. *He has to get some sleep,* I thought. *If he doesn't, he's going to collapse.* So I got out of bed and went into the room. I am far from being a tidy person, but the state of that room was appalling: papers all over the place, half-drunk cups of tea and the odd beer glass, room-service trays with the remains of sandwiches, jackets here and there, and some very gray faces.

"Tony," I said, "you have got to come to bed, because you must get some sleep. And as for you lot," I said, pointing at Alastair, Anji, and the rest of them, "out. You've all got to go." As it was, he barely slept anyway, and I spent a wakeful night with him tossing and turning in bed beside me.

Finally, it was time for Tony's big speech. The Clause IV moment had come. As he began to speak, a hush descended, and I felt a shiver of anticipation. It was only at the end, however, that it became clear just how momentous it was. There was a brief moment of shock, and then the hall erupted. I felt the excitement all round me — the most brilliant speech a new leader had ever given. I felt ridiculously proud. There was nothing fake or phony about my clinging to my husband's arm, but at that moment a pattern had been set, with the press making comments along these lines: "She's supposed to be this successful career woman, yet she behaves like a love-sick teenager." They had me "clinging to his hand like the adoring wife." I was seen as a "breath of fresh air." My clothes were approved of, I was approved of. Everyone was happy.

And then, within only a couple of hours, it all began to unravel.

"Where is she?" Alastair's voice boomed down the corridor. Then he came storming in.

What was he talking about? Who?

"Carole," he bellowed. "Where the fuck is she!"

Just then she emerged from the bathroom.

"I thought I told you to stay away from the limelight. But oh, no, you knew better. And now the press are onto you. Not only have they seen you; they know exactly what you are doing and who you are. And now our beautiful day has been ruined by this ridiculous woman." He was literally spitting.

"What do you mean?" Carole said, looking aghast.

"What I mean is that you're a topless model!"

I froze. "I don't believe it," I said, but nobody heard me.

"I'm not a topless model," Carole said.

"Yes, you are! And what's more, the *Sun* has pictures of you, and tomorrow no doubt the whole world will have the benefit of seeing your tits. I want you out of here. Now," he said. (The *Sun* was not only one of our more gossipy tabloids, but it had the largest daily circulation of any English-language newspaper in the world.)

Slowly the story emerged. Several years before, when Carole was in the music video business, a boyfriend had taken pictures of her topless. She was eighteen. They were never published, but they would be now, as he had just sold them to the *Sun*.

By this time Carole was in tears. She left the room, saying she was going to pack.

"How dare you?" I said to Alastair, his arms now folded across his chest. "Don't think I don't know about you writing for a porn magazine. If we were all held accountable for what we did at eighteen, then it's a wonder you didn't disqualify yourself from this job on several counts, frankly."

"Cherie, listen to me. I'm a journalist. I've got a nose for these things. That woman is trouble. You can't possibly trust her. I don't want anything to do with her, do you hear? There's bound to be more coming out, and if you want to know what I think, I think she's only here to sell her story."

"So you're about to expel her from the Garden of Eden, is that it?"

"Your words, not mine."

Then Tony came in, and suddenly I felt dreadful. He had been so happy, exultant. All those desperate hours working on the speech had paid off, and now here he was, looking like thunder. He wanted to talk to me alone, he said. Alastair bowed out. We went into the bedroom, and he shut the door. I felt sick.

"I cannot believe this, Cherie. My God, this woman has been in our house! She's been in our bedroom sorting through your clothes. I mean, who is this person? What do you know about her? Come on, think about it. What do you actually know about her?"

"You know who she is. She's an exercise teacher. I've been going to her classes for years. I was hardly going to cross-examine her about what she'd done when she was eighteen."

"And to think I let you talk me into having a massage." He sat down on the edge of the bed with his head in his hands.

"We all did pretty stupid things when we were young. As for Alastair, he was an alcoholic, for God's sake. I don't condemn him for that, and I don't see why he should condemn Carole for being a bit careless."

"Careless!" was all he could say in reply.

The next day it got worse. Part of me was hoping that it wouldn't be her or that the pictures had been faked or something. But it was obviously Carole. Alastair continued his attack.

"You have to drop her, Cherie. It's as simple as that."

"Well, sorry to disappoint you, but I'm not going to. It wouldn't be fair. She has done nothing wrong, and what's more, she's done a good job and been incredibly helpful to me. You've even said yourself that I look great.

"And by what right do you tell me what company I should keep? It may surprise you to know that I have a life of my own, that I actually enjoy the company of people who couldn't give a stuff about politics, and I intend to hang on to it."

Shortly after breakfast the phone rang. It was Carole. Her mother had just called, she said. The house was surrounded by photographers. Later it came out that she'd been involved with this cult called Exegesis. What this was, or is, I still have no idea. But by that time she was gone. It had been decided to get her into a safe house. She couldn't go back to her mum's, as the press was parked outside. Hilary Coffman and Tony's researcher, Liz Lloyd, had been deputed to take her out through the kitchens, and she stayed at Liz's for a few days.

As far as the press impact was concerned, Alastair had managed to keep Tony distanced from it all. But I felt really bad about the whole thing, particularly since my role was to make things easier for him, not more difficult.

As for Carole, I was not about to give her up. She had promised me I'd have more energy, and I did. And now I knew I was going to need it. There was no mileage to be gained in rubbing anyone's face in it, but I continued going to the gym three times a week for an hour before work, and gradually the furor around Carole Caplin seemed to die down.

The press showed no signs of letting up on their interest in Tony and me as a couple, but increasingly I needed clothes to wear. So Carole would search things out, and I would pay her to go. Realistically, who else could I ask? Most of my friends were working mothers like me. In terms of their clothes, their horizons were limited. I didn't know ladies who lunched.

CHAPTER 17

Home Life

Back in Richmond Crescent, life continued much as usual, except that now Daddy didn't take the kids to school in the morning. All three were still in school in Highbury, though this would be Euan's last year. The question was, where would he go next?

Planning your children's education is always difficult, but after factoring in all the Blair imponderables, it became a nightmare. Wherever Euan went, he would start a new school in the autumn of 1995, and if the Major government decided to follow the normal pattern, the election could be in May 1996. I had to be practical. If the unimaginable did happen and we found ourselves in Downing Street in 1996 or 1997, that would be upheaval enough for our kids. Continuity would be crucial, and changing schools would not be an option. Also, with Nicky only two years behind Euan, we didn't want them going to different schools. In the end we opted for the London Oratory School in west London, which was a reasonable journey from both Richmond Crescent and Westminster.

When Tony told Alastair, he went ballistic. It would be disastrous for Tony's reputation, he said. He had a duty to send his children to a neighborhood school, not to a school on the other side of London, operating independently of the local education system. The fact that the Oratory was funded by the state and nonselective in terms of ability did not impress him. The fact that it was a faith school was enough to put him off. Alastair famously "doesn't do" religion, so he never understood why it mattered to me that my children received a Catholic education. Catholic schools continued to have religious assemblies, and the children observed the feast days, things that no longer happened in nonreligious schools. This sort of thing wasn't important only to me; it was important to Tony as well. Although he wasn't Catholic, he had been coming to Mass with us since the children were little. At St. Joan of Arc, as at most Catholic churches up and down the country, the Sunday morning Mass was family Mass: a genuinely warm and friendly affair, if a little chaotic. It was a chance for the children and their parents to worship and socialize together. In fact, Tony used to take Communion with the kids on a regular basis. He was a member of our church community; few, if any, in the congregation knew he wasn't Catholic. By this time Euan and Nicky had made their first Holy Communion. It would have been very odd for Euan to go to a non-Catholic school after being at a Catholic primary.

I don't know if Alastair thought this was me flexing my muscles because of the disagreement over Carole. Frankly, I think it unlikely. I might have been the official Catholic in our family, and Tony might have been dissuaded from brandishing his religious beliefs in public, but this was not politics, this was private and nonnegotiable, and Tony told Alastair so in no uncertain terms. Alastair gave him dire warnings, saying, "You will live to regret this," but the truth is, we never did. It was the right thing for our family.

Of course the story leaked, and on December 1, 1994, it was front-page news in the *Daily Mail*. But Tony stuck to his guns. The London Oratory was not a fee-paying school. It was not selective. It was still funded by the state, if not the local education authority. His children's education was not a political football.

There was a broader point, too. Tony wanted to bring a good standard of education to everyone, whatever their religion or lack of religion. That was another of his goals: to show people that they could be aspirational yet at the same time care about what happened to others. Above all, he wanted to jettison the idea that once people did better in life, the Labour Party was no longer their natural home.

When John Smith took over as leader from Neil Kinnock in 1992, the party paid £70,000 for his apartment to be redecorated, on the grounds that he needed somewhere suitable for official entertaining. Now that Tony was Leader of the Opposition, someone from the party came to look over our house in Richmond Crescent and, taking a dim view of the holes in the carpet, suggested we should use John Smith's flat.

"If I'm having to entertain," I said, "I am not going to entertain in somebody else's house. It has to be done in ours." As for bringing Richmond Crescent up to scratch, neither of us felt we could take any more money from the party, which only two years previously had spent so much doing up John Smith's place.

The moment we began to look beneath the surface, it was apparent that a face-lift would not be sufficient. My dad was always complaining that he got ill every time he stayed in our spare room in the basement, that it was damp and unhealthy. It turned out he was right. The whole of the downstairs had to be damp-proofed and replastered, which involved borrowing £30,000 from the bank. Tony's attitude toward money has always been "I just want to do what's right, and somehow or other we'll sort it out." Although I had long before accepted that I was the major breadwinner, it sometimes rankled that he would get the credit for maintaining the moral high ground while the responsibility of funding an increased mortgage, as in this case, would fall on me. It didn't strike me as odd, however. It was how things had been when I was growing up. My grandma was always in charge of the family finances. Grandad would hand over most of his pay, and my mum would hand over half of hers.

When I moved to Michael Beloff's chambers in Gray's Inn Square in 1991, Leslie Page, the chief clerk, told me that chambers' "game plan" was that within the next five years, I would take silk. As we were now coming up on 1995, it was time to think seriously about what I should do.

Acceptance as a Queen's Counsel, or silk, was far from automatic. At that time, the view of the senior judges was what ultimately decided the matter, so if a junior barrister was thinking of applying, it was a good idea to talk to a senior member of the Bench to see what he or she thought.

Becoming a Queen's Counsel wasn't guaranteed to give a junior a higher income. There was even a risk he or she would see a drop. Someone with a good junior practice could earn well in excess of a silk whose practice was limited. In those days silks couldn't work without a junior. Not only could they not appear in court without a junior supporting them, but they could no longer do pleadings or draft court documents. And it was often the case that the junior brought in the work in the first place. If a junior didn't like a silk, he or she was in trouble.

By 1995, however, such rules were already bending because of murmurings concerning restrictive practices, and by the end of the nineties, they were largely gone. Even so, after I made silk, I rarely did things on my own, simply because the economics were better for the client. A junior was cheaper than I was and could easily do the background stuff. Why pay my hourly rate for this work? Roughly speaking, a silk is paid to shape the case and provide the eventual advocacy. Once in court, the junior is there to assist the silk, to make sure he or she covers all the points and generally to act as the silk's assistant. Whereas the junior will help the silk draft the written argument that is filed with the court, the silk presents the oral argument. When a trial involves examining witnesses, the silk might even let the junior do some of the minor witness evidence. In my situation, however, most of the cases I dealt with didn't involve witnesses, because they were about legal points, so my work mainly involved arguing the point of law.

I had moved chambers in order to give my practice a boost, and the move had certainly been effective. I had stopped doing the routine stuff and was doing more High Court work, specifically judicial review cases, which were both interesting and — because they often involved challenging government decisions — quite political and high profile. As a consequence, they brought me to the attention of the High Court judges, the people who ultimately decide who gets silk and who doesn't.

A classic example of public law was the poll tax. Officially known as the community charge, it had been brought in by Margaret Thatcher's government in 1989 and levied on every citizen. The tax was unrelated to an individual's wealth or ability to pay and so was perceived as being grossly unfair by the majority of the population.

People sometimes ask me how I deal with cases involving a law I don't particularly like. While I didn't think the poll tax was a good idea politically, I also believed that as Parliament had passed that bill, people had to pay the tax. That is, you can change the law, but you don't disobey the law. It's the old question that all law students have to decide: do you have an obligation to obey the law? For example, Gandhi and his followers, who flagrantly disobeyed the law, accepted that as a consequence, they would be sent to prison.

A friendly solicitor in Manchester brought me a series of interesting cases against a body called ICSTIS, set up to monitor child chat lines in order to prevent children from running up huge phone bills that their parents would have to pay. Some of these lines turned out to be sex lines, so I found myself defending the existence of sex lines that were being closed down by ICSTIS. It would start with a nice intellectual argument, but then the judge would say, "Well, let's see some of these transcripts," and I'd have to read out what people were actually saying on the sex lines. And as I was standing there, reading out this stuff, I could see my case disappearing down the plughole. The judge, being only human, would think, *I don't care how clever this legal argument is; those lines must stay closed.* And that's what usually happened. Often in such instances, I knew I was not going to win. Good as the intellectual case might be, it was morally indefensible.

The reason I took on these cases — and others that I didn't necessarily approve of — was the cab-rank rule. It arose in the eighteenth century, when John Wilkes and others like him were being tried for sedition and couldn't find lawyers to represent them, because the lawyers were frightened of being punished by the government. If the legal system was to work properly, it was reckoned, the defendants had a right to be represented. According to the cab-rank rule, it is a matter of professional misconduct to turn down a case if you are available and if you have been offered a reasonable fee.

Some barristers say, "I will not represent rapists" or "I won't do this or that." To me, the advantage of the cab-rank rule is that no one can claim that I picked a particular case because I espouse the cause. Of course, sometimes I do espouse the cause, and it could be argued that I am likely to make a better job of it. But that's completely and utterly irrelevant.

Once Tony was Leader of the Opposition, it became even more important that I stick to this rule. I had to ensure that I remained totally untainted by politics, especially when my field was so bound up with governmental decisions.

It was through doing public law that I also started doing education law. In the 1990s a whole system of special-needs education was starting up, responding to children with physical, mental, or behavioral difficulties. Because I was experienced in family law and was thought to be good with children, many of these cases came my way. In one case, we managed to get the court to overturn the local authority's decision to move a girl out of her special school. This girl had cerebral palsy. There was nothing wrong with her brain; it was just her body that was damaged. I also did the first case concerning a dyslexic girl who sued her local authority for failing to diagnose her condition. The issue was whether the local authority was liable to a charge of negligence. In 2002 I wrote a book on the subject. As the field was so new, there wasn't one that dealt with it.

Because education was a very new field in terms of the law, I argued before the highest courts in the land, which meant that my visibility was becoming much greater among the judges. I'd got to know several of them quite well, so I went to talk to some of them about applying for Queen's Counsel. Their response was encouraging. My practice, they felt, would justify my taking silk, and they suggested that it would be better to apply while there was still a Tory government. If I waited until Labour was in power, it would be harder to avoid allegations of favoritism.

I applied in 1995 — one of only six women who took silk that year. By sheer chance, on the day it was announced, Tony and I had been invited to Windsor Castle. Traditionally the Leader of the Opposition stays the night, but that year — much to our relief — this was impossible because of ongoing repairs following a serious fire in 1992. It wasn't that we had anything against staying, but the following day was Easter, and we wanted to set off early for the constituency.

So it was that on the day it was announced that "Her Majesty is pleased to have appointed . . . Cherie Booth as her Counsel," I had dinner with the Queen. It wasn't the first time I had met her. New MPs are always invited to Buckingham Palace with their spouses, and at that first meeting I remember being struck dumb, not knowing what to say and getting terribly confused as to how to curtsy. When I was little, I had been taught to curtsy in ballet class, but a ballet curtsy seemed a bit over-the-top for this particular occasion, so I managed a vague kind of bob. (The accusation that I refused to curtsy, either then or later, is a complete load of rubbish, though now I tend to bow. As a barrister, I bow all the time — lady barristers are not expected to curtsy — out of respect to the court and respect to the Crown, so that comes completely naturally.)

The ceremony where you actually take silk immediately follows the Easter bank holiday and takes place at the Palace of Westminster. This requires a trip to Ede & Ravenscroft to purchase a new silk gown and a full-bottom wig. Lady barristers traditionally wore long skirts for the ceremony, but since 1991 we had been allowed to wear the men's costume of knickerbockers, which were much jollier, so I decided to go for them. When I tried them on, I was surprised at how ill fitting they were at the front, with so much loose material. A red-faced assistant had to explain to me why. In the end I got a pair specially made.

It was a real family celebration. My dad came down, and my mum, Lyndsey, and all three of my children were there. Tony couldn't be there for the whole ceremony, as he was needed in the House of Commons, but at about eleven o'clock he came over to Westminster Hall to watch the proceedings.

After a little celebration in chambers, we went over to the Lord Chief Justice's court. There, in precedent order, we were presented to the Lord Chief Justice. By this time the kids were getting a bit restless and were rather bemused by all the bowing and scraping, not to mention their mum in this ridiculous outfit looking like a pantomime Prince Charming. My dad, meanwhile, was getting himself photographed by the waiting press: no show without Punch. Even so, I knew he was very pleased. I remember him saying, "Your grandma would have been so thrilled that you matched Rose Heilbron." And it's true; she would have been.

Finally it was party time. The car took us back to the house, and everyone — friends and family — turned up to celebrate. Later that evening we ended up at Tony's brother Bill's and had Chinese takeout. It was the end of a fantastic day: a very proud moment for me, a proud moment for my mum, and even the kids were marginally impressed. They were used to their dad being the Big Thing, but at least I got to dress up for my moment in the sun.

Around the time the London Oratory story first broke, I had a phone call from a very irate Fiona. Anji Hunter had told her that I thought Alastair had leaked the story. I had no idea where Anji had got that, I said. Certainly not from me, because it wasn't the case. Fiona was clearly very upset and stressed, and it emerged that despite what I had promised her about not losing sight of family obligations, life in the Campbell-Millar household had gone rapidly downhill.

"He goes off in the morning, then when I've just about given up on him ever coming back, he reappears. And when he is here, he's on the phone. Frankly, I could be an umbrella stand for all the notice he takes of me," Fiona said. This sounded all too familiar. Tony was doing his best to stay involved, but his job was an endless series of obligations, morning, noon, and night. I thought, *Join the club.*

"Believe me, Fiona," I said, "I know exactly how you feel."

After this conversation the idea emerged that if she was more involved, things might improve on the home front. Perhaps, Tony suggested, I could do with some extra help? Fiona was a freelance reporter. She had started on the *Daily Express*, where her father had been a journalist. She sometimes did things for the in-house magazine for the House of Commons and had always been political.

Fiona is very attractive, with a shock of blond hair, and also strongminded and determined. But she can be very unforgiving. At that time it's fair to say I didn't know her very well, but we were friendly, and I trusted her. The first thing she did in her new role was to get Philip Gould, the Labour Party's poll adviser, to slip a few questions into some of his focus groups to find out what people thought of me. As she was friendly with Lindsay Nicholson, then editor of *Prima*, a women's magazine, Fiona arranged for me to be a guest editor for the tenth-anniversary issue. Lindsay's husband, John Merritt, had been a trainee reporter with Alastair, and they had become great friends. John had died of leukemia in 1993, leaving Lindsay with a three-year-old and pregnant with their second daughter — a terrible story. I took to Lindsay immediately — a really nice woman, a fantastically capable editor, and a good Catholic girl like me.

What had emerged from Philip's focus groups was that I needed to project a softer image, to show that I was an ordinary mum, which I fundamentally was (though the idea that ordinary mums go round guest editing glossy magazines was another matter). At first I thought "guest editing" meant that I had physically to edit the magazine, but Lindsay remained very firmly in the driver's seat. "My" issue of *Prima* would be built round my interests, she explained. On the lighter side, knitting emerged as the front-runner. I had been given my first knitting needles by Grandma when I was three. Tea cozies were my pièces de résistance and — I liked to think — much sought after as collector's items. For this exercise, however, they wanted something that involved a pattern, so we went for a cable-knit sweater. (I didn't actually knit it, though I would have enjoyed the challenge. There just wasn't enough time.) Then there were my more serious interests: the abuse of women and children. I had recently been approached by Refuge, a charity for battered wives, and asked whether I would join its board. Until then the charity work I had done had been directly related to my work as a lawyer: giving free advice to the Child Poverty Action Group and the National Centre for Citizenship and the Law, and of course my Wednesday evening sessions in Tower Hamlets.

Veena, whose parents' flat I had borrowed in Maida Vale, had by this time divorced her first husband and married a charismatic barrister called Gareth Williams, and there was talk of him becoming Attorney General or Solicitor General. It was Gareth who approached me about getting involved with the Justice for Children campaign of the National Society for the Prevention of Cruelty to Children (NSPCC). Its aim was to get lawyers to raise funds for an NSPCC facility, which traced child-abuse rings and had specialist social workers who would support the kids through the court process. For a child, giving evidence in a criminal trial is always difficult and sometimes traumatic, and part of what we were looking for — in addition to raising funds — was a change in the way defense counsel cross-examined, because many barristers were still aggressive with even quite young witnesses.

Although it might appear self-defeating to bully a child with a jury present, if the child contradicts himself or herself, he or she is branded a liar, and the abuser gets off. We wanted to change that climate. The Tories had already started exploring whether we could make things easier for children, and after Labour came in, we did quite a lot to support victims in court, including battered women and rape victims, and to change the rules so that they could give evidence behind a screen. All that began with the Justice for Children campaign.

Prima also allowed me to build on a campaign by Refuge to raise its profile. I wrote an article about how I had become involved as a young lawyer and how important it was for me and for women in general.

Alas, Tony's office was very dubious about the article. Why should I draw attention to myself? A woman brought in to look at the thorny issue of how I should present myself decided I was asking for trouble. "People are going to assume that the reason you got involved is that your father beat your mother."

"But he didn't," I said. "And that is not why I am doing this." (In fact, in all these years, nobody has once suggested that it was.) Thanks to Fiona fighting on my side, the office finally agreed, but they remained decidedly apprehensive, muttering under their breath about not needing the extra hassle. They didn't get any hassle, and my getting involved in the campaign started a relationship with Refuge that continues to this day.

In this, as in so much else, having Fiona there to champion my cause made all the difference. Over those early years she kept me sane: not only in the obvious way — keeping the mail under control and running my schedule once we got into Downing Street — but most important in fighting for family life to be included in the thinking of Tony's office, something she and I had a common interest in.

In September 1995 Euan duly started at the London Oratory School. On the first day of term, those mothers among us who could went with our sons on the subway. They were only eleven, and most of them had never traveled on the underground on their own. We left home at ten to seven, having arranged to meet up with Euan's friend at Arsenal station. At Earls Court we changed onto the District Line. By now the carriage was filled with boys dressed in the same uniform, and they were chatting and joking with each other.

"Did you hear?" one boy said to his friend opposite.

"Hear what?"

"Tony Blair's son's going to be in our school today."

Euan said nothing but nudged me, and I gave him a little smile.

From West Brompton station it's about an eight-minute walk to the school, and that morning our route was lined with older students to mark out the way for the new pupils. As we walked down Seagrave Road, the atmosphere was jocular and lively. A happy start, I thought, to this new chapter in my son's life. As we approached the school, there was a flurry of activity, and other

163

mothers walking in front of me pulled their children to one side. Then I saw them: three photographers — paparazzi — shouting out my name and running toward us. It was a horrible feeling. It was as if the Red Sea had parted, and Euan and I had to walk up the middle, everyone turning to look and these guys running, their cameras held up against their faces. What could I do? If I tried to join the other mothers, it would end up with their children getting photographed as well, which would get me in even more trouble. I kept walking. By the time we got to the gate, Euan was close to tears, and while everybody else waited until all the new pupils had arrived, we were bundled in, then I was smuggled out another entrance. I got back on the underground feeling upset and angry — upset for my son, but furious with myself because I had failed to protect him.

Once back in chambers, I called Tony's office, told them what had happened, and said that, in my view, it was a breach of the Press Complaints Code, a set of journalistic standards established by the media to govern how the news should be covered. It worked. After pressure from the office, no English newspaper printed the pictures, although the "story" was reported. I couldn't believe it. This was an eleven-year-old boy who was going to be traveling every day through central London on his own. Did I really want him to be recognized? Would any mother? Two years later, when Nicky went to the Oratory, he refused point-blank to allow me to go with him on the first day, and who could blame him?

CHAPTER 18

Election Fever

Now that Tony was Leader of the Opposition, our visits to Sedgefield became less frequent. Looking back from the vantage point of a woman now in her fifties, I don't really know how I coped. Although we kept basic clothes at Myrobella, there was still a lot to take with us, not least the hamsters that, for some reason lost in the annals of the Blair family history, always came, too. Live animals weren't the only thing to think about.

One Friday I was doing a tribunal in Cambridge against Charlie Falconer. As we had a dinner party in the constituency that evening, I'd done the shopping for it in London the night before. I thought the case was going to settle, but it didn't, and so we were fighting. So there I was fishing out my brief from my bulging briefcase, and Charlie remembers watching in horror as a leg of lamb emerged, dripping blood all over the inside of my sleeve.

As the children grew older, Tony would increasingly go to Sedgefield on his own, leaving on Friday and returning early on Saturday evening. On weekends like those, when the nanny was having her well-deserved time off, I would finally have time to be a normal mother. A favorite Saturday activity was the Sumix Centre, a children's choir based in Thornhill Square, where Bill and Katy Blair lived. After dropping the kids off at Sumix, I'd pop into Bill and Katy's for a cup of coffee, then pick up the kids and go home via

Lyndsey's. Then it would be back to Richmond Crescent to help make supper for when Daddy got home.

I have always enjoyed cooking. Roasts were the Myrobella specialty, and on a Sunday I would busy myself in the kitchen while Tony took the children for a walk, often to a place that we called "Wind in the Willows," a house his parents had always hoped to buy but never did. In London my repertoire revolved around spaghetti and lasagne. We always needed things that could stretch because we never knew who would drop in. I would often experiment, not always successfully it must be admitted. On weekends we would eat together as a family. During the week the nanny usually cooked for the kids, while I did dinner for Tony and me.

By the end of 1995, election fever was mounting. John Major's government lurched from crisis to crisis, and the general feeling was that it was hanging by a thread. The Tory majority in Parliament was down to twenty-one members and falling; rebels were defying the party line; dissent within the Cabinet over Europe was rife (Major called the Euroskeptics "the bastards"); and there was a tide of sleaze, culminating in a trail of brown envelopes originally reported to be stuffed with cash intended as bribes for several MPs in the "cash for questions" scandal. In addition, the repercussions of the Black Wednesday stock market crash continued to affect both business and individuals, including our family.

Meanwhile I worked on losing weight, while Carole helped me build up my wardrobe. This was not as flip or self-centered as some people might think. The days of thinking that Tony could go to a function on his own while I slobbed out in front of the television were long gone. I was part of the package. Everything would be judged, often cruelly.

Suddenly we were on everybody's list. Tony's view was that if an event had political implications, we had to go. So we did, and of course our picture got taken. I can remember the writer Ken Follett, a very public Labour supporter, inviting us to his house: a private dinner, or so we thought. The press had prior notice, however, and the moment we opened the car doors, cameras were clicking. Alastair was furious and gave Ken a tongue-lashing. No doubt he was rude in the way that only Alastair can be, and I don't think Ken ever forgave him. Alastair took the view that the Folletts were doing it for their own publicity; the Folletts said they hadn't tipped anyone off and were offended that he'd said they had.

The clothes-buying routine was slowly evolving into something less hit-and-miss. I was using Ronit Zilkha, Caroline Charles, Betty Jackson, Ally Capellino, Paddy Campbell, and Paul Costelloe, all British designers. The clothes would usually have to be altered (that bottom, those hips), and soon a more organized approach evolved. By the time I got to Downing Street, I'd choose from the collections six months before they appeared in the shops. (I'd go to the offices and warehouses once the particular designs had been earmarked.) In September it would be things for the following summer. In January or February I'd be buying for the following autumn/winter season.

It was fascinating to get a glimpse of how the fashion industry works. There I was in the thick of it, talking to buyers and models as well as designers. I saw just how thin the models really were and how they smoked nonstop, and although I never saw them doing cocaine myself, I knew from what others told me that it was rife. I became very friendly with some of the designers. Paddy Campbell, for example, is a fascinating woman who started off as an actress, and we found we had a lot in common.

I didn't specifically look for women designers, but apart from one or two, it ended up that way. The lovely Paul Costelloe was an exception, a real Irish flirt. I've also bought things from Paul Smith. In 1995 Tony and I were invited to an event in the Indian community, and they suggested that it might be nice if I could wear a sari. I mentioned this to Bharti Vyas, the woman who ran the beauty clinic where I'd had my first facial, and one of her staff — a cousin, I think — was persuaded to lend me one of hers. I loved it. A sari is incredibly flattering for my kind of shape; it really makes you stand properly and feel a bit like a princess. A few weeks later, we went to a reception in the Sikh community, and a young woman came up and introduced herself. She was a designer, she said, and would like to work with me.

"The thing is," she said, "you and I are the same shape, so if something works on me, it would probably work well on you." That was how I met the fantastic Babs Mahil, who has designed all my Indian things ever since.

Early in 1997 Tony and I met Diana, Princess of Wales. Maggie Rae, by then a partner at another firm, had been involved in her divorce, and Diana had told her that she wanted to meet Tony. She was keen to show that she had something to offer this country, she said, and believed she could do a lot to help promote a more modern image of Britain. As the need for Britain to engage with the modern world was central to Tony's mission, he was quite taken with the idea.

It was all conducted in the utmost secrecy. Maggie invited Diana to her place for dinner, and Tony and I were invited, as well as Alastair and Fiona. By this time Maggie had moved from her original wreck, but not very far. Diana had already got there by the time Tony and I arrived, and she was down in the kitchen chatting with everybody. She seemed perfectly at home in ordinary surroundings, even making Alastair a cup of tea at one point. What most struck me was how completely obsessed Alastair was by the idea that she fancied him. She was certainly flirting with him (more than with Tony), much to Fiona's irritation, but every time she moved out of earshot, he'd say to Tony, "She really fancies me, and she's only asked you so that she can see me." Although he was doing it in a jokey way, such is his ego that part of him probably wanted to believe it.

There is no doubt that Diana was beautiful, more so in the flesh, perhaps, than came across in photographs. She was tall and slim and immaculately turned out. With me, I think, she was anxious to show her serious side. (No doubt she'd worked out that this would go down better than the flirtatious eyelash fluttering that had Alastair drooling.) Although she said she was no great intellectual, she projected the image of someone who had something to offer. And I believe she did have something to offer. If you have that kind of charisma, it makes sense to use it. Tony certainly saw this, and no doubt in Tony she saw someone who had a similar allure and magnetism.

I remember the one thing that came over strongly was how she felt about her boys and how close to them she was, how much a part of her life they were. She was concerned that William should be brought up in a more modern way than his father had been, and she wanted to see a modern monarchy. She was keen to stress that she, too, was a modern person. By this time she was involved in the land mine issue, and she put forward the idea that she could have a role in promoting Britain in the wider world as a sort of roving ambassador. Tony was certainly considering whether there was a way we could use her talents for the benefit of the country. Although she didn't say she was actually a supporter of New Labour, she certainly implied that she was, though whether she really was, is another question.

A few weeks later I met Norma Major at the *Daily Star* Gold Awards. We were both presenting awards — it was the first time I had been asked to do something like that on my own account. I hadn't met her before, but she came over and shook my hand (the press took a picture that appeared everywhere the next day), which I thought was incredibly gracious of her. She didn't have to do it.

Over the eighteen months since Tony had become leader, his office had coalesced into a very strong team that became like an extended family. Anji Hunter — known, not entirely affectionately, as "the gatekeeper" — ran his office, with Kate Garvey under her as diary secretary. Liz Lloyd did research. Jonathan Powell had arrived a month or so after Alastair to serve as chief of staff. Tony wanted someone who knew about the Civil Service, and Jonathan had been a diplomat, working in our embassy in Washington, which was where Tony first met him. What always struck people as particularly amusing, however, was that his brother Charles had been Margaret Thatcher's right-hand man.

It was clear that Anji and Alastair were resentful of Jonathan. They were incredibly dismissive, saying that because he'd been in the Foreign Office, he didn't understand politics. But the point was that he knew how the Civil Service operated, and that was why Tony needed him. For a while there was a definite jockeying for position, a "We were here first" attitude and "Can you really be on our side because you've been working for the government all this time?" I was inclined to take Jonathan's part, first because I'm a bit perverse, but also because I thought they were giving him far too much of a hard time. He's a lovely person to have around, a Tigger-like character, and charming in the way that Alastair is charming — the difference being that Alastair is a charming thug, and Jonathan doesn't have an ounce of thuggery in him. I also like him because he's eccentric — tall, gangly, and always terribly untidy. Jonathan never cares what he wears, and once we were in Downing Street, Tony was always giving Jonathan his old shirts and ties.

Jonathan's role was to prepare our people for government, which he did brilliantly. He is a public-school boy, clever and fantastic on policy. He was Tony's right-hand man all the way through the Northern Ireland peace process.

After their initial shadowboxing Jonathan and Alastair got on very well, not least because their areas of expertise were entirely different. Jonathan was in charge of the policy people, and he handled the details of policy and the niceties of negotiating very well. Alastair hasn't the slightest interest in policy; he either loves you or he hates you, and people either love or hate him.

With all this going on, it is not perhaps surprising that the office was intruding more into our family life than it had before. If there was work to be done, Tony had a choice: either he stayed in his office in Westminster, or he came home and the people he needed to see came with him. His visits to Trimdon became more infrequent, and John Burton was left to keep constituency matters ticking over. Everyone was so focused on winning the forthcoming general election that it became all-consuming. Almost the only person who didn't assume that Tony was going to win was Tony. His mantras were "No complacency" and "Do not take anything for granted." At some point before the election, a television reporter from ITV interviewed us in Richmond Crescent and asked me how I thought Downing Street would cope with having young children living there.

"Well," I said, "Downing Street will just have to get used to the idea of having noise and piano practice and friends round for tea."

Alastair got very upset. I shouldn't have answered the question, he said, as it made the assumption that we were going to win. While we were doing the interview in the garden, Euan had been playing the piano inside, so Alastair negotiated that ITV could have a shot of Euan practicing in return for their not broadcasting my remark. I was not happy. I considered my comment perfectly harmless, and I would rather not have had Euan involved in any way. Alastair just kept repeating, "You can't take the electorate for granted."

Inevitably Alastair won these arguments. Nevertheless, I think he found me a bit of a dilemma. He once said that I had the brains of a man and the emotions of a woman, and he found that very difficult to deal with. The truth is, he never believed that women have equal capacity.

CHAPTER 19

Endgame

From 1996 on, we were on an election footing, and when it wasn't called that October, we knew it would be May or June of 1997. The only piece of information lacking was the exact date. Then on March 17, John Major went to Buckingham Palace, and Parliament was dissolved. He had hung on till the very last minute. Polling Day would be Thursday, May 1 — a six-week campaign, though campaigns can be as little as three weeks. The view among Tony's staff was that the other side hoped we would run out of resources and steam. Not if Tony had anything to do with it.

Each morning, after an hour in his makeshift gym in Nick's room, Tony would leave around eight o'clock for the daily press conference at Millbank Tower, the Labour Party campaign headquarters. Most mornings I would go straight to the Albany gym, a former chapel near Regent's Park. I'd exercise for an hour, shower, dress, sort out my hair and makeup, and then go to meet Tony at Millbank.

In the months leading up to the election, the routine had been pretty much the same. Once the campaign proper began, after my workout I would leave the gym with one of the trainers who lived nearby and have a shower and change at her place, just to have a bit more privacy. Years later, when this woman needed the money, she sold a story to the Sunday tabloid the *News of the World* claiming that Carole and I had had showers together, which is a complete load of rubbish. (I knew the editor, Rebekah Wade, and the next time I saw her, I decided to have it out. "You don't seriously think that I was taking showers with Carole Caplin, do you, Rebekah?" I asked. She shrugged, then laughed. "It's only a story," she said.)

That was much, much later, but even as early as 1994, negative stories had started to appear in the tabloid press, usually about my appearance. I didn't save them — I'm not a masochist — but I did keep the letters that colleagues at the Bar sent me at the time, generally commiserating and expressing solidarity. One actually used the saying "Don't let the bastards grind you down." Little did I know that this grinding would be done on an industrial scale once we were inside Number 10 Downing Street.

The campaign "battle bus," an old coach customized to the office's specifications, was cramped and uncomfortable. There was a semicircle of seats all the way round at the back, where the windows were blacked out; this was where Tony and I sat. There was also a table with a fax machine and a television. At the front were tables and seats for the people who were with us and for members of the press, who would get on from time to time.

For security reasons, Terry always followed in the Rover behind us, and at the end of the day — if we could — Tony and I would get out of the bus and have Terry drive us back to London, while the other poor souls had to lurch on a bit longer. Tony tried to arrange the itinerary so that we could be home every night for the sake of the kids, but it didn't always happen.

For six weeks we crisscrossed the country, seemingly nonstop. In the election campaigns that followed, I did much more on my own, but 1997 was the first, and Tony and I largely stayed together. Every evening Tony would give a set-piece speech to the party faithful which he and Alastair had worked on during the day. He always spoke so well, and so passionately, that each night there was this extraordinary feeling of moving forward, a momentum that was unstoppable.

Not all our campaigning was together. At one point I made a solo visit to Crosby. Crosby was not on our list of potentially winnable seats — all of which Tony visited — so I just went with my dad. We got a tremendous welcome. Claire Curtis-Thomas, the Labour parliamentary candidate, was her usual dynamic self. "Cherie," she said, "we can win this seat! I know we can!" She was a good candidate, but how could we possibly win Crosby? It had been Tory since the beginning of time.

The last burst was a five-day campaign covering the last weekend of April. Alastair had one final idea, which he considered a brilliant coup because nobody ever did it. We would go and visit night workers, he said, starting with Smithfield meat market — a place my dad used to work when he was an out-of-work actor. This time I put my foot down.

"No, Alastair. Not unless you want to kill him. He needs to sleep." No doubt it was a wonderful idea, but you cannot campaign all day and all night when you're on the final leg of a six-week marathon and still be breathing at the end of it.

Those last five days the crowds grew bigger and bigger. Every place we visited, there seemed to be more people on the streets, and the pressure was building. The last day of campaigning found us in Scotland, a short hop from our roost in the northeast. In a town called Stockton-on-Tees a platform had been erected in the marketplace. We stood there, surrounded by a sea of faces, all shouting "Ton-ee, Ton-ee" and "We're on our way." The sheer emotion, the goodwill, and the intensity of it all were amazing. It was as if everyone's hopes were pinned on Tony, as if he were a boxer or a long-distance runner, a feeling that everything depended on this one man. I must have realized this before, or sensed at least some of it, but standing in the marketplace in Stockton was when it really hit home. I, too, felt very emotional and so proud. But I was also worried about him, because it was such a powerful thing that was happening. How could he possibly fulfill these people's dreams? It was a huge sense of responsibility, and I could sense Tony becoming more concentrated. He was pulling back into himself, becoming almost quiet, realizing that there was a real possibility that he was going to become leader of our country and that the people expected him to make a difference.

The previous Christmas we had taken a long-promised trip to Australia and visited our old friends Geoff and Bev Gallop and their kids. Tony had lived there for some years as a boy but had very little memory of it until he went back, and he loved it. He was struck by how young the country felt, and that's how he wanted Britain to be. So many things back home were stuck in the past, and we weren't moving forward. In fact, under the current administration we seemed to be moving backward. John Major's most recent conference speech had conjured up a vision of ladies riding bicycles in English country lanes and cricket on the lawns, whereas Tony wanted Britain to embrace modern technology. Then there had been the Tories' nastiness over immigration and gay rights, inherent in the Clause 28 question. The idea that we should still be uncomfortable about homosexuality had to go, he believed. There was an atmosphere of negativity in Britain that Tony was keen to change.

As MP for Sedgefield, he knew only too well the feeling in the north that the south didn't really care what was going on in the rest of the country as long as it was doing okay. I knew firsthand of the disparity of opportunity. I had brought up my own children, had been a school governor, and knew that most schools literally had to make a choice between books and teachers, because there simply wasn't enough money. Traveling round the country, being shown the state of school buildings, I saw how much of the infrastructure was close to collapse. And then there were the hospitals. In 1997 a number of health service authorities were in severe crisis with their funding. All round the nation, citizens were suffering. There were reports of elderly men and women unable to pay for heat and dying of hypothermia. We were told we couldn't afford a minimum wage, so there were people working as night watchmen and caretakers, for example, and women working in shops, all for £1 or £2 an hour. Things had to change.

Tony was now being seen as the instrument for that change, and there was a huge expectation that with a change of government, we would have a change of culture, that the country would change practically overnight. It was completely unrealistic, and one person who wasn't swept up in the fantasy was Tony.

Since he was first elected to Parliament in 1983, he had never had power, because the Labour Party had never been in power. Tony was still thinking that it could all go horribly wrong, as it had in 1992, when Neil Kinnock was convinced he was going to win. That last day of the campaign, Tony was the least buoyed up of any of us, I think.

After Stockton-on-Tees it was only a few miles back to Trimdon and Myrobella. The house was already full of Labour people when we arrived.

I could feel that Tony was still keeping himself back, but he knew plans had to be made, things had to be done — and quickly. The most immediate issue was making the Bank of England independent, which Tony emphatically believed was the vital emblem of Labour becoming economically respectable. He'd wanted it to be announced during the election campaign, but Gordon had thought it better to wait.

Around nine o'clock the kids arrived with Ros. They were amazed to see that Myrobella was now ringed by armed guards, sent by the Durham police. The mobile incident trailer that served as their headquarters was parked in the field next to the house, which in the summer was a mass of buttercups. We took the children over to see it, where we were shown an assortment of gas masks, bullet-proof vests, and night-vision rifles. The police let the kids look down the sights, but there was no great excitement. All three of them were rather subdued — as we all were, with reason. The whole experience freaked us out. Floodlights had been put up, and we could see shadowy figures here and there, and police dogs sniffing round. From time to time a siren would sound when a motion detector was inadvertently tripped. Myrobella had always been an open house, and suddenly it was being closed off. We weren't closing it, but it was being closed around us.

A few weeks earlier the security people had been to look over Richmond Crescent, and they had produced horrendous plans, which included putting a police box on our front porch and one at the back, because, they said, there were potential sniper positions from a block of flats looking over the park. There would also need to be a provision for a "siege containment" room, they said, and they would have to roof over our small back garden.

"But that's preposterous," I said. "What's the point of having a garden with a roof over it?" I almost wasn't taking it seriously, because I couldn't believe they really meant it, and I didn't think that people could possibly live like that. At the start of the campaign, our battered old cars had both been equipped with improvised explosive device (IED) detectors, as IRA car bombs were still a real threat. For the previous two weeks, two policemen had been permanently on guard outside our house, and apparently there were also a couple in the park. Even so, when we arrived at Myrobella on that Wednesday, I was shocked. There had been no discussion that I was aware of; they had just done what they felt they needed to do. They were even arranging with John Burton to buy the house nearest us at the end of the terrace, as a police house. The owners were more than happy to sell, John said. And who could blame them? It might be the safest house in the north of England, but who would want to live next door to something ringed in steel, looking like a young offenders' institution rather than a quirky Victorian family home with seven fireplaces and a hand pump?

We had already sorted out the following days' clothes. For the family walk to the polling station the next morning, I had a Betty Jackson outfit, and for the count that evening, a brown trouser suit with a long jacket by Ally Capellino. Ronit Zilkha was responsible for several things I had worn during the campaign, and she made the red suit that I planned to wear in London on Tony's first day as Prime Minister (God willing). All were in keeping with the British designers theme.

The next day, as the hours ticked by, our families began to turn up. Myrobella was crammed. Alastair and Jonathan kept popping in, and Fiona drifted in and out. That afternoon they all went away to have a rest. Tony was supposed to have a sleep, too, but I don't think he managed to do more than lie down and close his eyes. A guesthouse up the road had a small indoor swimming pool, which the owners said we could use, and the kids and I left him in peace. Meanwhile first indications of the turnout were beginning to come in. Philip Gould called to say that BBC exit polls were giving us a ten-point lead over the Tories.

Looking back, I don't know how I stood it. It felt almost as though I were in a bubble, instinctively trying to keep some sort of distance so that the whole thing wouldn't overwhelm us. The atmosphere was almost unnaturally calm.

We had to decide what to do with the kids. There was never any question that they shouldn't be involved. It wouldn't be like it had been with my father: once he became famous, we were completely cut off from anything to do with his life. I was determined that history would not repeat itself, that our kids would not be incidental extras to what was happening to their father. This was something that we were doing together as a family. Later I would be accused of double standards, of wanting to maintain their privacy while parading them before the cameras. But to have kept them out of those iconic pictures would have been to deny them their place in what would affect them all their lives. This was a journey we were going on together, and they had to know they were as important to us now as they were before. Leaving them out was not an option.

That said, they were too young to stay up all night, so we put them to bed and promised them that we'd get them up for the results, which wouldn't be until nearly midnight. Euan barely slept, but Nicky certainly did, because I remember the trouble we had waking him and how Tony had to carry him downstairs. He was only eleven then and still half asleep. Euan was already thirteen and so had taken a lot more interest in the campaign, while Kathryn was still a little girl at nine, and just very excited, largely because she loved the new outfit I'd got her from Marks & Spencer. I felt very shaky. While everyone around was focused on Tony, the party, and the country, I thought increasingly of what lay before me, of those three little people who hadn't asked for any of this, who hadn't been canvassed for their opinion, and who had no concept of what the future held. It was now my job, as never before, to make family life work. However much he wanted to, realistically Tony would not be there in the way he had been before.

I thought it might be a bit difficult for my mum and dad to be there together, but in the end it was fine. One thing my mum had always known was that the old rogue was completely devoted to the party, so for him this was a Big Thing.

At 10:00 p.m. the polls closed, and we all gathered round the television. Tony was upstairs in our bedroom, just lying on the bed staring at the ceiling. He didn't want to come down. When *News at Ten* came on, somebody went up to get him. He shambled in and stood at the door, and the newscaster began to speak.

"The predictions are that it's going to be a Labour landslide."

"Don't be ridiculous," Tony said. "I accept that we're going to win, but a landslide, no. It's ridiculous."

At about eleven-thirty John Burton arrived with Tony's security. During the last two weeks of the campaign, he had been provided with five protection officers (known as "'tecs") who would be on duty two at a time. They had been on the bus, but as we were constantly surrounded by people, we hadn't taken much notice. What were five more among so many? It wasn't as if this was going to be our life. (It was, of course, but we didn't realize it then.)

We went down to Newton Aycliffe Leisure Centre, where the vote counting for Sedgefield and the neighboring constituency was being held. Outside there was a feeling of Mardi Gras. Inside it was even more the case — everyone was ecstatic. Meanwhile Tony was pacing about, talking to people about what they had to do tomorrow and what the first things on the agenda would be. By now he had accepted that we had won, but he barely managed a smile. I was sitting with the family in a room at the back watching television, when there was a news flash: "Labour Gains Crosby."

My sister and I sat there open-mouthed, then clasped each other in near hysterics and jumped up and down. We just couldn't believe it; the whole Booth family was amazed, delighted, and astonished in equal measure.

And then it dawned on me: if we've won Crosby, anything is possible!

Sedgefield was a foregone conclusion, but Tony won it with an increased margin of twenty-five thousand votes. His only regret, he said when the crowd had quieted enough to let him speak, was that his mother was not there to see it. But his father was.

As soon as we could, I got the children into the waiting car and, with my mum and Ros in charge, waved them off to the airport. They were going home, I told them, but I would see them in the morning. From there it was back to Trimdon, to the Labour club, just to say thank you to our supporters, and then to Myrobella.

The phone rang at about two in the morning.

"This is Downing Street," the voice said. "We have the Prime Minister for you." It was John Major conceding defeat and wishing Tony well. I was in the room, but I didn't hear what he said, just Tony's muted response.

He and I were there alone, and I clasped both his hands in mine. "I know this is a huge responsibility," I said, "but you'll be fantastic." He was very calm, very much in awe of what was happening, because the vote of confidence was so big. I believe he'd always secretly thought he would win, but he'd never imagined he'd do so by such a huge margin.

A private plane was waiting at Teesside airport to fly us to London. The party at the Royal Festival Hall was already in full swing, but there was no risk that it would be over by the time we got there. As we flew down, results were still coming in, and Alastair was keeping everyone up-to-date. Gradually the scale of the victory became impossible to ignore, and at one point Tony put his head in his hands and said, "What have we done?"

There's a picture of the two of us on the plane, taken by the photographer Tom Stoddart, who'd been with us throughout the campaign, with Tony scribbling a few notes for what he was going to say. All I could do was put my arms round him and say, "It'll be all right. We're all coming, too."

That was how it was going to be. Whatever else happened, his family would be there with him, and indeed we were. We went in together, and we came out together. And we're still together, and that's really important.

As we crossed Westminster Bridge, dawn was glinting along the river. The streets round the South Bank were packed with people, and I thought that it must have been like this in 1945 when the war ended. Terry was driving, and either because of the excitement or because of barriers blocking off streets, we went the wrong way and had to turn round and back up.

We were both very subdued. Tony says that he never really got to enjoy that night. He made his speech about the new dawn rising over London and a new dawn for Britain. It was six o'clock in the morning by the time we left, and we emerged from the smoky, raucous atmosphere inside the Festival Hall into the clean light of the early morning. Someone gave us a glass of champagne, the first either of us had had. None of what was happening seemed real.

We went home and tried to grab a couple of hours of sleep. We slept fitfully, even though we were exhausted. Jonathan was the first to arrive later that morning, then came Alastair. In the meantime Ros had got the kids up and dressed. Then it was time to go.

"See you next at Number Ten!" I said, and kissed the kids goodbye. Ros was going to take them there later. First Tony had an appointment with the Queen, the ceremony known as "kissing hands," the formal invitation to the new Prime Minister to form a government.

As we walked out our front door, shouts rang out, and I realized what all the banging had been about while we'd been trying to get some sleep. Across the road a scaffolding had been erected for scores of photographers. All our neighbors were out in the street to cheer us off, and when we walked up to shake their hands, I suddenly had the feeling that we were saying good-bye — and we were, really. That's what it was. I heard Kathryn shouting, "Hey, Mum! Up here!" and saw her waving down to us from the second floor, her red hair glinting in the sun. Then Tony and I got into the Rover, with a police car behind us and Jonathan and Alastair bringing up the rear. And as we drove down through King's Cross, a motorbike escort with us all the way, cars stopped to let us through, drivers beeped their horns, and people on the streets waved. And all the time, above our heads, was the sound of a helicopter. I thought it must be the police, but now I realize it was one of the television channels filming us, the rotors pounding the air.

I'll never forget that journey, through all those bits of London that are normally in gridlock. We didn't stop, just drove straight down past Euston heading toward Buckingham Palace. I had been there before, to a diplomatic reception, but not to this part, the Queen's audience rooms overlooking the garden at the back. As the car swung in past the Victoria Memorial, I couldn't get over the crowds. Tony and I didn't dare speak; we just held hands.

Once inside the palace, we were taken up to the first floor, where I was introduced to the Queen's lady-in-waiting Lady Susan Hussey. The Queen's private secretary and press secretary then explained to Tony what would happen, while the lady-in-waiting told me what I had to do, which was basically to wait outside until the Queen rang the bell — the sign that I should go in. The Queen would receive me briefly, and that would be it.

Tony was in there on his own for about twenty minutes. Then the bell rang, and I went in, the door being opened by a footman. I can't remember not curtsying — something one would well recall — so I probably did. It was a big room, and the sun was shining through the large windows, and this iconic figure was standing there next to Tony, looking tiny beside him.

"Well, Mrs. Blair," she said, "I have just been congratulating your husband. With all this excitement, you must be tired."

"Tired but happy, Ma'am."

"And tell me, have you decided yet where you are going to live?"

"Well, I think we'll probably move into Number Ten, but we won't make up our minds until we've actually seen what it's like."

"You mean you haven't seen inside Downing Street? That does

surprise me." She smiled, then picked up the bell: the audience was over. We were escorted back downstairs, and I fully expected to see Terry and the Rover waiting for us. But there was no sign of the Rover, just a Jaguar — the Prime Minister's Jaguar. Then I saw it was Terry in the driver's seat looking as pleased as Punch. It turned out that they had tried to persuade Tony to change and take John Major's driver, but he'd said no. He wanted to keep Terry and Sylvie.

As we pulled out of the palace, a great roar went up — around the Victoria Memorial the crowds were going mad. Up the Mall, then turning into Whitehall, the noise was deafening. The car stopped at the bottom of Downing Street. For once people had been allowed in past the big gates, and the pavements on either side were packed with people shouting "Ton-ee, Ton-ee" and "Labour's coming home." As we made our slow way up that street, clasping the hands that were thrust out to us, I realized that these were staff and members of the Labour Party, as I recognized many of the faces. Above their heads, the windows of the Foreign Office were filled with more hands waving. I looked up the street to see if the kids had got here safely, and there they were, waiting for us to come up, little flags in their hands, their bright faces grinning, shining with excitement.

I stood with the children, and Tony walked a pace in front of us while he waited for the hubbub to calm down. Then he spoke.

"For eighteen years — for eighteen long years — my Party has been in opposition. It could only say, it could not 'do.' Today we are charged with the deep responsibility of government. Today, enough of talking — it is time now to do."

He turned round and walked over to us. We posed for a press shot, then somebody banged on that great heavy knocker, and the door opened.

CHAPTER 20

New Dawn

Over the last few days of the campaign, Tony had been getting memos from the Cabinet office at Number 10, setting out how things actually worked. From the most basic (there was no direct dialing, for example; all calls went through the switchboard, which, we were told, was always known as "switch"), through to the "cast list": who people were, what they did, whom they answered to — from the Cabinet secretary to messengers and "garden girls" (as, to my horror, the women who provided secretarial help were known). Ultimately, of course, they all answered to the Prime Minister, and now that was Tony.

Nothing can describe my mixture of emotions as the door closed behind me: not only awe in the historical sense — the knowledge that everyone from William Pitt to Winston Churchill had been there — but anxiety — that their baton, heavy with responsibility, had now been passed to Tony. There was also an undercurrent of unease. I felt like the unnamed narrator of Daphne du Maurier's *Rebecca* must have when she arrived at Manderley for the first time. As the new Mrs. de Winter, she might have been the mistress of the house on paper, but in reality she was utterly powerless, because she had no idea what she was up against.

As we walked down the corridor lined with staff, I was reminded of the scene from the Hitchcock film of du Maurier's novel: the old house, the servants lined up to greet their gawky, unsophisticated new mistress. And just as at Manderley, where the staff had all previously worked for Rebecca, these people now clapping us in were civil servants who'd been working for a Tory government for years and years, and there must certainly have been some among them who were hoping that our tenure would be short. None of our own people were there. It really felt like walking into the lion's den. Later I realized that it was just as unsettling for them having to deal with us. While Sir Robin Butler, the head of the Civil Service, and Alex Allan, the principal private secretary to the Prime Minister, talked to Tony privately, the kids and I hung round in the corridor outside making faces at each other. After only a few minutes Tony emerged, raised his eyebrows, and took my hand in his. We were off to inspect the accommodations.

We'd been sent the ground plans several months before as part of the standard preelection contact between the Civil Service and the opposition, so to some degree I knew what to expect, though I have always found architects' plans hard to visualize. Then, a few weeks previously, Jonathan had been allowed in to take a look. From what he'd seen, he thought the Number 10 flat would be too small for us, and although Number 11 — traditionally the domain of the Chancellor of the Exchequer — was definitely in need of a lick of paint, it was a much better place for a family. Our first stop, because it was nearer, was Number 10, so recently vacated by the Majors. Jonathan was right. Two bedrooms were a reasonable size, but the other two were very small. The five of us might just have squeezed in, but what about when my mum came to stay? Or Ros, come to that, without whom I could not function? Norma Major had redone the kitchen and knocked two rooms into one, but it, too, was a bit cramped, not helped by having such low ceilings.

The nicest thing about the flat was the bottle of champagne left there for us by the Majors, with a note saying, "Good luck. It's a great job. Enjoy it." A generous gesture and one I wouldn't forget.

Number 11 was the only real option, we decided. It was on three floors, with rooms set round a central staircase. It turned out to be a whole house minus the ground floor, and although the shell was original, it had been gutted and totally rebuilt in the 1960s.

From the outside, Downing Street looks like a sedate Georgian terrace. The frontage, certainly, dates from the seventeenth century, but behind it everything opens out in a way one would never expect.

Once inside, the only sign that these were originally individual residences are the multiple staircases. In 1735 the various individual buildings were connected by long corridors by the Prime Minister Sir Robert Walpole. Directly beneath the grand first-floor reception rooms, overlooking the garden and Horse Guards Parade, are the equally grand Cabinet room and the Prime Minister's private office. Directly above the grand reception rooms are the distinctly ungrand rooms that make up the Number 10 flat.

The black-and-white-marble-floored entrance hall that lies immediately behind the front door is the domain of the custodians, as the doorkeepers are known, and all visitors to Downing Street enter this way before being escorted to their eventual destinations. Go straight ahead, and at the end of a long corridor, you arrive at the Cabinet room and the offices of the Prime Minister and his staff. Turn left, and you are in Number 11, the offices of the Chancellor of the Exchequer, and, beyond that, the press office in Number 12. (What is known as the Number 11 flat actually extends above Number 12.)

We were introduced to this labyrinth of staircases and passages by Carol Allan, the house manager, and John Holroyd, in charge of protocol. They had both been at Downing Street a long time and knew the building well. I told them that I hadn't made up my mind about what we were going to do. Above all, I said, we didn't want to disrupt the children too much, and we certainly didn't want to move their schools. Nicky was in his last term at St. Joan of Arc, so in the back of my mind I was thinking that we would possibly stay in Richmond Crescent at least till the end of term, and maybe we'd move in over the summer.

Apart from the hall, Number 11 had plenty of light, and the rooms were all high ceilinged and generally spacious. As we walked round, I realized that it was a good deal bigger than Richmond Crescent. Yes, it was very old-fashioned — it had last been done up many years before with an unattractive mustard-colored carpet and flocked wallpaper — but we'd already been told it could be redecorated. The worst thing was the haze of cigar smoke that clung to everything. It was like going into a jazz club on a Sunday morning before the cleaners arrived — an all-too-enduring legacy of John Major's last Chancellor.

The children, however, were entranced. They'd already discovered a secret spiral staircase that led directly down to the garden.

And what a garden! "It's as big as the park," I overheard an excited Kathryn telling a friend later. The bedrooms had already been divvied up. Shrieks of "Bags, I have this one!" rang out from upstairs. Euan had gone for one with an enormous desk, only to discover later that once the desk had been removed, the room itself was smaller than his younger brother's. The problem with the bedrooms was the lack of storage, beyond a series of heavy mahogany wardrobes that smelled of mothballs and cedar. My heart sank at the sight of the kitchen. It might have been state-of-the-art in the sixties, but that was then. The sink had ancient faucets you could barely get a kettle under, and everything was incredibly utilitarian and bleak, with a beat-up pine table in the middle.

Then every so often it would hit me: what was I thinking of, complaining about sinks, when our little family was about to embark on an extraordinary voyage? In some ways I was too overwhelmed to take it all in, and I needed the children's excitement to bring home what had really happened and where we were. Tony was Prime Minister! This was Downing Street! Who cared about faucets!

"You've given me food for thought," I told Carol as we made our way down the staircase outside the front door of the flat on the first floor.

"When you know what you want to do, just give me a call," she said. The trouble was that I had no idea what I wanted to do. Tony was anxious to keep everything the same as it was, for both him and the kids. It was barely two years since we'd got Richmond Crescent as we wanted it. Even the idea of going through all that again made my heart sink. And yet I knew that the most important thing was for us all to be together as a family, as we had always been. And although it would involve a lot of work, Number 11 had an amazing amount of space. But it had to be a family decision, and that meant the kids' opinions were vitally important.

By the time we got down from our tour, friends and family were milling around the state dining room, already making inroads into the buffet lunch that had been laid on. The kids, faced with this huge table of food, had gone completely wild. The hubbub was tremendous — adults, children, everyone buzzing — and admonishments to calm down were totally disregarded. The whole building seemed to be ringing with shrieks and laughter, and I remember wondering whether it had ever seen such a day in its entire history.

Outside, the sun continued to shine, and while the children careered around, the bemused and slightly shell-shocked grown-ups sat in the garden, took photographs, and generally marveled at where we were and what had happened. I'd be chatting normally, then suddenly catch someone's eye, and we would both burst into fits of spontaneous laughter. I felt like punching the sky! He had done it! My husband had done it!

Around five it was time to go. After all the pumping of adrenaline and excitement, we had run out of steam, and we simply went home. It was surreal. One moment we were sitting on the terrace outside the Cabinet room at Number 10, and the next moment I was in the kitchen at Richmond Crescent, poking round in the fridge, wondering what to do about supper.

Lying in bed later that night, trying to get to sleep, I thought back over our day: so many extraordinary moments I was determined not to forget. As we'd come out of the audience with the Queen, I'd asked Tony what had happened. "I mean, did you really have to kiss hands?"

"Not exactly," he said. Before he went in, the Lord Chamberlain had explained that actual kissing wasn't required. It was more like "a brushing of lips over her hand." Next thing, Tony was ushered into her presence. Seeing the outstretched hand, he began to move forward, then somehow — feeling both bemused and nervous — he tripped over the edge of the carpet and ended up falling on top of the hand with an ardor that neither he nor Her Majesty was anticipating.

Her composure was quite unruffled, he said, and with a reassuring smile, she told him that he was her tenth Prime Minister and that her first, Winston Churchill, had been in office before Tony was even born.

"Don't worry," I told him, as we settled into the car on our way to Downing Street. "I know that her tenth Prime Minister is going to be as good as the first, even if his hand-kissing technique could do with brushing up."

Though exhausted, we slept not much better than we had the night before. Our bedroom was on the first floor, the bed between the two front windows, and the nonstop racket in the street — police needing to chat and talk every two hours when they changed shifts —

made sleep practically impossible. As I lay there, staring at the ceiling, it became obvious, as it hadn't been before, that staying in our old house wasn't viable if we were to have any privacy at all. Tony couldn't possibly run the country from here, and we didn't want to be separated, which meant that we would all have to move into Downing Street. The security people had made it clear that if we stayed in Richmond Crescent, it would be turned into something resembling a detention center. The glass in all the windows had already been changed, and special curtains had been put up. The road itself was cordoned off with bollards at both ends. It was unfair to expect our neighbors to put up with this. They hadn't asked for any of it.

At around six o'clock a truck arrived, and some men began to dismantle the scaffolding erected for the press. As I lay there, listening to the clanging and banging outside, I thought about the logistics of it all. The best time to do the move, I decided, would be half term, which was in about three weeks.

I can't remember now exactly what time the bell went off, sometime around eight-thirty. Ros was two floors up, still asleep — officially she was off-duty on weekends — and as nobody else was getting it, I pressed the intercom.

"Flower delivery for you, Mrs. Blair." It was one of the policemen.

"Can't you just put them inside the door?"

"'Fraid not. I'm here on my own."

I padded down to the front door and opened it, yawning, hair like a bird's nest, and bleary-eyed.

What awaited me outside was more than a nice bouquet from the governing body of St. Joan of Arc. If the marketing people wanted me to be like the woman in the street, they couldn't have planned it better. The photographer outside my door clicked away, and soon every tabloid editor in the world knew exactly what picture would go on the front page that Sunday. No doubt the photographer made a fortune.

As I shut the door, I remember leaning my forehead against the back of it, my eyes closed, thinking, *Oh, my God, Tony will kill me.* I could just hear him saying, "How could you be so stupid as to go down in your nightdress without even putting on a dressing gown?" In fact, he didn't. He had more pressing matters to attend to. Nevertheless, despite all the effort over the past weeks to turn me into a suitable consort for the Prime Minister, I ended up looking like the madwoman from the attic. (I did object to how my nightdress was mocked, however. It was a perfectly respectable gray cotton nightie — all natural fibers, not remotely cheap and nasty as the press claimed.)

Over breakfast I told the kids how I felt. The business with the flowers had put the final nail in the coffin of any idea I'd clung to of staying where we were. We couldn't. The press would be there the whole time; the entire neighborhood would be disrupted. I told them that I thought we should probably move to Downing Street, and I was wondering about half term.

"Why wait till then?" they chorused. "We've chosen our bedrooms, so why don't we just move in now?" They were very firm. If we did it on Monday, the May bank holiday, they'd be back in school by Tuesday.

I called Carol Allan. She would meet me at Number 10 in an hour, she said. With Nicky and Kathryn safely off to their music lessons, Ros and I left for Downing Street to play musical chairs. The Civil Service considers Number 10 and Number 11 government property and didn't want us to bring our own furniture into the building. This presented problems. The two sofas in the former Chancellor's sitting room were very down-at-heel, and nothing had been touched for years. Knowing that Gordon wasn't going to be using the Majors' flat, I felt quite comfortable about taking what we needed from there. I arranged for a sideboard, some lamps, and two sofas to be brought over, though they were a bit too small. Kathryn inherited the twin beds from the Majors' spare room, complete with Laura Ashley sprigged bedcovers. I wanted each of the kids to have two beds so that friends could stay, and it turned out there were a couple in storage that we could have. The same with desks and wardrobes.

The kitchen cupboards had less to offer in the way of equipment than a holiday cottage. In the short term Ros and I could bring things over from Richmond Crescent. I had not even begun to think about what was going to happen to everything there.

Tony spent the rest of the weekend closeted with Jonathan and Alastair, working out his Cabinet appointments. I tried to make sense of how I was going to move the whole caboodle in on Monday. Carol Allan agreed that they would open the windows and fumigate the rooms before we came in, so that was a start. There was no time to organize a moving van, not that we really needed one; all we were taking was our personal possessions, clothes, the kids' toys, and general bits and pieces, which all went in one of the regular Number 10 vans — what they call a comms wagon, which is used to transport secure telecommunications equipment for the Prime Minister when he's traveling. With the help of Ros, her mum, and her brother, we managed to accomplish all that on Monday morning. John Holroyd came in with a hammer and helped the kids put some of their posters and pictures on the wall, so it was quite sweet. But Number 11 was not set up for a family; that would take several years.

There was one near disaster. Kathryn and her friend Bella Mostyn-Williams, having decided that her wardrobe was exactly like the one in *The Lion, the Witch and the Wardrobe*, climbed in looking for adventure Narnia-style. An almighty shudder echoed through the building as the whole vast edifice crashed to the ground, with them within. Fortunately neither girl was injured, but if it hadn't been clear before, it was now: this was no way to furnish a kid's room.

That Monday evening Bill and Katy Blair came round bearing their usual gift of Chinese takeout. Over the following ten years, they never appeared without it. The next day being Tony's forty-fourth birthday, we squashed round that terrible table and raised our glasses to him and to the first night in our new home. And, incredibly, it was already beginning to feel like ours. The party had given us a framed poster, and the kids had stuck it up in pride of place beside the sink: "New Labour. Britain just got better." And it was true — we felt it in the streets, in the smiles of the people, in the air of jauntiness. It was as if a great weight had suddenly been lifted from everyone's shoulders.

The following morning, a huge birthday cake arrived courtesy of the *Mirror*, and somebody sent an even more enormous bouquet of red roses, about 350 of them, one for every Labour MP.

I didn't see them delivered, as for me it was business as usual, this time in the Court of Appeal. It was a big case about a European Union measure that protects employees when their companies are bought out. The reporters' bench was unusually full. When I stood up to open the case, I remarked how gratifying it was to see so much press interest in the technicalities of the Transfer of Undertakings Protection of Employment Regulations. Some of the reporters were there for the right reasons — it was an important case in terms of industrial relations. But most were political reporters, all wanting to see what I would do. (They lasted about fifteen minutes.)

Little did I know as I stood there discussing the finer points of employment law that a bombshell awaited me when I got back to Downing Street.

At the end of 1996, when the move to Number 10 became a probability rather than a possibility, the accountant had suggested that I undertake an income and expenditure exercise, such as you might do when applying for a mortgage. The results weren't exactly encouraging. Whereas Tony's income would go up, mine would go down. I didn't know exactly how being the Prime Minister's wife would affect the number of cases I could take, but it would certainly be lower. And with the official duties I'd have to carry out, I knew I'd have less time to devote to my career.

We'd been told that living in Downing Street would be treated as payment in kind and would, therefore, be taxed. Yet we still had a big mortgage to pay on Richmond Crescent, plus the loan I'd taken out for the refurbishment. I didn't want to give up our home. I had no idea how long Tony would be Prime Minister, so I needed to make sure that we had a home to return to if Labour lost the next election. On the plus side, I knew that MPs and ministers were about to get a 26 percent salary raise, which Parliament had approved a few months earlier and which was due to take effect following the 1997 election. With that increase, I decided, we could probably manage.

Then Gordon threw a wrench in the works.

At the first Cabinet meeting of the new Labour government, the new Chancellor announced that he was not going to take the salary increase, and he put pressure on the others not to accept it either. Tony told me as soon as he got back to the flat. I couldn't believe it; all my calculations had been based on the increase. This wasn't an optional perk: Parliament had endorsed it. Ministers had been specifically mentioned: "We believe that additional recognition of the job weight of the Prime Minister and Cabinet ministers is long overdue." As the Leader of the Opposition, William Hague, did take his increase, this meant that Tony was now earning less than Hague.

I remember sitting at the kitchen table at Number 10, putting my head in my hands, and staring at the now completely redundant financial breakdown, as Tony tried to calm me down. But I wouldn't be calmed down: How dare Gordon do that? What did he know about financial commitments? He was a bachelor living on his own in a flat with a small mortgage. Tony admitted it was a problem, but every problem, he said, has a solution — I just had to find one. He wanted to get on with the business of governing.

Despite my reluctance, it seemed like the obvious solution was to rent out the house in Richmond Crescent to cover the mortgage. But it wasn't that simple. First, the advice was that this should be done through the Foreign Office. As I would later discover when we needed a new nanny, we could no longer go through the *Northern Echo* or *Lady*. From now on, we could use Civil Service–vetted agencies only. It was a security issue.

"Your problem," the Foreign Office official explained, "is that the people we deal with don't want to live in Islington. They want to live in Kensington or Knightsbridge." Surely, I thought, there might be a junior official who wouldn't mind slumming it in our neighborhood. The Foreign Office came to have a look.

"If you're going to rent out this house, it'll have to be completely redecorated, because it's not suitable for the sort of families it would be suitable for." I was entering the world of doublespeak.

Okay, I decided, we'd rent it privately. "Forget it," said Alastair. When the Tory Chancellor of the Exchequer Norman Lamont had rented out his house, the tenant had been revealed as some sort of Miss Whiplash — manna from heaven for the tabloids.

"So what do we do?" I asked him. "We can't afford to go on paying the mortgage. It's as simple as that."

"Why don't you have a word with Michael," he suggested.

Michael Levy was the Labour Party's fund-raiser in chief, and also a friend and a successful businessman. If anyone would know what to do, he would.

Michael had been very good to us during the run-up to the election, letting the kids use the swimming pool at his house in north London, just to give them a break from Richmond Crescent.

"Sell," he said. No other options? "No. Sell."

We put it on the market, got an offer in fairly quickly, and accepted it. I didn't want to leave our home, and I worried about losing our footing on the property ladder. After the sale of the house, we had £200,000 left, so I suggested putting the money into another, smaller property. No. As Prime Minister, Tony was not allowed to have any investments, and if we bought a house without living in it, this would be classed as an investment. We were obliged to put the money into a blind trust, with me as the sole beneficiary.

The one bright spot on the housing front was Chequers. When Tony first became Leader of the Opposition, I remember Jill Craigie, Michael Foot's wife, coming up to me at some do and saying, "I don't envy you much, but I do envy you Chequers." As the wife of a Cabinet minister in the last Labour government, she had been there. With that kind of recommendation, I couldn't wait to see it.

The Friday of our first visit, the auguries did not look good. The curator whom Mrs. Thatcher had chosen to run Chequers had been a career naval officer — bizarrely, Chequers is officially considered a ship and is staffed by naval and air force personnel — and we'd heard that she had no experience with children. Sadly, she had taken over from her predecessor just as Mrs. Thatcher was ousted, and Mrs. Thatcher's successors, the Majors, hardly ever went there. When they did, they found things rather more regimented than they were used to. Meals had to be at regular times, and the curator believed in staying up until the Majors went to bed, which they found less than relaxing. It didn't sound to me like the kind of system that would go down too well with our kids, and I wondered how she would cope with having children running round the place, let alone going a bit wild.

John Holroyd did his best to allay my fears. "We very much want you to use Chequers," he said. "It hasn't been used recently as much as one would hope, so staff morale has gone down as a result, and I do assure you, they're all looking forward enormously to your coming. While it's true that the curator isn't used to having children around, there is no reason to think they won't charm her as they are already charming everyone here. Unfortunately," he continued, "she won't be able to welcome you herself this weekend, as she's injured her back." (In fact, the injury was serious enough that she never returned.)

The moment we arrived, driving up through the Victory Gate, with this historic Tudor pile standing right ahead of us, I couldn't believe it. We left the children outside kicking a soccer ball, relishing the acres and acres of space, while Linda, the housekeeper, showed us around: all ancient paneling, gorgeous oil paintings, ornate carvings, mullioned windows, and rooms big enough to run races in.

As we went back to the children, Tony began shaking his head. "We can't possibly bring the kids into this place," he said. "They'll wreck it." From outside we heard the sounds of squabbling and decided they needed to walk off the excess adrenaline. Grass led away from all sides of the house, apart from the front, into woodland — wonderful and unsettling at the same time. By now the kids were really playing up, and Tony began to raise his voice, shouting at them to "just behave!" Suddenly he looked round and saw that we were being followed by the protection officers. And he went stiff with frustration and bewilderment.

"I don't believe it," he said through clenched teeth. "I can't even yell at my own kids, because the police will hear." Never again would Tony be able to walk anywhere without being followed, albeit at a discreet distance.

By the end of the weekend, it was obvious to us that Chequers was a good place to be. There was an indoor swimming pool. Did we want to use it? Under Mrs. Thatcher it had been drained because she didn't swim. The Majors had used it, and in fact Norma had learned to swim there, but because they hardly ever went, the heating had been turned off. Our answer was a resounding yes.

The pool had been presented to Chequers by Walter Annenberg, the American Ambassador to Britain, in memory of Richard Nixon's visit in October 1970. It's built like an orangery, with a glass roof and glass sides that open completely in the summer. But because it's basically an indoor pool, you can swim there all year round. As far as the kids were concerned, it was complete heaven.

For ten years Chequers became our refuge. Although it might look like a stately home, inside the atmosphere is far more comfortable and domesticated than the outside view suggests. We would all breathe a huge sigh of relief when, on a Friday evening, the Jaguar turned through the gate into the east courtyard. Linda or Ann, her successor, would come out to greet us, and the children would run in, throw off their coats, and rush off to their bedrooms, or to see the rabbits, or to search the kitchen for treats they could scrounge.

Chequers was the one place where Tony could be just a dad and kick a ball round with his children like any other father. It was an illusion, of course. As we were quickly learning, police and security people were always round, but at least at Chequers, we didn't see them. At least there, we had the space to lead a normal life.

CHAPTER 21

Special Relationship

The first official visitors we hosted at Downing Street were, appropriately enough, the Clintons. It was barely a month after Tony took office, and I remember everyone being very excited, because everyone wanted to meet Bill: the kids, the nanny, my sister, and my mother. For the benefit of the press, we greeted the most powerful political couple in the world outside on the front steps. I had a special outfit made by Ronit Zilkha: "nonthreatening" was the brief from the office. Heaven forbid that I should look like a career woman. The office was terrified that I might turn into Hillary Clinton.

The Downing Street administration also had concerns about Hillary, albeit on a more pragmatic level. She would need somewhere to "park" herself, they said. The Number 11 downstairs toilet was deemed unsuitable for the wife of the American President. Only the bathroom off Ros's room met the standard, the former Chancellor's guest room being the sole part of the flat that had been decorated in the past ten years.

At least by the time Hillary took a look round, Number 11 had improved noticeably in terms of the jazz-club haze. When I recounted to her my run-ins with Downing Street over the most modest improvements (such as built-in wardrobes for the kids and a new kitchen), she was amazed. In America, she told me, the incoming President's wife had the choice of keeping the White House the way it was or redecorating. There was a charitable fund entirely devoted to its refurbishment, for which the First Lady would actively seek donations — and get them. When I suggested to the Cabinet secretary that we might do something similar to refurbish the state rooms in Downing Street or Chequers and save the taxpayers money, the answer was no.

Rather than some overly formal dinner in Downing Street, we decided to take the golden couple out to a restaurant — a far more personal way, Tony felt, of getting to know them. The Pont de la Tour has a fantastic position on the river, overlooking Tower Bridge, part of a refurbished warehouse complex. As we arrived, people were hanging from apartment windows and packing the open walkways to cheer both Tony and Bill, who was a huge international superstar.

Bill Clinton is an incredibly sociable person who loves ideas and loves talking, but who only really gets going after ten. If the evening takes off, you are guaranteed a fantastically interesting discussion, though you might regret it the next day. That evening did take off, the first of many we would enjoy together, and like so many others, it went on far longer than anyone expected. I found Hillary Clinton to be much warmer than her public persona might suggest. She has tremendous dignity and cares passionately about her and Bill's joint project, which is to make the United States once again the land of opportunity not just for the advantaged, but for everyone.

Part of the restaurant had been sectioned off for us, though it had been agreed that we would order from the ordinary menu. What we ate, however, would not be revealed — at least that was the intention. The next morning, however, "Cherie Eats Foie Gras" was front-page news. Apart from the usual eye rolling from Alastair, the result was a torrent of abusive letters from animal lovers. The venom they unleashed shook me to the core. There were so many letters that we decided to set up a standard reply.

Until this incident I had replied to every letter personally. Indeed, before we moved into Downing Street, Fiona and Roz Preston had shared the job of looking after me, paid for by the Labour Party, and one of the first things we'd done on arrival was to see what Downing Street could offer in terms of secretarial support. After a great struggle, Norma Major had persuaded the government to fund a secretary for her four days a week. Like so much in Downing Street, we were never told what might be available; it was up to us to find out.

Nor were we told what things cost. Chequers came with a full complement of staff, yet there were charges that would arrive out of the blue, such as the cost of laundering napkins. It all depended on who had used the napkins. If it had been family or official visitors, the laundering was paid for. If the napkins had been used by somebody not on the official list, we were billed. The system was confusing, to say the least.

We had a nanny for the children — Ros and later Jackie, who succeeded her in 1998 — and a housecleaner for three hours every day. I remember laughing when Hillary told me that the White House had four chefs. At Number 11, just as in Richmond Crescent, the nanny would usually shop, and she and I would share the cooking. On Sunday nights I would get back from Chequers loaded down, like a teenager returning to college after a weekend at home, with dishes that the cook there had prepared (for which we paid) to help me through our busy Monday and Tuesday nights, when we had receptions.

No previous Prime Minister's wife had had a full-time career. No previous Prime Minister's wife had had school-age children living at home. Since Euan was born, I'd had two demanding jobs: mother and barrister. Now I had three, and juggling three balls is not the same as juggling two. My role as the Prime Minister's wife might have not been official — as I was never allowed to forget — but it was time-consuming and important, and I had no intention of letting Tony down. We were in this together.

When the animal rights letters arrived, I asked if we might get help answering them from the garden girls, so called because their office on the lower ground floor overlooks the garden. My request was turned down. I was reminded that their role was to service the Prime Minister's office, not his wife. Then I asked about ordering some Downing Street notepaper. They agreed to a heading reading "from the office of Mrs Cherie Blair, QC" but wouldn't sanction "from the office of Cherie Booth, QC." In Downing Street terms, I was Mrs. Blair, the head garden girl explained.

"Agreed," I said, "but I am not Cherie Blair, QC. You could search with a magnifying glass, but no such person exists in the annals of the English Bar." A compromise was eventually reached. I could use the address, but not the crest. If I wanted to use the crest, I would have to be Mrs. Blair.

Now, more than ten years later, I no longer feel the need to make the point. But in 1997 I felt I was hanging on to my identity by the thinnest of threads. I was entering a system that seemed to proclaim, "You are a nonperson except in as far as you are an appendage to the PM."

What is certainly true is that the garden girls were under severe strain. When John Major was in Downing Street, letters to the Prime Minister ran around five thousand year. Once Tony arrived, the trickle became a flood, and the garden girls simply couldn't cope. Not surprisingly, given the pressure they were under, the occasional mistake crept in. One example was a letter from a school for the deaf asking if Tony could visit the school. Although the letter had been written by the children themselves, they had received only a two-line standard reply. As I was known to have an interest in special-needs schools, the head wrote to me, enclosing copies of the original request and Downing Street's reply. She accepted that the Prime Minister was busy, she said, but the children had made such an effort that maybe they deserved a better response. I couldn't have agreed more.

From then on, it was agreed that any letters from children would be passed on to my office, so that even if Tony couldn't send them a personal reply, I would. We ended up with a vast correspondence, as I soon discovered that the more you answer people, the more they tend to write back.

Within a matter of weeks, we attended our first international summit, the G7 (now G8). This annual meeting is hosted by one of the seven (now eight, including Russia) most powerful nations in the world — Canada, France, Germany, Italy, Japan, the United Kingdom, and the United States — and in 1997 it was America's turn. Thus Denver, Colorado, was the setting for Tony's first major appearance on the world stage. For me, flying over on the Concorde was a dream come true. (I still find it incredible that some way hasn't been found to keep this masterpiece of engineering in the air.) The pilot and his crew were clearly the best of the best, and they invited me to go into the cockpit as it landed — a real privilege and something I will never forget.

The welcoming event was a country-and-western concert. In the presence of assembled Denver worthies, the ceremony began with

197

the various leaders and their wives being trundled onto the stage in order of protocol and time in office. Tony, being the newest, was last.

"The Prime Minister of Great Britain and Northern Ireland, the Right Honourable Tony Blair, MP, and Mrs. Cherie Blair," the unseen speaker announced. As the spotlight picked us out, we walked onto the stage to thunderous applause. It was a totally surreal experience, similar to the one we'd had a few hours earlier as we'd walked down the steps from the Concorde, and the welcoming band had struck up "God Save the Queen."

The G7/G8 is unusual among summits in that the wives (or husbands) are an intrinsic part of the event, and a separate, parallel program is organized by the host wife. As the G7 the following year would be ours to host, Tony and I were making the most of this opportunity to see how it worked. Tony had his team, and I had Fiona, although she hated flying and hated even more leaving her daughter Grace, who was still a toddler. My hairdresser, André, was also with me, though Alastair had made it clear that his presence was to be kept strictly under wraps. He hadn't even been allowed to come on the same flight. We were lucky he made the trip, however; it was André who vetoed the cowgirl outfit, complete with tasseled boots and cowboy hat, that greeted me on arrival.

"You are *not* wearing that, Cherie," he said as soon as he saw it. And he was right. It was basically a Halloween costume with what André described as a tablecloth for a skirt. Tony's outfit was equally over-the-top, but he decided that the shirt was bearable, so he wore that with a pair of his own jeans. Unfortunately mine was an all-or-nothing situation, and to go out representing my country looking like Doris Day cracking her whip on the Deadwood stage just wasn't appropriate. The Denver stage would have to make do with smart casual.

In spite of Alastair's warnings that André should maintain a low profile, somebody saw him. Alastair's response was that Mrs. Blair was paying for her hairdresser herself, as indeed I was. Then the story became spendthrift Cherie, chucking money away like nobody's business. It was a steep learning curve: whatever I did, it seemed, I couldn't win. It was the twentieth-century equivalent of the stocks: anything could be thrown at me with impunity.

The spouses' program started on day two. I set off with the other wives (there were no husbands at this time) on one of those trains that you often see in Westerns, complete with viewing platform at the back. As we chugged up into the Rockies to gaze at the magnificent scenery, I was struck by how Hillary worked the crowds lined up along the embankments. Suddenly, something caught my eye, and at the same time Hillary said, "I think we should go back in now." As we all trooped back inside, I mouthed, "Did you see what I saw?" She laughed and nodded. A man had "mooned" the passing train, but apparently none of the other ladies had noticed.

A line-dancing exhibition put on by a local pensioners' group awaited us at our destination, and once again I saw how Hillary took the initiative, introducing us with an off-the-cuff speech. Even then I realized I was watching a master at work.

What I would have done without André I do not know. Although for a visit of this length, the Prime Minister always travels with an entourage of policy advisers, press officers, duty clerks, garden girls, 'tecs, and comms (communications) people, they were there to help him conduct his business. Their sole contribution to the domestic side of things was a note saying what time the luggage had to be ready for collection. In this regard, that last morning in Denver, André found me in a state of panic and began to help, folding Tony's shirts, collecting the little piles of things he would take out of his pockets at night, and sorting out his suits, while I scrabbled round trying to retrieve odd shoes and socks from under the bed.

Next stop was Washington, where Tony and Bill were having bilateral talks. When I unpacked, I realized there was nothing he could wear; it all needed to be professionally pressed or re-ironed. This time André wasn't there to help: Alastair had forbidden him to travel on the same plane, and he'd had to fly via Chicago. In the end the furor over André was so intense that Alastair banned him from coming on the next overseas trip. I would have to make do with local hairdressers like everybody else, he said.

Hillary asked if I'd be interested in seeing how she did things. By this time she had been First Lady for five years, so she and her staff had a huge amount of experience. Although there were obviously big differences between Downing Street and the White House, I thought I could learn from the way she handled the workload.

Her office was situated in the East Wing, where an entire department was devoted to invitations and menus. Being invited to the

White House, she explained, was seen as an honor: invitations became like family heirlooms, lasting long after the dinner was forgotten. This hive of activity was known as the calligraphy department. Everything was printed from copper plates, and envelopes were addressed by hand in the most beautiful italic script.

"But it must be so labor-intensive," I said, looking round at the mass of heads bent over their work. She explained that most of them were volunteers, old and young, who worked in the White House for the love of it. Some of them stayed for years, serving each president faithfully, like the person I met whose job it was to answer the mail addressed to Socks, the Clintons' cat. Others were interns, young college graduates who spent around six months working in the White House solely for the experience. This system (pre-Monica Lewinsky) seemed an entirely good idea, and on my return to Downing Street, I put forward a proposal to the Cabinet office about the possibility of using interns as a way of coping with the rising tide of correspondence and associated work that we were struggling to deal with. This proposal was adopted, and interns were brought into a number of departments, though after a few years it became apparent that it wasn't really saving the government that much money. Although the interns weren't being paid, we had to have people to supervise them and plan everything. The program was stopped in 1999.

My tour round the First Lady's office was incredibly useful. Hillary showed me the White House gifts they would take with them when traveling. These were not the gifts that would be exchanged on official visits, but smaller things, such as White House key rings, given to people who had generally been helpful. None of these gifts was very costly, just a token that was much appreciated. She also told me that she was planning a series of lectures in the White House, which would start in 1998, to commemorate the millennium. I later did the same.

Her final piece of advice would resonate the longest. "You've got to recognize," she said, "that you're not going to please everyone the whole time, and you're certainly not going to please the press, and therefore you should just do what feels right to you. And so long as you feel it's right for you, then don't get too upset about what other people say."

*　　　*　　　*

At the end of July 1997, after 150 years, Hong Kong was being handed back to China. It was both a political and a royal occasion, and it involved a mass exodus of senior personnel from Britain, including the Prince of Wales. As a result, there was a problem of transport. The Queen had the royal yacht *Britannia*, and she also had an aircraft. As the plane was nearing the end of its life, there had been talk of getting a new one, to be shared with the Prime Minister. This was eventually shelved for PR reasons, and from then on planes had to be chartered from British Airways (BA). In this case, however, Prince Charles would be returning on the royal yacht, which was already moored in Hong Kong, so it was decided that the Prime Minister would use the royal plane. The Prince would travel out with Robin Cook, the Foreign Secretary, on a chartered BA plane. (This was the occasion when Prince Charles famously was obliged to travel business class, as Cook, his wife, and Foreign Office officials had commandeered the first-class cabin. In a highly amusing, if ill-advised, epistle to friends, the Prince later complained about how small and cramped he'd found it.)

The royal plane was old and slow. The good news was that the front cabin could be transformed into a bedroom with two beds. The bad news was that it took nearly twice as long to get to Hong Kong as it normally did, as we had to refuel in Vladivostok. When we got out to stretch our legs, we were instructed not to move beyond a small area round the plane — not that we would have wanted to, it being ringed by Russian soldiers toting machine guns and looking distinctly menacing.

As always in these circumstances, as we came in to land in Hong Kong, there was a queue for the bathroom. By now I knew that the red carpet and a slew of photographers would be waiting, and I needed to look the part. Carole had worked out all my outfits, including the arrival one, which had been brought on board in a suit carrier. Suddenly, it was "Cabin crew, seats for landing," and I was still in the bathroom making myself look respectable. There was nothing to do but just get on with it, I decided. At the moment of touchdown, I was standing on one leg, my bum hard up against the folding door and my other leg on the toilet seat, desperately trying to pull on my tights before emerging in the official outfit for the walk down the steps.

On the way back from that trip, Alastair said, "We can't do that again." André's presence, he belatedly realized, had certain advantages. By the time the plane landed, I would be appropriately dressed and immaculately coiffed, no matter how long the flight or befuddled my head. No hair dryers were allowed on board, but André became a deft hand with gas-heated curling tongs.

As the handover ceremony began, just before midnight, the heavens opened, and I watched in admiration as Prince Charles began reading out a message from the Queen, which, thanks to the tropical downpour, was disintegrating in his hands. He was standing directly in front of me, his white tropical suit becoming increasingly diaphanous, which afforded me an interesting perspective on the future monarch. At midnight the flag of the People's Republic of China and the regional flag of Hong Kong were raised simultaneously to the unfamiliar strains of the Chinese national anthem, and as the People's Liberation Army goose-stepped their way into the hall, I felt a shiver run up my spine.

CHAPTER 22

Journeys

Princess Diana had been determined not to lose touch with Tony. Shortly after we moved into Number 10, Maggie Rae let us know that the Princess was keen to see him again, and she wanted to bring William and Harry to Chequers. Alex Allan, Tony's principal private secretary, nearly had apoplexy when he found out.

It would be quite wrong, he said, for Tony to see Diana before he'd officially seen Prince Charles. So sometime in those few weeks, Tony did in fact see the Prince, and Diana and William duly turned up at Chequers one Sunday in early July.

Over lunch she talked again about wanting to play a more prominent role in public life. She was determined that William be given a normal, modern upbringing, to make him, as she put it, "fit to be king."

Again she was very relaxed, this time chatting with my mum and being lovely with Kathryn. She talked about how she would like to have more children and how she longed for a little girl. We sat there on the grass, with Kathryn tucked between Diana's knees, watching the three boys and Tony play soccer on the north lawn. Later, when she and Tony went for a walk, William came with us to the swimming pool, where my lot all had a great time showing off. William was really sweet to Kathryn. She was totally in awe, not because he was a prince, but because he was a handsome fifteen-year-old, and she was only nine.

The afternoon was deemed a success, relaxed and normal, and in the Blair household Princess Diana was regarded as a good thing.

That summer we went to Tuscany for our vacation, staying at a friend's house, and had the usual jolly, relaxing time. Nothing had really changed, we told ourselves, as Ros's swimming gala got under way. Yes, we had to pose for the press at the beginning of the trip — for which it agreed to leave us in peace for the rest of the time — and yes, the garden girls were somewhere in the village and the 'tecs were somewhere in the shadows, but we could forget about them. Or at least try to.

Arriving back in England at the end of August, we went straight to Myrobella. The following weekend was the annual Prime Minister's visit to Balmoral, so we had a few days to relax. The Prime Minister is never really on vacation, however. The *Mail on Sunday* was threatening to publish the name of a British spy in some far-flung part of the world, and Tony became convinced that if his name was revealed, the guy would be killed.

That Saturday night we went to bed in the hope that Alastair had managed to sort it out, but at around three in the morning the phone rang. I have a vague memory of it ringing somewhere out of reach, then I drifted back into a deep sleep. The next thing I heard was the intercom buzzing outside our bedroom. As Tony rushed to the landing, I thought, *Oh, God. The Mail has done it. It's printed the spy's name, and he's been killed.*

A minute later he was back, as white as a sheet. It was the police, he said. There had been an accident. "It's Diana." The bell on our bedside phone hadn't been working, which was why we hadn't heard it. He picked up the receiver and called the duty clerk in Downing Street.

I watched him as he listened, saying nothing.

"A car crash in Paris," he said eventually. "She's in a coma. They don't think she'll pull through."

It was awful. I saw her sitting there on the grass, hugging her knees, only a few weeks back, and thought how full of life she'd been, talking about wanting to have more kids.

Finally the call nobody wanted. All I heard was Tony repeating, "I can't believe this. I can't believe this." We were to say nothing to anyone. It would be announced to the press shortly.

He was shocked and genuinely upset. During what remained of the night, Tony was on the phone, watching television, or doing both. There were so many things to think about. There was the issue of the photographers, but he didn't want to make a knee-jerk response. He didn't know whether he should speak to the Queen or to Prince Charles.

When the kids woke up, we told them what had happened. They were so upset, because they felt they knew her, and they liked her.

Tony agreed with Alastair that he should make a statement before morning service. Alastair was usually anti anything that involved the church or God, but on this occasion even he agreed it might be appropriate. Diana's death had sent a shudder through the nation, and Tony needed to say something to express what people were feeling.

St. John Fisher, the Catholic church in Sedgefield, was deemed inappropriate for his statement, as there was nowhere for the press to stand. So we went to St. Mary Magdalene in Trimdon, where Lily Burton, John's wife, played the organ. By the time we arrived, the television cameras were in position. Tony delivered his statement and, it's fair to say, caught the mood of the nation with his observation "She was the people's princess."

We returned to London that night and got Terry to drive us past Buckingham Palace to see the flowers that were already piling up round the base of the gates. Back in Downing Street, we opened a book of condolences, which everyone signed.

Now, of course, the film *The Queen* has somehow become the official record of that extraordinary week, but it wasn't quite like that. For example, from a pedantic perspective, the way that Number 10 is portrayed in the film is completely wrong, not to mention the way Tony and I are portrayed. (I never swear, and Tony is a good deal taller than Michael Sheen, the actor who plays him.) But there are more serious points to be made.

For a start, I never felt there was any opposition from Buckingham Palace to what Tony was suggesting; in fact he had been asked to become involved in the arrangements, for both the return of the princess's body and the funeral. The royal family's main concern over those first few days was to protect the boys, because they were so young and so upset and the family really didn't want them exposed to anything more. They weren't thinking beyond that. They just wanted to pull together as a family and didn't see why they should share their grief with the rest of the world. And in a sense, why should they have? I think they hoped that they could just get on with it — accept what had happened, do what had to be done.

I think that's what Tony really wanted, too, but as the days went by, it became apparent that this wouldn't be enough.

When we had first arrived at Number 10, we were told of detailed plans that existed in the event of the death of the Queen Mother. The protocol people had it all set out, exactly what was to happen and when. Tony and I even had to take suitable black outfits with us on holiday every year in case she died. And now, with the death of Princess Diana, they were treating this as a similar event. Their main concern was that the plan should be carried out with all due deference to precedent and protocol, including the business about how Diana wasn't Her Royal Highness — even in death, that had to be observed. When the body was flown back to England, the question arose of who was going to meet it. Tony suggested that he do so, and the Queen agreed. But then Prince Charles decided that he wanted to go, although the protocol people clearly would rather he didn't.

The last remaining question was the flag. Protocol decreed that it should be flown at half-mast only when the sovereign dies. Princess Diana was not the sovereign, QED.

The business of who should be invited to the funeral was another protocol issue, yet it seemed important to Tony that Diana's charities be given priority over foreign dignitaries, and even members of the government, who had had no involvement with her. I don't believe the family themselves had much to do with this scrabbling and squabbling. They were really too upset to do anything except hold themselves and the children together. Of course Tony did talk to the Queen, but she's a reserved sort of person, and from my understanding, it was less her personally than the system that was creating the difficulties.

Throughout it all, Tony believed that as Prime Minister, his priority was to make sure that all this didn't damage the monarchy, that the royal family got through unscathed, and he succeeded.

For obvious reasons, the traditional Balmoral weekend didn't happen that year. Instead we were invited for lunch. It was very lowkey, just the Queen and Prince Philip and some old family friends, with the conversation revolving around agriculture, stag hunting, and fishing. Sitting there, I thought, *This is really weird. Yesterday, at the lunch in Number 10 following the funeral, there I was sitting next to Hillary Clinton and Queen Noor of Jordan, talking about current affairs, and here I am today with our head of state talking about the price of sheep.*

No mention was made of Princess Diana or of the previous day's events. The Queen and Prince Philip were very kind, however. The Queen loves driving, and that afternoon she drove us in her Range Rover on a tour round the Balmoral estate, with the Queen providing a running commentary, talking about the landscape that she had known since she was a girl.

At one point I made a real faux pas, butting in when the Queen was talking to somebody else. We had been given a list of instructions of what to do and how to behave, but what with one thing and another, the rule that you talk to the Queen only when the Queen talks to you had slipped my mind. It never would again: one of the courtiers gave me a look I will never forget.

That winter I learned that Tony's driver Sylvie had breast cancer. Not that it stopped her from living. Motorbikes had always been her thing — there was always a specialist magazine in the glove compartment of the Jaguar — and shortly after the diagnosis, she went out and bought a Ducati, the ultimate Italian bike. Then, on December 3, came news of a tragic accident. Sylvie was in a collision with a truck and didn't survive. We went to her funeral a week later, and Tony spoke for everyone who knew her.

For both of us, the people we work with are central to our lives. This is nothing to do with politics — although it should be. I never forget that my grandma worked as a housecleaner, and I never want anybody to be treated as she was treated in Blundellsands. What is important is not what people do for a living, but that they are treated with respect.

Christmas 1997 was our first at Chequers. Everybody came to us, as they had at Myrobella, and in some ways it was just the same, although on a much bigger scale, starting with the tree. At about twenty feet tall, it took several people just to get it in the front door. Its home was the corner of the Great Hall, and by the time Christmas Eve arrived, it was decorated and surrounded by the usual array of colorful presents. With all that, and the kids' stockings hanging up beside the great fireplace, it's hard to imagine there could be anywhere more perfect to spend Christmas.

Rituals developed over the ten years we were there. We still went to midnight Mass, and there was still the usual early-morning chaos as in any family with young children. We paid a visit to the police bothy, beside the entrance, before lunch to hand over our presents for the officers. Then it was more presents and champagne for the staff on duty, including, at my insistence, a few carols to get us in the mood. Finally, our cook Alan served his wonderful lunch. This was one definite change in the proceedings from Myrobella: my turkey routine was no longer needed. Alan's Christmas puddings were in a class of their own. As early as October, the children would help him prepare both the puddings and the cake, everyone taking their turn stirring the huge bowl of sticky mixture.

That first December, however, Alan came to me very perturbed.

"Whatever is the matter, Alan? Why so down in the mouth?"

"Number Ten has said I can't have the usual Christmas turkey," he said. Every year, he told me, representatives of the British Turkey Federation would turn up at Downing Street with a huge bird to be given to charity, and a photograph would be taken of them presenting it to the Prime Minister. They would also present a smaller bird for use by the family and staff on Christmas Day; this was the one that was sent down to Alan. It turned out that Alastair had seen this in the schedule and vetoed it. His worst nightmare, he said, was having a photograph of Tony and a turkey, looking foolish, on the front cover of *Private Eye*, Britain's leading satirical magazine. As I was quite used to looking foolish by then, I offered myself up as an alternative. Luckily the Turkey Federation agreed, so that became a regular fixture on my Advent calendar, and Alan got his turkey.

The plan had been for Tony and me to go away on our own — a week in the Seychelles — just after Boxing Day, the British holiday celebrated the day after Christmas. Everything was organized. My mum would look after the kids, and then Ros would take over for the last few days. It didn't happen. In the end I couldn't bear the thought of being without them, so we all went: Tony and me, my mum, and three extremely lucky kids. We had a wonderful time, despite the fact that the press had a field day when it discovered that twenty years earlier, the villa we were staying in had been used as a location for the infamous soft-porn movie *Emmanuelle*.

In January 1998 the Monica Lewinsky scandal finally broke, and my heart bled for Hillary Clinton, coming on top, as it did, of the Paula Jones sexual harassment suit. Inevitably I thought back to all those young interns and our guided tour of the West Wing by the President himself, of the Oval Office and the little room off it with the photocopier. My reaction was basically *Oh, Bill, how could you?*

From the young woman's point of view, I can quite see how it happened. Bill Clinton is a tremendously charismatic man, who is able to mesmerize almost everybody he meets and make them feel that he is totally interested in them and what they are saying, which is clearly not always the case. As for him, I thought he was bloody stupid.

Just a few weeks later, we were due in Washington for Tony's first formal visit as head of government. If I had been impressed by Hillary before, I was doubly impressed by her now. Dignity is not the word.

Yet I could see for myself how angry she was with him, not just for humiliating her, but for jeopardizing their joint project, and I could also see how desperately he was trying to win back her approval. The shining light in all this was Chelsea. She is a fantastic young woman, incredibly sensible, intelligent, and talented, and very much her own person, with her feet firmly on the ground. I think that says something about the parenting they've both given her. In many ways she reminds me of Tony's brother, Bill, one of those people who was always grown-up, even when he was a boy. Chelsea is terribly reliable, and you know exactly where you are with her. During this time she was a very important link between her parents. I think the fact that Chelsea was both supportive of her mum, understanding how she was feeling, and yet able to forgive her dad was a very important part of why they stayed together.

People have wondered whether Tony or I felt ourselves placed in a difficult situation with them, given our Christian beliefs. The same thing had been asked a few months earlier when Robin Cook, Tony's Foreign Secretary, was outed by the press as being involved in an extramarital affair. The answer in both cases is no. Obviously we both believe in marriage. Once that ring is on your finger and the promises are made before God, you should be faithful. But how people conduct their lives is ultimately their own business, and as far as Bill Clinton is concerned, a British Prime Minister is never going to undermine an American President. As for me, I was never even tempted to raise the subject with him — nothing to do with him being President of the United States. It wasn't me he had betrayed, and with my father's track record, I am not unused to men's infidelity.

I did, however, discuss it with Hillary. In her view, the way the right wing relentlessly pursued the affair was all part of a wider attempt by their enemies to discredit Bill. The most important aspect, she said, was not to let it undermine the presidency. So on a political, strategic level, that was the line they took. On a personal level, however, there was no doubt that she was furious and hurt.

The idea that men just can't help behaving like that is nonsense. It's a myth that actually leads to a lot of mischief in the world. It's why women are stuck behind burkas. I don't for a second believe that men are inflamed by the slightest glimpse of an available body. Uncontrollable sexual urges are nothing of the sort. Of course men can control them, just as women can. What I find particularly worrying is that so often these situations involve the powerful boss and the vulnerable young woman.

When Tony was still Leader of the Opposition, I was approached in chambers for help by Catherine Laylle. Her children, ages seven and nine, had been abducted by their German father, and in a breach of all the conventions, the German courts had done nothing to help her get them back. Sadly, I could do little for her at the time. Later she sent me a book she had written about her experiences. And imagine my surprise when, in 1998, I met the newly appointed British Ambassador to the United States, Christopher Meyer, and his wife in Washington.

"You probably don't remember me," she said. It was Catherine. She was determined to ensure that other parents did not suffer as she was, and she asked Hillary and me to be among the first patrons of Parents and Children Together (PACT), the charity she was setting up to deal with the tragedy of abducted children. That afternoon we both spoke at PACT's inaugural reception. For a woman

1960. A St. Edmund's school photo. Grandma had a thing about bows, the fancier the better as far as she was concerned.

My parents met on tour with a small theater company. Here the two young ingenues star in *The Princess and the Swineberd*.

Mum and me in the park at the end of our road in Waterloo. My dad took the picture.

A rare trip back to my old school, aged fourteen, in Girl Guide uniform. I'd been asked to help out at the church fête.

Tony and me in Crown Office Row, the chambers in which we were both pupils.

Lyndsey (center) and me with Mum, Grandma, and Grandad on holiday at Butlins, Pwllheli, Wales. Until we started going abroad, Mum rarely managed to escape her parents-in-law.

Christmas 1979 with Lyndsey and my mum at her house in Oxford, a few months before our wedding.

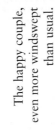

The happy couple, even more windswept than usual.

Classic photo of the bride's family: Auntie Audrey, Uncle Bob, Mum, Lyndsey, Tony and me, my grandma, Uncle Bill, and my cousin Catherine.

Tony and Euan climbing in the Pyrenees — something we did every summer when staying at Maggie Rae's house in France.

January 1984. Picture taken for the local paper only hours after Euan's birth. I managed a smile thanks to a rubber ring.

May 1982. The candidate for Beaconsfield, his wife, and the campaign team. A lost cause from the start.

Kathryn, Tony, and me on the stairs at Myrobella. My first experience of publicity — this accompanied the profile by Barbara Amiel.

Nicky and me on holiday in France.

Blackpool, 1994. Tony's first Labour Party Conference as leader. After his triumphant speech doing away with Clause IV, I felt ridiculously proud.

Princess Diana with Kathryn at Chequers, taken by my mum.

The first photograph taken at Number 10.

The third of May 1997. The ultimate bad-hair day.

After the euphoria, the trepidation. At this point we hadn't even seen inside our future home.

At least when I'm working I don't have to worry about what to wear.

April 1995. A proud day for the Booth family. Lyndsey, Mum, and Dad joined Tony and the kids for the official photo when I took silk.

The new grandparents: a proud Leo Blair holds his namesake. Tony's stepmother, Olwyn, and my mum were equally delighted.

Jacques Chirac sent us this photograph of Bill Clinton holding Leo at the United Nations. Our new baby had everyone smiling.

June 1997. The Clintons' first visit to us in Downing Street. My mum and Lyndsey (left) were among Bill's staunchest fans.

Family life in the Great Hall at Chequers. Bill continued to drop in on us long after he left office.

Sitting on the steps outside the front door at Chequers. Although it looked very grand, Chequers was where we had the most freedom to be ourselves.

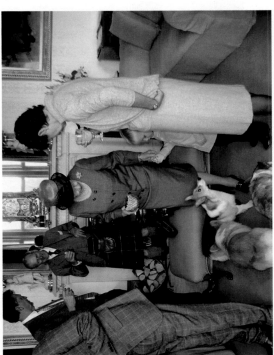

Leo endears himself to the corgis at Balmoral.

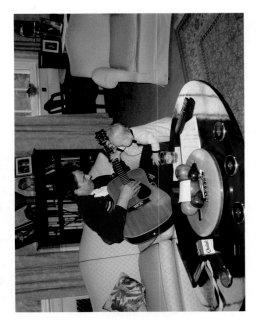

Like father, like son. A moment of relaxation in the sitting room of the Number 11 flat.

The launch of Matrix Chambers. As specialists in human rights, we were determined to be non-hierarchical.

The Bushes arrive by helicopter on the lawn at Chequers. We only came by helicopter once — with the Aznars — flying from the barracks between Downing Street and Buckingham Palace.

Bromley-by-Bow, London. While I no longer practice family law, the welfare of women and children continues to be very important to me.

My study in the Number 11 flat. With the heightened security following September 2001, I increasingly found myself working at home rather than going to chambers.

André and unidentifiable alien in the kitchen at Downing Street.

Greeting the Putins in front of Number 10.

Horseplay with Leo and Kathryn in the hall of the flat. Tony has always been a hands-on dad.

Leo stands guard over his daddy's red boxes in the Number 11 flat. Sometimes four or five would arrive at the same time, all equally beaten up.

July 2006. The G8 Summit in St. Petersburg and the traditional photo of spouses, though Angela Merkel's husband is missing. From left: Laura Bush, Bernadette Chirac, Maria Barroso, Flavia Prodi, Lyudmila Putina, and Laureen Harper.

Laura Bush and I were always happy to have a chance to catch up.

A quartet of Downing Street wives: Lady Wilson, Norma Major, the Countess of Avon (Clarissa Eden), and me, in Lincoln's Inn for the launch of *The Goldfish Bowl*.

I try to meet children wherever I go. These schoolchildren in Kuala Lumpur show why: you can't help but be buoyed up in their company.

There was no disguising the presence of children in the Number 11 flat.

May 2005. It was my good luck to be in my home town when Liverpool won the Champions League in a nail-biting penalty shoot-out against AC Milan.

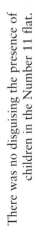

Bagram air base, January 2002, with Sima Samar, Afghanistan's Minister for Women, and two impressive young servicewomen.

July 2005. David Beckham may have caught more eyes as an ambassador in Singapore, but Tony was tireless in persuading International Olympic Committee delegates to give London their vote.

Kofi Annan with Raj and Veena Loomba at the launch of the campaign for International Widows Day at the UN, spearheaded by the Loomba Trust, of which I am honored to be president.

Nelson Mandela with Leo in the Pillared room at Number 10 in July 2003. Mandela is old-fashioned courtesy personified.

A school for street children in South India. The Foreign Office eventually figured out that I could be useful.

With Tony celebrating my sister-in-law Katy Blair's fiftieth birthday.

May 2005. Outside the back door at Myrobella. This was the last time I would cast a vote for my husband. Note the camera behind us. We were under constant surveillance.

Sharing a happy moment with Zara Willis. My work in education law first brought me into contact with children with disabilities, and I continue to be involved through specialist charities, in this case the Children's Trust.

My fiftieth-birthday party. Chequers had never seen (or heard) anything like it.

Chinese takeaway: the favorite Blair standby.

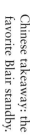

It was with mixed feelings that we left Downing Street for the last time.

With the Queen outside Number 10 after the Golden Jubilee dinner in 2002 to which all her former Prime Ministers were invited.

The photograph that caused the uproar. I went straight from giving my lecture to meet Pope Benedict as requested.

under extraordinary emotional pressure, Hillary coped magnificently. I could only thank her for being such a wonderful role model, both for career women in general and for me in particular. Thanks to her example, I was getting better at making off-the-cuff speeches. In America this was expected of the First Lady, whereas Number 10 was still coming to grips with the fact that I could walk and talk. The system was simply not geared to a Prime Minister's spouse who wanted to be involved. As for Catherine Meyer, her story eventually had a happy ending, although it would be nearly ten years before she saw her boys again.

That night an official banquet was held in our honor. It was one of those times when you are skin-tinglingly aware that what is happening is extraordinary. There we were, lined up beside the President and First Lady, shaking hands with some of America's finest entertainers, including Barbra Streisand, Robert Redford, Harrison Ford, and Steven Spielberg. The dinner was followed by a full-length concert, in which Elton John and Stevie Wonder performed, although Stevie's version of "My Cherie Amour" couldn't match the classic Tony Blair rendition. Sitting there, with the Union Jack and the Stars and Stripes both very much in evidence, I experienced a feeling of awe.

That trip was the first time André was acknowledged as a semiofficial member of our party, in that his name appeared on schedule lists as "A. Suard, Personal Assistant to Mrs. Blair." Even so, he was always treated differently from the rest of the group, and that still makes me angry.

What triggered the change in attitude was our first trip to Japan a few days into the new year. I had insisted on his coming along. Alastair could stamp his feet as much as he wanted; I was not going to turn up looking anything less than my best. And it wasn't only that. There was the constant packing and unpacking, not to mention the sheer organization required to keep us looking up to the mark. We were representing the country after all. André was more than happy to do it, and God knows we needed him.

The NATO summits and other bilateral visits Tony had made without me in the previous six months had been personally chaotic. He was traveling more than any Prime Minister had before — everyone wanted to meet Britain's new, dynamic leader, and his schedule was ridiculous — yet he was operating in a twentieth-century world with nineteenth-century backup. When the bags weren't outside his door at the appropriate time, the garden girls would end up throwing whatever they could find into his suitcases. It wasn't their fault — that wasn't their job — but things were disappearing at an alarming rate: watches, cuff links, socks, the odd shoe, shirts, and trousers. At the next stop on the itinerary, it would all need pressing, and crucial things couldn't be found. Gradually it dawned on them that having André around wasn't such a bad idea after all.

After years of being reasonably laid-back when it came to the Blairs and travel, these visits were unbelievably concentrated. You might leave Heathrow in the winter, then land in glaring sunshine with temperatures in the nineties, yet be forbidden to wear sunglasses or even blink. The clothes you had left in were stashed away in suit carriers before you landed, while those you would arrive in were ready to put on, crease-free and appropriate for both the temperature and the welcoming committee.

There were so many things that needed to be thought of when traveling — jet lag, getting up in the middle of the night, preparing in advance what you were going to wear coming down the steps onto the tarmac when all you could think of was throwing off the previous night's outfit and crashing into bed before a dawn flight to the next destination. André took care of everything. In the morning he would come in and wake us up, then run the bath.

"Just five minutes more, André . . ."

"No. Get up. If you don't, I'll open the curtains." The ultimate cruelty. Somehow he'd always manage to find a fresh lemon for my morning hot water. (I don't drink tea.) Ordering such a basic thing from room service was more or less impossible, and I rarely succeeded.

Also, Tony was used to André. After all, he'd been part of our lives since 1994. Tony could write his speeches — as he often did on those trips — sitting in his underpants, and if André was around, it didn't matter. But if an unknown chambermaid or hairdresser walked in, he'd freeze. In those early days, things were so disorganized. We couldn't guarantee we'd get a separate sitting room, so Tony would be having a meeting while I'd need to get dressed. (Much as I love my country, I draw the line at displaying my fleshier parts to senior members of the Foreign Office.) I'd just end up grabbing my clothes and going along to André's room.

He was also good company. The second night in Tokyo, as Tony was at a men-only function, André and I joined some of the other nonparticipants from the office and went to a noodle bar. I loved it, particularly the warm drink that came in a small bottle, which I didn't realize you were supposed to share. Tony's staff members were far better traveled than I was and later admitted that they didn't know how to tell me that sake wasn't just a Japanese version of tea, even though it did come in little cups.

By the time I got back to our room, I was feeling very happy indeed, having laughed and sung my way through the second half of the evening. My poor husband was not impressed — largely, I suspect, because he'd had an extremely dull dinner himself.

I was beginning to realize that I didn't have to be simply an appendage on these trips, that I could play a role that would be of real benefit. It didn't happen overnight. It's fair to say, however, that the Foreign Office proved much more open to my having a public role than did Civil Service, perhaps because ambassadors' wives have always had a public role, whereas wives of UK-based civil servants remain largely anonymous. Although our embassies abroad often found that I was useful, once back in Blighty, I was surplus baggage.

From the moment Tony arrived in Downing Street, Northern Ireland was a priority. Within six months of Mo Mowlam beginning talks with Sinn Féin, Gerry Adams and Martin McGuinness were in and out of Number 10.

The children made full use of the "secret staircase" that led directly from the Number 11 flat to the Downing Street garden. Once, I had brought Euan and Nicholas skateboards from a trip to Washington, and they were trying out their skills one day after school when I had an irate phone call from Alastair.

"Get those kids out of the garden," he said.

"Whatever for? They're just having a bit of fun."

"Well, take a look out the window, then get them out before the press gets wind of it."

So I did. And there, to my astonishment, were Gerry and Martin on the skateboards, showing the boys a few tricks.

A few weeks later, I happened to be taking Ralph Lauren around, and as we came into the White Room, there were Gerry and Martin. Naturally I introduced them to my visitor and was intrigued when Gerry began talking rather knowledgeably about clothes. Nothing daunted, I carried on with my tour patter.

"This room has a very famous ceiling," I continued. "Each corner has an emblem representing part of the United Kingdom." And one by one I pointed them out. "The rose is for England, the daffodil for Wales, the thistle for Scotland —"

"And I think the last one," Gerry butted in, "is about to fall off!"

This was the flax, the emblem of Northern Ireland.

"No, no," I said, smiling. "It's the symbol of friendship between our people." Then I whisked Ralph away before I did permanent damage to the peace process.

Easter 1998 was crunch time in regard to Northern Ireland. Tony was still in Belfast when the children and I set off on our planned Easter break to Spain. First we had an official visit with the Spanish premier, José María Aznar, and his wife, then we were on to Cordoba to stay with our friend Paco Peña, the Spanish flamenco guitarist, and his wife, Karin, whom we had got to know through Derry many years before.

We arrived at the Spanish Premier's official country residence outside Seville on Wednesday. Located within the boundaries of the Doñana, a national nature reserve and World Heritage site, it's right by the Mediterranean, utterly wild and with fabulous dunes. The whole area was closed to the public, so the kids and I were able to spend time there feeling unfettered. We were supposed to be staying only one night, but the talks at Hillsborough Castle, the official government residence in Northern Ireland, were still going on, and Tony was determined not to let this chance slip through his fingers. He felt that if he were to leave, the whole thing might fall apart. Thursday came and went, then Friday. The Aznars were very understanding; there was no question of our having to move on, they said. Children are a wonderful bridge at times like this, and as the Aznars' children were similar in age to ours, everyone was getting on fine, including my mother, who had come with us. Then, with a huge sense of relief all around, came what became known as the Good Friday Agreement, a major step forward in the journey toward a lasting peace in Northern Ireland.

Tony finally arrived on Saturday, and it's fair to say that by then the Aznars and the Blairs knew each other pretty well. Perhaps it helped that we were all lawyers. José María's wife, Ana Botella, was also a TV journalist, very independent and popular in her own right. On Maundy Thursday she had taken us to watch the traditional Easter parade, and everywhere we went, she was greeted warmly by the crowds. She had achieved a lot in her role as the premier's wife, and I was not surprised when, a few years later, she was elected to the Madrid City Council. Over those few days we had some useful discussions, and I became even more determined not to sit on the sidelines and do nothing.

People often wonder how politicians on one side of the political spectrum deal with politicians on the other side — something that happens all the time at the head-of-government level. The answer is, pretty well. Foreign policy is largely concerned with mutual interests. With America, for example, whether the administration is right or left, chances are that the mutual interests with outside powers remain the same. Obviously there can be areas of dissent, and in the case of Spain, Gibraltar comes to mind.

That Easter Euan had just turned fourteen, and although the *Today* program was no longer required listening in the Blair household, he was comparatively well-informed politically. With the insouciance of youth, he decided to bring up the issue of Gibraltar with José María. After the first shocked gulp on both sides — the hosts and an embarrassed mum — there was much laughter, and we went on to have an interesting discussion, something that would never have happened in ordinary diplomatic circumstances.

When Alastair heard the story, he decided it was too good to waste, but as we had long since agreed that our kids would stay beneath the parapet and out of the newspapers, my mum agreed to take the "blame" on this occasion.

Immediately after our return from Spain, Tony and I set off for the Middle East, first Egypt and then Israel. The embassy there had asked if there was anything I particularly wanted to do. As a result of the various special education cases I'd been involved in, I'd heard of a diagnostic process called the Feuerstein method, named after a psychologist practicing in Jerusalem. I asked if I could meet him. It was a fascinating encounter. He ran a center that helped both Israeli and Arab children with disabilities, particularly Down syndrome.

Expectations for these children, he believed, were too low and they could do far more than people imagined. They also had a particular empathy with the elderly. The center had developed a program in which these young people would visit older people in their homes. He told me how one old man had collapsed when he was being visited by a boy with quite severe Down syndrome, and this young man had been able to ring the emergency services and get him aid. Through my charity work I had met a lot of Down's children, and it was a joy to see how happy they appeared.

The contrast with what I saw the following day couldn't have been starker. Gaza is essentially just one big refugee camp, and I was taken by Yasir Arafat's wife to a school for special-needs children in Ramallah which she herself had set up. The children were provided with loving care but little else, and they were desperately in need of equipment and toys. As a result of the constant shelling, she explained, the proportion of premature babies in Gaza is high, and many babies are damaged at birth. It was all very upsetting, particularly when I thought of the facilities I had just seen only a few miles away.

The entire visit kept switching from one extreme to the other. That evening we landed in Saudi Arabia. As a special sign of respect for Tony, not only was I allowed to walk by his side but the Foreign Minister also shook my hand. That night, however, it was Saudi business as usual. While Tony went off to a men-only dinner, I attended a women-only dinner, where even the servers were women.

When in the male world, these women were completely covered up, but underneath, I discovered, they were far better dressed than I was. One woman recounted how her small son would pay great attention to what shoes she was wearing before they went out, as he was terrified that he would lose her. Once she was covered up, the shoes were the only way he had of identifying her. We were talking in English, and it was clear that many of these women were well educated and were familiar with London and Paris.

"Don't you find it restricting not being able to drive or go out?" I asked.

Not at all, they answered, with a laugh. "We live such easy lives, it's fine."

Yet over the following years, when I met these same educated women again — and others like them — it was clear it was increasingly *not* so fine. They were in a gilded cage, and once they had seen a broader horizon, it was hard to put up with the cage. This is why I think change will come as people realize there are other things they can do.

The next day, back in London, when I was donning my own black robe before going into court, I couldn't help but think of both the similarities and the differences between these women and me.

CHAPTER 23

Changing Gears

Involvement with a particular charity often stems from personal tragedy, and in this I am no exception. My auntie Audrey was only the first of many wonderful women whose lives, having touched mine in one way or another, were cut short by breast cancer. I can't remember now the first time I talked about her in public, but in 1997, shortly after we moved into Downing Street, I became a patron of Breast Cancer Care. I am also a patron of the Restoration of Appearance and Function Trust (RAFT), an organization devoted to helping patients in need of reconstructive plastic surgery. RAFT is based at the hospital where my dad had such fantastic treatment following his horrific accident.

Money is only part of what enables a charity to achieve its objectives. Equally important — sometimes more so — is raising public consciousness and, eventually, changing perceptions. In my early years, spare cash was never much in evidence, but I was able to help various charities in other ways: as a schoolgirl through practical help, working with Down syndrome children, and later through my legal expertise. Now the man I had married opened up another avenue. Well-known names, from royals to media personalities to someone like me who is less easily pigeonholed, can focus press attention in a way that, sadly, individual case histories cannot.

Even in the 1990s, breast cancer was not really talked about beyond the medical pages of serious newspapers. As I saw it, my job was to get women to talk openly about it. Only by removing the taboo, by making the vocabulary of self-examination and mammograms, of lumpectomies and prosthetics, part of the language of every woman, whatever her age, nationality, or background, could progress in early detection be made. Thanks to Alastair's decision that where Cherie was concerned, less was more, I had become a bit of an enigma. As a result, when I did speak or write, it was published and noticed.

The death of David Attwood's brother Michael at such a young age had never left me, and in the spring of 1998, I heard from Fiona that her friend Lindsay Nicholson's daughter, Ellie, whom I'd got to know when I'd "edited" *Prima*, was suffering from the same kind of leukemia that her father, John Merritt, had died of. When I went to visit her in Great Ormond Street, London's children's hospital, I was incredibly impressed by the work of Sargent Cancer Care, a foundation focused on children with cancer, and asked if I could be of help. I have been involved with that organization ever since. Sadly, Ellie died on June 9, 1998.

That summer of 1998, I was able to extend my charitable networking in an unexpected quarter. One day, when Prince Charles and I were walking round the grounds at Highgrove, the Prince's country home, he told me that he would sometimes allow groups in to look at the gardens. My cousin Paul Thompson, one of the family priests, had been working for many years for the Supportive Help and Development Organisation (SHADO), a drug prevention charity based at Liverpool Cathedral. He had recently died, still only in his forties, from an embolism following an injury to his knee, and I'd been asked if I would like to get involved in the charity. Each year, one of SHADO's main fund-raising events was a sponsored walk ending up at a stately home. In 1997 I'd welcomed the walkers for tea at Chequers. Plucking up courage, I asked the Prince whether he would consider allowing SHADO to look round his garden. Drug-related charities find it extremely difficult to attract funds, and I was quite prepared for him to say no. He didn't, and in 1999 SHADO's sponsored walk ended with tea and cakes at Highgrove.

It was now time, I decided, to unlock the potential of Downing Street itself. Although Margaret Thatcher and Norma Major had used Number 10 to host charitable receptions, I felt we could do a good deal more. The great state rooms on the first floor were empty for so much of the time. Why not put them to greater use?

In particular, both Tony and I were keen to extend the range of people who saw behind the famous facade. Gradually a system evolved whereby on Monday nights, Tony and I would host a large reception for more than two hundred people who came from a particular work sector — such as the police or social workers. Then every Tuesday I would host a reception for a charity. Initially they were "mine" — that is, charities of which I was a patron or was otherwise officially involved with. But that was purely practical: I offered and they accepted. As word spread of these Tuesday evenings, however, requests from other charities began to come in, and between 1998 and 2007, I hosted one every week, apart from August and the holiday periods. Regulations governing the use of public buildings prevented these evenings from being direct fundraising events, but a charity could use the event to raise its profile or as a thank-you to major donors. The charity paid for whatever food or drink was involved. The number of guests was limited to a maximum of forty, so that I could talk to each of them personally. I would also address the guests about the charity, its aims, its successes, and how they could help, and I would offer to have my photograph taken with each one. These events were never advertised, never mentioned in the press, but somehow word of them got around, and over the following years I was able to learn much about the fantastic unsung work that goes on up and down our country and overseas.

Furthermore, from the contacts I was making during Tony's official visits abroad, I became increasingly aware of the potential of what is loosely — and often disparagingly — called networking. On my return to England following my trip to Gaza, for example, I was able to arrange for equipment and supplies to be sent out to a girls' school run by Mrs. Arafat and the center for special-needs children I'd visited.

I was also aware of how the average constituent had no chance of visiting Downing Street, so every month I invited ten MPs from across the parties each to bring three children, each accompanied by a parent, to tea. It was a way of ensuring that kids from all over the country had the opportunity. I always told the children that I hoped that at least one of them would return here one day as Prime Minister and asked them to promise me that if they did, they would invite me back.

That summer we did our usual lurch across Europe, made less spontaneous by the constant presence of our security detail — nice though they were — and garden girls. By mid-August our increasingly unwieldy cavalcade was back in France. We were there when news came through of the Omagh car bombing.

Omagh continues to appall. Twenty-nine people died, and more than two hundred were injured in the blast. Responsibility was later claimed by a nationalist splinter group calling itself the Real IRA, as opposed to the Provisional IRA, whose political arm, Sinn Féin, had been party to the Good Friday Agreement. Tony borrowed a suit and black tie for the immediate television response, then flew straight to Belfast from Toulouse airport.

Though not physically present at Hillsborough during the talks, Bill Clinton had played a key part in the negotiations, and two weeks after the atrocity, on September 3, Bill, Hillary, Tony, and I flew into Omagh to see for ourselves the devastation that had been achieved by just one bomb attached to an old car parked in the main shopping street on a Saturday afternoon. Hillary is not as spontaneously charming as her husband, and this was the first time I saw her compassionate side. She was moved beyond words by what we heard and saw. It brought tears to our eyes to talk to the people who had lost loved ones.

But this was not tragedy tourism: Tony knew that it was imperative to get Sinn Féin to condemn the bombers and at the same time persuade the Protestants not to react. He also knew that Bill's physical presence, his unequivocal condemnation of the atrocity, and his renewed commitment to the peace talks would be crucial if the terrorists were not to achieve their aim.

Until we arrived at Number 10, I had considered chambers as archaic a setup as was possible to imagine at the end of the twentieth century. I was wrong. Downing Street was positively feudal. On the technical side, computers featured hardly at all. That obviously had to change, as by 1997 everyone in Tony's office was using a computer. Then there were the garden girls. They were the crème de la crème of the Civil Service secretarial elite, and until we moved in, they were obliged to wear skirts; trousers were even forbidden at Chequers.

"This is just nonsense," I told the Cabinet secretary. "There are Tony and I in our jeans. It's ridiculous to expect the garden girls to be wearing twinsets and pearls." Grudgingly that was allowed.

Then there was the question of rooms. The best and largest in Number 10 was the domain of the two principal private secretaries: one from the Foreign Office and one from the Treasury. John Major had worked in the Cabinet room itself, so this had a certain logic, as there were big double doors connecting the two rooms. Tony, however, preferred something less grandiose. All that was available was a former waiting room to the left of the Cabinet room, so that was where he was put. When I found out where he was spending his workday, I couldn't believe it. "Why are those two civil servants having the big room while the Prime Minister is in this little cubbyhole?" I asked.

The problem was simply lack of space. Downing Street was cracking at the seams, and no amount of shuffling people around would change that.

It was around this time that I had a brain wave. What about the Number 10 flat? That was completely vacant. Though officially Gordon's, he didn't use it. I had also noticed that a room opposite the entrance to our own flat, Number 11, seemed to be used by the Treasury simply for storing chairs. Meanwhile, personnel had a room the size of a large cupboard off a corridor next to the main entrance of Number 10, and visitors were having to hang round the entrance hall because there was no waiting room. I thought, *This is completely ludicrous.* So I put all these ideas to Tony and said he should talk to Gordon about it. "You've got to do something," I said. "It's simply not fair to your staff."

"Cherie, please listen to me. I'm sure you mean well, but don't get involved. At some point we'll get round to it, but frankly there are more important things on the agenda."

I wasn't surprised. I'd had plenty of experience of my ideas being discounted. This time, however, I decided to take the law into my own hands. So I picked up the phone and spoke to Sue Nye, Gordon's longtime aide. "I want to come and see Gordon," I said. Consternation in the Treasury! They immediately rang Tony to

222

SPEAKING FOR MYSELF

find out what was going on. He then called me and asked me to explain myself.

"I simply want to make the case that it's in everyone's interest, including his as Chancellor, to husband public resources. You won't go and see him, so I will."

By now I had my appointment, so it was too late to do anything to stop me. Off I trotted to the Treasury and was duly ushered in.

"Look, Gordon," I said, "we've got a real problem at Number Ten. It's overcrowded. The personnel department has nowhere they can talk to people alone. Yet there's a perfectly good room outside our flat which is currently unused." And if that wasn't acceptable, then what about the Number 10 flat? Surely part of that could be used, I suggested, if only as meeting rooms.

"I've got no objections personally," he explained, "but I owe it to future Chancellors of the Exchequer to preserve the integrity of the Chancellor of the Exchequer's rooms."

"Are you telling me you can't ease this terrible overcrowding because of some hypothetical situation in the future? Come on, Gordon. If only as a personal favor to me . . ."

No doubt he had a thousand more pressing matters to worry about than an empty room at Number 11. No doubt it wasn't my place to push. But the pressure on the staff at Number 10 was becoming unbearable. Even so, as I sat there getting nowhere, I began to think I had overstepped the mark. He said that he would think about it and left.

Later I was informed that he'd decided we could have the room opposite the flat entrance. Unbelievably, Number 10 then spent £10,000 redecorating it, but at least it released more space downstairs, so it was worth the embarrassment.

As for Tony, he did eventually move to the principal private secretaries' room, after which it became known as "the den."

By chance Tony's first visit to mainland China, in October 1998, coincided with an initiative organized by the Bar Council's international committee, relating to a conference in Beijing concerning the rights of the accused. My job was simply to introduce the session and generally explain what the delegates were going to see, which was a mock trial demonstrating how the British system worked. I then went off to see a group of women lawyers for a roundtable discussion about discrimination law in China. China was then still a country of bicycles and blue-Mao-suited workers — male and female, everyone looked the same. Just six years later, on my next visit, the consumer revolution was in full swing. Men and women could be clearly identified, and cars had transformed the look of the streets, though they were being driven as if they were bicycles. Color was everywhere, except in the sky, which remained an opaque gray whatever the weather — the result of the appalling pollution.

Before that first visit, Hillary Clinton had warned me about bugging. When she and Bill had been to Beijing, she told me, their security team had rigged up a soundproof tent in their bedroom, the only place, they were told, where they could talk safely. After a good night's sleep at the official guesthouse attached to the Forbidden City, Tony and I awoke to find André in a state of near hysteria. He'd woken in the small hours to find somebody in his room going through his things. Most of our delegation, we later heard, had had the same experience. If that wasn't enough, André said, he'd been having a shower when he noticed that instead of the mirror misting up, a large rectangle remained unnervingly clear. Apparently we were all under surveillance as well.

I had taken the decision fairly early on that there was not much point in swanning round the world as some sort of glorified tourist. If you're going to do it, you might as well do something useful. Increasingly, whenever Tony and I went away together on an official visit, it became standard for me to have my own program.

It was clearly important that I did nothing overtly political, but gradually the Foreign Office began to see how I might be useful. From its perspective, the great plus was my profession. As a barrister, I had the credentials to talk to other lawyers anywhere in the world. As our embassies would always have some sort of initiative in hand involving the law, my ability to talk to judges and senior lawyers proved useful: I could take soundings, testing the water at an informal (though informed) level. The promotion of women's rights, for example, is not always an easy subject to address, particularly in non-Christian countries. Yet not only would this fulfill the embassy's human rights objectives, but anything that encouraged people to use the common-law model was obviously good for our legal services, which are a large part of our "invisible" exports.

Early the following year, 1999, Tony and I paid our second visit to South Africa. We had first gone in the autumn of 1996, during his preelection tour of world leaders, and I was able during that week to visit Albie Sachs, who'd been appointed by Mandela two years earlier to lead the team writing the new South African constitution. As a human rights lawyer, I found it both a fascinating experience and a real privilege to be able to discuss the way the constitutional committee was drafting the human rights elements of the constitution. I also visited the Truth and Reconciliation Commission, the brainchild of Archbishop Desmond Tutu.

Nelson Mandela defies all preconceptions. In person he is tall and wiry, with a shock of white hair above a calm, near-beatific face. But what struck me most forcibly was his old-world courtesy, and not only to the great and the good. The first time he came to see us in Downing Street, Euan was off school with a cold but very anxious to meet the great man. When it came to it, our son was completely overawed and managed to stammer out, "It's so wonderful to meet you." With this gentle voice, Mandela replied, "And it's really nice to meet you, Euan." And I felt that he really meant it. On another occasion Euan introduced him to a friend from the London Oratory School, James Dove, whose father was from South Africa and had been involved with the African National Congress (ANC) during the apartheid years. Again Mandela was incredibly courteous to this young man. It was clear that this was something he did all the time.

Tony's last official visit as Prime Minister, in 2007, just before he stepped down, was to South Africa, and it was a great joy to find Mandela still alert though incredibly frail. The people around him were very protective. No one could use flash photography near him, for example; all those years spent breaking up stones in the glaring light of Robbin Island had affected his eyes. He still had the most incredible presence, but he was also still so gentle and unassuming.

During our visit in 1996, we were taken to an AIDS orphanage called Nazareth House in Cape Town, run by the same order of nuns as the orphanage just down from Seafield School in Crosby. Nuns, I have found, usually fall into two distinct categories: old battle-axes or really sweet. These were the sweet ones, and they were thrilled to see Tony. There was a little girl called Ntombi who for some reason attached herself to Tony. Then age three or four, she lifted up her arms and demanded to be carried, which he duly did.

When we asked about sponsoring her, we were warned that she was HIV positive. With sad smiles, the nuns reminded us of the graveyard we had seen, filled with names and dates recording tragically short lives. Tony and I looked at each other, and the decision was made. Thus Ntombi was the first child we sponsored from Nazareth House. Over the years we developed a close relationship with her. She did really well in school and at fifteen was able to return home to live with her grandmother and other members of her family. She is still very much alive.

We have also sponsored other children from Nazareth House. All of these children have been HIV positive, but many have had other disabilities as well. One little girl who we met on our first visit, for example, had been abandoned in the road, and ants had eaten out her eyes.

Children like Ntombi no longer live in the orphanage but are looked after by foster mothers in a nearby township, in "families" of around seven children each. These foster mothers are set up and funded by the nuns, while Nazareth House is used only for the most severely disabled children.

Taking a year off before starting university, our daughter, Kathryn, went to work at Nazareth House. I had told her the story of the little blind girl, and the first time we spoke on the telephone, she told me that the girl was still there. Sadly, however, she died shortly afterward of meningitis. Her death was a big blow for the nuns; they hadn't lost many children in recent years because of the dramatic improvements in the treatment of AIDS.

This is not the place to go into the vastly problematic question of Kosovo and its history as an ethnically Albanian province within Tito's Yugoslavia. Though predominantly Muslim, Kosovo is considered by the Serbs to be central to Serbia's identity as a Christian frontline state. Under Slobodan Milošević, Serbian forces had increased ethnic repression in Kosovo, but as the 1990s drew to a close, Kosovan freedom fighters (the Kosovo Liberation Army, or KLA) began striking back. By the end of 1998 the situation was acute. Demands that Serbia solve the problem fell on deaf ears, and the fighting intensified. Atrocities were occurring on both sides, and as a result, refugees were pouring out of the country into Macedonia, to the south. The hope was that if Serbia was threatened with

NATO air strikes, it would withdraw from Kosovo. But Tony was convinced — along with the British military — that only the threat of ground troops would shift Milošević. America, however, did not relish the idea of "body bags," and during the spring of 1999 Tony was putting all his energy into trying to persuade the Americans, via Bill Clinton, that the threat of ground troops was the only language that Milošević understood.

Throughout that time, Tony was constantly on the phone to America. Because of the timing, these calls would often come late in the evening, when he was in the flat. If he made the call, he would do so from our living room, where the special secure line to Washington was installed. When the calls originated from America, and came late at night or in the small hours of the morning, I would answer them, as the phone was always on my side of the bed. The disruption never bothered me, as I have always been more of a night person than Tony.

Although I never heard both sides of the conversation, I was very aware that Tony was constantly saying to Bill, "This cannot go on; we must do something. If we face Milošević down, not only will he back down, but the Russians will make him back down. But they have to understand that we really mean it." On March 24, 1999, bombing of the Serbian capital of Belgrade began. After that, the only further threat was a land invasion, increasingly the option preferred by NATO military personnel on the ground. Four NATO countries — Britain, France, Germany, and Italy — had troops on the Macedonian border ready to intervene, but America continued to stay out. "I feel like I'm out on a limb here," Tony used to say. "As if I'm on this big tree, at the end of a branch, and at any minute it's going to give. They'll saw through, and that will be me done for." ("They" were the more cautious Clinton advisers.)

On April 24 Tony went to Chicago to deliver a speech to the Economic Club of Chicago. The world, he said, is such that now we cannot just let these appalling things happen. We have to intervene, and in terms of Kosovo, success was the only exit strategy NATO was prepared to consider. "We will not have succeeded until an international force has entered Kosovo and allowed the refugees to return to their homes."

A week later we were in Macedonia. This was the first time since Tony had taken office that British troops were poised for action. By speaking to our soldiers on the front line — part of the Allied Rapid Reaction Corps led by General Mike Jackson — and seeing the refugee disaster for himself, he believed that he would be in a stronger position to argue the case for American involvement on the ground.

As with all such visits, Tony's itinerary was not broadcast in advance, and at the end of the previous week, I had spent two days in the House of Lords arguing an equal-pay case on behalf of part-time workers at Barclays Bank. Now, on Monday, we were in Skopje, the capital of the former Yugoslav Republic of Macedonia (as we had to be careful to call it, because of the sensitivity of the Greeks, who believe they have rights to the name). The capital was little more than a provincial outpost and our embassy little more than a consulate. Just talking to the staff, we realized that it had been quite difficult for Muslim and Christian staff members to work together with such terrible things going on just a few miles away.

A helicopter took us to a large refugee camp on the border with Kosovo. Everywhere we looked, there were white tents, rows of them stretching far off in the distance. The moment they realized who had arrived, the shouts rang out: "Ton-ee! Ton-ee! Ton-ee!" They already saw him as the man who was going to get them out of this horror. We moved from tent to tent with an interpreter, listening to stories of how these people had lived for years perfectly peaceably within their community, then how their neighbors — previously friends — had turned on them and threatened them with violence. We heard how they'd managed to get out, leaving everything behind. Although from the outside these tents were identical, inside they were all different. Each woman had done what she could to make her tent welcoming and comfortable for what remained of her family. It was humbling.

From there we were taken up to the crossing point, looking out across no-man's-land to the queue of refugees waiting to cross over into Macedonia and the sanctuary of the camp. The line snaked back as far as I could see. Everyone was laden with suitcases and bundles of what were probably clothes and linens. We were then taken to the head of the line, where people just wanted to shake our hands. The interpreter went with Tony, while I talked to people who spoke English, by definition educated. I remember a lawyer and a professor at Pristina University, both of whom had previously led uneventful lives. Life under communism may not have been particularly comfortable, they said, but they had never really known hardship. Now this had happened. They had no idea what awaited them — not a job in a university, that's for sure.

Even though I was born after World War II, when I was a child, games of Germans versus English were still commonplace, and I remember the stories my primary-school teacher Mr. Smerdon used to tell of the concentration camps. As I walked down this unending queue, faces marked by exhaustion and fear, I was deeply shocked. These people were being picked on because of their religion, because they were Muslims. What did Europe think it was doing? We had been there and done that. We didn't need to go back.

Three months later, at the end of July, Tony returned, this time to Pristina in Kosovo itself, and this time as a true hero. His plan had worked. America had agreed to commit ground troops, and the moment it had done so, Milošević had backed down. There are, apparently, hundreds of small boys called Tony running around the newly independent Kosovo.

CHAPTER 24

New Horizons

My post-1997 career at the Bar was progressing as well as could be expected given the difficulties of reconciling the Downing Street agenda with the Gray's Inn Square agenda. That wasn't my only problem. Shortly after we moved in, Number 10 decided to "take a view" on a case that I had been approached to do. I resisted. As a professional woman, I told them, I had to be allowed to get on with my profession. I invoked the cab-rank principle, my line being that as soon as I started making choices, I was in trouble. Even though they knew this was my position, over the next ten years the office would sometimes indicate that they would rather I did not do a particular case. I never knew exactly who it was "taking a view." Tony would simply deliver the message. As for who was standing behind Tony, it was "the office" or "Number 10." It was as if these anonymous people would all participate in a discussion — including my husband but excluding me — and come to "a view." The rationale was always the same: the press would write stories along the lines of "Cherie is suing the government," thus embarrassing the Prime Minister. My voice was never heard in these discussions. Nevertheless, the cab-rank argument was always accepted, until the next difficult case came along and we went through the whole thing again.

My fears that my career would suffer were already being justified. It wasn't so much the money; I loved my work. Not only were my official duties taking their toll, but while a few people wanted Cherie Booth, QC, because they wanted the attendant publicity, others wouldn't touch me with a barge pole, as publicity was the last thing they desired. It was rarely overt, but word got round.

Shortly after we moved into Downing Street, I sat as a recorder (a part-time judge), something senior barristers do to learn the ropes. The case concerned an old lady who had been evicted from her retirement home because she was being disruptive, going round complaining that the other old ladies were stupid. Before I passed judgment, she told me, "I want you to know that I have always voted Labour, and I voted for your husband in the general election." On the basis of the evidence, I imposed a suspended possession order on her, in effect delaying the eviction provided she behaved herself in the future, at which news her attitude toward me suddenly changed. "I will never vote Labour again!"

Arguing the same point of law but from the opposite point of view happens all the time, and it certainly keeps you intellectually focused. In 1997 I did a case in which a lesbian rail worker wanted to claim free rail travel for her partner. Heterosexual partners, even if they weren't married, were entitled to this perk, but Lisa Grant couldn't get it for her same-sex partner and claimed sex discrimination. I argued the case for her in the European Court in Luxembourg, but we eventually lost.

Under the British legal system, judges start life as barristers, then recorders. In 1996 I was made an assistant recorder, and in July 1999 I became a full recorder. Both recorders and judges are kept up-to-date by a body called the Judicial Studies Board, and toward the end of September I went on one of the three-yearly update courses. On the night of the twenty-third, a couple of old barrister friends and I went out for a birthday supper: my forty-fifth. I was feeling very positive. That summer we had had a good break in Italy, and Tony was feeling relaxed. All the energy he had expended over Kosovo had been worth it. Sitting there, raising a glass of champagne, I saw only one little shadow on my immediate horizon: my period. Where was it?

"It's a bit odd," I told Tony when he rang me that night from Chequers. "I'm usually so regular."

"So what does that mean?"

"Probably nothing," I said. "Probably just my age. Don't worry."

He wasn't about to. He was working on his Labour Party Conference speech and was paying little attention to anything else. But there was a little niggle at the back of my mind.

A few weeks before, we had been on the usual prime ministerial weekend at Balmoral. The first year we had been actually stayed overnight, in 1998, I had been extremely disconcerted to discover that everything of mine had been unpacked for me: not only my clothes but also the entire contents of my distinctly ancient toilet bag, with its range of unmentionables. This year I had been a little more circumspect and had not packed my contraceptive equipment, out of sheer embarrassment. As usual up there, it had been bitterly cold, and what with one thing and another . . .

But then I thought, *I can't be. I'm too old. It must be the menopause.*

Once back from the course, I met up with Carole at the gym. "I know it sounds odd," I said, "but do you think you could get me a pregnancy testing kit?" It was hardly something I could pop into the local chemist for. She brought it round on Thursday, and on Friday morning, lo and behold. I just couldn't believe it.

I rang Tony immediately. "The test," I said. "It's come up positive."

"So what does that mean?"

"It means I think I'm pregnant."

"Oh, my God."

That evening he came back from Chequers, and as soon as there was an opportunity, I showed him the little dipper and explained the significance of the blue line.

"How reliable is it?" he asked. I said I didn't know, but Carole had got me another one, though I'd have to wait to do that the following morning.

"We'll have to tell Alastair."

Alastair and Fiona came up the next morning before we set off for Bournemouth and the conference. The second test had shown the same little blue line.

"So how pregnant are you exactly?" Alastair asked.

"I don't know."

"Are we talking weeks or months?"

"Weeks."

He seemed more amused than anything else. They took the view that given it was still very early days, the best thing was to keep quiet. By chance I had already agreed to return to London on Monday for a Breast Cancer Care event. I'd leave a little earlier than planned to see my GP.

As arranged, Fiona and I took the train back to London on Monday. Rather than risk making a big deal of it, I went along to the general surgery at the Westminster Health Centre. It turned out that my usual doctor, Susan Rankin, wasn't there, so I saw another partner.

"So, Mrs. Blair," he said, "what can I do for you?"

"I think I'm pregnant," I replied with a smile. The poor man fell to pieces.

I had to calm him down. He didn't want to do an internal examination, he said. Feeling obliged to have at least a bit of a prod of my tummy, he kept saying, "Susan should be doing this."

"What about one of your tests?" I suggested. "Presumably it would be reliable?"

Relief flooded over him.

"Well?" Fiona said when I went out.

"End of May."

The next day it was very hard not to mention it. Traditionally we had a lunch for family and friends while Tony made the final adjustments to his speech. My half sister Sarah, who now worked as a journalist under the name Lauren Booth, had just had a miscarriage — she had written about it in a newspaper — so the last thing I wanted was to upset her further. I didn't tell my father for fear that he might let it slip.

Only those in the know would have spotted the twinkle in Tony's eye at a particular point in his speech that afternoon. By pure coincidence, one of his speechwriters had drafted a passage about children.

"To our children, we are irreplaceable. If anything happened to me, you'd soon find a new leader. But my kids wouldn't find a new dad. There is no more powerful symbol of our politics than the experience of being on a maternity ward. Seeing two babies side by side. Delivered by the same doctors and midwives. Yet two totally different lives ahead of them." As Tony spoke those lines, he glanced at me, because we both knew that very soon we would be in that hospital ward ourselves.

The plan was to keep the number of people in the loop very small. Now that it was confirmed, I decided I wanted a bit of private time with the idea of this baby. I also was conscious that, particularly at forty-five, things could go wrong, although I was personally convinced that everything was going to be all right. I had decided I wanted to get past the twelve- to thirteen-week mark before extending word beyond the tight-knit group. Also, we were due to go to Florence for a seminar that Tony and Bill Clinton had set up, and the last thing I wanted was for the focus to shift onto me. We'd wait till we came back from Florence, by which time it would probably be obvious, but at least we would be in control of the announcement.

I told my mum, my sister, and Jackie, our nanny. (Ros had left us in July 1998 to do a teacher-training course, a long-held ambition.) Jackie was thrilled. For any nanny worth the name, school-age children are all very well, but a baby is heaven.

I was a bit worried about telling the kids. I wanted them to know, but I remember thinking, *They are going to think this is disgusting. I mean, parents!* But they were fantastic about it and really excited. Kathryn came with me to an early scan, and as we walked along to the ultrasound department, I realized with a start that with me being so obviously middle-aged, people might think my prepubescent daughter was the one who was pregnant.

Once the Labour Party Conference was over, Susan Rankin gave me a proper examination. "You do realize," she said, "that the statistics for Down's and other abnormalities shoot up at your age."

I did, but having got this far, I didn't want to risk any damage to the baby, so I decided that an amniocentesis was out. I had a blood test and a scan, however, and all appeared well.

Over the next few days, the tight-knit group appeared to be stretching. Tony told Anji because, he said, she would be upset if he didn't. Then he told me he'd told Gordon.

"What business can it possibly be of Gordon's?" I remonstrated.

"You have to understand, Cherie. It's a very sensitive topic for him. The whole issue of my being a family man is very sensitive to him." He was only thinking of Gordon's feelings, he said.

Pregnant or not, we trundled on. As few people knew the news, there were no concessions to my delicate condition. Early on, I took the train from Liverpool Street station to Norwich to celebrate the opening of new offices for a big firm of legal-aid solicitors. Halfway there, overcome with nausea, I was sick all over everything. It was in the middle of the afternoon, and fortunately the carriage was empty, so I was able to go into the toilet and clean myself up. Then I went back to the carriage to scrub away at the seat and floor, all the time thinking, *This is hard, hard, hard.*

Another time we were up in the constituency, and I was with a Number 10 driver named Dave. Suddenly I knew I was going to be sick. Dave stopped the car, retrieved a bucket out of the back, and held it while I vomited my guts out. He was so kind that day that I swore then I would love him forever.

I was finding out the hard way that I wasn't thirty anymore. At one point I went up to Liverpool to do something for Jospice. Now a worldwide hospice movement, it had been started by Father Francis O'Leary, a Crosby boy born and bred. As always I stayed with my old friend Cathy, who has six kids, her youngest then being about four, while her oldest was older than Euan. Exhausted from the journey, I went upstairs to one of the girls' bedrooms where I'd be sleeping. The six-year-old had just got back from school, and the four-year-old was generally rushing about. I was sitting on the bed, trying to catch my breath, when Cathy came in with a cup of tea, and I burst into tears.

"What on earth is the matter?" she said.

"I'm pregnant. And I'm just remembering what it's like. The chaos, the noise. How can I possibly do all this in Downing Street?" It wasn't the first time I'd had such negative thoughts. It had taken over two years, but we had just got everything organized in Number 11 — the kitchen, our bathroom, the children's rooms — and now we were going to have dirty diapers and sleepless nights. Sitting there, I was overwhelmed by the immensity of it. And at the same time, I thought, *How dare I?* Here was Cathy, struggling to make ends meet. Her husband had just lost his job, and she was doing part-time teaching. But there she was, a good Catholic mother, bringing up these lovely, happy children.

One afternoon in mid-November, I had a call from Fiona. I was due to give a speech later that day.

"Just to warn you, there may be a slight problem," she said. Piers Morgan, editor of the *Daily Mirror*, had just spoken to Alastair and implied he knew I was pregnant. "He needs Alastair to confirm or deny it, and Alastair can't lie."

"I don't see why not," I said. "It's not his baby. Why doesn't he just say he doesn't know?"

"Because he does know."

"But who could have told the *Mirror*?"

"Lauren?"

"No. She doesn't know. I didn't tell her." And anyway, I knew that my half sister would never betray me, not over a thing like that. I went through everybody in my head. Sally Morgan wouldn't do it, nor Anji, even though I hadn't wanted her to know. I was sure it couldn't have come from the hospital. The scan had been registered under a different name, and they hadn't put me on the computer. That left Gordon. But what could he possibly have to gain by telling the *Daily Mirror*?

I called Alastair: "Why can't you just say that it's early days and we don't want to announce it yet?"

"Don't be ridiculous, Cherie. This is his big scoop."

"I don't want Piers Morgan to have a big scoop over my body, thank you very much."

"Okay, then we'll put it out over PA [Press Association]. The only way to handle it now is to make it a non-*Mirror* exclusive." This suited Alastair, because if Piers did get a scoop, the other papers would be furious. For Alastair, dealing with the tabloids was like juggling with raw eggs.

"We'll have a quote from Tony and a quote from you," he said, and hung up.

On the way to the meeting, Fiona's cell phone rang. It was Rebekah Wade, deputy editor of the *Sun*. "The announcement must be out — you might as well talk to her," Fiona mouthed.

I took the phone. I'd known Rebekah for some time and had a certain amount of respect for her: a woman making her way in the male world of Fleet Street.

We had a girly chat, along the usual just-pregnant lines, and that was that. The next morning this intimate girly conversation was plastered all over the *Sun*. From being a *Mirror* exclusive, it had become a *Sun* exclusive, and Piers was furious. To this day he remains convinced that I spoke to the *Sun* deliberately to thwart him. What I certainly didn't know when I talked to Rebekah was that at the time Fiona handed me the phone, the news had not gone out on PA. It did go out eventually that night, but not till later. Though I have my suspicions about how the *Sun* found out, they have never been confirmed.

The truth is that Piers still had his scoop. He made sure everyone knew that he had got the story and that it was he who had forced Number 10 to go public. But Rebekah was the only person who actually spoke to me. Piers never forgave me for spoiling his party, and over the years his resentment turned into outright hatred.

From then on, Cherie and the pregnancy were everywhere. The coverage was so positive that we heard there were some in Gordon's camp who thought we'd done it deliberately, to undermine Gordon. However, there was something rather unnerving about reading in the papers a score of doctors and professors going on about elderly mothers, the risks of brain damage, and the rest of it. "Of course she'll have a cesarean," the press said, and they had all the diagrams. But I thought, *Wait a minute, guys. This is my body and my decision!*

My obstetrician, Zoë Penn, said that as Kathryn had been a cesarean, normal practice would be to have another. But I was adamant that because the aftermath last time had been so grim, unless it was dangerous to the baby, I wanted a vaginal birth. The concern was that the stress of labor would open up the scar, which would be damaging to me.

We were always very clear that if the baby was a boy, we would name him for Tony's dad. He was going, as we declared, to be all the things that Grandpa Leo could have been but for the fact he'd had a stroke in his forties. Tony's father loved politics and had once had ambitions to stand for Parliament himself — as a Tory! Now he was finding life even more frustrating, as he'd recently had another stroke and had lost the ability to speak. I was so convinced the baby was a boy that we didn't really think of a girl's name. Bookmakers were by then taking bets, and I remember Euan coming to me and saying, "Why don't I just put a bet down?"

"Don't you dare!" I said. "The press would have a field day, and rightly so."

Among those who did put a bet on was a member of the Protestant negotiating team in the Northern Ireland talks. After the announcement he'd sidled up to Tony to congratulate him. "Great news, Tony. And what might you be thinking of calling the new arrival?"

Tony told him. A few months after Leo was born, Tony saw this same fellow, sporting an impressive tan. "You're looking well," he said. "Been on holiday?"

"Yes, indeed," he said. "And all thanks to you. I got very good odds on Leo if the Blair baby turned out to be a boy, and the whole family got to go away on the proceeds."

The other question that every parent is faced with is, where will the new baby go? The obvious place in our setup was Euan's room, next door to ours. As Euan had just turned sixteen, the sensible thing was to put him on the attic floor above. It was currently being used as offices and a bedroom for the duty officer, but it would make a nice little flat, with a small bathroom already there. The duty officer would need somewhere to sleep, and as the Number 10 flat was still unused, that appeared to offer a solution. This time no way was I going to see Gordon, so it was all done through the office. Although Gordon agreed to release the rooms, there were conditions attached: he wanted to make clear that this was a short-term arrangement and that when Euan went to university — at this stage more than two years away — he wanted those rooms back. Tony agreed.

"What do you mean, you agreed? Where's Euan going to live when he comes home for the holidays?" I demanded.

"Don't worry," he said. "It'll never happen. Once we've got the rooms, it'll never happen." And indeed it never did. Euan moved upstairs, feeling very grown-up and not ousted by the new arrival at all.

Every November, at a ceremony to mark the official opening of Parliament, the government sets out its program for the following year. This is known as the Queen's Speech, and it is indeed spoken by the Queen, although the words are written by the government. In 1997 one proposal in the Queen's Speech concerned the European Convention on Human Rights. Although Britain was already bound by the convention, new legislation was required to allow pertinent cases to be dealt with on home ground, rather than at the European Court in Strasbourg. This plan would not be fully implemented until October 2000, but from 1998 on, like-minded people began to talk about the possibility of setting up an interdisciplinary set of chambers that had human rights at its heart. At the same time, these chambers would be modern, with cutting-edge computer systems and clerks who didn't have to call us sir or miss. There were lawyers in London who did international law, but they were mainly commercial sets. There was also the odd barrister who did individual cases in Strasbourg, but these barristers were spread out across several sets of chambers and were all juniors. If this system was to take off, it needed a silk. Many of the people interested in the idea were either former pupils of mine or people I had brought on at Gray's Inn Square. In all, there were five or six of us interested in the proposal.

Things began to firm up in October 1999, when David Wolfe came to see me. The first official meeting in this regard was at the Russell Hotel in Russell Square. About ten people were present. I was the only silk, and we talked about who else we might approach.

While discussions continued, we heard that the old police station at the end of Gray's Inn, used by traffic wardens for the past few years, was being converted into offices by the Inn. One of the problems in setting up a new chambers with an entirely new ethos was finding a building that we wouldn't need to share. We had imagined we'd have to move outside the Inn and take on a commercial lease. Now that this rare opportunity had presented itself, we had to grab it, even though we weren't entirely ready. We all told our various chambers, and the die was cast.

As part of the belated modernization of our chambers at 4–5 Gray's Inn Square, we recruited Amanda Illing, who had previously worked as private secretary to the Director of Public Prosecutions, Barbara Mills. By the spring of 2000, she had learned the skills of clerking under Leslie Page and Michael Kaplan, who had clerked for me. So Amanda became our first clerk, although she was never called that, except by me through a slip of the tongue. Now she was our practice manager, later practice director, and has been a source of strength throughout.

Inevitably people interested in the new set of chambers fell by the wayside. Whereas some wanted a niche practice, I was among those who favored something more encompassing. In the end we had twenty-six practitioners, and those of us who were silks had to personally guarantee the bank debt that would be needed to start up a new set.

Usually chambers are called after their physical address or, occasionally, lawyers a long time dead. "The Old Police Station" hardly sent out the right signals. Clare Montgomery, QC, a successful criminal fraud practitioner, came up with Matrix, meaning, according to a definition she found in a dictionary, the intersection of ideas. By this time the Bar was increasingly split into criminal and civil sets. We were doing the opposite, bringing together the disciplines but focusing on human rights and civil liberties. A submeaning of "matrix" turned out to be fertility. As I was pregnant, and four other members' wives also were pregnant, this seemed a good omen. However, Matrix on its own, we decided, sounded a bit too radical. Thus Matrix Chambers was born.

Every aspect of the new chambers was subject to scrutiny. To start with, we were nonhierarchical. Instead of listing our members by seniority of call to the Bar, we were listed alphabetically, and the allocation of rooms was done by drawing lots. At the time, such innovations were seen as being radical and spurred much discussion.

By then, thanks to my familiarity with information technology, I was increasingly working from home. I finished my last case on May 17, 2000. To the delight of the press, it concerned parental leave. I was acting on behalf of the Trade Unions Congress (TUC) against the government, which, as we saw it, was taking too long to phase in parental leave under a European Union directive. Cartoonists went to town on the theme of *Blair v. Blair*. The hearing took place in the Lord Chief Justice's court, and as I stood up, the Lord Chief Justice said, "In the circumstances, Ms. Booth, would you like to sit down?" I replied, "Thank you, but I'm better on my feet."

I was, but he was right to ask: I was vast. I had been expecting the baby to come early — none of my other three having made forty weeks — and toward the end I was sleeping badly. I would get up, leaving Tony in bed, go next door into what would become the nursery, and sit in a rocking chair we had just bought. There, with the lights off, I would rock gently, looking out the window. At the back of the building, outside the back gate, I could see a photographer from the *Daily Mail*, waiting. The photographers came in shifts, day in, day out, for three weeks. I had this horror that when I went into labor, this photographer would burst in and take pictures. I thought, *I don't want to bring this baby into the world with the Mail peering into my room. Why can't I have this baby in private?*

Since the beginning, the *Mail* had been at the forefront of every negative story going. If an unflattering photograph came its way, the editors would print it. That March the *Mail* had been approached by somebody notorious in the publishing world who was offering the manuscript of a memoir written by our former nanny Ros Mark. The paper must have known that I would fight this tooth and nail, and the result was *Blair v. Associated Newspapers*, which the paper lost. Ros had been naive, but the *Daily Mail* didn't have that excuse.

The first we knew about the story was when Ros rang us in a panic. The *Mail* was outside the house in Lancaster where she was living as a student. The paper was trying to get an interview, she said. At this point we knew nothing about a book. We simply thought she was being harassed by the press, who'd found out about her connection with the Blairs. She didn't know what to do, so I suggested she ring Alastair. He in turn rang the *Mail* and asked what the hell they thought they were doing, harassing our former nanny. The *Mail* told him that she had written a memoir and was trying to sell it. The paper had been sent extracts, the spokesperson said.

We were astonished. Everybody, including Tony and Alastair. We all knew Ros so well. She was a sweet, sporty girl who had a lot of love in her, which she had given freely to the children. She had been with us for four years, and it was hard to imagine how we would have coped with the transition from Richmond Crescent to Downing Street without her. By now Alastair was in touch with the literary agent who had approached the *Mail*, who implied, Alastair said, that Ros herself wasn't the prime mover, but that her mother and brother were involved. Ros, it would seem, had simply provided the anecdotes and the details: the day-to-day life of a nanny in a chaotic but otherwise totally ordinary family that found itself in extraordinary circumstances.

In many ways it was a very warm depiction, but quite unpublishable as a book. From Tony's and my point of view, it risked being at worst embarrassing. But in terms of our kids, it was impossible. No matter who you are, you cannot write about children in that way — their personal habits, tantrums, foibles, and illnesses, their quirky ways — no matter how lovingly recounted. It was a total invasion of their privacy.

As an employment lawyer, I had always had proper contracts

with my nannies, all of which included a confidentiality agreement. In fact, when Tony became Leader of the Opposition, I had even had Ros sign another one, just to tie things up.

I spoke to the government's legal department, which said it was a private matter. I then got on to my old friend Val Davies, now a partner in a big City firm, and asked her to take out an injunction, which she did.

That Sunday the *Mail* ran a couple of paragraphs: nothing about the children — I'm not surprised, as it was all very domestic stuff — but an unguarded remark by Bill Clinton that Ros had overheard, and a couple of comments about different people who had come to stay in Downing Street.

We weren't able to stop the press reports — the fact that the Blairs' nanny had written a book — but everything concerning the manuscript had to be handed over to us, and the *Mail* was ordered to pay our court costs. We were also awarded costs against Ros, but I chose not to enforce them. It should really have ended there, but by this time Ros had become involved with a woman, whom the papers would later describe as a "fantasist," who tried to sell the manuscript elsewhere, in spite of the terms of the injunction. Extraordinary allegations started coming out. I then had to start taking out gag orders against this woman as well. It was a complete nightmare.

The baby was due on May 23, but on the morning of the nineteenth, I knew that labor had started. Always one for putting off the trip to the hospital until the last possible minute, I decided to do just one more thing. As Euan was taking his GCSEs, the headmaster had suggested that I come in to discuss how best to ensure that the press didn't get hold of his grades. Needless to say, we were followed, but Robbie, one of Tony's drivers, did a quick U-turn in Victoria Street and managed to lose them. Jackie came with me, as she was intimately involved in anything to do with the children's schools. Fiona came, too, as this was connected to the press.

My contractions were getting stronger. *Little does he realize,* I thought as I listened to the headmaster, *that as we sit here discussing how to keep my son's GCSEs out of the tabloids, I'm about to give birth in his office.*

When we were finished, I was so terrified about the press finding out, I refused to tell the hospital we were on our way. So Robbie just drove round the back, and we snuck in. I was taken straight into one of the delivery suites. Then there was the question of Tony. Obviously, the moment he arrived, the press would know what was happening. In fact, they had got wind of it anyway, and they were all gathering outside. When I found out, my contractions stopped immediately. Even the thought of that phalanx of photographers was enough to freeze me.

Sally Benatar, the only woman on Tony's protection team, had by now arrived, and she and Fiona waited outside as labor got well and truly under way. My other deliveries had all been fairly quiet births, but I made up for that with Leo! I remember the nursing staff saying that I didn't have to worry about how much noise I made because the room was soundproof. "No one will hear anything," they claimed. Only later did I realize that the room wasn't *that* soundproof, and poor Sally, who was in the early stages of her first pregnancy, was deeply regretting having volunteered to be present.

At around eight Tony said he couldn't wait any longer and came over. The 'tecs all put their heads round the door to say hello, and every one of them looked as if he was going to be sick. Leo was by far the longest of my four births. I think part of me was holding on because I was still terrified of being photographed. It was stupid, really, but when you're pregnant, you get these fixations, and I just thought, *I do not want to be photographed looking like that.* Giving birth is very private. You think you're ugly and the whole thing is horrendous. You think, *I don't want my husband to see me like this, let alone the entire world.* In the end, of course, you don't give a damn.

From Tony's point of view, it was the best birth, because it was entirely natural. Euan's was scary, as they had to use forceps. Kathryn's was scary, because I was being cut open. And Nicholas's — the only one that had been calm and natural — Tony had missed completely. I refused any drugs because my aim was to get out with the baby in complete privacy, and that meant as soon as possible.

Leo was born just after midnight, and at a few minutes after 2:00 a.m, I walked to the waiting car, the baby in my arms and Tony by my side. That was that. No one expected me to be released that night. The boys were waiting up for us — Kathryn was staying with a friend — and my mum was there to help. All was well with the world. As I fed my new baby for the first time, I felt totally safe. I was in my own bed, in my own home, and no one was going to come running through the door and snatch a picture.

We knew that there was a hunger for photographs, so I had asked Mary McCartney if she would come and take them. I had got to know her through Breast Cancer Care, her mother, Linda, having died of breast cancer. We decided we'd sell the images and give the proceeds to the charity. So the next day — shades of when Euan was born — André came in to make me look presentable. Mary took the photographs: one for the press and one with all the kids for us. Unfortunately they'd been up so late the night before that they were horribly badly behaved. Nicholas ended up with a bruised eye, thanks to Euan, and my mother was in tears.

CHAPTER 25

Future Imperfect

Leo's timing was impeccable. He arrived on the Friday before the bank holiday week. For ages I'd been pushing Tony to take some paternity leave, but he'd refused, saying, "I can't. I'm the Prime Minister." But from the moment he clapped eyes on his son, he was so besotted he wanted to spend time with him, and as Parliament wasn't sitting, it wasn't that difficult to cancel all his outside engagements. Of course he was still on the phone and read his papers, but basically he was based in the flat enjoying being a new dad.

When Leo was about six weeks old, I decided I needed to take a break and to start getting back in shape. The singer Cliff Richard, whom I had met at a charity event a year or so before, had said that if ever we wanted to get away, we could borrow his villa in Portugal. So while Tony stayed at home to keep an eye on the kids, Leo and I — together with Carole and my mum — flew off for a week's vacation. It was exactly what I needed: sunshine, good food, and gentle exercise. Everything was going well until the phone call from my husband on July 6, telling me he had just come back from the police station with Euan after he'd been found sprawled across the pavement in Leicester Square, the heart of London's entertainment district.

"But he's home now and he's safe," Tony said when he called to give me the glad tidings. "I won't suggest you try to speak to him because he's incoherent. But you don't have to worry, because I'm in charge."

"If you were really in charge, this wouldn't have happened."

It was a short conversation. When I put down the receiver, I turned on the television. The news had even reached Portugal.

Fortunately I was going back to England the following day, and it was a very shamefaced sixteen-year-old who greeted me. His father wasn't much better. I wasn't really cross. The press was making a lot of it, but the reality is that had he been the son of anybody else, they'd just have said, "Okay, don't do it again." As it was, because of press pressure, he had to be given a formal caution by the police.

The local police station was obviously out, so Euan and I were told to take the emergency escape route, a gloomy old tunnel that ran under Whitehall, right into the Ministry of Defence. In the event of a terrorist attack or a bomb scare, it would take us straight to the nuclear bunker.

A car was waiting on the far side of the Ministry of Defence, and we were taken to a police station in south London, where Euan made a statement and was given the caution.

"If you don't get into trouble again," the kindly police officer said, "when you're eighteen, this will be wiped off, and there'll be no record at all."

Euan looked decidedly cheered. "You mean once I've turned eighteen, no one need ever know?"

My heart sank. *My sweet, innocent boy,* I thought. *You don't realize that they'll never let you forget that at the age of sixteen, you were drunk and were cautioned.*

Because of giving birth to Leo, I missed that summer's G8 summit in Okinawa, which is why André wasn't there to prevent my husband from wearing a hideous Japanese shirt the British press delighted in. When he got home, Tony explained that they were all given a choice, and he had chosen the least offensive. To his amazement, when Bill Clinton appeared, Tony noticed that Bill had picked the most hideous of all.

"Why on earth did you choose that?" Tony asked.

"Take it from an old-timer," Bill said. "Sometimes when you go to these summits, you're in a rock-or-a-hard-place situation. If you don't wear it, you offend your host. If you do, you're made a mockery of at home. Now you, Tony, wearing that particular shirt, people at home might conceivably think that you actually chose to wear it. Me, wearing this shirt, everybody at home is going to think, *Boy, is that Clinton diplomatic, being so nice to those foreigners. There's no way he would have chosen to wear that. What a good man he is!*"

The UN doesn't go in for funny outfits, and as that September's Millennium General Assembly was a one-off, I was determined to go. I was still breast-feeding, however, so I would need to take Leo. The first question was, Can I take Jackie? The answer from the Cabinet office was absolutely not. Fortunately Leo has known André since the day he was born, and so André agreed to be his stand-in nanny. During that whole trip, whenever I had to be somewhere else, André looked after him: changed his diapers, gave him his bottle of expressed milk, everything.

André has had to put up with a lot from me over the years, but he never expected to have to introduce the British Prime Minister's son to the American President. We were staying in the UN Plaza Hotel, which because of its location doesn't have to try very hard. I was late returning to the room, a circumstance with which André was all too familiar. The baby bag was packed, and Leo was strapped to André's front in the sling, when two FBI men arrived at the door. They told André to bring the baby; Mrs. Blair would meet him at the destination. More than a little unnerved, he was ushered into a limousine — one of five, four of which were empty — and off they set. Then, disaster. Leo filled his diaper. Worst of all, it was of the explosive variety, and André had forgotten to pack an extra set of clothes. As André always points out, he is not a professional nanny, and he panicked.

"Excuse me," he said to the Secret Service man beside the driver. "I have a problem."

The man was totally unfazed, and seconds later they screeched to a halt. The door opened and André was ushered out, Leo still strapped to his front, to find himself being escorted into Ralph Lauren.

"My!" said the greeter — the place had been completely cleared of customers — "you must be important!" Then the penny dropped. "Oh, my God, it's Baby Blair!"

They were whisked into the back of the shop, and once André had cleaned Leo up and put on a new diaper, he was presented with a brand-new outfit, dungarees and a sweater resplendent with the American flag.

Next stop was the Waldorf Hotel, where he was assured I would be waiting. He was taken up through the kitchen entrance — the route of choice for American Presidents and their wives — then up to the presidential suite on the top floor, which was bristling, he says, with bodyguards, earpieces, and cell phones. Finally he arrived at a pair of double doors.

"The President will see you now," he was told, and the door was held open.

"What about Mrs. Blair?"

"She's not here yet. You're to go on in."

He was petrified. Making his way down the empty corridor, he began calling out, "Hello? Hello? Anybody there?"

"In here" came the reply. André pushed open the door to the room from which the voice was coming, only to see Bill and Hillary Clinton at the far end of a room the size of a tennis court.

I arrived about five minutes later, to find Bill holding Leo and generally cooing, although my son's red face showed that he had clearly been exercising his lungs until very recently. André gave me one of his looks.

"Cherie," he hissed, "don't you ever do that to me again."

We all then proceeded to the UN to meet up with Tony. The first group to emerge was the Chinese. They are usually very stiff and unforthcoming, but seeing Leo in his little American sweater was too much even for them. They stopped and talked and had their pictures taken with Baby Blair. Then French President Jacques Chirac came out, and it was the same thing. Tony couldn't believe it. "Why on earth," he said, "is the British Prime Minister's son wearing an American jumper?"

"It's a long story," I said.

The general election in 2001 was set for May 2, to coincide with local elections, but following a severe outbreak of foot-and-mouth disease, it was postponed until June 7. This outbreak was a major disaster for farmers, and the government was entirely right to wait until the situation was under control before going to the country. But it was singularly bad timing for me, as I was about to start a big case on May 8. When I had taken it on, I had assumed the election would be done and dusted by the time it began. Fortunately, as it was expected to be a very long case, the judge agreed we could have a "reading day" every Friday. In addition, a couple of public holidays were coming up.

As a result, although my campaigning with Tony was confined to the weekends, I was able to do some on my own with Angela Goodchild, who took over my schedule for the weeks of the campaign. As Fiona and Roz were "special advisers" paid for by the government, they were forbidden to do anything that might be deemed political. Angela had been a volunteer at Labour Party headquarters in the 1997 election and had then come in as a part-timer, a Labour Party employee in the political office, to help with Tony's more personal mail. With the publicity surrounding the founding of Matrix, members of the public increasingly saw me as a first port of call for legal advice, and I was flooded with queries. As Downing Street understandably couldn't help — anything to do with the law was clearly my professional domain — I negotiated to pay for Angela's services one day a week. We got on very well, and from then on, whenever I hit the campaign trail, Angela would accompany me.

For those four weeks in the run-up to the election, every Friday I'd visit marginals — those districts in which things were so close that a few votes in either direction might tip the scales — close to London. In the final week, thanks to a holiday and my junior on the case covering for me at the trial, I was able to be at Tony's side.

It was another landslide, with Labour losing only one seat to the Conservatives. The press, however, didn't look at the huge majority, but claimed instead that it was a victory for apathy because of the low turnout. Tony, rightly in my view, took it as a sign that the public was happy with the way he was going and hadn't thought there was much need to register their votes. Tony made some ministerial changes. Robin Cook was removed from the Foreign Office, and there was talk of Gordon Brown taking his place, though it didn't happen. Gordon, who had married Sarah Macaulay in August 2000, had recently been increasing pressure on Tony to commit to leaving office. But Tony knew he still had a lot to do, particularly in the area of public service reforms — namely, health and education — and he was determined to see them through.

The office was also given a shake-up. Tony moved Alastair out of day-to-day press management and gave Anji a new post as head of government relations. Fiona was promoted to head of events and visits. As a result, Angela began to take on more for me, and Sue Geddes joined the office to assist with my official schedule.

Everybody knows where they were on September 11, 2001. I was in chambers: I had two separate case conferences, one in the morning and one in the afternoon, and had just finished the morning conference when the news started to come through. My first instinct was to go back to Number 10. Whenever something important is happening, Downing Street is the place to be. Tony was in Brighton, where he had been due to address the TUC conference. As it was, his speech was simply handed out to delegates. He came straight back to London. His overriding feeling was that everything needed dampening down and confidence maintained, particularly in the financial sector. He was convinced that America would feel beleaguered, and we had to let the United States know it wasn't alone.

Tony remained very visible. From the start, his was the opposite of a bunker mentality. In his first television address, less than an hour after the news of the attacks came through, he said, "I hope you will join with me in sending our condolences to the people of America and to President Bush from the British people. This mass terrorism is the new evil in our world perpetrated by fanatics who are utterly indifferent to the sanctity of human life. All democratic countries must unite to eradicate this evil from our world."

Three days later, at a special session of the House of Commons, Tony made a fantastic speech, sending out a message not only to Britain but also to the world:

One thing should be very clear. By their acts, these terrorists and those behind them have made themselves the enemies of the civilized world. The objective will be to bring to account those who have organized, aided, abetted and incited this act of infamy; and those that harbor or help them have a choice: either to cease their protection of our enemies; or be treated as an enemy themselves. . . . We do not yet know the exact origin of this evil. But, if, as appears likely, it is so-called Islamic fundamentalists, we know they do not speak or act for the vast majority of decent law-abiding Muslims throughout the world. I say to our Arab and Muslim friends: neither you nor Islam is responsible for this; on the contrary, we know you share our shock at this terrorism; and we ask you as friends to make common cause with us in defeating this barbarism that is totally foreign to the true spirit and teachings of Islam.

Even before Tony was elected Prime Minister, he thought it important to learn about Islam. Britain has a sizable and important Muslim population, and, as far back as January 1997, Khawar Qureshi — a lawyer friend of mine and now a Queen's Counsel — took us to visit the Regent's Park mosque. He knew that we were interested and that Tony wanted to meet and talk to other Muslims. During the summer of 2001, while we were on holiday, Tony had in fact been reading the Koran.

The *Washington Post* was soon rating Tony alongside New York's Mayor Rudy Giuliani as "the only other political figure who broke through the world's stunned disbelief." Among the victims were two hundred from the UK, a small percentage of the total toll of three thousand, but 9/11 remains the largest terrorist attack ever on British citizens. That Friday we attended a memorial service at St. Paul's Cathedral. It was a powerful occasion: not only were we all in a state of shock, but it was so moving to see the relatives of the victims — mostly wives and children, because so many of the missing and the dead were reasonably young. As Tony was anxious to have a face-to-face meeting with the still relatively new President, George W. Bush, the following week we flew to America. By then Tony had already had meetings with all the key European leaders. He believed that the response to the attacks should be international rather than America going it alone.

On that long flight across the Atlantic, I remembered the conversation I'd had with President Bush, when he and Laura had stayed at Chequers the previous spring. We were all having dinner together, and the conversation had been extraordinarily open and frank, thanks in no small part to the presence of the children. George had been talking about the Star Wars missile defense system, initiated by President Ronald Reagan in the 1980s, and how he saw that as the ultimate shield.

But I had grown up under the shadow of IRA terrorism. "Surely," I'd said, "the real danger is not from Russia or any other country sending bombs, but from individual people in a terrorist attack?"

George had looked bemused at the suggestion. Americans had no sense that such a thing could ever happen to them, and that's what made September 11 so shocking.

On our arrival in New York, we went first to a processing center near the Hudson River. Everywhere we looked, people had put up pictures of their loved ones, with messages and contact phone numbers, in the hope that they would be found alive. It had been only nine days since the attack, and it was all very upsetting. Knots of people talked in hushed voices. A section of the center was being run by the British consulate, and we talked to those who were counseling the bereaved. The counselors themselves had barely slept in days. We wanted to go on to a fire station — New York firefighters, of course, having become the heroes of the tragedy — but with downtown Manhattan still in a state of paralysis, even with a police escort and motorcycle outriders, we were too short of time. So we went directly to St. Thomas's Church for a memorial service for the British dead.

We knew that Tony was expected to do a reading, but the question coming over on the plane had been, what? It would be very difficult to get the right tone. Magi Cleaver suggested an extract from a novel by the American writer Thornton Wilder called *The Bridge of San Luis Rey.* Magi had been shifted from the Foreign Office to manage the Civil Service side of the events and visits office. (The arcane regulations decreed that as a special adviser herself, Fiona could manage only other special advisers.) She was a tiny bossyboots of a person, and everybody seemed petrified of her, but she was charming and lovely to us. She took me under her wing, and I loved her. Having started her Foreign Office career in Chile during the presidency of Salvador Allende, she was interested in all things South American, which was why she happened to have the book with her. The reading ended like this: "There is a land of the living and a land of the dead, and the bridge is love, the only survival, the only meaning."

After the service I was able to talk to some of the victims' families, including wives who were pregnant and with whom, I am happy to say, I have been able to keep in touch as they have rebuilt their lives. At the time they were still hopeful that their husbands would be found alive. Tony went straight to Washington for talks with the President, while Bill Clinton agreed to come to the fire station with me in Tony's place. This particular fire station had been chosen because it had suffered such tremendous losses in the rescue operation, and in those kinds of circumstances, Bill is at his best. The men we met were just fantastic, brave and strong. One I talked to I recognized from one of the now iconic photographs taken that day. At the end they presented me with an American flag — for Tony — folded up in a triangle, with a plaque signaling their appreciation of his support, a thank-you from the firefighters of New York. For years it was on display in Downing Street, and now we have it at home. I was insistent that we take it when we left: a powerful memory of a very haunting visit.

By the time we got back to London, a whole new security regime was being put in place. It had been decided that from now on, I would have permanent police protection. What this meant in practical terms was that I stopped going into chambers every day. Like Tony, I could no longer drive; wherever I went, I had to have a Number 10 driver and a close security officer. Once I got back to Number 10, I had to stay there: no picking the children up from friends' houses, no dropping them off at sports activities, no popping out to the shops or going for a run in St. James's Park. If I wanted to do any of those things, a detective had to come with me. Everything had to be planned in advance and marked on the appropriate schedule.

The children were no longer permitted to travel by public transport. One of my main concerns in keeping their faces out of the newspapers was wanting them to lead as normal lives as possible, which meant subways and buses. In fact, we had managed surprisingly well. The nannies, too, were unknown, and could take the children for a hamburger without any fear of their being recognized.

Euan was far from pleased. He had been taking the underground to school since 1996, and the idea of being driven by the police did not go down well. Nicholas wasn't much happier. Kathryn, still only twelve, was less resistant, as she hadn't experienced the same kind of freedom the boys had.

Security at this level takes some adjusting to. If you have police protection, you have police protection; it is not some sort of optional perk. You cannot go anywhere without having somebody with you, and the police have to know where you are and what you

253

are doing all the time. One evening that autumn, on the spur of the moment, Kathryn and I decided to go to the theater, to see *Blood Brothers*. The play was written by Willy Russell, whom I knew when he ran a folk club in Liverpool. It starred Barbara Dickson, who, long before she became famous, did a gig at the Trimdon folk club. We were about to set off when I suddenly remembered the security. The 'tecs had left for the day, and I hadn't made any provision for late-night duties. Although I felt bad, I rang them up and said perhaps they could meet us at the theater. "I'll just get a taxi there," I said.

"Sorry, Mrs. B. You can't do that," the officer said. "You'll have to wait till I get there."

"But we'll be late."

"Well, then, you'll just have to be late."

Another issue was the nuclear bunker. When we'd first moved in, I had inspected it to see if it was suitable for children. It was totally underground and really spooky. There were army-style bunks, and I couldn't see how I could ever take the kids down there. Downing Street staff members were divided into groups: Red, Blue, Green, and Orange. In the event of an emergency, the Red group had to come down with us, the Blues were to muster on the lawn, the Greens were to go home but be on call, the Orange group were free to go home and not be on call. Alastair was in the Red group, but Fiona was in the Green group, and I thought, *No way is Alastair going to come in with us and leave Fiona and his kids at home if there's a nuclear Armageddon*. I'd told the powers that be as much and asked, "Just how realistic is this as a plan?" In response, they'd asked if I wanted to show the children the bunker, and I'd said no.

Now I had to address the matter seriously, so Jackie and I went down, as instructed, taking clothes and games and books for the children. Apart from the hum of the air-conditioning, it was as quiet as a grave. Jackie agreed with me that if it ever came to it, this place would completely freak them out.

In early December the *Daily Mail* ratcheted up its attacks on me. This time it was in relation to Leo. They demanded to know whether he had had the MMR (measles-mumps-rubella) vaccine. "Come Clean, Cherie" was the headline. The great issue of the day was whether the MMR vaccine causes autism. A report — since wholly discredited — had said that it could. Then the *Mirror* joined in. I had innocently responded to a letter sent to me by the mother of an autistic child, saying that I was "keeping an eye on things." It had seemed fairly innocuous at the time.

A number of people around me, whose views I respected, were vociferously against all forms of vaccination. Over the years I had listened to their side of the argument, and it's fair to say that I was of two minds. I did get Leo vaccinated, not least because it's irresponsible not to — there's absolutely no doubt that the incidence of a disease goes up if vaccinations go down — and he was given his MMR jab within the recommended time frame. I was adamant, however, that I would not give the press chapter and verse. I saw no reason to parade my family's vaccination records in front of the public. It would set a bad precedent, and everyone — by which I mean Alastair and Fiona — agreed.

CHAPTER 26

Frontiers

The invasion of Afghanistan began less than a month after 9/11. The destruction of the Twin Towers was generally acknowledged to have been the work of al-Qaeda, the terrorist organization run by Osama bin Laden. Their training camps were known to be in Afghanistan, funded in part at least by the Taliban, which provided support and safe haven. In 1998 President Bill Clinton had launched cruise missile attacks on these camps in retaliation for the al-Qaeda attacks on two U.S. embassies in East Africa, but with little effect. On October 7, 2001, the aerial bombing of Afghanistan began, and Kabul fell a little over a month later.

At the beginning of the new year, Tony and I set off on an official trip to Bangladesh, India, and Pakistan. By now the Foreign Office had acknowledged my usefulness, and while Tony talked with various officials, I visited a number of projects related to women.

Because of the color and vibrancy of the subcontinent, the poverty there always comes as a shock. Yet huge efforts were being made to harness the entrepreneurial skills of women. Near Dhaka I visited a microcredit program run by a nongovernmental organization (NGO) called BRAC, which had not only set up the cooperative where women learned to manage the microfinance loans they received but also delivered elementary health care and education to women. Some women would be trained in basic health-care principles and techniques and have access to things such as malaria tablets and contraception. Other women would be trained in women's basic human rights under Islamic law, learning, for example, that husbands don't own all their wives' property and that a husband's family can't take away the wife's property.

The British High Commission continues to be very involved in dealing with forced marriages and related issues, and I was taken to a refuge for women whose husbands' families had been in some way dissatisfied with them — perhaps because of their physical appearance or their dowries. To substantiate their claims that these women were substandard, the husbands' families poured acid from car batteries over the women's heads. According to Human Rights Watch, in Pakistan such attacks killed 280 women and injured 750 in 2002 alone. In Bangladesh there were 485 acid attacks that year. With the increasing availability of car batteries, these horrific incidents multiplied. The women's injuries defied description. They had no faces left, or at least no distinguishing features. It was as if their flesh had melted. Hugging these women was, for me, a way of defying their aggressors. I know how much it means to have human contact, and luckily I have never felt any physical repugnance toward any human being, though I believe that is the purpose of these cruel and cowardly attacks.

At that time in Bangladesh, both the Prime Minister and the Leader of the Opposition were women (though they hated each other with a passion). It seems extraordinary to me that in a country where being a woman is apparently no barrier to high office, individual women are treated as being of less value than animals.

Wanting both to be comfortable and to show respect, I asked Babs Mahil to make my clothes for this trip. She also wanted to make something for Tony — a Nehru-style suit that he wore to the state banquet in India. I thought he looked very handsome, but the British press, true to form, had a real go at him. Sadly, he never wore the suit again. Although Alastair had claimed to approve, he was in fact generally of the opinion that Tony could wear anything as long as it was an ordinary suit, and he was to be the final arbiter of Tony's attire.

Thus, when we arrived in Bangladesh, Tony wasn't even wearing his own suit. Alastair had deemed it too crumpled, and so Magi Cleaver had been dispatched to the terminal to find another one. Some bemused young man, who turned out to be from our Department of International Development, was persuaded to give up his suit for an hour so that the British Prime Minister would look suffi-ciently smart. For the rest of the trip, André was in charge, and it just went to show once again that when André wasn't there, things fell apart.

Our next destination, Kabul, was not on the official itinerary. Indeed, we were under a complete press embargo. "You don't have to go," Foreign Office officials had told me, but I was determined: "I'm going with Tony." It had been nearly two months since Kabul had been taken, but it was still far from safe, which was why we flew in the middle of the night and would go no further than Bagram air base.

Unsurprisingly, this was the first time I had traveled in an army plane. It was designed for carrying troops, and I'd been warned that it was lacking in even the most basic creature comforts. There were no regular seats, and the toilet was a bucket. Not that I saw it: I decided I would rather die than climb over the press — sworn to silence in exchange for being allowed in on the secret — to go to the bucket in the back.

In fact, there weren't that many of us, but Tony and I were lucky enough to be taken into the cockpit, and we were there from takeoff to landing. The crew members were special services people (elite SAS commandos) who had been flying in and out of Afghanistan on various missions since the war began, and they made it seem as easy as a school bus route. These were the kind of daredevil pilots beloved by writers, not faint of heart in any way.

Tony and I sat in the back of the cockpit where the engineer would normally sit, and above us was a sort of see-through dome where the gunner would stand and direct the fire. As we took off, Tony asked if he could stand up and watch. So there he was, peering out into the night and asking them about this and that. One of the pilots took on the mantle of tour guide, pointing out different peaks and telling us when we were crossing the Khyber Pass — an area that is lawless to this day. As we flew into Afghan airspace over the mountains of northern Pakistan, all the lights went off. Even though we might not be seen, the pilot helpfully explained, we could still be hit by a heat-seeking missile. An indication on the radar that we might have been spotted resulted in immediate avoidance tactics, and the plane began to swerve and sway, the idea being that any missile already deployed would be misled, aiming for where we had been rather than where we were now.

So Tony was standing up there, watching all of this, while I was strapped in, thinking, *Why did I come? I've got four children at home, one of whom is less than two years old. It was nutty of me to think this was a good idea.* Believe it or not, as I was sitting there, my entire life really did flash before my eyes. All I could think about was that if I hadn't come along, at least one of us would have been alive for the kids. Finally, at 1:30 a.m., we arrived at Bagram air base.

It's only when you land in a military plane that you realize that a commercial landing is basically done for the benefit of the passengers. There was no question that we had touched down — indeed, "touched" is much too mild a word for it.

Make no mistake, Afghanistan in January is cold. I had my big heavy coat on, but it wasn't enough.

The red carpet was out; I hadn't expected this kind of welcome. But I was soon disabused of its purpose. "Whatever you do," the copilot said as we walked down the steps, "stay on the carpet." Bagram had been mined by Taliban forces, and although some of the mines had been cleared, there was still a way to go. "We can guarantee that as long as you stay on the red carpet, you'll be okay." (Whenever I find myself walking on a red carpet, I remember that arrival at Bagram.)

Even though it was the middle of the night, we were greeted with due ceremony by President Karzai and his Cabinet. I was so grateful to have landed safely I could have kissed them all.

The SAS had played a very important part in the invasion, and I was totally enthralled by the stories of how they'd stormed Taliban hideouts, real tales of derring-do. It was impossible to imagine how close they'd been to death and how, against all odds, they'd managed to pull it off. Staff from our Department of International Development gave an impressive presentation on what we were going to do to help Afghanistan build itself up again. The Afghans said over and over how grateful they were and how fantastic our people were doing. If you want someone to help rebuild your country, they said, the British have the right stuff.

While Tony had a meeting with Karzai, I was introduced to the Minister for Women, Sima Samar, and together we spoke to a group of women soldiers who were helping with the peacekeeping. When we asked them what their impressions were, they told us that each day more and more women were visible on the streets, although few were uncovering their faces. The minister told them that for the people of Kabul, the very presence of these young women soldiers doing responsible peacekeeping work was an important step toward the recognition of women's right to see and be seen. When I asked her what I could do to help, what the women of Afghanistan wanted, her message was simple: Please make sure you keep the pressure on the men. Please don't forget the women of Afghanistan.

While we were talking with troops based at the airport, Tony took a call from Gordon Brown's office. I knew from his face what had happened. Gordon and Sarah's newborn baby, Jennifer, had died. We had been on our way to Hyderabad when the news had come through that she was dangerously ill. She had been born prematurely, and although she was a fighter, things were not looking good. Throughout the trip I had found it very hard to smile for the cameras knowing what they were facing back home. As a comparatively new father himself, Tony also was all too aware of the emotional strain they were under.

We arrived back in England on Tuesday and were in Scotland on Friday. We went first to their house. Sarah was so calm, and it was very brave of her to let us come. Whereas in the old days Gordon's flat had always been a bit of a mess, Sarah had made their house into a welcoming home. Losing a baby under any circumstances is terrible, and losing your first baby is utterly devastating. My heart went out to both of them.

From our visits to Washington, we had got to know Vice President Al Gore, the Democratic candidate for President in 2000, and his wife, Tipper, reasonably well. So I think it's fair to say that our hearts sank when the results of the 2000 election were finally in. In fact, Tony had felt very strongly that Gore had played it wrong during the campaign and that he should have used Bill Clinton more rather than distancing himself from the President. He seemed not to realize how much goodwill Bill still commanded and what a great communicator he was. Like the rest of the world, we followed the drama of the election, and for me, as a lawyer, it was fascinating to see the U.S. Supreme Court splitting along political lines. It would never have happened like that in the UK, because the appointment of our judges is not so politicized.

We had watched George W. Bush on television and felt that he didn't seem comfortable with foreign affairs, yet Tony was determined that they should have a good relationship. Others of our party, notably Alastair and Sally Morgan, had a more mixed view.

As we prepared for our first meeting with the Bushes at Camp David at the end of February 2001, I said to Tony, "Let's face it, he's probably not looking forward to it much either. He knows we're friends of the Clintons, and he also knows you're a Labour Prime Minister and all the rest of it, so everybody's going to be a bit nervous, everybody's going to want to try and get along."

The fact that the encounter was in the semirustic setting of Camp David was indicative, in a way, of the difference between the two presidents. The Clintons had entertained us lavishly with a formal banquet at the White House. And whereas they never really got going till late, the Bushes were tucked up in bed by ten. We had come from Ottawa, where I had been half-frozen, having no idea of how heart-stoppingly cold it would be. From Washington we were flown out to Camp David in the presidential helicopter *Marine One*, which is less like a helicopter and more like a small plane.

We had been to Camp David once before with the Clintons, and it had not been what I'd expected. Because it was the presidential equivalent of Chequers, I thought it would be a country home. But Camp David is a U.S. Marine base. Everyone stays in wooden "cabins" named after trees. Each cabin has a lounge, a bathroom, and two bedrooms, all decorated to a luxurious standard. (When the Clintons were there, the hand lotion and soap came from a supplier in Arkansas.) The cabins are all spread out, and whenever you venture outside, you're followed by military personnel.

That first night with the Bushes, we had an early dinner. The meal over, the President said, "Why don't we all watch a movie?" So we did. He got all the new releases on DVD, he explained, and that night we watched *Meet the Parents* with Robert De Niro. There were armchairs ranged around, and I sat next to George, who was soon laughing away. It was a perfectly friendly evening, very low-key. We were joined by our ambassador, Christopher Meyer, and his wife, Catherine, and of course by Jonathan Powell, Alastair, and the others.

In fact, the Prime Minister and the President got on remarkably well. George is actually a very funny, charming man with a quirky sense of humor. The reason he gets bad press, he says, is "because I talk Texan." Bush thinks Texan, too. Bill Clinton is also from the South, but while Clinton may talk southern, he doesn't think southern.

There had certainly been a slight sense of anxiety before the meeting, but by the time we left, the general consensus was that "he's a guy we can easily get on with." We may not have agreed in terms of domestic politics, but that is largely irrelevant in terms of international diplomacy. And the special relationship between the UK and the United States is precisely why, when Bush and the Republicans took over, there was never any question that we would do everything we could to get on well with them.

As we were escorted to *Marine One* after breakfast, I realized that we hadn't been back to our cabin to get André or our luggage.

"Don't worry," I was told. "He'll be on the helicopter." He wasn't, but by the time I found out, it was too late. André wasn't the only one who'd been left behind. There was a garden girl as well, not to mention our bags. Apparently they had both been waiting patiently for us to get back from breakfast. Somebody had to arrange for another helicopter to bring them back to Washington, and Christopher Meyer was not amused, claiming that it was somehow my fault.

The next time we saw the Bushes was at Chequers a month or so later. By then we knew that George didn't really like formal entertaining, and if they'd come to Number 10, we'd have to have had some kind of formal dinner. They were much happier in an informal setting, and we were very clear that we wanted it to be just *en famille*. When we were told that Condoleezza Rice wanted to stay the night, we said no. Everyone could come for the meetings, but there were to be no sleepovers apart from the family. The day they were arriving, Linda, who was then running Chequers, came to see me.

"I've managed to accommodate Mr. Bush's doctor," she said.

"What doctor?" I asked.

"Dr. Rice."

"Dr. Rice?" And then the penny dropped. Condi, as she is always known, had conned Linda into thinking the President needed to have his medical doctor close at hand.

Like us, the Bushes are very family oriented. Laura was an only child brought up by her mother, and she married into this big family, with everyone having loads of children. But she and George have only two children, twin daughters, one named for her mother and the other for his: Jenna and Barbara. That evening at Chequers was very much a family affair, and in addition to our children, James Dove, Euan's friend from the Oratory, was there. He had always been interested in politics, and perhaps because he was present, the conversation was more wide-ranging than it might have been if it had just been us. Certainly I can't see Tony or me raising the question of capital punishment, but that's exactly what one of the kids did. So there we were, discussing the death penalty: in one corner, an American President who believed in it; in the other, a human rights lawyer who very definitely did not. I stated my view, saying that the death penalty is inherently wrong and that if you make a mistake, you can't put it right.

"Well, that's not the way it is in America," George said. "We take the eye-for-an-eye view."

But it was completely and utterly good-hearted. The way George handled those kids and their questions, I thought, *All credit to him.* And I know that both James and Euan were pleasantly surprised that he could string an argument together and didn't turn into some sort of raging bigot. I often say that I must be the only person on the left that George Bush gets to socialize with. But no one can say — at least not me — that he doesn't have a sense of humor.

One of the last things Bill Clinton did when he stepped down from office was to sign the Rome Treaty, which set up the International Criminal Court (ICC). After the Balkans War and the Rwanda genocide, the UN had decided to set up the International Tribunal for the Former Yugoslavia and the International Tribunal for Rwanda. The success of these tribunals had led to the establishment of the ICC as a permanent court based in The Hague. The ICC would try people charged with crimes against humanity and genocide either when their own country had no infrastructure or when the country asked the international community to conduct the trial.

In recent years America has signed very few international charters, a pattern described as "American Exceptionalism." This is essentially an attitude of moral superiority, a belief that America is qualitatively different from other nations and so does not need to buy into international treaties. An example is the International Covenant on the Rights of the Child (CRC). This charter has been signed by every country in the world but two: Somalia, which has barely got a government, and the United States. One of the reasons America didn't sign the CRC was that, at the time, it was still executing juveniles. The Supreme Court has subsequently abolished this horror, but whoever the President is, it will be difficult for him or her to get Congress to change its attitude. Once a country has signed a treaty, it then has to ratify it. In the United States, this needs to be done with the approval of the Senate, and the Senate, it should be noted, is full of people who don't have passports. So when Clinton signed the Rome Treaty, he knew it wouldn't be ratified. It was simply his way of singeing Congress's beard.

Once an international treaty is signed, a minimum number of countries must ratify it before it comes into force. By 2002 it was becoming clear that the Rome Treaty would soon reach the magic number of countries. In addition to its other provisions, it was the first international treaty to require a minimum number of women judges. I had become involved in the campaign to make sure enough women were nominated to exceed the minimum figure. As very few international courts have women at all, this became a pet project of mine.

Everyone in the international legal community was resigned to the fact that the United States would not ratify the treaty and would thus be unable to nominate any judges. But then came rumors of something worse. George Bush, it was said, was going to formally unsign the treaty — that is, take America's signature off. One of Tony's advisers suggested that he approach George directly, on a personal level, saying, "This is just silly. Nothing is going to change. It just gives the wrong message to the international community; it makes them think you simply don't care."

I agreed. "You must raise it, Tony," I said, over and over, until the opportunity came for me to take matters into my own hands.

George and Laura had invited us to visit them after Easter 2002 at their ranch in Crawford, Texas. As Euan and Nicholas were both busy with schoolwork, I decided to take Kathryn and Leo on a trip to Disney World while Tony stayed with the boys in England and met me later in Texas. After four days of full-on fun, we spent Easter with an old friend of mine from the LSE who had a holiday home in

Florida. While Jackie stayed in the Sunshine State with the children, I set off for a breast cancer charity event in Dallas, which I was doing jointly with Laura.

Laura is a very warm, genuine person whom I liked the moment I met, and I immediately felt completely comfortable talking with her. It was clear that we had common ground; like me, she is interested in other women and women's issues generally. When we met, we would talk about our families and about literature, because we share a love of books. We had more of a "female friends" sort of relationship than I had with Hillary. My conversations with Hillary focused more on ideas, and of course we had our politics in common. To a degree, when I first met her, I was a little in awe. As Bill's wife, she had already been the First Lady for a number of years and was experienced in the job. But when Laura and I met, we were on a much more equal footing and have remained so. Our children, too, are more of an age.

Laura trained as a teacher, and in an exchange between colleges, she did part of her training in Oxfordshire, so she is surprisingly well-informed about life in England. I knew that Laura was involved in a breast cancer charity, but it was the American ambassador to Hungary who had suggested this joint event when she'd heard I was going to Texas. It was my first experience of the sheer professionalism of American fund-raising, and it was extraordinary: people paid at different levels to get different levels of access. At the reception Laura and I stood beside each other as people made their way along the line. *Just like one of my Downing Street receptions,* I decided, and I began chatting to those at the head of the queue. Immediately I heard a voice in my ear: "Mrs. Blair, you're to stop talking to these people. Just stand here, shake their hands, and let the photographer take the picture. That's all they've paid for. We've two hundred and twenty people to get through, so please understand. All they want is their picture with you and the First Lady. Please don't talk to them. That's not the point." So that's exactly what we did. It was a conveyor belt.

Then came dinner. Just about everyone was a Republican, and these were *Texas* Republicans. I found myself in a nearly intolerable situation. These women would start by saying how lovely Laura was, and I would concur, and then they'd start comparing her to "that terrible Clinton woman," going on and on about Hillary in the most disparaging way. I couldn't believe anyone could be so rude. I didn't say anything. There was absolutely no point, and I didn't want to make a scene, but I had to keep reminding myself that half the proceeds of that night were going to Breast Cancer Care. As I watched Laura being her usual charming self, I saw her in an entirely new light: she lived in a different world.

It was a big honor to be invited to Crawford. This was the Bushes' private home. I traveled from Dallas by car, but it soon became clear that most of those in the Bush circle — rich oil people — hopped around by helicopter. The road was like one you might see in an American movie about the West, just miles and miles of emptiness. Eventually we came to Crawford, the "town," where there's a café, a gas pump, and little else. The members of the press who had come out with Tony were furious because there was nowhere decent to stay. I remember thinking on the long drive out, *If I were the American President and could live anywhere, I don't think this is the place I would choose.* The house, however, was delightful: clean lines and modern, with paintings everywhere and no clutter; a really warm place.

Just before meeting for lunch on our last day, I had one final go at Tony: "Have you mentioned the thing about the International Criminal Court?"

"Don't fuss, woman. I've got important things to do."

Well, so had I.

As usual I was sitting next to George at lunch. "Look, George," I began, "I just wanted to talk to you about the International Criminal Court. People are saying that you're going to unsign. While everybody understands that the Senate is not going to ratify the treaty, do you really want to stick two fingers up to the international community? I know Clinton put you in this position, but it's not going to affect anyone in America, so why not leave it as it is? Then at least you'll seem to be part of it. But particularly now, when you've got all this goodwill from the international community, why rock the boat?"

George looked over at Condi, who was never far away, and beckoned her over.

"Condi," he said, "remind me to get you to tell me something about this."

Tony was sitting at another table with Laura and heard nothing.

As we said our good-byes, George put his hand on Tony's arm and said, "Tell you what, Tony. That wife of yours, she's very persistent on this international court thing."

Tony's smile faded as he hurried me toward the car. "Cherie, what can you have been thinking of?"

Just as the car was about to pull away, George came running out after us, and the driver wound down the window.

"And now," he said, "I understand why Clinton signed that bloody thing in the first place! It's all your fault, Cherie!" It wasn't true, of course. I had never raised it with Bill, but we all laughed, and he took it in good spirit.

Sadly, my little intervention made no difference. In the end the President did unsign it. But I think it's also the nature of the man that he didn't take my comments as a personal insult. It was my point of view; it just happened not to be the view of his adviser.

As for the campaign to get more women judges, we were very successful. In fact, we exceeded the quota.

CHAPTER 27

Collision Course

The Queen Mother died while Kathryn, Leo, and I were in Florida. We were back in Downing Street on April 8, and Kathryn and I walked to Westminster Abbey to the lying in state to pay our respects. The Queen Mum was always at Balmoral when we went there, and even in her late nineties, she was a formidable woman; there was a lot of steel in her. After Leo was born, I would take him with me, and that first year, when I asked the Queen if I could introduce him to her mother, she was more than happy. To my astonishment she said, "Mummy would allow Leo to have a picture taken with her." So we have a photograph of a queen born in 1900 holding a baby born in 2000.

The year 2002 must have been a difficult one for Queen Elizabeth. Those great celebrations — fifty years on the throne — and yet only weeks before the razzmatazz began, she lost both her mother and her sister, who had died in February.

The Queen Mother's funeral had been planned for years and was very different from Diana's. But inevitably, sitting there in the same seat, in the same coat, brought back memories. By chance the following day also focused on the past, when we gave a reception for former Prime Minister Jim Callaghan's ninetieth birthday. All the key figures of my political youth were assembled, though one important person was missing: Jim's wife, Audrey, who was suffering from Alzheimer's. The way Jim talked about her in his speech was so touching. Sadly, she died shortly afterward, and Jim died just ten days later. They had been partners for so long that he simply didn't want to carry on without her.

At the end of the month, Number 10 saw another similarly nostalgic celebration when Tony hosted a Golden Jubilee dinner for all the Queen's former Prime Ministers. Inviting those who were still with us was easy enough, but we also needed to involve representatives of those who had passed on: their widows or other family members. I hadn't realized how delicate this would be. To represent Alec Douglas-Home, a Conservative Prime Minister in the early 1960s, we invited his eldest son. Then a message came through from other members of the family who thought they should have been invited. The seating plan was also problematic, the key question being which Prime Minister should sit next to the Queen, and then who would flank Prince Philip. No way was Edward Heath about to sit next to Margaret Thatcher, who had ousted him as leader of the Conservative Party, and I imagined John Major had little desire to be near her either.

In the end Heath sat next to the Queen. (Although Jim Callaghan was fractionally older, Heath had been Prime Minister before him.) Tony was on her other side, as host. Margaret Thatcher was placed next to Prince Philip, and I was his other bookend.

By this time the redecoration of the state rooms at Number 10 was finished. This redecoration is done on a ten-year cycle, and a social anthropologist would no doubt have fun looking back through the various colors. What in Mrs. Thatcher's time was the Blue Room, the Majors had turned into the Green Room. It was now a rich terra-cotta, which the committee had been advised was "period appropriate." The design adviser wanted to remove the gilding that Mrs. Thatcher had put in, but this had been so expensive and so elaborately done, it would have cost a fortune to remove. Norma Major took one look at the new color and said she really liked it. Mrs. Thatcher was not so impressed.

"This is disgusting," she said.

Another room that displeased her was her former study on the first floor, which hadn't been involved in the recent refurbishment. "What have you done to my lovely room?" she barked. "It is just appalling." In this case she was right. It had been horribly brutalized in the intervening years, and I was determined to do something about it.

Her preferred color may have disappeared in the (now) Terra-cotta Room, but over the door, within the plaster frieze, is the figure of a little man going up a ladder with straw on his back — a nod to "Thatcher." I, too, have left my mark. Just before we departed Number 10, my plans to return Mrs. Thatcher's study to its former glory were finally completed, and the official opening was a tearful one, as this was one of the last things I did in Downing Street. I was known universally as Mrs. B, and if you look carefully, you can see a group of six bees carved into the wood of the bookcase: five big ones and a little one.

I had never seen the Queen more relaxed than on the evening of the dinner. She seemed always to be smiling. "What a relief," she said with a laugh as she came in. "No need for any introductions." Everyone was soon sharing reminiscences, and I found it fascinating to hear about different families' experiences of living in Number 10.

A few days later Tony and I had dinner with Roy and Jennifer Jenkins. Jennifer had been reading a history of the American First Ladies called *Hidden Power*. "Somebody should do a version for this country," she said. Coming so soon after that fascinating dinner with all the Prime Ministers and their families, it got me thinking. I had all the contacts, and, most important, I was about to have plenty of time on my hands: very disconcertingly, I had just discovered I was pregnant again.

Needless to say, I was astonished. Leo's birth had seemed like a miracle, and here I was nearly three years older. Although the idea was daunting to say the least, I realized that it would be nice for Leo not to be what amounted to an only child. As before, I went to see Susan Rankin, who arranged for me to have a scan in-house.

The radiographer was in raptures. "I have never seen a baby in a mother of your age that wasn't conceived by IVF [in vitro fertilization]," she said.

Tony was less enthralled. "I'm not sure I want to be a father at fifty," he said.

This time we decided to say nothing to anyone about the pregnancy. Not Alastair, not Fiona, certainly not Gordon. Not even my mum and dad. Only Jackie and the children knew. Unusually for me, I wasn't feeling at all well. It was going to be a hard pregnancy, I realized, and I was feeling grim most of the time. In fact, the *Mirror* published a picture of me sitting down after an official photo with the

COLLISION COURSE

Queen during a lunch at the Guildhall, part of the Jubilee celebrations. I'd been standing up for the picture but then had felt incredibly weak. This was taken as proof of how rude I was and how anti-monarchist, the caption being something like "Cherie Snubs Queen."

That year it was as if the past, the present, and the future were on a collision course. In May Tony attended a European Union meeting in Madrid, where José María Aznar told him he was planning to announce that he wouldn't be standing for a third term and that he'd be designating his successor. Aznar had first been elected Prime Minister exactly one year before Tony and was now two years into his second term. It had got Tony thinking. Even when we'd first arrived in Downing Street, he had said there would come a point where he would grow stale, and that after two terms — or a maximum of ten years — it would be time to move on. On a practical level it would mean I'd have got two of the kids through school and one even through university. Of course that was before Leo turned up.

Even during his first term, there had been tensions between Tony and Gordon. Many of these were provoked by the behavior of Charlie Whelan, Gordon's equivalent to Alastair. Whelan, it was claimed, spent half his time "briefing against" Tony — setting up the story that Gordon was the power behind the throne and the man taking all the decisions. Few believed that story, but it was irritating nonetheless. More damaging was the claim that Tony had done a deal with Gordon that he was now reneging on. Though Tony had always said that he felt two terms were probably enough, to my knowledge he never gave a guarantee on timing. Yet Gordon was always trying to pin Tony down with his "When are you going to go?"

So when Tony had this conversation with José María Aznar, he got very taken with the idea. It was not that he would be capitulating to Gordon's demands, he explained; it was rather that by making a public announcement, it might encourage Gordon to play ball. "It would reassure him that I am willing to go, and therefore he might start cooperating, and we could get the health and school reforms through."

"You must be mad," I said. "It might work for José María and his successor, but Gordon would only take advantage, and you'd be severely weakened in the eyes of the other people who count." Fortunately Sally, Jonathan, and Alastair all thought the same, and by

271

June Tony had accepted that if he wanted to get his reforms through, he needed to stay at Number 10, not announce that he was planning on packing his bags.

There were foreign policy concerns, too. The shadow over Iraq was becoming increasingly thunderous, and Tony was increasingly concerned. That spring America had renewed bombing in the no-fly zone in an attempt to disrupt Saddam Hussein's military command structure. In early June 2002, when Bill Clinton came to Chequers for the weekend, I found him and Tony crawling around the floor of the study, which was covered with maps. Bill was saying how he had always felt that Iraq was unfinished business, that Saddam Hussein was a dangerous person and a serious threat to world peace. From the intelligence he had seen, he was convinced that Iraq had weapons of mass destruction. He certainly wasn't advising caution — after all, he had initiated the bombing — but he was advising Tony that the UN was inevitably bound into the whole process. I could sense his frustration at no longer being in a position to take these decisions.

Carole was around that weekend. She was there to do some training with Tony, and I'll never forget her coming into the Great Hall and within seconds engaging the former President in conversation. "You need to remember the importance of stretching your back," she was saying, while arching her own, right in front of him, all white leggings and leotard at full stretch, her long hair sweeping the ground. I could see Bill's eyes widen, and I quickly moved her on.

The more I thought about it, the more I liked the idea of a book about the wives of Downing Street. I even had a title for it: *The Goldfish Bowl*, because that was what it felt like. I mentioned it to Fiona, but she was dead against it. What I needed, she said, was to lower my profile, not raise it. But I remained excited about the idea. As we planned to go up to the Lake District before going on holiday to France, I decided to run it past the social historian Cate Haste, wife of the broadcaster and writer Melvyn Bragg, to see what she thought.

Because the terrible foot-and-mouth epidemic had been causing so much damage to the British tourist industry, we'd arranged to spend a few days in the Lake District, though being on vacation in Britain was never particularly relaxing, particularly for Tony, as the media would never leave him alone. We took Leo to the Beatrix Potter museum, and the weather on the last day was glorious, reminding me of when I used to hitch my way on the M6 from Crosby all those years ago. In the end we had a good time.

On August 5 we were back at Chequers. I had a meeting at Matrix on the morning we were due to leave for France, so I had booked myself in for my next scan. It was the same ultrasound technician as before, and again she was really excited, going on about how rare it was for someone my age to have a naturally conceived baby. She was just moving the sensor across my oiled stomach when suddenly she stopped.

"There's no heartbeat," she said, still staring at the screen. For a moment I didn't understand.

"What did you say?"

"There's no heartbeat, Mrs. Blair. I'm afraid the baby's dead."

"Ah," I said. "So that's why I'm feeling better." Because I was. Recently the constant nausea had disappeared.

I told her I needed to go to the bathroom. She pointed me to one immediately off the room, and the moment I sat down, the bleeding started. Later I thought it was almost as if, now that I knew, my body could let go.

By the time I emerged from the cubicle, Dr. Rankin had appeared. They were going to have to do a scrape, a D & C, she said. "We'll try to get you in and out as soon as possible." Nobody need know. For the time being, I should go back to Downing Street and rest.

I stood numbly by the door in the waiting room, and the 'tec came over.

"Come on now, Mrs. B, no dawdling. You've got that holiday to think of. Can't have you missing that flight."

"I don't think I'll be going on holiday," I said. I felt embarrassed. He didn't even know I was pregnant, and I didn't know what to do or say. "I need to speak to the PM."

"Are you all right, Mrs. B?"

"Just get me the PM and take me back to Number Ten."

The flat was empty and silent. Leo's toys were stashed away in hampers. We weren't meant to be coming back for several weeks. There was usually so much noise — music coming from the kids' bedrooms, piano practice, the kettle, the washing machine, a TV on in the background somewhere. Ordinary sounds of family life. I walked upstairs, suddenly feeling very, very old, and crawled between the sheets and just lay there, strange sounds ringing in my ears. Only when Tony got through did I let go.

He said he'd come up to London straightaway after explaining things to my mum and the kids. Twenty minutes later he called back. The kids were okay, he said, and he hoped I understood, but he had to tell Alastair. Ah, yes. Alastair. I lay there waiting. Then the phone again: this time the two of them on the line. There were implications in not going on holiday, they said. It was all to do with Iraq. There had been talk that we might be sending in troops. If we didn't go on vacation, the concern was that it would send the wrong message. They had decided that the best thing was to tell the press that I'd had a miscarriage.

I couldn't believe it. There I was, bleeding, and they were talking about what was going to be the line to the press. I put down the receiver and lay there staring at the ceiling, as pain began to grip.

Finally, Susan Rankin rang. I should get to the hospital as soon as possible.

When I began to come round from the anesthetic and was being wheeled out of the operating theater, who should I see but Gary, one of the 'tecs. He was looking so distressed that I burst into tears, sobbing and sobbing, and saying, "But I really want my husband." In fact, Tony was there, but because of the security issues, it was Gary I saw first.

As for Tony, his main emotion appeared to be relief. "You know you felt there was something not quite right, Cherie," he said. "So it's probably all for the best." I realize now he was simply trying to make me feel better; it just came out a bit oddly. Of course he was right, but I was surprised at just how badly it hit me. It wasn't as if I were childless. I had four lovely, healthy children. But I was overwhelmed by this great sense of loss. To me, more than anyone else, this baby was real. I had seen it. I still have the scan.

I decided to go ahead with the book. It seemed appropriate. While in the Lake District, I had talked to Cate Haste, and she thought it a good idea. It would be based on interviews with the former wives. I had met them all and sensed they had strong, idiosyncratic views and real stories to tell. Fiona was still against the idea. She thought I'd be accused of taking advantage of my position. I pointed out that there was a precedent: Norma Major had written a book about Chequers, and no one had criticized her. After that wonderful Golden Jubilee dinner, I really wanted to share the history of these fascinating people. I found them inspiring. Perhaps Fiona didn't see it that way. Perhaps she felt that I should have suggested doing it with her. But I believe her unhappiness had less to do with me than with Alastair. She was getting progressively resentful of the time that he was spending with Tony, and this in turn was affecting her relationship with me, which was rapidly deteriorating.

Fiona was firmly in the camp of those who believed that Britain should not get involved in Iraq. It was a nonstop tirade. "Why don't you just tell Tony to stop it? He'll listen to you," she'd say. She harangued Alastair, too. If it was bad for me, it must have been terrible for him — no letup at work or at home. My response was always the same: "Listen, Fiona. I don't see Tony. I don't see what Tony and Alastair see. If Tony tells me, as he does, that if we don't stop Saddam Hussein, the world will be a more dangerous place, I believe him. And in my view you and I should be supporting our men in these difficult decisions, not making it worse by nagging them."

The discussions over the possibility of Tony not standing for a third term had certainly made me aware of just how vulnerable we were. The bald truth was that however comfortable we had made the Number 11 flat, it was only a grand version of a tied cottage. We had no tenure. Once we were out, we were out with nowhere to live. Certainly there was Myrobella, but no way could I carry on my career from county Durham, and with three children in school in central London, we had to stay in the area. Other Prime Ministers hadn't been faced with either of these problems. Thanks to Denis, the Thatchers were wealthy long before they took up residence in Downing Street, and the Majors had kept their house outside Cambridge.

Over the past year the talk at every dinner party was house prices. Between 1997 and 2002, particularly in London, they had risen dramatically, and our old home in Richmond Crescent was now worth more than £1 million. Our friends would tease us about our lack of a house, but it was no joke. To make matters worse, the stock market had taken a tumble after 9/11, and the money in our blind trust had gone down. The blunt truth was that we were substantially worse off than we had been when Tony became Prime Minister five years earlier. At the time I was pondering all this, I was pregnant with my fifth child, which further concentrated my mind.

That August we returned to our favorite corner of France for our summer holiday, this time to a rented house. Renting a house on the open market with the security features the protection guys required was difficult. We eventually found one, but it wasn't ideal, and as I was feeling generally very low, I can't say it was the best holiday of our lives. We had friends in the area, however, and as my miscarriage was now public knowledge, people were very sympathetic.

Jackie was taking some well-earned rest with her family, so Maureen, our household help and babysitter, came along. Her surprisingly bluesy Scottish voice, coming from such a pint-size person, enlivened many an evening's singing and playing by the local guitar wannabes, who naturally included Tony.

Among the mix of familiar faces was an English girl called Caroline, married to a Frenchman who ran a foie gras business. Euan's examination results had just come through, and he had decided on Bristol University, a hundred or so miles west of London. While Caroline and I were chatting, she asked if I'd thought about buying something there for Euan rather than renting. The short answer was no, I hadn't. Well, you should think about it, she said. Why throw money away on rent if you have the potential to buy? At least that way you could have capital growth. She had a friend in Bristol, called Sheila Murison, who taught at the university and, as a business sideline, bought places and then let them out to students. I decided it was certainly worth investigating, and I asked her to ask her friend to keep her eyes open. That night I mentioned it to Tony. I wasn't supposed to talk about investments at all, but I thought a general question was reasonable. Did he think it was a good idea in principle? No, he didn't. He thought it was ridiculous.

Well, it wasn't his decision. The main reason for the blind trust was that I was the sole beneficiary, and the more I thought about it, the more doable it seemed.

I wasn't much cheerier when the time came for Euan to go to Bristol. Within two months I had lost my last baby, and now I was losing my first. It may sound stupid and sentimental, but that was how it felt. It was thirty years exactly since I had pushed my poor old mum out the door of Passfield Hall, her face streaming with tears, and I remembered how embarrassed I had felt and how I'd just wanted her to go so that I could get on with my new life. Now here I was at another hall of residence. I didn't cry when I said goodbye to Euan, although he clearly knew that tears weren't far away, saying, "Mum, I think it's time you left now."

Tony, who hadn't been able to come to Bristol, wasn't exactly sympathetic to any of this. Iraq was looming ever larger, and the tension both in the flat and in Number 10 was palpable. Leo, delightful though he was, didn't make life any easier. The phone would ring in the night, and Leo would wake up and cry. I'd get up and go to his room to comfort him, and as often as not, I'd end up lying beside him and falling asleep, squashed uncomfortably into the wooden bed designed as a racing car, waking a few hours later with numb limbs.

Shortly after I got back from France, Caroline's friend Sheila got in touch, and we had an exchange of e-mails about what I was looking for in terms of a flat. I was thinking of two bedrooms, between £225,000 and £275,000. At the beginning of October she e-mailed me to say she'd found a development called the Panoramic, which I might be interested in, and she forwarded me the brochure. Although the list price for a two-bedroom, £295,000, was more than my maximum budget, she was thinking of buying one herself, and the builder had already quoted her a discounted price. As there were only five left of an original fifty-five, she was sure she could get this for me. And she did. On October 6 she said she'd negotiated a price of £269,000, a reduction of £26,000. She added that as a garage was included, the price could probably be structured to pay separately for that and thus get the flat itself below the £250,000 threshold, at which point certain taxes kicked in. Of course any such manipulation would clearly be tax evasion, and I couldn't do that. Later it was claimed that I got a special discount, but that wasn't the case.

I then discovered that the Web price was only £275,000 and e-mailed Sheila to say that the reduction was, therefore, only £6,000, and presumably we could do better than that. I left it in her hands, as I was about to accompany Tony on a trip to Moscow. He would be meeting with Russian President Vladimir Putin for talks about Iraq following the publication two weeks previously of a dossier based on various intelligence agencies' assessments of Saddam Hussein's arsenal of weapons of mass destruction.

In the meantime the protection people had to look at the security implications of the flat. From their point of view it was fine. They did say, however, that if possible, it should be bought in another name, preferably that of a company. I told them it would be bought in the name of the trust. I had already spoken in principle to the trustees, and they were happy to release £100,000. I would fund the rest with a mortgage. I hadn't intended to buy so quickly, but the money was sitting there. As I couldn't speak to Tony about it, I asked Fiona what she thought.

"It's a risk going to see it yourself," she said. "Someone is bound to spot you."

"I could always ask Carole to go for me."

She shrugged and said, "Up to you." Things between us were becoming really tense.

It worked out perfectly. Carole told me that she was going to Bath the following weekend with a friend, and Bristol was just down the road. I contacted the developers and made an appointment for her to see the flat with Euan. After all, he was the one who was going to be living there. As it happened, I couldn't have gone anyway, as I was in Bermuda for a week on a commercial case, leaving on the nineteenth. When I called Carole to confirm the time, she said that she might take her friend along — her new man, she confessed, an Australian called Peter Foster. I said fine. I had guessed there was someone around — I'd recognized the signs — though she had been unusually coy.

She called me in Bermuda. She'd had a look at a couple of the flats and thought they were okay. Euan hadn't gone with her in the end. "But," she said, "I took my friend along. He's a businessman and knows about these things, so I thought that could be useful. He thinks it's a good deal. In fact, he's thinking of getting one himself. Here, he can tell you."

The new man came on the phone, confirmed what Carole had said, and added that he thought I could get the price down. I knew that already, of course, but I didn't say so. He also told me, just as Sheila had, how with a bit of manipulation with the garage, I could avoid some taxes. Again I made it quite clear that I wasn't interested. I thought he sounded a bit pushy, but I thanked him for his help, and that was that. Or so I thought.

CHAPTER 28

Mea Culpa

A week later, on October 28, the day after I got back from Bermuda, I had an e-mail from Peter Foster, the new man in Carole's life, attaching copies of floor plans of the Panoramic. He appeared to have been talking to the developers on my behalf, which was ridiculous — Sheila Murison was handling all that. I supposed he had been talking to them anyway about his own possible purchase, and talking about mine as well strengthened his hand. In another e-mail, he put his mortgage broker in touch with me, and I passed the details on to my own accountant, whom I'd been with since 1982. Again there seemed little harm in it.

The business of the blind trust was very difficult. I couldn't discuss it with Tony, yet I couldn't spend a quarter of a million pounds on a stranger's say-so, however much Carole might sing his praises, which she did nonstop. So I made an appointment the following Saturday to view the property myself. I also contacted a couple of real estate agents and arranged to see another place the same morning.

So I went. Two of the available flats were next door to each other, and it occurred to me that if I got both, I might trigger a discount. Then Euan could be in one, and I could let out the other. Mortgage rates were low, and I needed somehow to build up capital so we could eventually buy a house. I discussed the possibility there and then with the person showing me round and offered an overall figure of £430,000, which in the end was what I paid.

The next day an e-mail arrived from Peter Foster. Carole was obviously relaying everything that was going on, but given that she had just told me she was pregnant, this wasn't the time to be prickly. I knew how much she longed for a baby, and my heart went out to her. This was probably her last chance. Her boyfriend was obviously pitching for a job, but the truth was that I didn't have any need of him. In one of his e-mails, he said he knew some rental agencies, so to keep Carole happy and him out of my hair, I said he could forward me their details. I was puzzled by his wanting to get involved and started feeling distinctly uneasy.

The administrators of the trust agreed to allow £100,000 to be invested, and, as planned, I raised the rest by mortgage in the normal way through my bank. We exchanged contracts on November 22 and completed the deal a week after.

On Sunday, November 24, the Downing Street special protection officers received a report from colleagues in Cheshire. They'd had a tip-off: a convicted con man called Peter Foster was claiming he was involved with the Blairs through Carole Caplin. He planned to involve her in a scam concerning a diet tea, which had already landed him in prison. There was also some talk of involvement in a property deal, and he'd boasted that he'd met the Blairs' son Euan. Then Alastair rang. He'd just had a call from a former newspaper colleague, Ian Monk, now working in PR. He was advising Carole and Peter Foster, he said. Foster had just lost a deportation case, and as Carole was now expecting his child, he was looking for "advice." Foster also claimed he was being blackmailed, by the man who had tipped off the police about Foster's questionable dealings, and having contacted the *News of the World*, they were planning to set up a "sting" — that is, to record a meeting between me and Carole and Peter Foster.

I felt sick, Tony was beside himself, and Alastair was merely grim. Sooner or later, probably sooner, he said, it would come out. For him this was the ultimate "I told you so." Carole would now have to go. We saw Carole at Chequers that Sunday and confronted her with the information. She confessed that she knew all about Foster's past but claimed that he was completely innocent: he'd been stitched up by the security services.

"Please, Carole," Tony said, clearly exasperated. "This is ridiculous. The man is a fantasist. You've got to understand; we cannot be connected with a criminal."

She then presented Tony with an extraordinary letter from a lawyer in Fiji, "putting into context" Foster's shady past. This was hardly reassuring to anybody who had ever spent time around villains and criminals, as both Tony and I had done as barristers. It was classic stuff. To say he was dodgy would be putting it mildly, and we told her so.

"You're talking about the father of my unborn child," she said, and burst into tears. It was horrible. It was as if it had just occurred to her that if he went away, she'd be left literally holding the baby. Frankly, neither of us could spare the emotional energy. Tony had Iraq to contend with. Politically things were very hot, with antiwar groups becoming increasingly vociferous. The last thing he needed was this, and I knew it. I was supposed to be his support, not his undoing. As for me, in addition to my official engagements, for two weeks from November 25 to December 5, I was sitting as a recorder in Isleworth Crown Court. I also had late-afternoon appointments with former Prime Ministers' wives for the book.

We told Carole that although it was her life, that man was never coming near any of us. It was all we could do. She agreed that she would keep away from Downing Street. Indeed, for the time being, I kept away from her entirely. This was a shock to both our systems: we had worked out together at the gym most days when I was in London for as long as I could remember.

On Saturday, November 28, the headline in the *Daily Mail* ran "Cherie's Style Guru Has Fallen for a Fraudster." That afternoon the *Mail on Sunday* sent through a list of twenty-two questions to the Downing Street press office, all Foster related. It was horrendous, and Tony was fuming.

"I told you not to buy any bloody flats."

"He had nothing to do with the bloody flats. I have never met the guy. He has never been here; he has never been to Downing Street. What more can I say? I can't believe you'd believe a convicted con man rather than your own wife! Telling lies is what the man does for a living!"

"So you categorically deny you have had any contact?"

"Apart from a few e-mails, no. I'll show them to you if you like." Technology and Tony are like oil and water, and waving that offer aside, he dashed off the form, filling in yeses and nos — mostly nos — then faxed it back. Unfortunately I think he told Alastair in very firm terms that I'd had no contact with Foster whatsoever — a version that Alastair confidently relayed to the press. I didn't talk to Alastair at all.

For the next few days a stream of denials issued from Downing Street. Then, on Thursday, December 5, the *Daily Mail* published the exchange of e-mails between Peter Foster and me. Alastair's look of superior satisfaction changed completely. I had never seen him so angry. As he saw it, he had lied to save my face, and he was determined that if anyone went down for this, it wasn't going to be Alastair Campbell.

That morning Hilary Coffman came to my bedroom while André was doing my hair. She knew time was short: I had to be in court at Isleworth at 9:30 a.m. Within seconds she was giving me the third degree, clearly on instructions. I have known her for a long time as a faithful servant of the Labour Party, and she was clearly uncomfortable about doing it, not least because she was a friend of mine professing not to accept what I was saying.

"But Hilary, don't you see, there isn't a scandal. It's you lot who are making it into a scandal. Look, I've used my own money to buy two flats. I've paid the going rate for them. Nobody paid £295,000. Okay, so I got a discount on the published price, but that's standard — it's a marketing ploy to make you feel you've got a bargain. No, I didn't know him. No, I have never met him — I once said hello to him in passing at the gym. No, he has never met Euan. No, he has never been to Chequers. No, I did not ask him to help me avoid paying stamp duty. No, he was not my financial adviser. No, I did not find him a barrister. No, I did not intervene with immigration or any government official or legal representative on his behalf. No, no, no, no, NO, NO."

There came a point where André could stand it no longer. "How can you do this to her? Just look at what you are doing to her! I'm going to tell someone. You cannot do this to her," he said, and stormed off.

In the mirror was a face I barely recognized. My chin was wobbling. My reflection was blurred as I blinked to try to control the tears. On my dressing table were photographs of all the children. If things had gone differently, in two months' time there would have been another one . . .

I was forced to issue a statement saying that Peter Foster was involved. "Damage limitation" is the term, I think.

I bumped into one of the press officers in the corridor beneath the flat at the entrance to the press office. "I'm so sorry all this is going on, Cherie," he said.

Fiona's take was slightly different. "Everyone in the press office hates you," she told me. "They've told lies on your behalf, and none of them ever wants to work for you again. They want nothing more to do with you."

We passed a frosty weekend at Chequers. Tony was on the phone most of the time, in his study, the door closed. Iraq. Alan was making his usual Christmas puddings, and I went with the children to have a stir and make a wish, while Jackie was keeping everybody cheerful. I found it all very, very hard. It was about to get worse. On Sunday the *News of the World* got in on the act. We later discovered that they had offered Peter Foster £100,000 to tell his story. Now they were questioning the discounts on my clothes. That night Bill Clinton dropped in at Downing Street and gave me a big hug.

On Monday the ninth Peter Foster's solicitors issued a statement saying that I had contacted them about his deportation case but that I hadn't intervened in any way, that it had been only to reassure Ms. Caplin. This, of course, did more harm than good. But it was true. I had phoned them, but all I was doing was checking that everything that should have been done had been done. I knew perfectly well that he hadn't a chance of winning his appeal. His record — prison terms on three continents, including in Britain — spoke for itself, but I wasn't going to say that to my friend. And she *was* still my friend. I had just heard that she had lost her baby.

André arrived at 8.00 a.m. to do my hair. That night I had a reception for the Loomba Trust, whose aim it is to educate the children of widows in India. In the afternoon I had my annual children's Christmas party. Every year children from one charity are invited for tea. Father Christmas comes and there's an entertainer, and at the end we turn on the lights on the tree outside the front door. I'd try to enjoy myself, but I felt like a pariah.

André was just getting started when Alastair came storming into the bedroom. Until now he had refused to talk to me, either sending in Hilary to do his dirty work or using Tony as a go-between. I think even Tony didn't want him to talk to me, instead putting himself between us as a shield because he knew Alastair was so angry.

"That's it," Alastair said, his arms folded, as he looked at me via the mirror. "It's now political. The Tories are asking questions, and your husband is going to have to answer them. One more time, Cherie, did you at any point have anything whatever to do with the immigration case?"

"I've told you, no. You're determined to humiliate me, aren't you? I know you've been briefing against me."

"Apologize," I said.

"I don't think so." Alastair snorted. "For the last time, I want that woman out of your life."

"She has just lost a baby; her boyfriend is threatened with deportation. I'm not going to abandon her. I've said I won't talk to her, isn't that enough?"

"Don't forget, you brought all of this on yourself."

I felt terrible for Carole and very weepy. The news about the miscarriage had taken me straight back to that dreadful afternoon, only a few months before, when I'd been lying upstairs bleeding. Even with four children already, I had felt utterly bereft. How Carole was feeling, I could only imagine. Banned as I was from any contact, I couldn't even comfort her. The whole situation was ridiculous. Tony could talk to her, but I couldn't.

That morning I spent an hour with Lady Wilson, the wife of former Prime Minister Harold Wilson, talking about her life in Number 10 in the 1960s and 1970s. Listening to her, I realized that little had changed in forty years. She had often been lonely and unhappy. She was the first of the Downing Street wives who came from a background that wasn't "establishment." Her son Giles had been a teenager when they'd moved into the Number 10 flat, and even after all these years, it pained her to remember the impossibility of him simply getting in and out without a great song and dance being made of it. She remembered how she would wake in the middle of the night to find a garden girl at the end of the bed taking dictation from her husband. To retain her sanity, she told me, she would take

"I don't need to. You do it all on your own."

"Don't you dare talk to Cherie like that!" André exploded.

"You mind your own business," Alastair retorted. "Remember, you're just a fucking hairdresser."

the bus to north London, where they used to live, and cry on the shoulders of friends. The lack of privacy, the loss of identity — I heard the same stories over and over again: different women, different backgrounds, different generations, but all bound together by a strong sense of public service, seeing their role as that of support and comfort to the Prime Minister.

Just before lunch André called me from the salon. "How are you feeling?"

"Not great, André."

"You know I'm not her greatest fan, but I think you need to see Carole."

"She's banned."

"That's my idea. You meet at my flat!"

"But when?"

"This afternoon. I have it all worked out. You turn the Christmas lights on with the kids, and I'll be waiting out back."

"You mean just walk out?"

"I mean just walk out. Don't tell anybody. Be very naughty. Give them the slip!"

"But I've got the Loomba Trust reception."

"I'll get you back for that. Promise."

So that's what happened. Between three and four-thirty I was down in Number 10 for the children's Christmas party. Once the tree ceremony was over, I walked back in through the Downing Street front door, turned left, and pushed the button for the Number 11 lift. I didn't normally bother to take the lift up one flight of stairs, and this was no exception: I didn't go up; I went down, down into the basement, through the comms office, and out into the back parking lot, where André was waiting. Nobody stopped me; nobody even seemed to notice. His flat is in Berwick Street, in Soho. Carole was already there, he said. He'd be waiting in the café across the road. But we didn't have much time. "Half an hour tops," he warned me. It was a few minutes after five.

She was in a bad way. Very upset, very contrite, very tearful, not least because she had lost the baby. I told her that I wouldn't abandon her, that as far as I was concerned, she had done no wrong. Did it do any good? I don't know. But we both had a cry, and I think we both felt better. She showed me the contract that Ian Monk had negotiated with the *Mail on Sunday* for her to contribute a weekly column. She pointed out the bit that said, "Any reference to Mrs Cherie Blair shall appear only after prior approval." She would never talk about us, she said. Then I had to go. Any idea that I wouldn't be found out was ridiculous, of course. I had been seen leaving on the security cameras, but at least they hadn't had time to follow us and didn't know where I was going. It felt like a victory.

When we got back, André gave me a hug. Then I opened the car door and walked in the way I'd left. I nodded to the uniformed officer on duty. He nodded back and picked up the phone. The prisoner had returned.

The next day it got worse. The Tories were calling for an official inquiry. I couldn't stand it anymore; I was just shaking. Alastair had had more questions through from the *Daily Mail*, implying that I had been trying to exert pressure on a judge. The law was my life! How could anybody think I could do such a thing? Yet Alastair was asking me as if it were a real possibility. I felt so angry that when they said they wanted me to make a statement, I agreed. They wrote it.

Eventually I added in some stuff about Carole. Alastair wasn't happy, but I didn't care. It was supposed to be my statement, after all. That evening I was due to present the Partners in Excellence awards, which as patron I did every year, to organizations involved with affordable child care and associated services. The venue was the Atrium restaurant, just beyond the House of Commons. Fiona suggested that we use it as a platform.

As I got into the car, Fiona sat grim-faced beside me. From the moment we passed the barriers into Whitehall, it began: flashlights against the windows of the car, the shouts of the photographers. Never before or since have I felt so hounded. I was their prey. It was that simple. Past the House of Commons, on to the Embankment, then finally we were there. The nice new 'tec opened the door, and an arm from somewhere guided me in, the lights blinding me, the voices shouting. Once inside, I stood there trembling, checking to see if the microphone was turned on. My statement had been timed at nine minutes. Just another nine minutes, and it would all be over. And these good people thought they were getting a speech on children and excellence. I thought, *They are the ones I should be apologizing to. All their hard work, and they get this charade.* A nod from Fiona, and I'm on.

"In view of all the controversy around me at the moment, I hope you don't mind me using this event to say a few words. . . . You can't fail to know that there have been a lot of allegations about me and I haven't said anything, but when I got back to Downing Street today and discovered that some of the press are effectively suggesting that I tried to influence a judge, I knew that the time had come for me to say something. It is not fair to Tony or the government that the entire focus of political debate at the moment is about me."

Tony was at his weekly audience with the Queen, but he saw it later on the news. There was a moment toward the end when I nearly broke down, when I mentioned Euan having left home. What we'd wanted for him in Bristol, most of all, was that he would be safe, that he would be away from the press. He'd had all that furor over going to school, then there had been the drinking episode, and he'd gone to Bristol to get away from all that. And now here he was, tangentially at least, caught up in this. I'd dragged my son, whom I'd wanted to protect, into the news. My girlfriend, who had just lost a much-wanted baby, was being hounded by the press. And on top of all that, I had to try to keep going with all my official engagements and keep relatively calm at home so that the other children didn't get too upset. All of that I could cope with, but the mention of Euan's name was the thing that tipped me over.

One day, a few months before the 1997 election, Philip Gould had told me that Tony was going on a long journey, and that neither his past friends nor the office could go all the way with him. The only one who could do that was me, and I needed to make sure I was by his side supporting him. I took those words to heart and vowed always to be there for him. So the worst aspect for me of the whole Bristol flats nightmare was that I had let Tony down. At the moment in his life when he needed me most, I was a drag on his energies rather than a source of support.

Yet however bad things were, I never felt that he had abandoned me. For a quarter of a century, we had been not only lovers but best friends. I always knew there would be things that Tony couldn't talk about, but I also knew that he would never lie to me, which was why I was 100 percent behind him over Iraq and the threat Saddam Hussein represented to world order. His preoccupation with what he had to do and the consequences for individual lives, both British troops and Iraqi civilians, weighed on him night and day, awake and asleep. In trying to get the UN Security Council to force Saddam to comply with its resolutions, he faced a titanic struggle. He was tireless in his efforts to persuade the Americans not to act unilaterally, while at the same time attempting to galvanize the rest of the world into action when it was clear that the language of diplomacy was no longer enough. Although 2002 had undoubtedly been a bad year for me, whatever problems I had faded into insignificance compared to what he had on his plate.

Following that splendid tenet of tabloid journalism "no smoke without fire," "Cheriegate," as it was wittily dubbed, dragged on for weeks, until eventually the press just got bored. The only positive thing to emerge were the letters I received in commiseration: the charities I was involved with, colleagues at the Bar and on the Bench, politicians from both sides of the House, priests and vicars, monks and nuns, friends and people I had never met and never would. I even got a kind letter from Prince Charles. I replied to them all, but those people will never know just how much their support meant to me.

Eventually Peter Foster was deported. (One of his more spectacular claims, worth including for its sheer audacity, was that Tony was the father of Carole's baby.) He is now in Australia, serving a four-and-a-half-year sentence for fraud. A few months after he was deported, he was in touch with the *Mail* again, sending it copies of fabricated e-mails purporting to show that I had tried to channel funds through an offshore tax haven. He clearly had no idea of how little money we had. The *Mail*, naturally, demanded yet more answers. This time, thanks to my accountant's thorough forensic investigation of my entire computer system, Downing Street was able categorically to deny the whole thing. The *Mail* decided not to run the story.

The reverberations continued to rumble round Downing Street. There were more cross-examinations by Hilary Coffman. There was a belief that Carole had taken clothes either for me or herself without paying for them. I was required to contact everyone who had ever supplied me with clothes and get written assurance that the discounts I'd been given were standard, that there had been no special favors. That turned out not to be sufficient. The new Cabinet secretary, Sir Andrew Turnbull, told me that I had to repay the discounts. I refused. I wanted to know on what authority he was able to interfere with personal contracts I had made. "You show me the law that says that I have to pay this back, and I will do it. Otherwise I will not." Eventually a private secretary was assigned to investigate the whole business of the clothes. She told me that she would try to work out a better scheme, where the rules would be clearly set out.

I had done my homework. From ambassadors' wives to the Queen's ladies-in-waiting, nobody else carried the burden of having to dress well for official duties without financial help and under such constant media scrutiny. As for other leaders' wives, they expressed total disbelief that I didn't have a budget for formal occasions. A report was apparently written and presented, but in spite of several requests, I never got a glimpse of it.

While all this nonsense was going on, the situation in Iraq was becoming increasingly tense, involving Tony not only in telephone calls round the clock but also in an endless series of bilateral talks, some of which I had to attend.

On October 11 we had flown to Moscow for Tony to see Vladimir Putin. We had first met the Putins in February 2000. Putin was then the heir apparent, and this was a getting-to-know-you trip to St. Petersburg, his hometown and power base. After a whistle-stop tour of the Hermitage, we were taken to *War and Peace*, a four-hour opera by Prokofiev. Refreshments during the two intervals had consisted solely of champagne and caviar. As I was then six months pregnant with Leo the trip wasn't easy, and although the hotel was like an oven, outside it was bitterly cold.

My next visit couldn't have been more different. It was the three hundredth anniversary of the founding of the city. In the short time since assuming the presidency, Putin had poured money into St. Petersburg and totally transformed it, or so it appeared. Much of it, we later discovered, was no more substantial than a film set: the facades of some of the houses had been painted and others disguised to make them look totally restored. It was the end of May, and the weather was lovely. (A few years later they actually sent up airplanes to disperse the clouds so that the sun could shine for the G8.)

The idea was to show St. Petersburg in all its former magnificence, and in that Putin certainly succeeded. The most extraordinary of the reconstructions I saw was the amber room in Catherine Palace. The original had dated from the early eighteenth century — a room completely lined with amber and semiprecious stones — but it had been looted by the Germans during World War II, and no trace of the contents has ever been found. In terms of the entertainment, expense was no object — ballet, fireworks, vodka and caviar wherever you looked. Rather surprisingly, I found I liked caviar. When our host saw me spooning some up, he hastened over. "You don't want this stuff," he said, removing my plate and bringing me some beluga.

It was a mind-boggling display of Russian power. Once again I was grateful and amazed to have been granted a ringside seat to history, to incredible people and incredible events.

Three weeks later the Putins arrived on their first state visit to Britain, and I was down to entertain Lyudmila one afternoon. As we had been taken to *War and Peace* in St. Petersburg, I arranged to visit the Royal Opera House in Covent Garden, where we would be joined by an array of cultural people for lunch. On the Putins' arrival in London, however, I was informed through an aide that Mrs. Putina would really like to go shopping. From what I knew of her, I judged that Burberry's might hit the spot, so I arranged a discreet visit to their showroom just off Piccadilly Circus immediately after the lunch. Unfortunately this being a state visit, transport had been provided by Buckingham Palace, and Lyudmila arrived at Downing Street in the royal Bentley, glass everywhere, designed to provide an unrestricted view of the occupants. Discreet it was not.

The aide had been right, however; the opera wasn't her thing. But she perked up immediately when we got to Burberry's. No sooner had we arrived in the showroom than she stripped off down to her underwear. In the interests of diplomacy, I decided I had better keep her company. As she didn't have any money on her, I put her considerable purchases on my credit card. The next day I was informed that a large packet had arrived from Mrs. Putina. She was repaying me in cash. I had never seen so many £50 notes. Our friendship was undoubtedly consolidated that afternoon in our knickers.

In those early days Lyudmila Putina was very unsure of herself. Her husband had fairly chauvinistic views about the role of a wife. He had two basic rules, she confided: "A woman must do everything at home" and "Never praise a woman; it will only spoil her." Language was important to her; she had studied modern languages at Leningrad University's philology department and spoke fluent German, the Putins having lived in Germany for several years.

After the Berlin Wall came down, she told me, she had feared for the future of Russian literature and language. In 2002 she had visited the United States to take part in the second annual National Book Festival hosted by Laura Bush, and she decided to replicate the idea. I promised that I would support her, and I did, going over with Laura for the launch and on two further occasions, when I met the First Lady of Armenia, Bella Kocharian, and the First Lady of Bulgaria, Zorka Purvanova. Without my support, Lyudmila later admitted, she probably wouldn't have gone through with it. There's no doubt that her book festival gave a huge boost to her confidence and, I think, her status. As a thank-you she gave us lunch in the state rooms of the Kremlin and an extraordinary private tour. By "us" I mean my "entourage": to wit, André and Sue Geddes. (To his credit, our ambassador, who was also invited, did not balk at this unusual arrangement.) We were taken high up onto the roof by the famous golden domes, from which we could look down at the cathedral. Having been razed by Communist apparatchiks because they didn't want to look out on it, the cathedral had been restored by Boris Yeltsin in the 1990s after its ignominious decades as a public swimming pool.

The aim of Tony's current meeting with Putin was to persuade him that the UN needed to demonstrate unity so that America did not feel it would have to act unilaterally. It was a chance, Tony said, to show that in the new world order, the UN did have power and could make things happen. We met at Putin's private dacha. That evening, I remember, he was at pains to point out that far from being a convinced communist, he had always been a man of religious faith with a strong attachment to the Orthodox Church. I was not entirely convinced. I sensed that the former KGB chief was still there under the surface. (He has a very powerful presence — he's broad-shouldered and keeps himself fit with judo. He puts a lot of value on physical strength, his own and Russia's. This is not a man you would want to cross.)

The invitation to his private cottage was a sign of favor, and that night, apart from the interpreter, there were just the four of us. The dacha was, in fact, a hunting lodge, and Lyudmila had never even been there before, their main dacha being outside St. Petersburg. The meal was heavy in the traditional Russian manner: meat and no vegetables, unless you count pickles. When it was over, Putin stood up and stretched. "And now," he said, "I want to take you wild boar hunting."

By this time it was about half-past ten. No one had said anything about hunting wild boars or anything else. I was dressed for dinner in high heels and a dress, and the temperature outside was well below freezing. Tony came to help me on with my coat. "Buckle down, girl," he said, "and stop complaining."

Lyudmila gave me a look: this wasn't her idea of fun either. Outside it was pitch-dark, and there was nothing I could do to prevent my heels from click-clacking on the concrete path while everyone else was creeping along with exaggerated stealth. I was petrified. The machine-gun-toting Russian bodyguards were behind us, while our own protection officers were presumably somewhere behind them — at least I hoped so, in case we were about to be ceremonially assassinated. I didn't know whether to be more frightened of the guns or the wild boars, which I'd seen pictures of and which I knew to be particularly vicious creatures.

Putin led us down to a hide and was explaining the finer points of boar hunting as he peered down the sights of a night-vision rifle. *One day*, I thought, *I will tell my grandchildren about this.* No doubt to their disappointment (but not mine), there would be no violent denouement to the evening. Not one wild boar was seen, let alone killed.

Russian hospitality is not for the fainthearted. The next day we were told we were going on a picnic. Again the temperature was subzero, but the area was very beautiful, with a huge lake and waterbirds everywhere; everything glistened with hoarfrost. A wild boar was being roasted over a roaring fire, next to which, in a kind of bower, a table had been laid, complete with white tablecloth and silver cutlery. Seeing that I was shivering, Putin ordered one of his soldiers to give me his greatcoat, which was not very different from the ones in *Dr. Zhivago*. I was faced with one further practical problem. In order to cut the meat, I had to take off my gloves, but if I took off my gloves, the cutlery stuck to my hands. The wild boar was delicious, but the cold was so overwhelming that I can't say I really enjoyed it.

The meeting was generally deemed a success. Tony felt that Putin had an understanding of where he was coming from and that he wasn't just doing this as an acolyte of the American President, but because he wanted to make the UN work.

In December, immediately after the Peter Foster nightmare, we went on a similar mission to visit the Schröders in Berlin. Gerhard Schröder had come to power in 1998, and as he was a social democrat and a modernizer, there was a natural affinity with him. His wife, Doris, had been a journalist, although she looked very fragile, with short blond hair. Unusually, we were invited to their home, where we met her daughter from a previous marriage. Again the meeting was very convivial, with just the four of us. Gerhard assured Tony that while he had to tread carefully because of his own political position, he wasn't going to cause difficulties for the Americans in the UN. In the event, however, Schröder, Jacques Chirac, and Putin formed an alliance that torpedoed Tony's attempts for unity. On February 24, 2003, the United States, the UK, and Spain sponsored another UN resolution. France said that it would veto the resolution "whatever the circumstances," and it was thus never ratified.

Following that evening with the Schröders, Tony gave an interview with British Forces Radio in Germany, just before Christmas. They, more than anybody else, knew that preparations were well under way for an invasion of Iraq. When asked about the final decision about whether to go to war and how difficult it would be to make, Tony replied, "These are the hardest decisions because you are aware that you are putting people's lives at risk and that is why we should never undertake conflict unless we have exhausted all other options and possibilities."

And that is truly how he felt and what he had done for months and months. At the same time as Tony was trying to make an alliance with the European leaders, he was also talking with Chile, Cameroon, and Angola, all of which were then on the Security Council. Having conversations late into the night, Tony desperately sought to keep a united front, in order that Saddam Hussein would back down. That was the message. That's why when Chirac said that he would not support the second resolution "whatever the circumstances," Tony knew that all his careful negotiating had come to nothing. He also knew that if Saddam Hussein didn't back down, the Americans were going to go in anyway. And that, of course, is exactly what happened. George Bush did offer Tony a way out. Via the U.S. embassy in London, the President had been told that the controversy over Iraq risked bringing Tony down. He called Tony and said that Britain did not need to be part of the invasion, that he would find a lesser role for us to play. But Tony was not going to back out. He was determined that we would support America, because he thought it was the right thing to do. He could not let Saddam Hussein get away with defying the international community and making his own people's lives a misery. So the die was cast. After that it was only a matter of time.

On the evening of March 10, 2003, the secure phone line rang in the flat. It was the call Tony had been expecting. The Americans were going in.

CHAPTER 29

Family Matters

Next came the storm. Criticism of the impending Iraq War reached its peak on February 15, 2003, when thousands of people took to the streets of London in opposition to the military action. According to the police, it was the largest demonstration the UK has ever known. Criticism of Tony flooded in, and there were anti-Blair slogans everywhere. The kids were badly affected. To see their father portrayed as "B-Liar" every time they left the house was upsetting, to say the least. We shielded them as much as we could, but it was difficult. They couldn't be wrapped in cotton wool. As all this was happening, we had a warning about a threat against Euan in Bristol. I had arranged to go down to see him for lunch on his nineteenth birthday, and I remember having to ring him up and needing to be very vague. There was a change of plans, I said. He should bring some clothes and meet me at a hotel in Bristol. Once he got there, I told him what the situation was, that there had been a threat, and that he had to go to a safe house until we found out whether the threat was real.

"But what about my party?"

"I'm sorry, but the police are insisting."

Gary was the protection officer designated to stay with him. For the first few days the two of them were cooped up in the safe house, unable to go anywhere. After that Gary went round with him until things quieted down.

The prohibition on my seeing Carole had lapsed, largely because I rarely saw her anymore outside the gym. Alastair and Fiona wanted her cast into the outer darkness, but Tony agreed that I could still exercise with her, as long as it was done well away from the public eye. Carole had recently participated in the making of a documentary film with Peter Foster. As the woman making it was one of her clients, she thought this would be her vindication. It wasn't. Alastair was, rightly, dead against it.

The Conman, His Lover and the Prime Minister's Wife was broadcast in February. Watching this man who had created so much havoc in our lives was oddly gripping. On the screen he came over as a complete shyster.

Sitting through that program had an unforeseen effect on me. For the first time I found myself looking at Carole objectively and querying her judgment. She knew this man's track record, and staying with him for the sake of the baby no longer applied. Could she really not see what a liability he was? It was nothing sudden, but over the next few months I found myself backing away from her. I went to the gym less often. As for my wardrobe, Angela Goodchild and I managed all that ourselves with the designers I had been working with for years. Unfortunately there was one last chapter still to come.

Sometime that spring, the press office from Barnardo's, an English charity devoted to improving the lives of disadvantaged and orphaned children, got in touch with Fiona. They were launching a campaign in relation to child prostitution, they explained. The magazine *Marie Claire* was supporting the campaign and had asked Barnardo's if I, as president, could give them an interview. Part of the interview would include a visit to a project in Islington that dealt with fourteen- and fifteen-year-old girls. Naturally I said yes. A few days later the magazine changed its tune. It would prefer "A Day in the Life" sort of piece. Nobody was very keen — the access was unprecedented — but in the end it was agreed.

André came to do my hair that morning at eight o'clock. The *Marie Claire* photographer took some pictures as I left Number 10 on my way to the gym. Next stop was Matrix, where I talked with some of the team — more photos — then it was back to Number 10, where we broke for lunch. We all agreed to meet up again at 2:00 p.m. before heading off to the Barnardo's project.

Around one-thirty Carole popped up to the flat. I had seen her at the gym that morning, and she'd suggested she come by before the afternoon session to make sure I was still looking all right. She had often done my makeup for photo shoots, so I said fine. Shortly after she arrived, the custodian rang through from the Number 10 front hall. Was I expecting some people from *Marie Claire*? Yes, I was.

Carole and I were upstairs when I heard voices. Peering down from the landing, I realized to my dismay that while the writer and the photographer were there, Fiona wasn't, and that somewhere downstairs Leo was playing. The last thing I wanted was them getting into a conversation with my three-year-old son, or even seeing him. I had to act quickly to lure them away. "I'm not quite ready for you," I called out. "You'd better come up." Hurriedly I phoned down to Jackie and asked her to keep Leo in his room. I then phoned Angela and suggested that she come up to the flat to be introduced: anything to keep them from wandering round.

They were early, they admitted when they reached the bedroom. Carole quickly redid my makeup for the photo session that would follow downstairs. As the photographer raised her camera to take a picture, Carole put up her hand and said, "No." As soon as I heard Angela's voice, I took them down to the study to meet her, then suggested she might like to take them to see the garden, hoping to get them out of the flat. At that moment Fiona turned up. Except in relation to Iraq, I had never seen her so angry. Her fire was initially directed against poor Angela, who, she wrongly assumed, had let the two women in. (The poor custodian who gave them access to the building ultimately got the blame.)

A few weeks later the magazine sent over a spread of the photographs they wanted to use. I was horrified. It included the picture of Carole touching up my lipstick, even though her hand and her saying "No" is clearly visible. Worse, there was a picture of our bed. We rang the magazine immediately and said we didn't want those particular pictures used, that they constituted an invasion of our privacy. The editor's response was, Sorry, but these are our pictures, and we intend to use them. It turned out that Fiona hadn't agreed that we would have picture approval. It wasn't how Downing Street worked, she later explained. Usually she would have been present with the photographer so the situation wouldn't arise. Except, of course, this time she wasn't and it had.

The August issue of *Marie Claire* duly appeared in July 2003, and the picture of Carole retouching my lipstick became front-page news. "Lippygate" was the tabloid shorthand this time. I was really angry. It may not have been Fiona's fault, but nonetheless she had been in charge, and I felt that, one way or another, she had landed me in this mess. It proved to be the last straw. After she left for the summer, she never returned. It was a sad ending. As someone who knew only too well the pressures I was under, because they paralleled her own with Alastair, she was invaluable, and it's hard to imagine how I would have coped without her in those early years. I will always be grateful for that.

Meanwhile, over at *Hello!* magazine, Carole was breezily commenting on various outfits that I had worn since Tony had been elected, who the designers were, and so on. Providing such information had been expressly forbidden by Number 10 right from the start, and she knew it. This was the moment I finally decided that she was less innocent than I had always believed. I had been a loyal friend to her, but the time had come to call it a day.

"This is doing neither of us any good, Carole," I told her. "As long as you are linked to me, you are not able to be independent in your own right." All in all, we thought it best to put some distance between us. Another sad ending.

Fiona's job was taken over by Jo Gibbons. She was quite a different character from Fiona. Jo had no interest whatever in my charity work, so she was perfectly happy for Angela and Sue to handle me on their own. From then on, they did everything, from organizing my schedule and charity events to sorting out my wardrobe and accompanying me on trips, both in the UK and abroad. They stayed with me right to end of our time in Downing Street and beyond. With this new arrangement, our little team suddenly started to work a whole lot better.

July 18, 2003, was a momentous day for Tony. On that date, he became the first British Prime Minister since Winston Churchill to be awarded the Congressional Gold Medal for being "a staunch and steadfast ally of the United States." We were allowed to take several guests to the Capitol. I invited my half sisters Jenia and Bronwen, who both live in America, and was able to introduce them to Laura

Bush and Hillary Clinton. The moment Tony walked onstage, the whole audience rose and gave him the most extraordinary standing ovation. It would have been moving in any circumstances, but coming as it did after all the heartbreak and negativity, it made my heart sing.

Washington was only the first stop on our itinerary. Next came Japan, South Korea, China, and Hong Kong. For once Alastair didn't come with us. He was increasingly disaffected, and Fiona had made it abundantly clear that they both wanted out of Downing Street. So the moment the Washington event was over, he flew back to London, while we went on to Tokyo. We were all so cheerful, happy, and laughing, and were just settling down to go to sleep, when the first call came through. A comms person came forward from the back of the plane and handed Tony the phone. It was Downing Street: David Kelly, the scientist at the center of a bitter row between Number 10 and the BBC, was missing.

A year before, Kelly, an employee of the Ministry of Defence who had been a weapons inspector in Iraq, had spoken to a BBC journalist "off the record." In a subsequent news item on the *Today* program, the journalist had claimed that Number 10 — subtext for Alastair — had deliberately inserted false information about Saddam Hussein's arsenal into the government's weapons of mass destruction dossier, against the wishes of the intelligence service. The bosses at the BBC believed that Kelly had been the source of this information. For the past few weeks, Alastair had been involved in a hideous and very public shouting match with the BBC. They had called him a liar, and he objected very strongly to that. The "source" of the story had remained anonymous until the previous week, then Kelly had been named. And now he was missing.

Within a few hours there was another call. As I watched Tony hand back the phone, I saw him slump into his seat. David Kelly was dead, he said. His body had been found in a woodland close to his home. It was awful. He decided there and then that there had to be an investigation and spoke to our old friend Charlie Falconer, now Lord Chancellor, from the plane to see which judge might be available. I have never seen Tony so distraught, and I felt helpless to do anything. Eventually he spoke to Alastair, who had just arrived back in London. Alastair said he couldn't handle any more and wanted out.

After a night in Tokyo during which he barely slept, Tony had a meeting with the Japanese Prime Minister, Junichiro Koizumi, while I visited a center for disadvantaged children. I found it hard to give the staff and the children the attention they deserved. We then flew by helicopter to Hakone, just below Mount Fuji. The Prime Minister had long wanted us to have a traditional Japanese experience, and the Ryuguden Hotel certainly was that. It was utterly beautiful, looking out over Lake Ashinoko and surrounded by hot springs. Koizumi is very unusual among politicians, especially Japanese politicians. He looks like the young Richard Gere and has a passion for Elvis and Cliff Richard. I had brought him a CD that Cliff had signed especially for him.

It should have been a great trip, but we realized soon enough that it was going to be quite the opposite. In the twenty-five years I had known Tony, I had never seen him so badly shaken. At the Tokyo press conference, the *Mail on Sunday* had shouted at him, "What is it like, Mr. Blair, to have blood on your hands?"

Our next stop was South Korea, where we had dinner with the newly elected President Roh and his wife. She was incredibly nervous, though once we got chatting, she gradually relaxed. They clearly had no idea what Tony was going through, and I tried my best to keep up the small talk. At the end of the dinner, when I admired Mrs. Roh's earrings, she immediately took them off and handed them to me. There are strict rules in Downing Street about gifts, and anything over £140 has either to be paid for or deposited in the strong room, to be borrowed for special occasions. I couldn't possibly take them, I told her. But she insisted. They were not expensive, she said. They had been made in Korea, and she could easily get another pair. This was her first official visit, and she wanted to thank me for making it all so easy. I took the earrings. I wear them all the time.

After a stay of only a few hours, we were on our way to Beijing. Before we left, I had time to attend Mass, where I prayed for David Kelly, for his family, and for Tony.

Throughout the trip Tony did his best to look cheerful for the sake of his hosts, but it was desperate. In Beijing we saw an installation of hand-size terra-cotta figures made by the British artist Antony Gormley. There is a photograph of the two of us taken that morning which I keep in my study: Tony crouching down among the thousands of tiny figures, me behind him, my arms around him, giving him the support he needed.

"You are a good man," I told him as we crouched there, the cameras whirring. "And God knows your motives are pure, even if the consequences are not as you had hoped." Tony knew that David Kelly had been a loyal public servant, driven to despair because of all the furor, caught up in something he could never have imagined.

At Tsinghua University in Beijing, we met with a group of students, who threw all sorts of questions at Tony. As we were about to leave, one last voice rang out: "Sing us a song!" From a Western perspective, this may sound like a very strange request, given the seriousness of the issues he'd been dealing with till that moment. But I have come across it often in the East — the home of karaoke. Knowing that Shanghai, our next stop, was linked to Liverpool as a sister city, they asked for a Beatles song. Tony kept saying no, then finally said, "Ask my wife. She can sing." The atmosphere was so tense, I would have done anything to lift the mood. I gave him a look, as if to say, Is this what you really want? "Whatever you like," he said. Then he added, "'When I'm Sixty-four.'" So that's what I sang. As far as I was concerned, the tour couldn't get over fast enough.

Back in London, Alastair was going to pieces, and Tony spent half the time on the phone trying to calm him down: physically and emotionally, he was exhausted. We had lunch in Shanghai, then set off for Hong Kong. Although it was only a six-day trip, Tony seemed to age ten years. The stress was written on his face, however much he tried to keep up appearances. It wasn't fair, he said, to take it out on these people who had put so much time and effort into our visit.

When we got to Hong Kong, we had a day's downtime inked into our schedule — or that was the idea. However, a hurricane was on its way, and if we wanted to get out, we were told, it had to be now. The rest of the visit was canceled. As I always do (if the crew will let me), I was in the cockpit for takeoff. The wind was already picking up when the plane in front of us suddenly stopped halfway through takeoff. "If we don't get the PM out now, he'll be stuck here," the pilot said. "I'm going to try." As our speed increased, the brand-new automatic warning system kicked in: there was a buzzing; lights flashed ABORT, ABORT, ABORT; and the plane swerved. The pilot looked bemused. "That's the first time that's ever happened," he said. "I'm going to try again." Even I was scared, but this time we rose steeply into the air — over the end of the runway and above the churning China Sea — banked, and headed for home.

As a postscript to David Kelly's tragic death, his widow and grown-up children came to visit us at Chequers. We wanted to say personally how very sorry we were about what had happened. It was clear to me that what had made the Kellys' lives even more intolerable was the behavior of the press after he had killed himself, to the point of taking pictures through their front windows. An official inquiry later established that Kelly had leaked no information to the BBC after all.

Whatever else is going on, a visit to Balmoral is a fixed point in the Prime Minister's calendar. Built by Queen Victoria in the valley of the river Dee, it's where the Queen and Prince Philip spend the summer, and it's probably the nearest thing they have to a private home.

Balmoral felt almost like a film set the first time I went there, in 1997. Everywhere I looked were stags' heads and tartan. And being in the Scottish Highlands, it was always cold — even in the first week of September. That first year we went only for lunch, rather than the full weekend, because of Diana's death.

The atmosphere the next year, the first year we stayed overnight, was noticeably tenser than it was in subsequent years, as 1998 marked the first anniversary of Diana's death and William and Harry were both visiting their grandmother. Other members of the family were also in evidence. Prince Edward had just got engaged to Sophie Rhys-Jones, I remember, so they were there, as were Princess Anne and Princess Margaret, while the Queen Mother was a fixture until she died. The Queen herself was always very approachable. She has never been anything other than gracious and charming to me, and I admire her enormously. From what I've seen, she isn't half as stuffy as some of her courtiers.

We usually stayed in what was known as the Prime Minister's Suite, which was warmed by an electric heater, not dissimilar to one my grandma had in Ferndale Road. We had two rooms, one with a double bed, the other with a single. The big bed came complete with feather pillows, which, unfortunately, I am allergic to, though later these were kindly changed. Beside the bed were two bells, one marked "maid" and the other "valet." The maid who was allocated to me the first year was very young and kept curtsying and calling me "my lady." "Please don't call me my lady," I insisted, but this only flustered her more.

The visit would always start with tea, a proper sit-down affair, with the Queen at the head of a large table, in charge of an urn bubbling with water. She would make the tea herself, from putting the leaves into the pot to the pouring. To eat, there would be cucumber sandwiches, bread, Balmoral honey, and Duchy preserves. (Prince Charles, also known as the Duke of Cornwall, has a commercial venture that makes these jams and chutneys.) It was all delicately done, and the first time, I watched to see what other people did before daring to lift a finger, let alone a teacup.

At six o'clock the Queen would have her audience with Tony, so I would go back to our room to get ready for dinner. Tony would join me later. On our first visit, I was horrified to discover that my suitcase had been unpacked and everything put away in drawers or hung up. We were both puzzled by what turned out to be the traditional country-house practice of laying out the husband's belongings in the single room. Was he supposed to sleep there? we wondered. Or was he allowed to come and visit me in my double bed?

Bath done and suitably attired, we would go downstairs. Saturday evening was usually a barbecue, but in the event of bad weather, it would be switched to a formal black-tie dinner. Although we always brought the necessary clothes for both, the barbecue was never canceled. As it was, trousers and sweaters were de rigueur, so press reports about the Queen being shocked at my wearing trousers were pure invention.

When Tony and I arrived downstairs on our first visit, it struck me that we had been invited into a private home. The Queen presumably didn't mind at all — and certainly must have been used to it — but I couldn't help feeling I was somehow encroaching. Yet everything looked very normal. The Queen was playing cards with the boys, and Prince Edward was tackling a crossword. Family life was just going on, and round the edges were us, the guests — not only Tony and me, but other people, too.

At one point that first year, Princess Anne came over and said something that included "Mrs. Blair."

"Oh, please call me Cherie," I said.

"I'd rather not," she replied. "It's not the way I've been brought up."

"What a shame," I said.

My relationship with the Queen's only daughter went rapidly downhill after that and never recovered.

I got the distinct impression that the Queen Mother thought I didn't know the first thing about protocol, and she was right. I never really got the hang of it in terms of what you call people and how you greet them. Diana I called "Diana." Charles I called "Charles," and in fact I would always kiss him, though I'm not convinced he really liked it. The Queen, however, was always "Ma'am."

I would watch other people go through the rigmarole. That first weekend, Sophie Rhys-Jones was still clearly finding her feet. When Charles came in, she'd bob. When Anne came in, she'd bob. I decided I'd limit my bobbing to the Queen and the Queen Mother and leave it at that.

The highlight of the visit was undoubtedly the barbecue, though it was not remotely what I'd expected. The barbecue itself was an amazing design, and I was so impressed that I asked where it came from. The answer was unexpected to say the least: Prince Philip had designed it himself, and in fact he very kindly gave us one.

The arrangements never changed. The Queen herself would take the wheel and drive Tony and me across the moor. We'd arrive at about eight. Being so far north, it was still reasonably light, even in September. Prince Philip and his equerry (an officer allocated from one of the services, who spends about a year filling a role somewhere between private secretary, companion, and looker-after) had gone ahead, and by the time we arrived at the little house where the barbecue was held, the grouse stuffed with haggis were already on the flame. (Not traditional barbecue fare, perhaps, but something I can highly recommend.) Venison sausages also were featured regularly on the menu. Plates, cutlery, and salads in plastic containers arrived in a massive hamper on wheels, which was towed behind the Range Rover. Everyone had a job. That first year Prince Edward was in charge of the first course and did a thing with prawns. The Queen laid the table, which was set up in the kitchen near a big wood-burning stove, and I helped her. There was no electricity, and as the light faded, candles took over. There were no staff at all, except the

Queen's equerry. As the evening wore on, the light faded slowly, and we all helped clear up before driving back. It was just fabulous: wonderful landscape, completely empty, and the air so clean.

In September 2002, following the Queen Mother's death in the spring, I asked the Queen whether she would mind if we had a picture of Leo with her, and so we did. She is very good with small children, and she liked Leo, who really loved her dogs. I remember when he was about eighteen months old, the Queen was showing him how to throw a biscuit to one of the corgis. After he successfully tossed the treat, she told him that they all had to have one now, so he took a handful and flung them across the room. The corgis went wild. "Oh," she said, "that wasn't quite what I meant." But she wasn't remotely cross at the ensuing mayhem.

By the time Leo was two and a half, he had learned the words to "God Save the Queen," and at the end of our stay he sang it to her on his own. Her Majesty was very gracious and congratulated him. (All praise to Jackie, who had taken a lot of trouble over it.)

Leo was really the person who broke the ice at Balmoral. Once he came along, the whole atmosphere completely changed. Indeed, during our first visit I was on edge the whole time, thinking, *Oh, my God, what faux pas am I going to make next?* But over the years we got used to each other. The Queen was clearly very fond of Tony, and the last time we went, I was really sad to think that we would never go there again.

Whereas the Queen is very approachable, I can't say the same about her sister, Princess Margaret, whom I met several times at Balmoral. One evening I was at the Royal Opera House for some gala performance. As I was talking to her about what we'd seen, Chris Smith came over.

"Have you met Chris Smith, our culture secretary, Ma'am?" I asked.

She peered at him.

"And this is his partner," I continued.

"Partner for what?"

I took a breath. "Sex, Ma'am."

She stalked off. She knew exactly what kind of partner I meant. She was just trying to catch me out.

Her niece, Princess Anne, and I similarly never found an accord. The reason, I think, was less our slightly awkward meeting when we were first introduced at Balmoral than her perception that I was was egging Tony on with a proposed ban on foxhunting. Anne had very strong feelings about the matter, which she made clear to me when Tony and I attended a state banquet at Windsor Castle while the bill was going through Parliament. Prince Charles and Prince Andrew, by contrast, who also had strong views on the subject, were extremely civilized about it.

I actually had no feelings on the issue whatsoever, but that message did not get through to the pro-foxhunting lobby. In September 2004 my fiftieth birthday party at Chequers was stormed by a group of hunt supporters. The party had been due to start at seven-thirty, but with protesters blocking the gates, only three guests somehow managed to beat the blockade. It looked as if we were in for a quiet evening.

Tony was in a pessimistic mood. "I warned you, Cherie. I told you we shouldn't have a party in our position." We certainly hadn't had one the previous year for his fiftieth, because of the Iraq War.

Eventually, after inviting the leader of the protesters in, Tony charmed her into seeing reason. They had made their point, he said, so perhaps now they could unblock the road. From then on, his mood lightened considerably. Gradually the friends who had been diverted by the police to a nearby supermarket parking lot started drifting in, but it was nine o'clock before the party got going. For many of our guests, it was a strange experience: in their youth they more likely would have been on the picket line. In the end everyone agreed that this was one birthday party they would never forget, between the picketers and Tony himself up with the band and having a brilliant time, letting his hair down for what seemed like the first time in years.

CHAPTER 30

Going the Distance

In September 2003, no sooner were we back from Balmoral than Tony was off again, this time to Berlin for talks with Jacques Chirac and Gerhard Schröder on the rebuilding of Iraq. It was no wonder he always seemed so tired: no world leader before him had undertaken so much traveling. Next in the round of talks were the Aznars. At least they were coming to us. That evening over dinner, the conversation again came round to José Maria's decision to stand down at the end of his second term in 2004.

A few weeks later, we were at Chequers for the weekend. Tony had been down at the local Royal Air Force base, where they had a small gym, exercising on the running machine, and he came back looking distinctly gray. He had a pain in his chest, he said. He didn't understand: no matter how much effort he put in, he was short of breath and didn't seem to be getting any fitter. I said I was going to call the doctor. He told me not to be ridiculous, but I did anyway.

Dr. Shah was the resident GP at the local Royal Air Force base, and he expressed amazement that the Prime Minister didn't have his own doctor on hand. I told him that he had probably been offered one but, knowing my husband, had said no. Dr. Shah arranged for him to go immediately to the local hospital. I went with him.

At the hospital they erred on the side of caution, saying they'd prefer to send him to London. A garden girl arrived at Hammersmith Hospital in London shortly after we did and sat outside the consulting room throughout, with the prime ministerial red box. Tony's condition, the consultant explained, was an irregular heartbeat, which was usually cured by an electric shock. The procedure would take seconds, so we didn't need to involve John Prescott, whose job, as Tony's deputy, was to take charge if Tony couldn't. Tony immediately felt a lot better.

Although he'd been advised to take a daily aspirin as a precaution, he thereafter made no effort to do so. Not surprisingly, the pain came back a year later. Now it was decided that an operation was necessary. Again it was something quite simple, though he would need to have a general anesthetic, albeit for a matter of minutes. This time John would have to be involved.

The 2004 Labour Party Conference was coming up, and Tony was determined to wait to have surgery until it was over. In my view, the stress of having to write that speech was unlikely to improve matters, and I told him I'd rather they did it straightaway. Again he took no notice. I took matters into my own hands and fixed for him to go into the hospital on the Friday after conference ended, which is usually a very quiet day.

In 1997, at his first Labour Party Conference as Prime Minister, Tony both promised and warned that his tenure would be a time of "high ideals and hard choices." Never was that truer than in Iraq. There were times when I faltered, when I was worried about the direction that things were taking in Iraq, and I would have to remind myself that I did not have the overall picture that Tony did. But because I believed in his judgment, I was prepared to put aside the doubts; I knew him and knew he would never do the wrong thing. He had enormous strength of conviction, a quality I had recognized very early on, and my job as his wife was to support him.

Although in 2004 conference had voted four to one against pulling our troops out of Iraq, over the previous year the pressure on Tony had become increasingly intense. There was Iraq, and there was Gordon. Gordon wanted to become Prime Minister so much that he failed to understand that had he merely been prepared to implement Tony's programs involving education, health care, and pensions, Tony would have stood down, no question. Instead Tony felt that he had no option but to stay on and fight for the things he believed in.

As the tension began to mount inside Number 10, Tony once

again began to consider standing down, and I felt helpless to do anything. Of course such a close relationship in the hothouse atmosphere of politics was always going to be difficult. Gordon wanted to be leader, and he had a perfect right to want that. Yet my sympathies inevitably lay with Tony, and I wanted him to go on his own terms. The effect that the constant friction had on my husband colored my feelings. I accept that I am not objective on this — and, frankly, it would be odd if I were. Nor am I blind to the many good qualities Gordon has. But I am intensely loyal to Tony and resented any pressure that was put on him.

This time, at least, there was a positive focus: the job of President of the European Commission needed to be filled by June. Tony had always been fired up by the idea of a united Europe, and we started to talk about whether he should throw his hat in the ring. I even went so far as to look up schooling possibilities for Leo on the Internet. In the end, however, Tony decided to throw his weight behind the candidacy of José Manuel Barroso, the Prime Minister of Portugal, whom he admired, who shared his views on the future of Europe, and who was an ally of the United States.

There had been a point, around the time of the debate on Iraq in March 2003, where Tony felt that he might actually get pushed out. With the Tories supporting the invasion, he never believed that the vote would go against him, but had there been a major Labour revolt, he would have had to resign. The idea of our being cast out in the wilderness with nowhere to live was terrifying to me, and I knew that, somehow or another, we had to buy a place in London. This time Tony agreed. My recent history with property buying being so dire, Tony decided to ask our friend Martha Greene to help.

I first met Martha in 2001 through Carole, at the gym. Then in 2002 she developed breast cancer, and we became closer as a result. Martha is an American, an expatriate who came to London when she was young and never left. When I first met her, she was running a restaurant called Villandry, which she had turned around. She catered for our twenty-first wedding anniversary, and she would also bring in supper for Tony when I wasn't there. As a result, she became a family friend. Tony and I put great trust in her ability with all things culinary and financial.

Where to start looking for a new house presented a bit of a

conundrum. Tony had no wish to stay in Westminster, while I was determined that Leo wouldn't change schools. I also needed to be within hitting distance of chambers, and Tony wanted to be near the Heathrow Express to the airport. Connaught Square, north of Hyde Park, fulfilled all the criteria except one: price. Although it didn't have a garden, it looked out on one, and by now we knew that for security reasons, Tony would never be able to use it anyway.

The purchase of a house of this size and price represented a major leap of faith. Yet we had to have something. If we had to move out suddenly from Number 10, we needed somewhere to go. I had to work, as did Tony. Three years on from 9/11, we were only too aware of the security implications of wherever we lived once Tony stepped down. The usual rules about cutting your coat according to your cloth, drummed into me by my grandma, didn't apply.

To raise this kind of money, Martha put together a business plan. In the long term Tony had "prospects." In the short term we still had to meet mortgage payments. The rent we could obtain would not cover the whole mortgage. We also realized, again for security reasons, that at some point we would have to buy the carriage house behind the original house. As Tony's income was fixed, somehow I would have to increase my earnings dramatically to cover the balance, hence a series of speaking engagements, which Martha arranged through her contacts in America.

Public speaking seemed an ideal way of doing something I felt passionate about while at the same time resolving a pressing financial situation. As a barrister, I am no stranger to making speeches, and I particularly enjoy discussing women's rights. In America I would speak on these issues and other legal matters at conferences.

Although I still refute the idea that I had no right to be paid for these speaking engagements, they proved disastrous from a PR point of view, particularly the series I did in Australia. I was just one "item" on a road-show agenda that included dinner, entertainment, and an auction. For this I received a set fee, as did the four other "performers" on the program. The road show went to several cities, the idea being to raise money for the Children's Cancer Institute of Australia, which in the end it did. The tour was far from the disaster the British press made it out to be, and in fact it exceeded expectations. Altogether the profits from the tour of Australia and New Zealand were £350,000, the most money the charity had ever raised. But though being paid a fee to speak at a charity event may be standard practice in the charity world, it was a painful lesson that "standard practice" did not apply to me.

There was no doubt that in April 2004, with Gordon rattling the keys above his head, Tony suffered a crisis of confidence as to whether he was still an asset to the Labour Party. I remained determined that he not resign, that he fight the next election and win, and in this I was helped hugely by our closest friends in the Cabinet. It wasn't just for the sake of his reputation that he should stay on, but for the sake of the New Labour agenda — most important, for public services. As before, when he had failed to win a seat or when he was uncertain about whether he would win the leadership, I reminded him that he needed to "pick himself up, dust himself off, and start all over again." Among many others, I was convinced that if Tony failed to stand for a third term, it would be seen as a response to the negative criticism of the war. It would be read by history as a tacit admission of failure. There was a certain type of intelligentsia who would never forgive him for Iraq, even if he were to flagellate himself in front of them, who would just say, "I told you so. We should never have trusted him." I always felt strongly that he should not apologize for something he believed to be right. He could regret the lives lost in Iraq, but he should not apologize for taking the right decision for the country.

In an interview with Andrew Marr, the BBC's political editor, on the last night of the Labour Party Conference, Tony said that if he were elected, he would serve a full third term but would not serve a fourth. He also explained that he had a heart flutter and that he would be having surgery the next day. At the same time, Downing Street announced that we had bought a house in Connaught Square.

That Friday evening, after conference ended, we made our way back to Hammersmith Hospital. I stayed beside Tony until he grew woozy, then returned to the room he would occupy after the operation. I went down on my knees with my rosary, and I didn't stop praying until the garden girl came up to tell me that all was well.

Without support from the government, the London bid for the 2012 Olympic Games could never have reached the starting line, let alone the finish line. And although my husband is not as keen on athletics as

I am, he was very much in favor from the beginning, reflecting not only on what it would mean to London and Londoners but also on the impact it would have on young people, on sports in general, and on the country's own self-image. And then there was what is known as the "legacy," not only for London's East End (where much of the necessary construction would be done) but for the country as a whole. As a showcase, it's hard to imagine anything more globally visible.

For some years Silvio Berlusconi, the controversial Italian Prime Minister, had been inviting us to stay as his personal guests. As Italy was a key player in the International Olympic Committee (IOC), Tony felt that if he played his cards right, there was a good chance we could get its three votes for London. So he had agreed to an overnight visit at Berlusconi's summer villa on Sardinia. Downing Street was naturally horrified, fearing bad publicity, but Tony was insistent. Berlusconi had stood with us on Iraq, one of the "coalition of the willing," and if visiting him could get us the Italian IOC votes, Tony would do it, he said, and "bugger the opprobrium."

Silvio Berlusconi never does anything by halves, and the yacht that awaited us in the harbor at Olbia put the royal yacht in the shade. And there was Silvio, on board waiting for us. Suddenly I felt Tony tense beside me, and no wonder: our host was wearing what looked like a pirate outfit, complete with a multicolored bandanna around his head.

"Oh, my God," he muttered, as we made our way across the gangplank. "The office is going to have a fit."

He was right. It had "foolish photograph" written all over it.

"Whatever happens," I said, "I'll make sure he stands next to me." I sighed. Not only did I have to give up time with my children to go on this trip, but I also had to make myself look ridiculous. "At least," I said, "the boat isn't exactly public, and nobody knows you're coming." Famous last words.

"Now I am going to show you something of the island," Silvio announced as we swooshed out of the harbor. This wasn't going to be a beaches-and-headlands cruise, we realized, as the boat raced into a thriving port. "Please excuse me for a moment," our host said. "I must just go below and change."

Tony breathed a sigh of relief. Common sense had prevailed. But when Silvio reemerged minutes later, the only difference was that the bandanna was now white to match the rest of his outfit.

The docks were crammed. No way was this going to remain a private visit. There was no possibility that Tony could entirely escape the cameras, but I did as promised, and a casual observer would have assumed I was besotted with our Italian host, as I never left his side.

The port was extremely well-to-do. Rather than ship chandlers, however, the predominant shops were luxury boutiques, into one of which we were propelled. Silvio wanted to buy me some jewelry, he said.

"It's very kind," I protested, "but I can't accept. It's not allowed. I won't be able to keep it."

"What you mean you can't keep it! This is not from my government; it is from me. A personal gift of friendship, Cherie."

"I'm really sorry, Silvio, but I can't."

"Nonsense. Here. What about this?" He held up a really expensive piece of jewelry. I realized it would have been insulting to keep saying no, so I desperately started looking for something cheap while trying to explain that if he gave me anything over £140, it would go straight into the Downing Street vault.

"Well, this is lovely," I said, pointing at an insubstantial-looking piece of gold wirework.

"No, no, no," Berlusconi protested. "This one is so much nicer. Trust Silvio."

"Honestly, this is much more me."

He clearly thought I was a madwoman.

Villa Certosa is as extraordinary as its larger-than-life owner. On our initial tour, we were serenaded by Silvio's personal guitarist-troubadour, and every so often Berlusconi himself would break into song. Many of the tunes, it turned out, he had written. Dinner also came with musical accompaniment, the grand piano being on a raft moored in the middle of a vast lagoon. I had never met Silvio's wife, Veronica Lario, before. She generally kept a low profile, and Villa Certosa was very much her husband's project, she said. Their house in Milan was more her domain.

After the meal we had *limoncello* from Berlusconi's own lemon groves, before once again music appeared on the menu. "Do you play, Tony? Do you sing?"

"No. But Cherie does."

Thanks, I thought.

Our host's face lit up. The pianist would accompany me, he said. Fortunately my expression was hidden in the dark. I opted for "Summertime." After a few bars he joined in. In fact he has a very good voice of the "O Sole Mio" variety. Then Tony and I exchanged glances. We were ready for bed.

It was not to be.

"But what about the concert?" Berlusconi exclaimed. The evening's event was apparently the inauguration of a four-hundred-seat auditorium carved out of the cliff. An orchestra had been flown in especially from the mainland, he said, not to mention the soprano and the tenor. There was nothing to be done. Among the audience were the 'tecs, garden girls, and comms people. I was glad I couldn't see their faces when Silvio demanded that I do a repeat performance of "Summertime."

The "just a few fireworks" turned out to be one of the most magnificent displays I have ever seen, lasting at least twenty minutes and ending with "Viva Tony" emblazoned across the sky. So much for discretion. Tony was mortified.

The next morning was a bit lower-key. For me, a whole series of thalassotherapy pools, while Tony played soccer with Berlusconi and the 'tecs. The final hurdle was the masseur. My husband has a horror of male masseurs, but this was the masseur for the legendary Italian soccer team AC Milan. "Look, Tony," I said. "He does footballers. Believe me, he's not after your body." Later he was forced to admit that it was a really great massage.

Was it worth it? As experiences go, it falls into the category of ultrasurreal. As for the IOC votes, Berlusconi promised nothing, and of course the IOC members are independent, but he said he would do what he could. We will never know for sure, but for all his eccentricities, Silvio Berlusconi is a man who does what he says he will.

The 2005 election, held on May 7, was a vindication of my belief that whatever the press might say, the British public still had faith in Tony. Our majority in Parliament was reduced — hardly surprising after eight years in office — but Labour achieved a third successive term for the first time in its history. As for the Conservatives, although they increased their presence in the House, their percentage of the overall vote was below 35 percent for the third time.

During this campaign I made sure that I had no commitments in court and was able to visit fifty marginals, largely on my own, as the party wanted Tony and Gordon to be the story. It was a poignant few weeks for me, as it would be the last time I would be campaigning for the Labour Party in the role of Prime Minister's wife.

The host of the 2012 summer games would be announced on July 6 in Singapore. As far as Tony and I were concerned, the timing was as bad as it could be: the same day, Britain was hosting the G8 in Edinburgh, seven thousand miles away. The G8 leaders were due to assemble at Gleneagles on July 6. The big question in the run-up to Singapore was, should Tony go? Some voices in Downing Street were saying no: just before the G8, what was the point? Although by now Tony was used to long-haul travel, the constant crossing of time zones — grabbing sleep when you can, grabbing food when you can rather than when you need it — does nobody any good. The risk was that he would end up being tired and unfocused both in Singapore and in Scotland. The 2005 Gleneagles G8 was particularly important for Tony because, in addition to the usual heads of state involved, he had invited the leaders of China, India, Brazil, South Africa, and Mexico — known as G8 + 5 — as well as representatives from Africa and Asia. It was the first time, too, that the focus would be less on the issues of the day and more on the future, namely Africa and climate change. We also knew that because we needed to be back in Gleneagles before the first guests arrived (I was hosting the spouse program), we wouldn't be able to stay in Singapore for the final vote. But then neither would President Chirac, who would be representing the rival Paris bid.

I remember going through the pros and cons with Tony way into the night. I don't know what decided him. Perhaps the gut feeling that his presence could tip the balance, that we'd come so far, it was really important to give it a final push. Or perhaps the sense that if he didn't go and we lost, he would always feel that he could have made the difference. It was a bit like athletics itself. There is no point in competing if you don't want to win, even though you know you may not — and in this case, the odds were definitely against us. The risk of failure, however, has never caused Tony to back down. He would rather stick his neck out and risk success, which ultimately is what makes him a great leader.

The roll call of support in Singapore covered a spectrum unimaginable in any other world: from Princess Anne to London Mayor Ken Livingstone to soccer star David Beckham, looking wonderful in an extraordinary white and silver tracksuit. We knew we were running neck and neck with Paris, and as this was the third time Paris had been in the last six, there was a real sense that its time had come.

The voting was done by a process of elimination. Round by round, the lowest-scoring city was eliminated. The dark horse was Madrid, which would be heavily supported by Spanish-speaking South American countries, but should it go out before us, the feeling was that those South American votes would come to us rather than Paris.

Tony's determination to leave no stone unturned — or in this instance, no committee member unspoken to — was extraordinary. Of about 110 IOC delegates, he was scheduled to meet 40. Sitting in adjacent suites, we divided them up between us, one every twenty minutes. With my husband turning on the charm and determination as only he can, I was very happy dealing with the smaller fry — but of course their votes were worth no less.

People really wanted to meet Tony and were genuinely astonished that he was so approachable — very different from Chirac, whom I watched sweeping presidentially through the hall, not staying to mingle, there just to be seen, as if he were doing them a favor simply by turning up. Tony made people feel they were doing *him* a favor by letting him come along. There was a definite sense that the contrasting styles might make a difference. Chirac's final blunder may have been Paris's undoing: on remarking that British cuisine was second only in ghastliness to Finnish cuisine, he waved good-bye to Finland's two votes.

We could not stay for the announcement of the winner. Rushing on our way, we flew directly from Singapore into Glasgow airport, arriving at Gleneagles at eight in the morning, when Tony went straight into a meeting.

The G8 moves from country to country. We had hosted our first in 1998, in Birmingham. It had been a baptism of fire for me in terms of hosting the spouse program. By then I had two examples to consider. The first was Hillary Clinton's G7 in Denver, where, in addition to our ride on the train, the wives had been to a craft fair and had had a group discussion. From that I knew we were all intelligent, interested, and, on the whole, educated women. I was determined that when it was my turn, I would treat the ladies as though they had a brain rather than just a husband.

The second example had come just three months later, when Britain had hosted the annual Commonwealth Heads of Government meeting in Edinburgh. Here were fifty women from fifty-two Commonwealth countries, where many of them operated like First Ladies. In Africa, in particular, the role is more like that of a queen: the wife can have real power, initiating and funding really important work, particularly in relation to women, children, and disability. That the Foreign Office had considered us worth only a visit to a tartan factory, a cookery demonstration, and a fashion show was, frankly, patronizing.

Thus, for my first G8, I decided to give the wives a rather more serious program. After dinner a group from the Royal Shakespeare Company performed extracts under the title "Shakespeare's Women," which went down very well. Obviously Hillary Clinton and Aline Chrétien (Canada) had no problem with the language. Nor indeed did Flavia Prodi. Like her husband, the Prime Minister of Italy, she was a university professor, and her English was excellent. Although Mrs. Hashimoto and Mrs. Yeltsin needed interpreters, I felt that it was better to aim high than be patronizing.

The next day I had been given permission to use the royal train, and I took everyone to Chequers for lunch. Sticking with what I knew, I invited Rosalind Higgins, a professor at the LSE (later a judge at the International Court of Justice), to talk to us about international human rights. (I don't believe I am the only wife of a leader whose husband expects her to be able to discuss things with him.)

Now, in 2005, my general attitude remained the same. After two days of nonstop IOC campaigning, followed by a twelve-hour flight, I was shattered and jet-lagged. Sleep, however, seemed impossible. The vote from Singapore could come in at any time, so I decided to have a massage to calm down. Lying there, oiled up and generally not fit to be seen, I was finally drifting off to sleep when there was a knock at the door. It was Gary, the 'tec.

"Mrs. B? Just thought you'd like to know, we're in the last two."

I lay there, the guy pummeling away, every muscle tensed. Another knock.

"Mrs. B? I'm sorry to have to tell you, but . . . we've won!"

If I'd been stung by a swarm of bees, I could not have leapt higher. Pulling on my sweatshirt, I hopped to the door and started running down the corridor, Gary laughing behind me, continuing through the public areas to our suite and my wonderful husband.

We were both nearly delirious. "It was all down to you," I said when we finally stopped laughing. And it was true. However many representatives I had been nice to, it was Tony who had made the difference.

A moment of panic flitted across Tony's face. "Oh, my God," he said. "What am I going to say to Chirac?"

The relationship with the French leader was already strained because of Iraq. "Whatever else we do," he said, wagging his finger and giggling, "there must be no crowing!"

That night the Queen was hosting the dinner. Toward the end of the first course, my Elvis-loving friend Mr. Koizumi leaned across the table, waving his fork.

"What do you think, Jacques?" he piped up, loud enough for everyone to hear, including the Queen. "Very good food here!" At which he began laughing. I looked round at the various faces. Chirac's was a study in diplomacy. The Queen's reflected total mystification.

"I didn't say it," Chirac explained to Her Majesty.

"Say what?" she replied.

Prime Minister Koizumi was in relentlessly high spirits throughout the meal, finally getting everyone to sing "Happy Birthday" to George Bush, whose birthday it was.

As the evening was winding down, the Queen and Prince Philip caught my eye. "Marvelous news, Mrs. Blair," she said quietly, giving Chirac a covert look.

"Of course," said the Prince, "I'm so old, I won't be here then."

"Oh, sir, please don't say that. I certainly hope you will." And I did. I'm actually quite fond of the old boy.

"Well, one needs to be realistic," added the Queen. "It'll be for Charles and the boys, not for us."

How terrible, I thought. *How can we possibly have the Olympics without the Queen?* She smiled and moved away. I found the idea that the Queen might not be there quite upsetting.

The spouses' program was surprisingly royal, I realized. The following morning we were going to Glamis Castle, where the Queen Mother was born and brought up. In line with the G8's theme of Africa and climate change, I had arranged that a tree be planted in the name of each spouse, mirroring a plan in Burkina Faso that encouraged the planting of income-producing trees.

The following morning I was chatting with André as he was trying to restore some order to my hair, when his cell phone rang. He listened, said nothing, and then crossed to the TV and turned it on. It was his boyfriend, he told me, saying he was okay, but there had been some kind of explosion in London. Like any mother, my first thought was for the safety of my children. I called Jackie but couldn't get through on her cell phone. The Downing Street phones were working, however: Leo and Kathryn were fine. The 'tecs had picked them up from school, and they were on their way home. Next I got hold of Nick, who was in Oxford, and finally Euan in America. Although the two older boys weren't in any more danger than they had been a day or a week before, when something so terrifying strikes at the heart of all you hold dear, there's comfort to be found in just hearing your family's voices. As the enormity of what had happened began to come through, I felt both angry and numb.

A series of four coordinated bombs had gone off during rush hour, killing fifty-six people and injuring seven hundred. Among the dead were the suicide bombers. These were streets I knew. The bomb on the Piccadilly Line was beneath Russell Square, where the first meetings about Matrix had been held. The bus that was so callously targeted after the underground was closed was in Upper Woburn Place, where the old industrial tribunal building used to be.

The summit was to go ahead, it was decided; otherwise the terrorists would be seen to have won. But all the leaders immediately understood that Tony had to go to London, leaving our Foreign Secretary, Jack Straw, to chair the climate change session that morning.

The spouses' program also went ahead, but the atmosphere was far from the one I had planned and expected. Among the guests I had invited that evening was Alexander McCall Smith, author of the popular No. 1 Ladies' Detective Agency series and emeritus professor of medical law and bioethics at Edinburgh University. We ended up discussing the finer points of moral philosophy.

That night I lay in a luxurious hotel, surrounded by every kind of security imaginable, and it was dreadful. I thought of all those hundreds, perhaps thousands, of people who tonight wouldn't sleep because they had lost someone close to them, someone they were never able to say good-bye to. To go from the euphoria of the previous day to this terrible tragedy was beyond comprehension.

CHAPTER 31

Benediction

When tragedy strikes, there's a profound need to make sense of it. It wasn't long, however, before my "What are we doing here?" turned into "What am I doing here?" Increasingly I knew I needed to find my own voice.

One of my last conversations with Fiona in the summer of 2003 had made me acutely aware that something had to change. "You have to go underground," she said. "Go back to being a mother and a barrister and nothing more. The press all hate you. They have all the cards, and you will never win." But how could I do anything in terms of the press if that was how she felt? Once the team changed, things gradually got better.

Decisions often emerge from negative experiences, and at least I knew now what I was *not* prepared to do. I was not prepared to spend the rest of my life worrying about what people thought about the way I dressed. It didn't matter in real terms, and it certainly didn't matter to me. What did matter to me, I realized, was helping other women find their voices. Women make up half the world's population and yet continue to be underused at best, and abused and defiled at worst.

By the summer of 2005, Laura Bush and I had known each other for more than four years, and although our politics were different, we were definitely friends — always delighted to see each other and catch up.

At the Gleneagles summit, Laura had proposed that I join her on a visit to Africa immediately following the G8. She was going with her daughter Jenna to visit South Africa, where her other daughter, Barbara, had been working in an AIDS clinic. They were then going on to a number of other countries before visiting Rwanda. Having been involved with the International Criminal Court, I was interested to see what impact the Rwanda tribunal had made, and everyone — which is to say Tony and the Foreign Office — seemed keen that I should go. Then came the inevitable question: who was going to pay? Laura's offer of a lift was rejected as "inappropriate," and in any event, I couldn't do the whole trip, as I had legal commitments. Obviously Rwanda was too poor even to think about paying. The Foreign Office said it wouldn't pay. Downing Street said, "We don't have a budget." So after going round the houses, Sue Geddes was informed that I would have to pay my own way.

This was the final straw. "You claim to want to highlight the cause of Africa, yet you won't back it up," I told the private secretary concerned. "And as for handing over two thousand pounds of my own money for Sue and me to represent Britain, I am simply not doing it. I shall tell Laura Bush that I can't go because the British government doesn't think it sufficiently important."

It was ridiculous. The UK was Rwanda's main development partner, with direct aid running at more than £34 million a year. On many levels it was a success story, an oasis of stability and economic growth, and if we wanted to have influence in the areas of concern — democratization and human rights — then it made sense for me to visit at the same time as the First Lady of the United States. Not to go would be a wasted opportunity to fly the flag for Britain. Fortunately Gus O'Donnell, Cabinet secretary and head of the Civil Service, finally decided that the visit should be paid for by the British government. Once that was agreed, everything fell into place.

I flew via Nairobi and, following the success of our Olympic bid, decided to visit a project for young soccer players in a local township. I took as many 2012 T-shirts and soccer balls as I could stuff into my suitcases and, with a local hero by my side — the great marathon runner Paul Tergat — consolidated the message that the Olympics weren't just about London but about sports round the world, and that they have the ability to lift the impoverished everywhere. That night, at a dinner at the Kenyan High Commission, I met both the Chief Justice and human rights lawyers and learned firsthand about the rapidly deteriorating situation in the country. At that point this situation was not generally known, and I left the next morning feeling thoroughly depressed. When I'd landed, I'd been quickly spirited along, but now, back at the airport, I realized the inroads China was making when I saw every sign translated into Chinese.

An idiosyncratic rendition of the national anthem greeted our arrival at Kigali airport, and as the red carpet was unrolled, I realized we were in for a full state visit, with Janet Kagame, the President of Rwanda's wife, there to greet me with her welcoming delegation. As for the British delegation, it consisted of myself, Sue, and Ken McKenzie, our protection officer. Twenty minutes later the band struck up "The Star-Spangled Banner" as the First Lady's plane whispered to a halt. The door opened, and out poured fifty people, with Laura and Jenna bringing up the rear. Among the welcoming party was the British Ambassador, and all four of us squashed into his Range Rover, while helicopters patrolled overhead. Anything that moved had been commandeered by the American Secret Service, including fire engines. As for the ceremonial exit from the airport, we had no alternative but to sneak into the slipstream of the American convoy.

Our first stop was the Gisozi Genocide Memorial, where we laid a wreath before going into the museum itself. Set up with the help of the UK-based Aegis Trust, it presented the background and history of the civil war that had devastated the country and shamed the rest of the world. More than 800,000 Tutsis had been murdered and a lesser number of Hutus. In most conflicts children are absolved of responsibility and are treated with compassion, but in Rwanda that had not been the case. As with rape, infanticide had become a weapon of war. Tutsis were like cockroaches, the propaganda went, and to eradicate them, babies and toddlers had been held by their legs and their heads cracked against walls. It is hard to imagine a more hideous example of a crime against humanity, and Laura and I stood in this room and wept. Later we met some survivors — mothers and rape victims — who even ten years on found it hard to talk about the genocide.

When Laura left, I stayed an extra day, wearing my legal hat. The leaders of the genocide were facing trial at the International Criminal Court for Rwanda in Arusha, Tanzania, but the cases handled there were only the tip of the iceberg. Back in Rwanda there was a huge backlog of cases waiting to be dealt with by the internal courts, but the system could not cope. Based on numbers alone, it would take two hundred years to process all of the cases currently before the courts. While those awaiting trial in Arusha were, rightly, receiving proper medical treatment for illnesses such as HIV/AIDS, their victims, mainly women who had been repeatedly and brutally raped, were dying before they could give evidence, unable to get similar treatment.

While the tribunal deals with the major perpetrators, Rwanda itself is pioneering a system for the "lesser players" known as Gacaca courts, based partly on traditional tribal methods of solving disputes and partly on the Truth and Reconciliation Commission in South Africa. I went to see one of these courts in operation, accompanied by Janet Kagame, a tall, imposing mother of four in her forties.

We watched as men accused of individual crimes of violence and theft were brought before a village gathering of what appeared to be many hundreds of people. My abiding impression was one of color: the dresses of the women, the forest of umbrellas used as sunshades, and the accused, who were dressed entirely in pink. Witnesses were called, the accused answered questions, and an appointed group of nine elders from the locality gave judgment. It all takes place within the course of a day. There is no capital punishment, but individuals who are found guilty can be sentenced to more then twenty years in prison. Rough justice indeed.

The idea behind the Gacaca courts is that the harm caused by the genocide was done to the community as a whole, and so the community as a whole should judge what happens to the perpetrators. For lawyers brought up on the common-law view of due process, there is some disquiet. Issues of bias and the rights of the accused come to mind. But what is the alternative? How do you heal a country after a civil war of such magnitude and horror? I'm not saying the Rwandans have the answer, but it was both instructive and fascinating to talk about what works and what doesn't. One thing is clear to me: on such a grand scale, in a country as poor as this, the idea of trial by jury, or even trial by a tribunal of three judges, is not really a practical possibility. Yet to throw up your hands and not deal with these crimes at all is no answer either. Not to acknowledge them would leave festering resentment. At least giving these victims the opportunity to tell their stories is an acknowledgment of what they went through.

I can't pretend that I know the answer, but part of the solution must be to go along with the grain of the society concerned, to go along with a system that is already embedded in its culture, rather than imposing one from the outside. This is not an uncontroversial view, however. Following my visit I addressed an international law college in Geneva, and it was clear from the response that not all the professors and students were willing to see this as a way forward. For some due process was all.

On my next visit to Rwanda, in March 2007, I opened a survivors' center, provided by the British government and run by a foundation that provides not only practical advice but training for trauma counselors. Now that the country's immediate needs for shelter and food are beginning to be met, there is a real need for psychological counseling.

The focus of that second visit was a seminar of women parliamentarians from across the world, but particularly from Africa. Ellen Johnson-Sirleaf, the President of Liberia, is a shining example, a true role model. To take up the reins of a country so devastated by war, with no infrastructure to speak of, is a huge task at any age, let alone at sixty-eight. I had been invited to speak on violence against women, and listening to other delegates, I realized how far we had traveled in the UK. In the Sudan, for example, there isn't even a word for rape.

As a result of the war, women outnumber men six to four in Rwanda. One positive consequence is that 49 percent of the MPs are now women, which inevitably changes the government's priorities. In stark contrast, the Kenyan delegate was one of only six women MPs in Kenya's parliament. She explained how she had been trying to get through a law on wife beating and rape for years, but the attitude in the Kenyan parliament, she explained, was no different from that of the male population as a whole. She quoted a male MP as saying, "It is well known that when an African woman says no, she means yes."

The night of the official dinner was one of the most extraordinary of my life. Toward the end of the evening, the charismatic and legendary "Princess of Africa," Yvonne Chaka Chaka, began to sing. Little encouragement was needed for the delegates to take to the floor, and soon even the two Presidents were dancing, while I was handed the microphone to join in with "No Woman No Cry." And so, in spite of the difficulties that women in Africa face, this was a joyous celebration of life, a spontaneous display of warmhearted exuberance.

The retreat by the Cabinet office over that first visit to Rwanda in the summer of 2005 marked a turning point, not only in my relationship with Downing Street but also, to some extent, in my relationship with the press. From then on, I felt I was being heard on issues I was highlighting, issues that increasingly related to women.

Every year Breast Cancer Care focuses on a particular area of concern, and in October 2005 it produced a report showing that the organization was still not getting its message across in minority and ethnic communities. Within the Muslim community, in particular, the taboo against discussing women's bodies made it hard to achieve the breast awareness that is so necessary for early diagnosis. With this in mind, Breast Cancer Care invited the Pakistani High Commissioner to share the findings. The problem was even greater in Pakistan, she said, and as a result, she invited me to visit her country early the following year, with the aim of highlighting the breast-awareness message. Breast Cancer Care paid my travel expenses, and the government agreed to pay Sue's expenses so the charity didn't lose money. The Foreign Office also agreed that I could continue on to Afghanistan. I had maintained contact with the Minister for Women there, and she was very keen for me to see for myself what was being achieved in the wake of years of Taliban rule.

As all women with a growing family can attest, the crunch comes when your children start to leave home — and let no one underestimate how hard that is. Just as they have to learn to live without you, so you have to learn to live without them. Painful though it is, there are advantages. When I had four children at home, I rarely went away for more than three days at a time, but I was now able to take longer trips. By the time of my visit to Pakistan and Afghanistan, Euan and Nicky were away at university. For me it was never a case of "out of sight, out of mind," though, and I would speak to Leo and Kathryn daily, timing the calls so that they could tell me about their days. Even in the ten years since we'd arrived at Number 10, communications had totally changed. Now the kids knew that wherever I was in the world, I was always reachable by cell phone. There was something both surreal and grounding about finding myself in a truck negotiating a mountain pass or smearing antimosquito cream on my arms in equatorial Africa, and having Leo on the line asking where I'd put his goggles, or Kathryn asking if she could borrow a pair of my shoes and did I think black or brown mascara was better.

The two destinations of that trip in early 2006 couldn't have been more different. Among the Pakistani middle class, gender is no barrier to high achievement, and the women I met included a general, three newly qualified fighter pilots, and the governor of the central bank. They lived in an entirely different world, however, from those who packed the refugee camps set up in the wake of the 2005 earthquake and those who lived in Kashmir, where the women I met were completely covered, so conservative is their culture.

Pakistan has the highest rate of breast cancer in Asia, due partly to environmental conditions but also because they don't examine their breasts. In the developed world 80 percent of women going to the doctor with a nonbenign breast lump have a stage 1 or 2 tumor, for which there are many good treatments leading to a positive prognosis. In Pakistan, by contrast, 80 percent of the women presenting with a lump already have a grade 3 or 4 tumor. As a result, the prognosis is not good, and many can be offered only palliative care.

I talked to one woman sharing a bed with another woman, lying top to tail. She was crying. When I asked about her condition, she pulled aside her hospital gown and showed me a suppurating tumor on her left breast. She was forty-two with young children. She had only come to the hospital, the British doctor told me, once she could no longer ignore the pain. There was very little they could do for her. In the UK, he said, doctors would rarely see a tumor like this, as it would be unlikely to get that far without treatment.

I had been due to meet Madame Chirac in Kabul; however, Sue and I turned up at the airport to find that our flight had been canceled. Luckily a UN flight was going there early the following morning, and we were allowed to hitch a lift.

We drove in from the airport through a capital laid waste by war. The Minister for Women had arranged for me to visit the largest girls' school in the city, where the age range went from five to twenty-one. There were eight thousand pupils, and in order to accommodate them all, the school functioned on a shift system. Many classrooms were filled with rubble, and there was no glass in the windows, yet classes continued, as they needed to make up for lost time. The school was desperately in need of a science lab, the head told me, as well as sports equipment. As for books, I saw girls reading dog-eared copies of low-grade Pakistani magazines and the Koran, and that was it. Accompanying us on the trip was a *Times* journalist, and on our return to England, enough money was raised to provide six new classrooms and a science lab. A Swiss charity called Smiling Children has since taken up the school's cause and is providing training for the teachers.

I knew there was an issue in Afghanistan concerning the appointment of women judges to the Afghan supreme court. Chief Justice Shinwari was an old-fashioned conservative who was claiming that women did not possess the necessary qualifications in Sharia law. Taking the bull by the horns, I raised the issue with President Karzai. He wasn't surprised, and later that afternoon a group of women MPs told me they'd been bending his ear about this very subject for some time. Afghanistan's new constitution stipulates that one-third of MPs should be women, and they were already beginning to show their muscle. The men had wanted segregation in the debating chamber, but the women had simply refused, and all the MPs now sit alphabetically. Sitting literally beside the women MPs, the men were obliged to notice their existence. The women told me that they were determined to challenge the idea that no women were qualified to sit on the supreme court, and they did. I later learned that they had organized a campaign in the Afghan parliament, and when President Karzai renominated Shinwari for Chief Justice in 2006, the parliament refused to accept him, and a more liberal Chief Justice was appointed.

There is no doubt that President Karzai is under enormous pressure from the conservative elements within his government. One example of the concessions he is having to make on women's issues is his own wife. Before the Taliban came to power, she had worked as a doctor, but now she is no longer allowed to work.

I was granted the rare privilege of meeting Mrs. Karzai. I knew from the President that she longed for a baby — an admission that astonished me at the time — and that he feared that she wasn't able to have one. When I met her, I sensed a real aura of sadness. When I discussed the implications of living in a city so inherently dangerous, she told me that it didn't affect her because she never went beyond the palace. She hadn't even been permitted to join Madame Chirac at that morning's opening of a children's hospital. "It's not safe," she explained.

"But surely if it's safe for the French President's wife, it must be safe for you?"

She smiled and repeated, "I just don't go out."

On leaving I said that I hoped that one day she could visit me in the UK. It didn't happen. What did happen was that six months after my visit, she became pregnant. I hope that in due course she will find her voice and be able to play a bigger role in her country.

The role of leaders' wives is particularly important, I believe, in Muslim countries. When I was in Pakistan, the Prime Minister's wife gave her first public interview in which she used the word "breast" and in so doing may have saved thousands of lives. The work being done by Sheikha Mozah in Qatar is an example of what can be achieved. Her Shafallah Center for disabled children is world-class, with facilities that put the West to shame. In my role as patron of Scope, a UK charity that works for people with cerebral palsy, I addressed a conference at the Shafallah Center on the way forward for children with disabilities in the Gulf region. There the battle is not about money, but about removing the stigma of both physical and mental disabilities. In my discussions with the families at the center, a number of the young women spoke of how, as sisters of children with disabilities, their marriage prospects were considerably diminished, and this is one of the reasons families are prepared to keep these special children behind closed doors.

My colleagues from Scope could only marvel at the standard of the facilities available, yet they were also able to share their expertise about inclusion and integration, as well as their belief that this approach is not only better for the children but also a matter of basic human rights. Around 10 percent of the world's population, or 650 million people, live with a disability. They are the world's largest minority. Their special needs have now been recognized in the UN Convention on the Rights of Persons with Disabilities. I was able to speak about what the convention meant not only at the Shafallah conference but also on Al Jazeera TV. The UK was among the first countries to sign the convention, in March 2007, and Qatar followed in July.

Over the ten years we were in Downing Street, I had access to people with real power to make things happen, and I'm not ashamed to say that I made full use of it on behalf of the charities I was involved with. As an example, in April 2007 I visited both Qatar and Kuwait in my capacity as president of Barnardo's. Many people still think of Barnardo's as running orphanages, but in fact the last Barnardo's orphanage closed in the early 1970s. Barnardo's experience with disadvantaged children stretches back a century, yet it is always looking at innovation. Its mission today is to provide the services children need wherever and whenever they need them. Its main focus is keeping children with their families, and it runs a huge number of programs to help disadvantaged youngsters. I have been lucky enough to visit many of these programs, such as the Dr. B's restaurants, where young people with disabilities learn practical skills in the catering industry at a pace more suited to their abilities. Barnardo's always needs money, and in 2007 I accepted a check for £500,000 from the Kuwaiti government.

As I have seen everywhere I have traveled, women are tremendously resourceful. Not only do they keep their families together, but they are sources of wisdom and strength, prepared to walk miles to fetch water or carry their children to health centers where they know treatment is available. Yet so often these same women are at the mercy of unwanted pregnancies and sexually transmitted diseases. I remember visiting a labor ward with Salma Kikwele, the First Lady of Tanzania, and seeing a young girl, no more than sixteen, sitting by herself. Her baby had been stillborn. There was no chance of privacy here, either in birth or in death. We were being followed by local news photographers, and there was no sense that perhaps this wasn't appropriate. We also saw the last push of a baby being born, and we were introduced as the little girl was put on her mother's breast. We were told afterward that the woman was going to call her daughter Salma Cherie.

Each culture brings its problems. In countries where sexual activity is rife, you have HIV/AIDS. In countries where young women are married as soon as they become sexually active, too-early pregnancies result in fistulas — where the vagina is torn and the bladder leaks into it. It is relatively easy to repair, but for young women in the middle of nowhere, treatment is not available. Often leaking and smelling, they are considered unclean and rejected by their families. We in the West can't even begin to understand such problems.

My religion and my family are the two fixed planets that give my life meaning. Yet because my mother wasn't Catholic, I can hardly claim to have been brought up in a conventional Catholic household. Perhaps as a result, my views and the church's sometimes differ, usually for reasons of pragmatism. In the conventional sense, therefore, I cannot be considered a "good Catholic," and indeed for a period in my twenties, my attendance at Mass was sporadic to say the least. But once my children were born, that changed, and I have found that the weekly period of reflection that Mass affords me is incredibly important. After so many years the rituals are second nature to me, and that in itself brings solace and reassurance.

The Pope is seen by Catholics as the successor to Saint Peter, and to meet him is considered the ultimate benediction. As my faith deepened following the birth of Leo, I hoped that Tony and I might have the opportunity to meet him. The beginning of February 2003 was a hard time to be living in Downing Street. War drums were beating in the background, and every time we went out, it was to a chorus of jeers and shouts of "B-Liar" and "Blair Murderer." We were existing in an atmosphere of enormous tension and stress.

One of Tony's foreign policy advisers was Francis Campbell, a committed Catholic from Northern Ireland, who also worked with Tony on multifaith projects. By this time he knew that Tony was genuinely interested in religion. Downing Street had been very resistant to the idea of Tony meeting the Pope; drawing attention to his dubious practice of going to church was singularly ill-advised. But as the Iraq War loomed ever larger, even they saw that such a visit might serve a diplomatic purpose. Apart from anything else, the Vatican had contacts with Iraqi Christians.

As religion was such a contentious issue, however, it was decided not to announce the visit until the very last moment. This meant that we couldn't stay in the British embassy in Rome, so Francis arranged for us to stay at the Pontifical Irish College, which trains priests from Ireland. This solution also had its problems. Not only was the Irish College *very* Catholic but there was also the whole Irish dimension, the Catholic Church having always supported the cause of a united Ireland. It was the first time that a British Prime Minister had stayed there. We were originally put in the cardinal's room, but the implications of a married couple sleeping in the cardinal's bed proved too much, and we were moved next door.

As schools were on break, we were able to take the children, apart from Nicholas, who was away on vacation. John Paul II was not only the Pope but also a major historical figure, and I was delighted that several of our Catholic associates, from one of Tony's chief advisers to some of the 'tecs, were able to join us.

A papal audience is a big occasion, whatever the circumstances. But my emotions ran away with me when I thought of how proud my grandma would have been. All those admonitions to behave, to learn my catechism, had not been in vain.

Francis had briefed us as to what was going to happen, but the reality was so awe-inspiring that I felt as wonder struck as a child. The ritual had probably remained unchanged for hundreds of years. Once we were inside the Vatican, our private visit had become official, and we were led by the gentlemen of the guard in solemn procession through wonderfully decorated corridors into the medieval heart of the complex. In those surroundings — massive blocks of stone and marble — you cannot fail to be aware of history, but I was very conscious of just how historic Tony's coming here was. He was still a practicing Anglican, though he had been coming to Mass with the children for many years. I knew that Francis would have let this be known, and my fervent wish was that he be allowed to take Communion following our audience with the Pope. Under Francis's guidance I had written a letter to that effect, but whether it would happen, I did not know. Nor did I know whether we would be invited to kiss the Pope's ring.

I had been brought up to venerate the papacy and all that it stood for. The feeling was so deep, it was visceral, and part of me wondered whether Tony realized just how momentous it was. The history he had learned in school was Anglican history. For Catholics, the history of England was rather different: Elizabeth I was a bad Queen, and Mary Tudor was misunderstood. It was as if all my life had been leading up to this moment, leading down this endless succession of corridors and throne rooms. All these years, I thought, English Catholics had been in the minority, and suddenly I felt as if we weren't a minority anymore.

Finally we reached the Pope's private chambers. I realized that we were in the very heart of the Vatican, the room behind the balcony from which he blesses the crowds in St. Peter's Square. While Tony was having his private audience with the Pope as Prime Minister, Vatican officials asked whether Leo would like to sit on the papal throne, which of course he did (though he was too young to appreciate the honor). After about twenty minutes I was ushered in to join my husband. John Paul II was sitting in a chair, a very old man dressed in his papal white, frail and clearly very tired. He talked to me about my having Leo at such a late age and what a good example it was. Then everyone else in our group came in to be introduced, one by one. When it came to Leo's turn, the Pope stretched out his hand for the ring to be kissed, and Leo simply handed up a little picture he had done. We still have the most beautiful photograph of that moment, Leo looking straight into the Pope's eyes, and it is signed by John Paul himself. It is very precious.

In Tony's conversation with the Pope, the question of Iraq did come up, he told me later. The Holy Father made it clear that he was antiviolence but finished by saying, "In the end it's your decision and your conscience. It's your job to take these decisions, and whatever you do, I'm sure you'll do the right thing." I know that Tony took a lot of comfort from that.

The press later reported that the Pope gave Tony a hard time. That wasn't true. He actually gave him a very kind time, and as a sign of favor, we were taken to the Crying Room, the anteroom where the newly elected Pope is left for a few minutes to reflect on the immensity of what has just happened. Often, apparently, he cries.

While we were being shown some of the unseen corners of the Vatican, along with the magnificent Sistine Chapel and the catacombs, word came through that we were invited to join the Pope at Mass in his private chapel the following day and that Tony would be allowed to take Communion. That was another moment of pure joy for me. Francis Campbell and I had chosen some English hymns just in case, and as a thank-you for their hospitality, we invited two seminarians from the Irish College to join us, as well as two from the Scottish College and two from the English College. When we arrived in the chapel the following morning, the Pope was already before the altar, hunched over in a chair, bent nearly double. He had been praying for an hour, a nun explained in a whisper. He seemed to me then such an extraordinary symbol. In spite of his frailty, he was still Pope, and I sensed no diminishing of his power, as if within his weakness lay his strength. When he stood up and faced us, an enormous energy filled the chapel.

In my mind socialism and Catholicism have always been inextricably connected. The liberation theology of the Young Christian Students that so marked my girlhood was fundamental to my view of politics: Christ as the radical feeding the poor. This was where Tony and I had first come together, and this extraordinary man from the Polish working class, who had grown up under the cloud of Nazism, then communism, exemplified everything my husband and I believed in, political in the best sense of the word. Being given his blessing was of enormous comfort to us both.

Unlike the long-awaited audience with John Paul II, I had no expectation of meeting his successor, Benedict XVI. Three years later I was in Rome to address the Pontifical Council of Social Sciences. After my talk was over, an official from the Vatican approached me.

"The Holy Father would like to meet you," he said.

"But I'm not dressed appropriately," I said. "I haven't even got my head covered." The protocol surrounding papal visits is very exact. As a woman from a non-Catholic country on an official state visit, I was expected to wear black. White or cream can be worn only by queens from Catholic countries. And here I was wearing cream.

He brushed my objection aside. "The Holy Father won't mind at all," he said. "Just come along now and meet him." So I did, together with my two friends who were with me. I spoke with the Pope for about twenty minutes, about Tony's proposed conversion to Catholicism, and also about his plans for a faith foundation, for which I knew Tony hoped for the Pope's support. I said that I felt my husband would very much like to discuss both matters with him and asked if it would be possible. He said yes, of course, and one of the last visits we made during Tony's premiership was to Rome to meet Pope Benedict. This time I was in a long black skirt, black jacket, and mantilla, as custom decrees.

After that first audience with Pope Benedict, a photograph was published of me dressed in that cream outfit. The British press had a field day. A Conservative woman MP and high-profile Catholic convert chose to join in the hullabaloo, saying, "Who does she think she is? The Queen of Spain?"

No. Just a Crosby girl who got lucky.

CHAPTER 32

Leaving

One great pleasure of the past ten years has been my chancellorship of John Moores University. JMU is a grouping of several famous institutions: the Liverpool Mechanical Institute and the Liverpool College of Art (where John Lennon famously studied), to name just two. In March 2002 Yoko Ono and I unveiled a statue of Liverpool's most famous son at the newly named John Lennon Airport. When I introduced her to JMU's new vice chancellor, Michael Brown, he said, "You know that your husband used to go to our university." She looked at him, and her eyes opened wide. It turned out she'd been giving money to the wrong university all these years! She'd even endowed a scholarship in his honor.

My relationship with JMU began in 1997, when they offered me an honorary degree, confounding the aphorism from Saint Mark's Gospel that a prophet is not without honor except in his hometown. To be honored just down the road from where I grew up was for me the ultimate accolade. Two years later they asked if I would become chancellor, and I was delighted to accept. JMU has a great mission about access for young people whose families haven't been to university — in other words, for people like me. The role of chancellor is largely ceremonial, turning up once a year to award degrees and cutting the ribbon at the opening of new facilities and buildings.

Everything at JMU is wonderfully theatrical. Recipients of honorary degrees have a gown designed and made by the fashion department which is unique to them: When I was installed as chancellor, a special fanfare was composed and played. After two terms as chancellor I was obliged to stand down, and my successor, Dr. Brian May, famous virtuoso guitarist of the rock band Queen and less famous astrophysicist, is proof that academic excellence and popular culture are not mutually exclusive. My successor's appointment was highly appropriate: in addition to its well-known involvement in the artistic life of Liverpool — Phil Redmond of *Brookside* fame is an honorary professor — JMU has one of the most important astrophysics departments in the UK.

The Labour Party Conference in 2006 was my last as wife of the leader, and we all knew it: times they were definitely a-changing. For a start there were no bracing photo opportunities in front of a lashing sea, be it at Blackpool, Brighton, or Bournemouth. We were in landlocked Manchester. Not only that, but our old friend Bill Clinton came along — proof, if ever it was needed, that leaving high office is not the end by a long shot.

Then there was Tony's speech. It was greeted with a standing ovation, and no wonder. Even the archconservative *Daily Telegraph* called it "the most dazzling speech of his career." He urged the party not to turn in on itself. We had grown so used to things only getting better, he said, that it was salutary to remember just how grim things were in the bad old days before New Labour. "Take a step back and be proud," he said. "This is a changed country." The challenges in 1997, Tony reminded us, had been largely British, while the challenges before us now were largely global. What he didn't say was that he intended to be very much a part of it.

In Gordon's speech the previous day, he had said that he felt it had been a privilege to work with Tony. The news agency Bloomberg subsequently reported that I had been overheard saying, "Well, that's a lie," and the press went for it like starving rats tossed a single crust of bread. The truth is that whatever I might have felt, I never said it. It seemed as if the press had to have its "Cherie's crass-behavior moment," and that was it — another Labour Party Conference tradition that had hopefully come to an end.

As for the manner of our leaving, I would have preferred to stay in Downing Street for another month, but that was entirely for practical considerations: the end of the school term would have been less disruptive, and I had hoped that the house in Connaught Square might be ready for us to move into, though it wasn't. The fact was that Tony needed to resign his seat at least six weeks before the summer recess to give time for a successor to be elected, as elections can be held only while Parliament is sitting. He had been determined to go on his own terms and had achieved that, and he was passing the country on to his successor in good shape.

Unlike some previous tenants of Number 10, for whom leaving came as a shock and sometimes at barely twenty-four hours' notice, our move was carefully planned. The packing itself took months. In addition to the accumulated possessions of ten years of family life, there was a entire room full of mementos of government and charity visits. I must admit to being by nature a hoarder, and I found it hard to throw away these gifts that had been so thoughtfully given, many of them by children. We have them still.

Tony had chosen Wednesday, June 27, as his last day in office. Children are not usually permitted to attend Prime Minister's Questions, but the Speaker gave special dispensation for Leo and the older children to come along to hear their father face the Leader of the Opposition for the last time. (Nicky sadly missed it due to floods in Oxford.) It was a wonderful House of Commons occasion: dotted round the chamber I saw many of Tony's colleagues, past and present, who had come to share this moment — all so important to his years in power, all there to salute him and wish him well. When the House stood up to applaud, emotion got the better of me, and I found I could barely see.

Saying good-bye to our home after ten years was difficult, and we were all sad to leave. But in my case, it was less the building than the people. Although inevitably there are comings and goings in any government-run organization, among the nonpolitical staff there is some semblance of continuity, and the relationships that we'd built over ten years were not washed away like sand castles with the next tide. Before walking out of that famous front door for the last time, we had first to walk out of our own front door, the door to the Number 11 flat, which for a decade had formed the frontier between our home — with its scattered toys, PlayStations, guitars, iPods, computers, board games, and general family chaos (not to mention my collection of files and law books) — and the tight-lipped center of British political power, a frontier that far too many people seemed to think they could cross without knocking. There were times when all I'd wanted was to ram a bolt across the door and say, "Closed."

All that was now in the past. Pulling the door of the flat shut for the last time, we made our way, down and then up (there is no direct link between Number 11 and Number 10 on the first floor) to the state rooms, where the staff was already assembled. Tony made a speech thanking everybody for their hard work, and I made a short speech thanking them for being so good and welcoming to us as a family. Then we were asked to wait while everyone else went downstairs to clap us out — the final tradition for all outgoing Prime Ministers.

As we stood waiting for the word to proceed, Tony walked across to the window and stood there motionless and alone for a few moments, gazing out for the last time. Then, turning abruptly, he led us down that historic staircase lined with portraits of Prime Ministers — where a space now awaited "Tony Blair 1997–2007" — into the hall and corridors below, lined with all those familiar faces.

I hadn't anticipated how hard it was going to be to say good-bye, and how emotional. There had been times over the past ten years when the outside world had seemed a very hostile place indeed and the support of the people around me meant more than any of them will ever know. Garden girls, messengers, comms people, drivers, custodians, 'tecs — they came to be like an extended family, the only people in the world, apart from my blood relatives, who knew me as I really was: the Cherie they chatted to about family crises and joys; about relationships and careers; about parenting and children — not the Cherie they saw portrayed in the media. "It's a good thing you've got a sense of humor, Mrs. B," I remember one of the 'tecs saying after a particularly unflattering photo of me appeared.

"Luckily the ability to laugh is one thing I've never been short of," I replied. "I'm a Scouser, remember. It's hardwired, part of the DNA."

After all the hugs, the embraces that were hard to pull away from, the bowed heads, the wrists raised to eyes to wipe away tears, the occasional ripple of subdued laughter, there came a moment when it was only the six of us, simply there as a family, standing in that hall with its familiar black-and-white-checkered floor, the long corridor extending away toward the Cabinet room at the back of the building, looking at each other and thinking, *This is it.* Then Tony straightened his back, took hold of Kathryn's hand, and said, "Okay, guys, that's it. Let's do the business."

Sitting in the back of the Daimler, Tony stone-faced beside me, I stared out the window as we passed the Cenotaph, that haunting memorial to our unknown soldiers. He was right to be angry. Even though I had tossed my remark to the press lightheartedly — "Bye. I won't miss you!" — I didn't have the right. We had discussed it so often: leaving was to be on his terms and was to be done with dignity and grace, and what I had just done was neither gracious nor dignified. It was not my day; it was Tony's day. I knew it, and he knew it, and I sat beside him feeling both foolish and small. Then, just as the car turned into the Mall, he shrugged his shoulders, took my hand, and gave me a grin, that infectious grin that I have never been able to resist. He grinned because he loves me. Because he knows that I just couldn't help myself. In the end part of the reason he loves me is my unpredictable character. I am impulsive, and he is not. I am the abrasiveness against which he can spark.

He didn't say anything, nor did I expect him to. When you have known someone for thirty years, a lot of things go unsaid, because you know each other so well they don't need to be said. Tony has a very quick temper, which I have always suspected he inherited from his redheaded mother, but it flares up and is gone in a minute. When he says something unkind, I know he doesn't mean it. I know it's simply the tension talking. But when he asks me my opinion, I know he wants to make up.

In all those years, whatever strain he was under, Tony never lost his temper either in public or with his staff. The one place where he could release his frustration and anxiety was at home. Even the children understood and learned not to take it personally. He was under incredible pressure, and if he was short-tempered, we knew he wasn't really cross with us. And we were more than happy to pay that price to have him at home as much as we did. Home was always where he felt happiest, one of the reasons we'd had an open house from the beginning of our marriage and continuing at Number 10. Why have a meeting in an office when you can have a meeting at home?

As the Victoria Memorial came into view at the end of the Mall, I saw once again the jubilant crowd of ten years before. I'd felt proud of him then, and I feel proud of him now. I remembered the vulnerable young man I'd first met, who had just lost his mother, and the resilience and determination that took him all the way to Downing Street and across the globe. But more than anything, I am proud of what he has achieved for us as a family. We went in there together, saw our kids grow up and our family expand, and we came out the other side still happy and united, all of us, in our different ways, coming to terms with the weight of ten years of experience and looking forward to the next phase of our lives.

ACKNOWLEDGMENTS

First and foremost, this book is about a family on a journey, so I could not have written it without the blessings of Tony and our children, Euan, Nick, Kats, and Leo, who know they are the center of my life. My mother, my sisters (yes, all of them), and the wider Blair clan are always there for me, and I thank them for standing by me. I have shamelessly tapped into their memories for this project.

One question I'm always asked is how I keep so many balls in the air, and the truth is that I could not and do not do it on my own. There are many special people who have helped me on my way, some of whom are mentioned in these pages, some of whom are not. I certainly could not have coped without a wonderful group of women who have kept my life ticking over and helped care for the family, so thanks especially to Jackie and Maureen, but over the years to many others as well. Eternal gratitude, too, to Angela Goodchild and Sue Geddes, who together keep me organized and sane. To Martha Greene, who sorts out so many aspects of my life; to Hilary Coffman for her advice and support; to David Bradshaw for his speechwriting talents; to Faith O'Hara for her skill and understanding; and to the unflappable André Suard for his patience, loyalty, and unfailing good humor.

At work there is Amanda Illing and the great team at Matrix, who have had to cope with the disruption to my practice caused by writing this book just when they thought they had got my full attention. As for all those who have been such an inspiration and help to me in my charity work, to name individuals here would be invidious, as they are legion.

I could not have got through ten years at Number 10 without my girlfriends, and I thank them wholeheartedly for all their support; you know who you are! I want especially to thank the wonderful staff at the Labour Party, whose hard work got us to, and kept us in, Number 10; and all those at Downing Street, especially those in the events and visits department, who worked so closely with me on the Number 10 receptions, as well as overseeing our domestic and foreign visits. I am glad to have this opportunity to thank the unsung heroes of the corner of Whitehall I got to know so well: The members of the information technology and comms department, who put up with my amateur interest in the subject of computers with such good humor. The garden girls and 'tecs, who over all those weekends at Chequers and family holidays became like our surrogate family — and not forgetting the drivers. David Heaton, the house manager at Downing Street, and all his staff, who helped the house function twenty-four hours a day. And to the wonderful "switch," without whom Number 10 would cease to function at all. A big thank-you to all the staff at Chequers — our refuge every weekend. As for my fears on arriving that first day at Number 10, they proved utterly groundless. I can guarantee that these loyal and hardworking people will serve every Prime Minister with the same dedication and professionalism they showed to us.

I should like to thank everyone at Little, Brown for their encouragement, advice, and patience, especially Ursula Mackenzie, Antonia Hodgson, and Vivien Redman. I couldn't have even contemplated writing this book without their stalwart support. They had much more to do than would usually be the case, and I am truly grateful for all their hard work.

Finally I should like to pay tribute to Kate Jones, my agent, who first had faith in this book and whose vision and encouragement got me started and kept me going. Although she read the early drafts, she never saw the completed version. Like so many other good people, she was taken by cancer far too young.